An Introduction to Literature

POETRY

An Introduction to Literature

DRAMA

EDITED BY

Edmond L. Volpe AND *Marvin Magalaner*

FICTION

EDITED BY

Theodore Gross AND *Norman Kelvin*

POETRY

EDITED BY

Edmond L. Volpe AND *Marvin Magalaner*

Selected from these three volumes

A one-volume omnibus anthology

POETRY, DRAMA, FICTION:

An Introduction to Literature

EDITED BY

Edmond L. Volpe, Marvin Magalaner,

Theodore Gross, AND *Norman Kelvin*

An Introduction to Literature

POETRY

Edited by

Edmond L. Volpe

and Marvin Magalaner

The City College of

The City University of New York

RANDOM HOUSE *New York*

FIRST PRINTING

Published in New York by Random House, Inc. and simultaneously in Toronto, Canada, by Random House of Canada Limited
Library of Congress Catalog Card Number: 67–12367
Manufactured in the United States of America by Kingsport Press, Inc., Kingsport, Tennessee
Typography by Leon Bolognese

ACKNOWLEDGMENTS

Gerard Manley Hopkins, from *Poems of Gerard Manley Hopkins.* Copyright 1948 by Oxford University Press, Inc. By permission of the publisher.

William Butler Yeats, reprinted by permission of the Macmillan Co., A. P. Watt & Son, the Macmillan Co. of Canada Ltd., and Mr. Michael Butler Yeats: "Sailing to Byzantium," "The Second Coming," and "Easter 1916" from *Collected Poems.* Copyright the Macmillan Co., 1928, renewed 1956 by Bertha Georgie Yeats; "The Lake Isle of Innisfree," "Never Give All the Heart," and "He Remembers Forgotten Beauty," from *Poetic Works.* Copyright the Macmillan Co., 1906, renewed 1934 by William Butler Yeats; "No Second Troy" from *The Green Helmet and Other Poems.* Copyright the Macmillan Co., 1912, renewed 1940 by Bertha Georgie Yeats; "Two Songs from a Play," "Leda and the Swan," and "Among School Children" from *The Tower.* Copyright the Macmillan Co., 1928, renewed 1956 by Bertha Georgie Yeats; "Byzantium" and "Death" from *The Winding Stair.* Copyright the Macmillan Co., 1933, renewed 1961 by Bertha Georgie Yeats; "September 1913" from *Responsibilities.* Copyright the Macmillan Co., 1916, renewed 1944 by Bertha Georgie Yeats.

Robert Frost, "Fire and Ice," "Stopping by Woods on a Snowy Evening," "After Apple-picking," "The Death of the Hired Man," and "West-running Brook," from *Complete Poems of Robert Frost.* Copyright 1923, 1928, 1930, 1939, by Holt, Rinehart and Winston, Inc. Copyright 1951, © 1956, 1958, by Robert Frost. © 1967, by Lesley Frost Ballantine. Reprinted by permission of Holt, Rinehart and Winston, Inc.

T. S. Eliot, "The Hollow Men," "The Love Song of J. Alfred Prufrock," "Journey of the Magi," "A Song for Simeon," and "Marina" from *Collected Poems 1909–1962.* By permission of Harcourt, Brace & World, Inc., and Faber and Faber Ltd.

Dylan Thomas, from *The Collected Poems of Dylan Thomas,* copyright 1953 by Dylan Thomas; © 1957 by New Directions. Reprinted by permission of the publishers, New Directions Publishing Corporation and J. M. Dent & Sons Ltd.

Robert Lowell, from *Lord Weary's Castle,* copyright 1944, 1946, by Robert Lowell. Reprinted by permission of Harcourt, Brace & World, Inc.

"A Handbook of Poetry," reprinted from *Encyclopedia of Poetry and Poetics,* Alex Preminger, Ed., by permission of Princeton University Press. Copyright © 1965 by Princeton University Press.

Contents

An Introduction to Literature

POETRY

Introduction

Poetry is perhaps the most difficult kind of literature. This is probably because the very nature of most poetry requires a compactness and intensity not ordinarily found in prose. Not only must each word bear a greater weight in meaning than in ordinary prose, it must also serve a second purpose in enhancing the sound and rhythm of the line in which it appears. Thus, poetry often departs, much more than prose does, from the language of everyday speech. The normal word order of ordinary speech may be inverted in poetry, or a word one would ordinarily expect to find in a sentence may be left out of a line in order to intensify meaning or maintain a rhyme or meter. Again, poetic diction sometimes incorporates obsolete or archaic words or phrases that ultimately enhance the meaning but make it less obvious at first. Finally, most poetry has a lyric quality that presents the poet's thoughts and feelings in an intensely personal way.

It is obvious, then, that poetry requires analysis if readers want to do more than merely skim the surface of its complex statements. Finding out what a poet has to say is often a process of examining the means he uses to say it, and for this kind of analysis one must have a knowledge of metrics and the poetic uses of language that reaches beyond the reading of any single poem. When a poem is a successful work of art it is always in some respects a unique experience for its reader, and for this reason he must often dissect the work in order to fully discover it. But such dissection is a constructive—not destructive—process provided that it is followed, as it must be, by a sympathetic and intelligent reconstitution of the poem with the added understanding obtained. Some students might object that this kind of dissection would destroy the beauty of a poem but, on the contrary, knowledge of the parts of a poem is what allows one to see the beauty of the whole. Experimental dissection of a frog in the school laboratory is done, after all, only to discover how the whole frog is made, and this its surface alone will never tell you. It is for this reason that the student who deals with poetry must be a scientist of language and must approach his material with the analytical intent of the scientist.

The work of the so-called New Critics in our time—among them I. A. Richards, Cleanth Brooks, and Robert Penn Warren—has made clear the need for close explication of the text of a poem. These critics have shown beyond question that a successful poem is a perfect blend of content with the form in which that content is presented. It becomes essential, therefore, to be as concerned as much with *how* the poet works as with *what* he has to say. Indeed, in a sense the form of the poem *is* what the poet has to say: the content is made convincing by the form in which it is rendered.

In order to describe more concretely what we mean by the elements of poetry that require analysis we have provided a discussion of them in the *Handbook of Poetry* at the back of this book. Here we shall try to demonstrate how these elements—meter and rhythm, imagery, symbolism, ambiguity, and tone—may be viewed in the analysis of a typical poem.

The Collar

I struck the board, and cried, No more.
  I will abroad,
 What? shall I ever sigh and pine?
My lines and life are free; free as the road,
 Loose as the wind, as large as store.
  Shall I be still in suit?
 Have I no harvest but a thorn
  To let me blood, and not restore
 What I have lost with cordial fruit?
   Sure there was wine   10
Before my sighs did dry it: there was corn
   Before my tears did drown it.
 Is the year only lost to me?
   Have I no bays to crown it?

l. 3. *ever:* forever.
l. 5. *store:* a great quantity; an abundance.

No flowers, no garlands gay? all blasted?
All wasted?
Not so, my heart: but there is fruit,
And thou hast hands.
Recover all thy sigh-blown age
On double pleasures: leave thy cold dispute 20
Of what is fit, and not. Forsake thy cage,
Thy rope of sands,
Which petty thoughts have made, and made to thee
Good cable, to enforce and draw,
And be thy law,
While thou didst wink and wouldst not see.
Away; take heed:
I will abroad.
Call in thy death's head there: tie up thy fears.
He that forbears 30
To suit and serve his need,
Deserves his load.
But as I raved and grew more fierce and wild
At every word,
Methought I heard one calling, *Child.*
And I replied, *My Lord.*

[*1633*]

This poem, by a seventeenth-century clergyman-poet, puts the case for throwing off spiritual restraint (symbolized by collars in general and the clerical collar in particular), and then, in a dramatic reversal, urges by example the necessity of submission to spiritual authority. A careful examination of the short selection will illustrate not only Herbert's techniques of composition but also the way in which most poets go about their task of creating a poem.

First, let us attempt a recapitulation in prose of the action of the poem. The narrator, restive and anxious, strikes the table and considers his state. There is no reason for him to continue in his unhappy way of life. Nothing holds him to his present existence, and he is physically free to go where he will. He asks why he no longer gets any return from the effort he expends ("no harvest but a thorn"). At one time, there was satisfaction—before the onset of his depression. The answer to his agonized crying comes to him: there is satisfaction awaiting him for the taking, but he must amend his state of mind in order to enjoy it. He must cease to have a conscience and to consider all sides of the question. He must stop thinking and simply enjoy the things of this world. Having made this decision, he is anxious to put his resolution into action and get away, for those who do not help themselves deserve to suffer. But just as he has steeled himself for the change, he hears the call of God. The restraint of the collar is too strong and ingrained, and, all thoughts of rebellion banished, he responds to the voice of his Master.

Assuming that the prose summary of the "plot" contains all the information that Herbert was trying to convey in the poem, where does it fall short of the artistry of the poem? To answer this question, we shall have to consider Herbert's (or any poet's) use of rhythm, language, image, symbol, rhyme, and tone color.

Herbert's employment of rhythm is particularly interesting and, even for the uninitiated student, quite obvious. The first lines of the poem, particularly, should be contrasted with the last two sentences. At the beginning, the narrator is frantic, banging tables, turning frenetically in all directions to escape the chafing of the collar. Appropriately, therefore, the lines are full of sharp pauses, choppy punctuation, exclamatory phrasing, and a kind of breathless nervousness. Notice that in the first line alone, consisting of only eight words, there are three separate marks of punctuation and three different thought groups. Though the reader normally expects a line of poetry to flow fairly evenly from beginning to end, perhaps with the intrusion of one slight rest, these lines are deliberately uneven and irregular. Near the end of the poem, however, as the voice from Heaven recalls the narrator to the peace of submission, the lines become quiet, the rhythm orderly—indeed, the rhythm and the meter are, for the most part, identical, and the mood created is one of regularity and rest after long exertion.

The strands of imagery which bind the parts of the poem together are particularly noteworthy. In a poem called "The Collar," one might expect to find imagery of confinement and restraint, as one does here. At the beginning, the narrator insists that "My lines and life are free; free as the road." His choice of the word "lines" is reinforced later on when Herbert speaks of "rope of sands" and "cable," and later he talks of tying up his fears. Yet nothing really holds the narrator if he wishes to go. This is indicated by his "rope of sands" image. Certainly such a rope would have no power to restrain. Moreover, if the reader considers what a rope of sand might literally be, he may conclude that

Herbert refers to the hourglass image, with the falling sand resembling a rope. In this event, the author may wish the reader to assume that what keeps the narrator immobile is simply the passage of time ("Is the year only lost to me?"). He has become confirmed in his stagnation by letting time pass him by, but now he hopes to recover his "sigh-blown age / On double pleasures."

Another stream of imagery, often raised to the level of symbol, is the Christian. It is interesting, and maybe significant, that the narrator feels persecuted, almost crucified, by his unsatisfyingly austere existence, and that he refers to the "thorn" which is his only harvest. When the reader recalls that Christ too received a thorn for his sufferings, a self-pitying identification might be implied. Further reinforcement of the Christian motif comes in the next few lines. The narrator loses blood through the pricks of the thorn, but does not replenish his supply with "cordial fruit," a phrase in which the adjective is used in the double sense of "congenial" and "wine producing." Continuing to speak of wine, he complains of its absence where he is concerned, and of the absence also of "corn." Herbert seems to be lamenting his loss of bread and wine—the two elements of the sacrament, the body and the blood of Christ. His inability to take Communion, or to be satisfied by it any more, would indeed be serious for a communicant and crucial for a clergyman. If the imagery may be interpreted in this way, the poet is bemoaning much more than the loss of the sensual pleasures of food and drink. He has apparently lost his faith, at least temporarily. How ironic, then, that in the first line he strikes "the board," the table on which meals should be served. Yet this is no more ironic than that he should wear the collar of the clergy without feeling the obligations of the faith. And when the narrator turns to the joys of the life of unrestraint which he now seeks, he puts these joys again as images of food: "but there is fruit, / And thou hast hands."

Less evident than Herbert's use of imagery and symbolism in the poem is his manipulation of sounds as reinforcement of the meaning of his lines. In this connection, note the deliberate use of harsh "r" and explosive "b" sounds in the first two lines ("Board," "struck," "cried," "abroad.") Contrast these lines with the following ones in which he postulates his freedom and mobility. Now the liquid sounds of "l" and "f" become prominent in "My lines and life are free; free as the road, / Loose as the wind . . ." And notice the simulation of his sighs in "there was w*i*ne / Before my s*i*ghs did d*ry* it." In this aural and, to some extent, subliminal reinforcement of the intellectual statement, Herbert's poetry (and poetry in general) does what ordinary prose is not fashioned to do.

It should be clear by now that what the poem says on the surface, though its determination is important to the student, is only one of many considerations which require confrontation. Herbert's simple, short poem is much more meaningful and complex than the prose summary of it given at the beginning of this analysis. It becomes the job of the reader to establish and question the relevance of everything about a poem: the form, the kinds of rhythm, the sounds, the sense, the strands of associated images, the symbolic content. In short, the fine, careless rapture that comes with reading a poem for the first time must be supplemented by deliberate intellectual analysis if one is to attain the true and most satisfying kind of appreciation, the kind that gives one the fullest knowledge and the deepest pleasure. It is appreciation of this sort that college courses in poetry hope to develop.

William Shakespeare

In 1564, William Shakespeare was born at Stratford-on-Avon, a rural town not far from London. John Shakespeare, his father, was a well-to-do, upper-middle-class businessman active in the civic life of the town; his mother was a gentlewoman. The records of Shakespeare's early life in Stratford are remarkably scanty, so that his childhood activities can only be reconstructed on the basis of probability. A youth of his status in the community would probably have studied at a "dame" school or grammar school where the principal subject would have been Latin literature and language. Rumor has it that Shakespeare had to flee from Stratford in order to avoid prosecution for deer poaching, but there is no definite evidence to prove this. It is known for certain that he married Anne Hathaway at the end of 1582 and that their three children, a girl and twin boys, were baptized between 1582 and 1585.

After Shakespeare left Stratford for London, his activities were much more fully recorded. In 1592, for instance, the writer Robert Greene wrote a letter bitterly attacking an "upstart crow" who had appeared upon the London scene and had attained great popularity suddenly, thus relegating to the shadows such former celebrities as Greene and his writer friends. In 1593, Shakespeare published *Venus and Adonis*. In the following year, he became an investor in the Lord Chamberlain's Company, which had a theater north of London. He was writing many of his most famous comedies at that time and was shortly to write *Romeo and Juliet, The Merchant of Venice, Richard*

II, and *Henry IV*. Also during these years, he was writing the sonnets. By the end of 1598, the Company had built the Globe Theater, and Shakespeare was acknowledged to be the outstanding playwright and literary figure in England.

With the death of Elizabeth I in 1603, Shakespeare found an even more enthusiastic patron in James I who, in a sense, adopted Shakespeare's company (which changed its name to the King's Men). This company often gave command performances at Court. During the first decade of the seventeenth century, at the height of his popularity and power, Shakespeare wrote *Othello, King Lear, Macbeth,* and *Antony and Cleopatra.*

For unknown reasons, Shakespeare apparently retired from active life with the players and returned to Stratford to live in 1608. He had earlier bought a large house in the town, purchased a coat of arms, and caused his family to be accorded the respect of gentlefolk. Now he became one of the distinguished citizens of Stratford. *The Tempest, The Winter's Tale,* and *Cymbeline* were produced during this semiretirement. On April 23, 1616, at the age of fifty-two, Shakespeare died in Stratford.

It is difficult to speak of the influences and experiences that moulded Shakespeare in the absence of meaningful biographical information. There can be no doubt that the move from sleepy Stratford to teeming London, gasping with Renaissance enthusiasm and recklessness, affected the impressionable young man powerfully. From being a provincial power—or, rather, a loose confederation of several power centers—England had emerged as a great nation and under Elizabeth was enjoying the fruits of strength and enterprise. Exploration, whether in seeking new lands or new verse forms, was the order of the age. Language was bursting the seams of conventional usage, and, like Marlowe's Faustus, ambitious intellects were pushing beyond traditional boundaries in science, law, the theater—in all areas of life. That excitement must have fired the playwright who, though building on the old myths, histories, theatrical traditions, and sources, yet added new dimensions of characterization, poetry, and dramatic subtlety to the theater.

Shakespeare's sonnets hint at several of the forces that helped to shape the poet's personal life. A loose series of over one hundred and fifty separate poems, the sonnets tell a story which is fragmentary at best. The vague "plot" of the series has been subject to varying interpretations. Most critics find in the sequence the story of a poet who is devoted to his young patron, a man of wealth and rank.

Shakespeare then introduces his mistress and shows his great love for her. There follows the betrayal of the poet by a liaison between the patron and the woman, with the consequent necessity for the poet to make a choice between them. He chooses the male friend. However, he turns again to address his mistress, sometimes with raillery, in the last section of the series. [See *Handbook:* sonnet cycle.]

How much the details of the sonnets match the details of Shakespeare's life is debatable, but it is true that sonnet sequences of the period traditionally dealt with the writer's innermost feelings and were expected to be at least emotionally autobiographical. Furthermore, the frequently noted sour tone of Shakespeare's dark comedies such as *Measure for Measure* and *Troilus and Cressida,* as well as his treatment of Ophelia in *Hamlet,* shows clearly that Shakespeare had suddenly and sharply altered his earlier sunny view of womanhood to a more cynical, realistic, earthy one. It is more than likely that Shakespeare had suffered a betrayal in his own life sufficient to alter the content and tone of his principal works.

Beyond the narrative line, certain persistent themes in the sonnets afford glimpses into Shakespeare's personal attitudes; and, since the sonnets were obviously written over a period of years, the pervasive motifs cannot be attributed to the mental or emotional vagaries of the passing moment. There is, first of all, the note of surpassing pride in the immortality of poetry and its consequent power to make immortal the subject it celebrates—in Shakespeare's case the young patron whom critics have, inconclusively, tried to identify for three centuries. The complementary theme is equally strong: the mortality of flesh, allowed a brief span in this world before Time destroys it utterly through natural decay and death:

> And, all in war with Time for love of you,
> As he takes from you, I engraft you new.

The first seven sonnets in the pages to follow form part of the series that expresses his devotion to his fair young patron and his desire that that fairness be perpetuated in the patron's progeny and in the poet's words: But even as Shakespeare lauds the power of the poet, his basic dissatisfaction with his profession as playwright and actor intrudes insistently. The poet seems to recognize that actors (in his day) have little higher status than beggars, thieves, and vagabonds, and he yearns, presumably, for a higher social position:

> When in disgrace with Fortune and men's eyes
> I all alone beweep my outcast state,

And trouble deaf heaven with my bootless cries,
And look upon myself, and curse my fate,
Wishing me like to one more rich in hope,
Featured like him, like him with friends possess'd,
Desiring this man's art, and that man's scope,
With what I most enjoy contented least—

Shakespeare's depressed state in this octave [see *Handbook:* octave], and the reasons for it, seem more sincere than the superficial turnabout of the sestet [see *Handbook:* sestet] in which, recalling the love of his patron, he scorns "to change my state with kings."

To appreciate Shakespeare's contribution to the sonnet form [see *Handbook:* sonnet], the reader has merely to read the florid, archaic, elaborately contrived efforts of two of his predecessors in the form, Wyatt and Surrey. To Shakespeare we owe the perfection of the rhyme scheme [see *Handbook:* rhyme scheme] which today serves to identify the Shakespearean or English sonnet as contrasted with the Petrarchan or Italian type. Shakespeare's rhyme arrangement, *abab cdcd efef* gg, helped to modernize the form. In the plays also he improved upon Marlowe's blank verse and thus made his own unrhymed iambic pentameter [see *Handbook:* iamb] most closely approximate the rhythms of modern English speech. The final couplet [see *Handbook:* couplet] of his sonnet acted as an effective clinching device for the burden of the poem while it served also as a bridge to the next sonnet. And Shakespeare's language, though rich and often vividly metaphorical, still conveys the crispness and firm certainty of modern discourse. The lines from a very well-known sonnet give evidence of this:

Shall I compare thee to a summers' day?
Thou art more lovely and more temperate.

. . .

So long as men can breathe or eyes can see,
So long lives this [poem] and this gives life to thee.

Shakespeare's sonnets were probably written by 1598; they are mentioned in a contemporary work of that year and several of them were published in a collection during 1599. The whole sonnet sequence was not published until 1609 and then only by a piratical publisher, Thomas Thorpe, who somehow obtained possession of the manuscript. Had the sonnets not been stolen, it is unlikely that the sequence would have appeared at all, for courtly writers of these lyrical revelations, while quite content to let their friends make copies of the poems for their personal pleasure and for distribution to others in the circle of friends, ordinarily did not subject their emotional verses to the indignity of commercial publication. How Thorpe got the sonnets is a mystery. His dedication of the pirated volume:

TO THE ONLY BEGETTER OF
THESE ENSUING SONNETS
MR. W. H. ALL HAPPINESS
AND THAT ETERNITY
PROMISED
BY
OUR EVER-LIVING POET
WISHETH
THE WELL-WISHING
ADVENTURER IN
SETTING
FORTH
T. T.

is one of the great mysteries of Shakespearean studies, for if "Mr. W. H." refers to the patron of the poet, it may contain a clue to the identity of the young man in the sonnets. Contemporary scholarship is still unsure of the reference.

Obviously, Shakespeare's reputation does not rest upon his sonnets. His genius as a playwright and as the chief dramatic poet in the English language often relegates his lyric poetry [see *Handbook:* lyric] to the shadows. But had they been written by a lesser artist, their distinctive contribution to English sonnet form would have been enough to bring fame to their originator.

BIBLIOGRAPHY

Hubler, Edward. *The Sense of Shakespeare's Sonnets.* Princeton, N.J.: Princeton University Press, 1952.

Rowse, A. L. *William Shakespeare: A Biography.* London: Macmillan, 1963.

Wilson, John Dover. *Shakespeare's Sonnets.* Cambridge, Eng.: Cambridge University Press, 1963.

146

Poor soul, the center of my sinful earth,
My sinful earth these rebel pow'rs that thee array,
Why dost thou pine within and suffer dearth,
Painting thy outward walls so costly gay?
Why so large cost, having so short a lease,
Dost thou upon thy fading mansion spend?
Shall worms, inheritors of this excess,
Eat up thy charge? Is this thy body's end?
Then, soul, live thou upon thy servant's loss,
And let that pine to aggravate thy store; 10
Buy terms divine in selling hours of dross;
Within be fed, without be rich no more:
  So shalt thou feed on Death, that feeds on men,
  And Death once dead, there's no more dying then.

Commentary

The poet is concerned at the undue attention paid to the needs of the physical body and at the consequent neglect of man's spirit. He advises that concentration upon the soul, which will result in attainment of eternal life, will mean the end of Death as a force.

It cannot be said that this theme is pervasive in Shakespeare's works, either in the other sonnets or in his plays. So eclectic is the dramatist, and (ostensibly) so detached, it is fruitless to ascribe to him personally the medieval platitude which is the burden of this sonnet. On the other hand, each of his tragic heroes is brought to his downfall by the existence of a flaw of character whose presence suggests failure on the hero's part to heed the admonition implicit in the sonnet. Had Macbeth not allowed wordly ambition to plague him, there would have been no tragedy. It is the same with Othello's jealousy and Antony's lust. In this sense only can the theme of the sonnet be thought to color Shakespeare's major work.

The sonnet contains relatively few difficulties. In line 1, "earth" may be taken as equivalent to "clay" or "body," sinful because mankind is subject to sin since Adam's fall, until grace restores him to the blissful state once more. In line 2, the "sinful earth" is the physical body of the speaker, surrounded by "rebel powers," the devilish enticements of the flesh. (Note the variation in meter in this line. Some critics have ascribed it to a printer's error in repeating "my sinful earth" rather than the two syllables Shakespeare wrote.) "Dearth" in line 3 means "famine" or "scarcity" in which the soul exists, though the surrounding body, "the outward walls," is expensively adorned. Now Shakespeare adopts the jargon of real estate and treats the body like a house: "large cost . . . short a lease . . . fading mansion." In line 7, the worms are inheritors of the lavish sums spent on physical pleasure in that after death they feed on the body. "Servant" in line 9 refers to the body. In line 10, "pine" has the force of "waste away" while "aggravate" has the opposite meaning of "increase." "Store" in that line refers to "abundance." In line 11, "terms divine" means "everlasting life," and "dross" is worthless stuff.

In this sonnet, Shakespeare is clearly concerned with presenting as forcefully and appealingly as possible the medieval Christian idea that existence in this world is merely a transitory condition—an affliction, almost—from which the untrammeled soul emerges at the death of the body to resume an eternal heavenly life. If this be true, said medieval writers like Chaucer, the satisfaction of the physical body is frivolous and often sinful, for it permits the individual to forget or ignore his spiritual elements, perhaps to his eternal detriment. To cater to the body is to starve the soul.

In sonnet 146, therefore, the poet seeks to assign practical business values to body and soul with a view toward convincing hardheaded readers of the concrete need to favor the spiritual over the temporal. He chooses the terminology of real estate in which to couch his appeal. The body is a property—a mansion—which houses the soul. But the soul will be a tenant for only a moment as eternal time is measured. Why then should the soul, which is everlasting, be deprived while the "outward walls" of the house are painted "so costly gay" with finery and cosmetics? Is this body-house worth the financial upkeep when the soul's "lease" is necessarily so temporary? Can the physical remains of the body-house be willed to a successor? Only worms can profit from what is left on earth.

The answer is for the soul to seek enrichment at the expense of the body, to liquidate the worthless physical frills and thus afford to purchase eternal life. To feed the soul is to starve the body. And by thus obtaining immortal life, the soul eliminates death. With death gone, dying is eliminated.

The reader will note that the poem is set up almost as a catechism except that the questions form the entire octave and are followed by all the responses in the sestet. Shakespeare was very likely impelled to arrange the poem in this way because of the sonnet tradition which called for the problem to be enunciated in the first eight lines [see *Handbook:* line], the last six supplying the answer. But the essential religious tone is maintained. The quality of turnabout between the octave and the sestet is expressed in other ways too. Contrast the description of the soul as weak and impotent at the beginning of the sonnet with its great strength at the end when it is powerful enough to devour dreaded death. At the start is is a "poor" soul, surrounded by devilish masters. It "pines" and diminishes. Before the end, however, it "aggravates," it becomes metaphorically the tycoon and conquers the strongest force man fears. The servant of the body has reduced the body to servitude, and the natural and proper order of man's private cosmos is established.

This sonnet illustrates several of Shakespeare's writing habits, and, at the same time, demonstrates many of the peculiarities of Renaissance poetic technique. The striving for balance, already mentioned, is nowhere more obvious in the sonnets: "Poor soul" and "sinful earth"; "pine within" and "outward walls"; "large" and "short"; "Buy" and "selling"; "terms divine" and "hours of dross"; "Within" and "without"; and so on. What Lyly, early in the period had elaborated into a frilly confection in verse has taken on in Shakespeare's work structural inevitability. His use of frequent adjective-noun combinations ("sinful earth," "fading mansion," and "terms divine") is characteristic of Shakespeare's literary technique, but is to be found in much of the blank verse [see *Handbook:* blank verse] of Marlowe and his contemporaries as well. Again the chief difference between Shakespeare and his generation seems to be in the poetic product: the reader feels all too often that the word combinations are, for the other writers, a flashy *tour de force* to demonstrate the writer's talent. In Shakespeare, the combinations are usually organically appropriate and quietly just. It is the misfortune of Shakespeare's contemporaries, no matter how talented, to be judged by the norms that he established. By those norms, Shakespeare remains supreme.

6

Then let not winter's ragged hand deface
In thee thy summer ere thou be distilled.
Make sweet some vial; treasure thou some place
With beauty's treasure ere it be self-killed.
That use is not forbidden usury
Which happies those that pay the willing loan;
That's for thyself to breed another thee,
Or ten times happier be it ten for one.
Ten times thyself were happier than thou art,
If ten of thine ten times refigured thee: 10
Then what could death do if thou shouldst depart,
Leaving thee living in posterity?
  Be not self-willed, for thou art much too fair,
  To be death's conquest and make worms thine heir.

l. 3. *treasure:* make rich.
l. 6. *happies:* makes happy.
l. 10. *refigured:* represented.

9

Is it for fear to wet a widow's eye
That thou consum'st thyself in single life?
Ah, if thou issueless shalt hap to die,
The world will wail thee like a makeless wife;
The world will be thy widow and still weep,
That thou no form of thee hast left behind,
When every private widow well may keep,
By children's eyes, her husband's shape in mind.
Look what an unthrift in the world doth spend,
Shifts but his place, for still the world enjoys it; 10
But beauty's waste hath in the world an end,

l. 4. *makeless:* mateless.
l. 7. *private:* separate.
l. 9. *Look what:* whatever. *unthrift:* spendthrift.
l. 10. *his:* its.

And kept unused, the user so destroys it:
  No love toward others in that bosom sits
  That on himself such murd'rous shame commits.

11

As fast as thou shalt wane, so fast thou grow'st
In one of thine, from that which thou departest;
And that fresh blood which youngly thou bestow'st
Thou mayst call thine, when thou from youth convertest.
Herein lives wisdom, beauty, and increase;
Without this, folly, age, and cold decay.
If all were minded so, the times should cease,
And threescore year would make the world away.
Let those whom Nature hath not made for store,
Harsh, featureless, and rude, barrenly perish. 10
Look whom she best endowed, she gave the more;
Which bounteous gift thou shouldst in bounty cherish.
  She carved thee for her seal, and meant thereby
  Thou shouldst print more, not let that copy die.

l. 7. *times:* generations.
l. 9. *store:* breeding; increase.
l. 11. *Look whom:* whomever.

12

When I do count the clock that tells the time,
And see the brave day sunk in hideous night;
When I behold the violet past prime,
And sable curls are silvered o'er with white;
When lofty trees I see barren of leaves,
Which erst from heat did canopy the herd,
And summer's green, all girded up in sheaves,
Borne on the bier with white and bristly beard;
Then of thy beauty do I question make,
That thou among the wastes of time must go, 10
Since sweets and beauties do themselves forsake,

l. 6. *erst:* in times past.

And die as fast as they see others grow,
  And nothing 'gainst Time's scythe can make defense,
  Save breed, to brave him when he takes thee hence.

l. 14. *Save breed:* except for his children.

14

Not from the stars do I my judgment pluck,
And yet methinks I have astronomy;
But not to tell of good or evil luck,
Of plagues, of dearths, or seasons' quality;
Nor can I fortune to brief minutes tell,
Pointing to each his thunder, rain, and wind,
Or say with princes if it shall go well
By oft predict that I in heaven find.
But from thine eyes my knowledge I derive,
And, constant stars, in them I read such art 10
As truth and beauty shall together thrive
If from thyself to store thou wouldst convert:
  Or else of thee this I prognosticate,
  Thy end is truth's and beauty's doom and date.

l. 2. *astronomy:* astrology.
l. 5. *fortune to brief minutes tell:* foretell the future precisely.
l. 6. *Pointing:* appointing or allotting.
l. 8. *oft predict:* frequent signs.
l. 12. *store:* producing a line of descendants.
l. 14. *doom and date:* Day of Judgment.

15

When I consider everything that grows
Holds in perfection but a little moment,
That this huge stage presenteth naught but shows
Whereon the stars in secret influence comment;
When I perceive that men as plants increase,
Cheerèd and checked even by the selfsame sky,
Vaunt in their youthful sap, at height decrease,

l. 4. *secret influence comment:* exercise secret power

And wear their brave state out of memory;
Then the conceit of this inconstant stay
Sets you most rich in youth before my sight, 10
Where wasteful Time debateth with Decay,
To change your day of youth to sullied night;
  And, all in war with Time for love of you,
  As he takes from you, I engraft you new.

l. 8. *out of memory:* until it is forgotten.
l. 9. *conceit:* notion.
l. 14. *engraft:* replenish your memory in my poetry.

16

But wherefore do not you a mightier way
Make war upon this bloody tyrant Time?
And fortify yourself in your decay
With means more blessèd than my barren rhyme?
Now stand you on the top of happy hours,
And many maiden gardens, yet unset,
With virtuous wish would bear your living flowers,
Much liker than your painted counterfeit.
So should the lines of life that life repair,
Which this time's pencil, or my pupil pen, 10
Neither in inward worth nor outward fair
Can make you live yourself in eyes of men.
  To give away yourself keeps yourself still,
  And you must live, drawn by your own sweet skill.

l. 6. *unset:* unsown.
l. 9. *lines of life:* offspring.
l. 13. *give away yourself:* produce children.

18

Shall I compare thee to a summer's day?
Thou art more lovely and more temperate.
Rough winds do shake the darling buds of May,
And summer's lease hath all too short a date.
Sometime too hot the eye of heaven shines,
And often is his gold complexion dimmed;

And every fair from fair sometimes declines,
By chance, or nature's changing course, untrimmed;
But thy eternal summer shall not fade,
Nor lose possession of that fair thou ow'st, 10
Nor shall Death brag thou wand'rest in his shade,
When in eternal lines to time thou grow'st.
  So long as men can breathe or eyes can see,
  So long lives this, and this gives life to thee.

l. 7. *fair:* beautiful object.
l. 8. *untrimmed:* shorn of its beauty.
l. 10. *ow'st:* own.

19

Devouring Time, blunt thou the lion's paws,
And make the earth devour her own sweet brood;
Pluck the keen teeth from the fierce tiger's jaws,
And burn the long-lived phoenix in her blood;
Make glad and sorry seasons as thou fleets,
And do whate'er thou wilt, swift-footed Time,
To the wide world and all her fading sweets;
But I forbid thee one most heinous crime,
O, carve not with thy hours my love's fair brow,
Nor draw no lines there with thine antique pen. 10
Him in thy course untainted do allow,
For beauty's pattern to succeeding men.
  Yet do thy worst, old Time; despite thy wrong,
  My love shall in my verse ever live young.

l. 4. *in her blood:* while she still lives.

23

As an unperfect actor on the stage,
Who with his fear is put besides his part,
Or some fierce thing replete with too much rage,
Whose strength's abundance weakens his own heart;
So I, for fear of trust, forget to say

l. 2. *put besides his part:* thrown off in his role.
l. 5. *for fear of trust:* afraid to trust myself.

The perfect ceremony of love's right,
And in mine own love's strength seem to decay,
O'ercharged with burden of mine own love's might.
O, let my books be then the eloquence
And dumb presagers of my speaking breast, 10
Who plead for love, and look for recompense,
More than that tongue that more hath more expressed.
  O, learn to read what silent love hath writ.
  To hear with eyes belongs to love's fine wit.

l. 6. *right:* perhaps a pun on "rite."
l. 10. *dumb presagers:* silent indicators.
l. 12. *more expressed:* more frequently expressed.

24

Mine eye hath played the painter and hath stell'd
Thy beauty's form in table of my heart;
My body is the frame wherein 'tis held,
And perspective it is best painter's art,
For through the painter must you see his skill,
To find where your true image pictured lies,
Which in my bosom's shop is hanging still,
That hath his windows glazèd with thine eyes.
Now see what good turns eyes for eyes have done:
Mine eyes have drawn thy shape, and thine for me 10
Are windows to my breast, wherethrough the sun
Delights to peep, to gaze therein on thee.
  Yet eyes this cunning want to grace their art,
  They draw but what they see, know not the heart.

l. 1. *stell'd:* fixed.
l. 2. *table:* the tablet.
l. 8. *glazèd:* glassed.
l. 13. *want:* lack.

25

Let those who are in favor with their stars
Of public honor and proud titles boast,
Whilst I whom fortune of such triumph bars,
Unlooked for joy in that I honor most.

l. 4. *joy in that:* enjoy what.

Great princes' favorites their fair leaves spread
But as the marigold at the sun's eye,
And in themselves their pride lies burièd,
For at a frown they in their glory die.
The painful warrior famousèd for might,
After a thousand victories once foiled, 10
Is from the book of honor rasèd quite,
And all the rest forget for which he toiled.
  Then happy I that love and am beloved
  Where I may not remove, nor be removed.

l. 6. *But as the marigold at the sun's eye:* as the marigold opens in the sun.

l. 11. *rasèd quite:* completely erased.

29

When, in disgrace with Fortune and men's eyes,
I all alone beweep my outcast state,
And trouble deaf heaven with my bootless cries,
And look upon myself and curse my fate,
Wishing me like to one more rich in hope,
Featured like him, like him with friends possessed,
Desiring this man's art, and that man's scope,
With what I most enjoy contented least;
Yet in these thoughts myself almost despising,
Haply I think on thee, and then my state, 10
Like to the lark at break of day arising
From sullen earth, sings hymns at heaven's gate;
  For thy sweet love rememb'red such wealth brings,
  That then I scorn to change my state with kings.

l. 3. *bootless:* unavailing.

30

When to the sessions of sweet silent thought
I summon up remembrance of things past,
I sigh the lack of many a thing I sought,
And with old woes new wail my dear Time's waste.
Then can I drown an eye, unused to flow,

l. 4. *Time's waste:* Time's eradication of beloved things.

For precious friends hid in death's dateless night,
And weep afresh love's long since canceled woe,
And moan th' expense of many a vanished sight;
Then can I grieve at grievances foregone,
And heavily from woe to woe tell o'er 10
The sad account of fore-bemoanèd moan,
Which I new pay as if not paid before.
  But if the while I think on thee, dear friend,
  All losses are restored and sorrows end.

l. 7. *canceled:* no longer owed because it has been paid.
l. 8. *expense:* loss.
l. 10. *tell o'er:* add up.

32

If thou survive my well-contented day,
When that churl Death my bones with dust shall cover,
And shalt by fortune once more resurvey
These poor rude lines of thy deceasèd lover,
Compare them with the bett'ring of the time,
And though they be outstripped by every pen,
Reserve them for my love, not for their rhyme,
Exceeded by the height of happier men.
O, then vouchsafe me but this loving thought:
"Had my friend's Muse grown with this growing age, 10
A dearer birth than this his love had brought,
To march in ranks of better equipage;
  But since he died, and poets better prove,
  Theirs for their style I'll read, his for his love."

l. 1. *my well-contented day:* the day on which I shall be content to die.
l. 5. *bett'ring:* better verse.
l. 8. *happier:* more talented.

40

Take all my loves, my love, yea take them all;
What hast thou then more than thou hadst before?

l. 1. *loves:* my own and that of my mistress. Shakespeare knows of his mistress' affair with his friend and patron.
  my love: the friend.

No love, my love, that thou mayst true love call;
All mine was thine, before thou hadst this more.
Then if for my love thou my love receivest,
I cannot blame thee for my love thou usest;
But yet be blamed, if thou this self deceivest
By willful taste of what thyself refusest.
I do forgive thy robb'ry, gentle thief,
Although thou steal thee all my poverty; 10
And yet love knows it is a greater grief
To bear love's wrong than hate's known injury.
Lascivious grace, in whom all ill well shows,
Kill me with spites; yet we must not be foes.

45

The other two, slight air and purging fire,
Are both with thee, wherever I abide;
The first my thought, the other my desire,
These present-absent with swift motion slide.
For when these quicker elements are gone
In tender embassy of love to thee,
My life, being made of four, with two alone
Sinks down to death, oppressed with melancholy;
Until life's composition be recured
By those swift messengers returned from thee, 10
Who even but now come back again, assured
Of thy fair health, recounting it to me
This told, I joy, but then no longer glad,
I send them back again, and straight grow sad.

l. 1. *other two:* in sonnet 44 earth and water, two of the four elements believed at that time to make up matter, were mentioned; the "other two" are air and fire.

55

Not marble, nor the gilded monuments
Of princes, shall outlive this pow'rful rhyme,
But you shall shine more bright in these contents
Than unswept stone, besmeared with sluttish time.

l. 4. *stone:* monument in a church.

When wasteful war shall statues overturn,
And broils root out the work of masonry,
Nor Mars his sword nor war's quick fire shall burn
The living record of your memory.
'Gainst death and all oblivious enmity
Shall you pace forth; your praise shall still find room 10
Even in the eyes of all posterity
That wear this world out to the ending doom.
  So, till the judgment that yourself arise,
  You live in this, and dwell in lovers' eyes.

l. 6. *broils:* battles.
l. 12. *ending doom:* Day of Judgment.
l. 13. *that:* when.

60

Like as the waves make towards the pebbled shore,
So do our minutes hasten to their end;
Each changing place with that which goes before,
In sequent toil all forwards do contend.
Nativity, once in the main of light,
Crawls to maturity, wherewith being crowned,
Crooked eclipses 'gainst his glory fight,
And Time that gave doth now his gift confound.
Time doth transfix the flourish set on youth,
And delves the parallels in beauty's brow, 10
Feeds on the rarities of nature's truth,
And nothing stands but for his scythe to mow:
  And yet to times in hope my verse shall stand,
  Praising thy worth, despite his cruel hand.

l. 5. *main:* sea.
l. 8. *confound:* destroy.
l. 9. *transfix the flourish:* cause the attractiveness to disappear.
l. 10. *delves the parallels:* makes wrinkles.
l. 13. *times in hope:* times to come.

71

No longer mourn for me when I am dead
Than you shall hear the surly sullen bell

Give warning to the world that I am fled
From this vile world with vilest worms to dwell.
Nay, if you read this line, remember not
The hand that writ it, for I love you so
That I in your sweet thoughts would be forgot,
If thinking on me then should make you woe.
O, if, I say, you look upon this verse,
When I, perhaps, compounded am with clay, 10
Do not so much as my poor name rehearse,
But let your love even with my life decay,
  Lest the wise world should look into your moan,
  And mock you with me after I am gone.

73

That time of year thou mayst in me behold
When yellow leaves, or none, or few, do hang
Upon those boughs which shake against the cold,
Bare ruined choirs where late the sweet birds sang.
In me thou seest the twilight of such day
As after sunset fadeth in the west,
Which by and by black night doth take away,
Death's second self, that seals up all in rest.
In me thou seest the glowing of such fire
That on the ashes of his youth doth lie, 10
As the deathbed whereon it must expire,
Consumed with that which it was nourished by.
  This thou perceiv'st, which makes thy love more strong,
  To love that well which thou must leave ere long.

97

How like a winter hath my absence been
From thee, the pleasure of the fleeting year!
What freezings have I felt, what dark days seen,
What old December's bareness everywhere!
And yet this time removed was summer's time,

l. 2. *pleasure:* the summer season.

The teeming autumn, big with rich increase,
Bearing the wanton burden of the prime,
Like widowed wombs after their lords' decease.
Yet this abundant issue seemed to me
But hope of orphans and unfathered fruit; 10
For summer and his pleasures wait on thee,
And, thou away, the very birds are mute;
  Or, if they sing, 'tis with so dull a cheer,
  That leaves look pale, dreading the winter's near.

l. 7. *prime:* the time of fertilization and conception; i.e., the spring.

99

The forward violet thus did I chide:
Sweet thief, whence didst thou steal thy sweet that smells
If not from my love's breath? The purple pride
Which on thy soft cheek for complexion dwells
In my love's veins thou hast too grossly dyed.
The lily I condemnèd for thy hand,
And buds of marjoram had stol'n thy hair;
The roses fearfully on thorns did stand,
One blushing shame, another white despair;
A third, nor red nor white, had stol'n of both, 10
And to his robb'ry had annexed thy breath;
But for his theft, in pride of all his growth
A vengeful canker eat him up to death.
  More flowers I noted, yet I none could see,
  But sweet or color it had stol'n from thee.

Note that sonnet 99 has fifteen lines, the first five rhyming *ababa*.
l. 1. *forward:* early.
l. 6. *condemnèd for thy hand:* blamed for stealing the color of your hand.

116

Let me not to the marriage of true minds
Admit impediments; love is not love
Which alters when it alteration finds,
Or bends with the remover to remove.

O, no, it is an ever-fixèd mark
That looks on tempests and is never shaken;
It is the star to every wand'ring bark,
Whose worth's unknown, although his height be taken.
Love's not Time's fool, though rosy lips and cheeks
Within his bending sickle's compass come; 10
Love alters not with his brief hours and weeks,
But bears it out even to the edge of doom.
 If this be error and upon me proved,
 I never writ, nor no man ever loved.

l. 10. *compass:* circle.
l. 11. *his:* Time's.

129

Th' expense of spirit in a waste of shame
Is lust in action; and, till action, lust
Is perjured, murd'rous, bloody, full of blame,
Savage, extreme, rude, cruel, not to trust;
Enjoyed no sooner but despisèd straight;
Past reason hunted, and no sooner had,
Past reason hated as a swallowed bait
On purpose laid to make the taker mad;
Mad in pursuit, and in possession so;
Had, having, and in quest to have, extreme; 10
A bliss in proof, and proved, a very woe,
Before, a joy proposed; behind, a dream.
 All this the world well knows, yet none knows well
 To shun the heaven that leads men to this hell.

l. 1. *Th' expense:* the using up.
 spirit: vital substance.
l. 14. *heaven:* the joy of sexual relationship.

134

So, now I have confessed that he is thine
And I myself am mortgaged to thy will,
Myself I'll forfeit, so that other mine

l. 3. *other mine:* my friend.

Thou wilt restore to be my comfort still.
But thou wilt not, nor he will not be free,
For thou art covetous, and he is kind;
He learned but surety-like to write for me
Under that bond that him as fast doth bind.
The statute of thy beauty thou wilt take,
Thou usurer that put'st forth all to use, 10
And sue a friend came debtor for my sake;
So him I lose through my unkind abuse.
  Him have I lost, thou hast both him and me;
  He pays the whole, and yet am I not free.

ll. 7–8. *He learned . . . bind:* He acted as my surrogate in making love but now he is in the bondage of love himself.
l. 9. *statute:* bail (?).
l. 10. *use:* usury.
l. 11. *friend came:* friend who became.
l. 12. *my unkind abuse:* cruel tricking of me.

interlude: 1. a short, humorous play formerly presented the parts of a miracle play or morality play. 2. a short play of a sort popular in the Tudor period (ruling family of Eng., 1485–1603, descended from Owen Tudor ?–1461, a Welsh nobleman who married the widow of Henry V) either farcical or moralistic in tone and with a plot typically derived from French farce or morality play.

a short poem with a witty or satirical point ←

John Donne

Eight years after Shakespeare's birth, John Donne was born in London in 1572. From his father, a wealthy tradesman, he gained, perhaps, his practical concern for money and for making a place for himself in the world of affairs. From his mother it is likely that he derived his artistic and literary inclinations as well as his eloquence in oratory. His mother was descended from Sir Thomas More and was the daughter of the dramatist John Heywood. The fact that Donne was born a Roman Catholic in the England of Queen Elizabeth worked against his chances of secular advancement, especially in terms of education and civil service. Thus, though his parents were able to send him to Oxford until he was sixteen, he was barred after that unless he could conscientiously sign the Thirty-nine Articles of the Anglican faith.

Donne's young adulthood was marked by a restless searching for his place in the Renaissance world. At nineteen, in 1591, he went up to London to study law and one year later was admitted to the Society of Lincoln's Inn. Four years later, he went on several military expeditions to destroy the Spanish fleet. He was attracted, his biographers believe, not so much by patriotism as by the hope of making a reputation and reaping the material rewards of fame at a time when Englishmen like Essex and Raleigh were being recognized and lionized for their deeds. His military career over in 1597, he became secretary to Sir Thomas Egerton, and through him, at the age of twenty-five, Lord Keeper of the Great Seal of England. In the process, it had been necessary for him to drop his association with Roman Catholicism and to embrace the Church of England.

Just when Donne's future seemed assured and his fortune made, he took a step which was to alter the tenor of his life: he wooed and secretly married a highborn sixteen-year-old girl, the niece of Thomas Egerton, without obtaining the necessary permission of the girl's father, Sir George More. The unrelenting father forced Egerton to dismiss Donne from his position. Furthermore, he refused to contribute to the support of his daughter, and he had Donne imprisoned for marrying without the consent of the father. Though the Archbishop of Canterbury himself declared the marriage legal in 1602 and Donne was freed, he emerged from prison with bleak prospects and no job.

Reestablishing himself as a citizen of consequence took several years. Immediately following his release, he took his family to a country house in Surrey lent to him by a cousin of his wife. Here he read widely, especially in theology. As a hobby, he continued to write poetry, an avocation that had occupied him since his eighteenth year. As the family increased, he moved to Mitcham, closer to London. The opportunity for employment and for patronage by the mighty came to him upon the accession of James I to the throne. It was Donne's task to reinforce James's repression of the Catholics by writing anti-Catholic propaganda for the State—an assignment particularly appropriate to an apostate Catholic who had grounded himself in theology. So successful was he in this employment that men of considerable power tried to convince him to enter the Church of England as a clergyman. But at thirty-five, with hopes of temporal preferment still high, Donne resisted the call:

> But, Sir, my refusal is not for that I think myself too good for that calling,—for which Kings, if they think so, are not good enough; nor for that my education and learning, though not eminent may not, being assisted with God's grace and humility, render me in some measure fit for it: but I dare make so dear a friend as you are my Confessor; some irregularities of my life have been so visible to some men, that though I have . . . made my peace with him be penitential resolutions against them . . . ; yet this, which God knows to be so, is not so visible to men as to free me from their censures, and it may be, that sacred calling from a dishonour. . . .

There may be truth in Donne's stated wish not to bring discredit upon the church through his former sins of the flesh, but more likely his hesitation stemmed from his continuing hope of temporal advancement.

The years that followed immediately brought no alleviation of his physical situation. He suffered from ill health and in fact wrote a tract in defense of suicide called *Biathanatos,* in which he says, "Whensoever any affliction assails me, methinks I have the keys of my prison in mine own hand, and no remedy presents itself so soon to my heart as mine own sword." Melancholy and ennui characterized him during these years, even though he could count among his good friends members of the distinguished Herbert family, Ben Jonson, the Countess of Bedford, and Sir Robert Drury, in honor of whose teen-aged daughter Donne wrote the famous Anniversary poems.

By 1609, Donne's fortunes had taken a turn for the better. His wife's father finally settled a dowry on his daughter. By 1612, the poet had decided upon ordination. He was already an old man by Renaissance standards—over forty—with a family to support. Moreover, he knew that the King himself wished him to take orders as a prelude to a semispiritual, semipolitical career in the church. In 1613 he formally requested a position in the church and two years later he was ordained. After his wife's death in 1617, Donne more and more withdrew from worldly affairs, devoting himself to theology and church matters. James I made him Dean of St. Paul's in 1621, a congenial post in which he could be close to the life of the city but at the same time could have a sanctuary for meditation and work. In extreme ill health, he dwelt often on death, identifying himself with sick humanity in his *Devotions.* Death came to him in March, 1631.

In a letter to the King's minister, Somerset, Donne described himself as an "independent and disobliged man." It was this independence of spirit which very largely shaped his life. Donne lived in an age when it was still necessary for the man of letters or the aspirant for a position in the church to court favor with people in high places, and he certainly hoped for patronage. Yet he refused to accept this kind of security if it meant compromising with principle. To adopt Anglicanism and shed Catholicism was rather a natural consequence of his changing religious and theological position—not a concession to economic necessity. Moreover, Donne knew very well that he might lose his hard-won place in Sir Thomas Egerton's service—with the bright future that seemed assured—if he married Ann More, but he placed the sacredness of their love above material advancement. Finally, though Donne was aware that the King himself wished him to enter the church as a first step to receiving the King's favor, he held back for five years before capitulating.

The poverty, deprivation, and frustration which his independence cost him affected his personality and, in turn, his poetry. Though his two major themes are usual in poetry—love and death—Donne made these motifs unmistakeably his own by his attitude toward them. Death had become for Donne an unwelcome familiar, a personage to be addressed in almost rowdy terms, an enemy of close acquaintance. It is not surprising that eyewitnesses to Donne's last sermon at St. Paul's recall that he preached, in effect, his own funeral sermon, his impassive face like a death mask. Nor is it hard to believe that he posed in his shroud, as though rehearsing the ritual of his end. His essay on suicide indicates also the morbid turn which his mind sometimes took. The first lines of poem after poem demonstrate his preoccupation:

> Before I sigh my last gasp, let me breathe,
> Great Love, some legacies . . .
>
> Whoever comes to shroud me, do not harm . . .
>
> When my grave is broke up again . . .
>
> When I am dead, and doctors know not why

The motif of love, often intermingled with that of death, is expressed in several ways. Least typical are the personal tender expressions of love, probably for his wife, which ring with sincerity and devotion. Much more typical are the cynical, intellectual exercises that play on the mysterious relationships of men and women. Many of these follow the mode of the seventeenth century in flippant allusion to this relationship as purely physical, inevitably temporary, and always changing. Constancy is mocked, variety lauded. It is difficult to say whether Donne is executing a literary convention here or whether he is describing what contemporary scandal took to be his own way of life. In any event, since the poems were not published till after Donne's death and cannot be properly dated—some of them having been written as early as 1590 and others well into the seventeenth century—it is dangerous to read any biographical allusion into most of them.

In Donne's own time, though he was reputed to be a poet of extraordinary talent, only a small circle of friends and literary acquaintances knew his work, for it circulated only in manuscript.

Hesitating as he did between life in the church and out of it, Donne may not have wished to give wider distribution to his often raw and sexually suggestive love lyrics [see *Handbook:* lyric]. Nor, perhaps, would the audience at large have grasped the meaning of the difficult poems. Apparently Donne preferred to win fame as an orator and preacher. His *Devotions* and other "divine" works are ample testimony to his genius as a writer of scholarly religious prose.

Donne's method of presentation in poetry is startling to readers unaccustomed to the style of the "Metaphysical School" of seventeenth-century lyricists, of whom Donne is the outstanding example. The poets of this group thought a poem an intellectual exercise even though the content might be primarily emotional. The poem became a kind of syllogism, a geometrical or algebraic proof, a step-by-step process of arriving at the solution to a verbal equation. Such a poem was constructed by bringing together, as Samuel Johnson said, "a combination of dissimilar images" [see *Handbook:* imagery] in which the poet, using wit and ingenuity, finds and reveals "occult resemblances." Thus, in Donne's "The Flea," the tiny insect is found to be both the human lover and his beloved, if the reader will but follow the complicated argument as to how such an analogy is possible.

The incongruities and surprises of this kind of poetry make for harsh and unmelodious lines. There is nothing comfortable in such verse, nor can the reader follow the poem without stringent and cooperative attention. One must likewise ignore Wordsworth's definition of poetry as the "spontaneous overflow of powerful feeling" as he attempts to penetrate the thick-textured intellectual complexity of Donne's lines. At the same time, one must admire the sheer verbal felicitousness of the poet and his ability, through metaphor [see *Handbook:* metaphor] extended into what is called "conceit," [see *Handbook:* conceit] through ambiguity, through plays on words, and through imaginative association of dissimilar elements, to produce a poem which is lyrical and emotionally meaningful.

Donne's reputation has fluctuated more than that of most major poets. The posthumous edition of his poems, published by his son, brought him critical approval, but subsequent alterations in taste reduced him to an unread minor poet in the nineteenth and early twentieth centuries. Largely through efforts of T. S. Eliot to counteract what he at one time considered the undesirable effect of Milton's poetry on the modern writer by proposing Donne's work as much worthier of imitation, Donne's reputation has been rehabilitated. His verbal pyrotechnics are in vogue today. His ability to think and feel at once in his emotionally charged intellectual exercises (Eliot's aim, too, in his verse) has made Donne a model. Finally, his difficulty and obscurity, his complex way of looking at and commenting on his world, have made him appear particularly modern and immediate to readers today.

It is easy to see the reflection of his age in Donne's own life and in poetry. That it was a disturbed and nervous age is clear: an age of unbounded possibilities but also of great anxieties which lack of restraint engenders. Scientific discoveries had shaken man's certainty about his place in the world even as they had promised him a new place in the cosmos. In the "Anniversary" poems Donne dwelt specifically on the chaos of his time. But even when his poetry ignores the political or social or scientific or religious world, as it often does in terms of theme, his verses bear the stamp of that world. The diction is often deliberately harsh, impatient, brutal. The rhythms are nervous and the rhymes crabbed. Godhead shares a page with an insect; a man may be a spider. Most of the poems rely on paradox [see *Handbook:* paradox], which, in itself, is a device for startling the reader into unaccustomed and often bizarre associations and equations. Indeed, several critics of Donne have suggested that his choice of paradox as a pervasive method is the poet's way of bringing order, at least in his own created universe of poetry, to the disorder of the universe around him. For if the poles of the paradox may be artistically reconciled—if there is Oneness in the apparent diversity—then a complete falling apart of our world is prevented, at least for the moment. If Donne did not succeed in rescuing his world, his use of the method did, at least, result in memorable poetry.

BIBLIOGRAPHY

Bennett, Joan. *Four Metaphysical Poets.* Cambridge, Eng.: Cambridge University Press, 1934.

Martz, L. L. *The Poetry of Meditation.* New Haven: Yale University Press, 1954.

Williamson, George. *The Donne Tradition.* New York: Noonday Press, 1958. Originally published by Harvard University Press in 1930.

The Flea

Marke but this flea, and marke in this,
How little that which thou deny'st me is;
It suck'd me first, and now sucks thee,
And in this flea, our two bloods mingled bee;
Thou know'st that this cannot be said
A sinne, nor shame, nor losse of maidenhead,
Yet this enjoyes before it wooe,
And pamper'd swells with one blood made of two,
And this, alas, is more than wee would doe.

Oh stay, three lives in one flea spare, 10
Where wee almost, yea more than maryed are.
This flea is you and I, and this
Our mariage bed, and mariage temple is;
Though parents grudge, and you, w'are met,
And cloysterd in these living walls of Jet.
Though use make you apt to kill mee,
Let not to that, selfe murder added bee,
And sacrilege, three sinnes in killing three.

Cruell and sodaine, hast thou since
Purpled thy naile, in blood of innocence? 20
Wherein could this flea guilty bee,
Except in that drop which it suckt from thee?
Yet thou triumph'st, and saist that thou
Find'st not thy selfe, nor mee the weaker now;
'Tis true, then learne how false, feares bee;
Just so much honor, when thou yeeld'st to mee,
Will wast, as this flea's death tooke life from thee.

Commentary

The subject matter of the poem is typical of seventeenth-century lyrical verse: the lover seeks to convince his love of the desirability of consummating their passion and assures her that yielding to him will not diminish her honor.

So little is known about the amorous entanglements of Donne during his early manhood that ascribing autobiographical significance to "The Flea" is unwise. By his own admission, the poet had lived a full and lusty life in youth. The unwillingness of his father-in-law to accept him as a member of the family may have been due partly to Donne's tarnished reputation, and some critics ascribe Donne's unwillingness to embrace ordination and life in the church to an uneasiness regarding the dissolute life he had formerly led. But all this is speculation and not particularly germane to a reading of the poem.

The point is that a verbally talented young man like Donne was expected, in the seventeenth century, to write poems in which the man—always the narrator—tries to seduce the lady by an appeal to her mind or her emotions. This set theme was the convention and it was employed by poets almost universally, whatever may have been their private views of amorous deportment. Donne's contribution to the established mode is the method of argument—the resort to extended metaphor and devious logic to prove intellectually a rather dubious emotional proposition. Andrew Marvell, in "To His Coy Mistress" makes the point openly and clearly. So do the "Gather ye rosebuds" poets. Donne must dazzle the reader through a display of circumlocution. He must demonstrate intellectual virtuosity by a witty linkage of apparently dissimilar and incongruous ideas and images. Thus, the biting of the lover and his beloved by a flea is equated to the copulation of man and woman, and the involved consequences of such a bizarre equation become the subject matter of the poem.

There are few verbal or syntactical pitfalls in "The Flea." Its difficulty lies in the deviousness of its argument. In line 4, normal usage would reverse the order of "mingled bee." The "this" in line 5 refers to the mingling of the blood of man and woman. In line 7, the word "this" refers to the flea. In line 10, "stay" is the lover's exhortation to the woman not to kill the flea. The second "this" of line 12 refers to the body of the flea in which both bloods now mix. The two lines that follow show the lovers together symbolically in the body of the insect regardless of opposition by parents or the beloved herself. "Use" in line 16 is a synonym for "habit." In line 17, "self murder" suggests suicide, for by killing the flea, the beloved would be killing herself since her blood is in the bloodstream of the creature. The "sacrilege" of line 18 sums up the triple killing: the murder of a

Trinity. "Purpled thy nail" in line 20 shows that the lady has already killed the flea. And in the last two lines, "Just so much honor . . . / Will wast [waste]" means "You will lose just so much honor. . . ."

It is more profitable to follow Donne's argument as the lover speaks. He points out to the beloved that a flea, which has bitten both of them and consequently has the blood of both within him, has succeeded in an enterprise which she has denied to her lover. Yet the accomplishment of the flea in no way shames the beloved nor renders her less virginal. At the same time, the engorged flea flourishes by reason of having within him the substance of both lovers. Yet the lady refuses to allow the healthy union of herself with the man. As the second stanza [see *Handbook:* stanza] begins, the beloved is about to kill the flea as her lover bids her restrain the impulse. His argument is that, in killing the flea, she would be killing three entities, for within the insect in symbolic union are the poet and his love. Neither the objections of relatives nor of the lady herself are of avail, for cohabitation is already taking place. It is true, the narrator goes on, that the lady is in the habit of "killing" her lover, but to do so under these circumstances would be to desecrate the marriage bed and to commit suicide too. As the final stanza begins, the beloved has already killed the flea, who is innocent of any wrongdoing. The lover must face a victorious beloved who insists that his entire argument has been disproved by her act: the flea is dead but lover and beloved continue to live undiminished in health. The lover counters this turn in the discussion with the final thrust: by seeing that what I feared would happen did not happen, you see that fears are often without foundation. In the same way, your fear of losing your honor in this seduction will prove groundless.

Several observations may be made concerning the terms of the argument. By choosing a flea Donne obviously widened the distance between the panting lover and his beloved, on the one hand, and the ostensibly sexless, minute, unattractive insect, on the other. That the choice was deliberate seems clear, for the gap between the opposing (yet related) images sharpens the wit of the conception. Donne is similarly triumphant in wit at the end of the poem when he has the beloved represented almost as speaking for the sated reader. Weary of following the intricacies of the argument, the reader detects the logical flaw: the flea is dead but the lovers remain alive. At this moment, the poet, who has led the reader into the trap, shifts the ground of his argument and capitalizes climacticly on the reader's, and the beloved's, temporary victory.

The Canonization

For Godsake hold your tongue, and let me love,
  Or chide my palsie, or my gout,
My five gray haires, or ruin'd fortune flout,
  With wealth your state, your minde with Arts improve,
    Take you a course, get you a place,
    Observe his honour, or his grace,
Or the Kings reall, or his stamped face
  Contemplate, what you will, approve,
  So you will let me love.

Alas, alas, who's injur'd by my love? 10
  What merchants ships have my sighs drown'd?
Who saies my teares have overflow'd his ground?
  When did my colds a forward spring remove?
    When did the heats which my veines fill
    Adde one more to the plaguie Bill?
Soldiers finde warres, and Lawyers finde out still
  Litigious men, which quarrels move,
  Though she and I do love.

Call us what you will, wee are made such by love;
  Call her one, mee another flye, 20
We'are Tapers too, and at our owne cost die,
  And wee in us finde the'Eagle and the Dove.
    The Phœnix ridle hath more wit
    By us, we two being one, are it.
So to one neutrall thing both sexes fit,
  Wee dye and rise the same, and prove
  Mysterious by this love.

Wee can dye by it, if not live by love,
  And if unfit for tombes and hearse

l. 7. *stamped face:* engraved on coins; Donne suggests life in the business world.
l. 15. *plaguie Bill:* an official list of those killed by the plague.

Our legend bee, it will be fit for verse; 30
  And if no peece of Chronicle wee prove,
    We'll build in sonnets pretty roomes;
    As well a well wrought urne becomes
The greatest ashes, as halfe-acre tombes,
  And by these hymnes, all shall approve
  Us *Canoniz'd* for Love:

And thus invoke us; You whom reverend love
  Made one anothers hermitage;
You, to whom love was peace, that now is rage;
  Who did the whole worlds soule contract, and drove 40
    Into the glasses of your eyes
    (So made such mirrors, and such spies,
That they did all to you epitomize,)
  Countries, Townes, Courts: Beg from above
  A patterne of your love!

l. 31. *Chronicle:* history.

A Valediction: Forbidding Mourning

As virtuous men passe mildly away,
  And whisper to their soules, to goe,
Whilst some of their sad friends doe say,
  The breath goes now, and some say, no:

So let us melt, and make no noise,
  No teare-floods, nor sigh-tempests move,
T'were prophanation of our joyes
  To tell the layetie our love.

Moving of th'earth brings harmes and feares,
  Men reckon what it did and meant, 10
But trepidation of the spheares,
  Though greater farre, is innocent.

ll. 9–12. *Moving . . . innocent:* earthquakes are dangerous and ought to be feared, but celestial movements are not harmful.

Dull sublunary lovers love
 (Whose soule is sense) cannot admit
Absence, because it doth remove
 Those things which elemented it.

But we by a love, so much refin'd,
 That our selves know not what it is,
Inter-assured of the mind,
 Care lesse, eyes, lips, and hands to misse. 20

Our two soules therefore, which are one,
 Though I must goe, endure not yet
A breach, but an expansion,
 Like gold to ayery thinnesse beate.

If they be two, they are two so
 As stiffe twin compasses are two,
Thy soule the fixt foot, makes no show
 To move, but doth, if th' other doe.

And though it in the center sit,
 Yet when the other far doth rome, 30
It leanes, and hearkens after it,
 And growes erect, as that comes home.

Such wilt thou be to mee, who must
 Like th'other foot, obliquely runne;
Thy firmnes drawes my circle just,
 And makes me end, where I begunne.

The Relique

When my grave is broke up againe
Some second ghest to entertaine,
(For graves have learn'd that woman-head
To be to more than one a Bed)
 And he that digs it, spies
A bracelet of bright haire about the bone,
 Will he not let'us alone,
And thinke that there a loving couple lies,

Who thought that this device might be some way
To make their soules, at the last busie day, 10
Meet at this grave, and make a little stay?

If this fall in a time, or land,
Where mis-devotion both command,
Then, he that digges us up, will bring
Us, to the Bishop, and the King,
To make us Reliques; then
Thou shalt be a Mary Magdalen, and I
A something else thereby;
All women shall adore us, and some men;
And since at such time, miracles are sought, 20
I would have that age by this paper taught
What miracles wee harmlesse lovers wrought.

First, we lov'd well and faithfully,
Yet knew not what wee lov'd, nor why,
Difference of sex no more wee knew,
Than our Guardian Angells doe;
Comming and going, wee
Perchance might kisse, but not between those meales:
Our hands ne'r toucht the seales,
Which nature, injur'd by late law, sets free: 30
These miracles wee did; but now alas,
All measure, and all language, I should passe,
Should I tell what a miracle shee was.

l. 13. *mis-devotion:* Roman Catholicism.

ll. 29–30. *Our hands . . . free:* though nature does not forbid free love, we refrained from sexual contact.

FROM AN ANATOMIE OF THE WORLD

The First Anniversary

Wherein, By Occasion of the Untimely Death of Mistress Elizabeth Drury, the Frailty and the Decay of this Whole World Is Represented

When that rich Soule which to her heaven is gone,
Whom all do celebrate, who know they have one,
(For who is sure he hath a Soule, unlesse
It see, and judge, and follow worthinesse,
And by Deedes praise it? hee who doth not this,
May lodge an In-mate soule, but 'tis not his.)
When that Queene ended here her progresse time,
And, as t'her standing house to heaven did climbe,
Where loath to make the Saints attend her long,
She's now a part both of the Quire, and Song, 10
This World, in that great earthquake languished;
For in a common bath of teares it bled,
Which drew the strongest vitall spirits out:
But succour'd then with a perplexed doubt,
Whether the world did lose, or gaine in this,
(Because since now no other way there is,
But goodnesse, to see her, whom all would see,
All must endeavour to be good as shee,)
This great consumption to a fever turn'd,
And so the world had fits; it joy'd, it mourn'd; 20
And, as men thinke, that Agues physick are,
And th'Ague being spent, give over care,
So thou sicke World, mistak'st thy selfe to bee
Well, when alas, thou'rt in a Lethargie.

Elizabeth Drury: in this elegy, Donne intended to go far beyond praise of a particular adolescent. He enlarges his subject to the "idea of a woman," and uses the poem to reveal his thoughts on his world.

l. 21. *Agues physick are:* these diseases were believed to be self-curing.

Her death did wound and tame thee then, and then
Thou might'st have better spar'd the Sunne, or Man.
That wound was deep, but 'tis more misery,
That thou hast lost thy sense and memory.
'Twas heavy then to heare thy voyce of mone,
But this is worse, that thou art speechlesse growne. 30
Thou hast forgot thy name, thou hadst; thou wast
Nothing but shee, and her thou hast o'rpast.
For as a child kept from the Font, untill
A prince, expected long, come to fulfill
The ceremonies, thou unnam'd had'st laid,
Had not her comming, thee her Palace made:
Her name defin'd thee, gave thee forme, and frame,
And thou forgett'st to celebrate thy name.
Some moneths she hath beene dead (but being dead,
Measures of times are all determined) 40
But long she'ath beene away, long, long, yet none
Offers to tell us who it is that's gone.
But as in states doubtfull of future heires,
When sicknesse without remedie empaires
The present Prince, they're loth it should be said,
The Prince doth languish, or the Prince is dead:
So mankinde feeling now a generall thaw,
A strong example gone, equall to law,
The Cyment which did faithfully compact,
And glue all vertues, now resolv'd, and slack'd, 50
Thought it some blasphemy to say sh'was dead,
Or that our weaknesse was discovered
In that confession; therefore spoke no more
Than tongues, the Soule being gone, the losse deplore.
But though it be too late to succour thee,
Sicke World, yea, dead, yea putrified, since shee
Thy'intrinsique balme, and thy preservative,
Can never be renew'd, thou never live,
I (since no man can make thee live) will try,
What wee may gaine by thy Anatomie. 60
Her death hath taught us dearely, that thou art
Corrupt and mortall in thy purest part.
Let no man say, the world it selfe being dead,

l. 60. *Anatomie:* analysis.

'Tis labour lost to have discovered
The worlds infirmities, since there is none
Alive to study this dissection;
For there's a kinde of World remaining still,
Though shee which did inanimate and fill
The world, be gone, yet in this last long night,
Her Ghost doth walke; that is, a glimmering light, 70
A faint weake love of vertue, and of good,
Reflects from her, on them which understood
Her worth; and though she have shut in all day,
The twilight of her memory doth stay;
Which, from the carcasse of the old world, free,
Creates a new world, and new creatures bee
Produc'd: the matter and the stuffe of this,
Her vertue, and the forme our practice is:
And though to be thus elemented, arme
These creatures, from home-borne intrinsique harme, 80
(For all assum'd unto this dignitie,
So many weedlesse Paradises bee,
Which of themselves produce no venemous sinne,
Except some forraine Serpent bring it in)
Yet, because outward stormes the strongest breake,
And strength it selfe by confidence growes weake,
This new world may be safer, being told
The dangers and diseases of the old:
For with due temper men doe then forgoe,
Or covet things, when they their true worth know. 90
There is no health; Physitians say that wee,
At best, enjoy but a neutralitie.
And can there be worse sicknesse, than to know
That we are never well, nor can be so?
Wee are borne ruinous: poor mothers cry,
That children come not right, nor orderly;
Except they headlong come and fall upon
An ominous precipitation.
How witty's ruine how importunate
Upon mankinde! it labour'd to frustrate 100
Even Gods purpose; and made woman, sent
For mans reliefe, cause of his languishment.
They were to good ends, and they are so still,
But accessory, and principall in ill;

For that first marriage was our funerall:
One woman at one blow, then kill'd us all,
And singly, one by one, they kill us now.
We doe delightfully our selves allow
To that consumption; and profusely blinde,
Wee kill our selves to propagate our kinde. 110
And yet we do not that; we are not men:
There is not now that mankinde, which was then,
When as, the Sunne and man did seeme to strive,
(Joynt tenants of the world) who should survive;
When, Stagge, and Raven, and the long-liv'd tree,
Compar'd with man, dy'd in minoritie;
When, if a slow pac'd starre had stolne away
From the observers marking, he might stay
Two or three hundred years to see't againe,
And then make up his observation plaine; 120
When, as the age was long, the sise was great;
Mans growth confess'd, and recompenc'd the meat;
So spacious and large, that every Soule
Did a faire Kingdome, and large Realme controule:
And when the very stature, thus erect,
Did that soule a good way towards heaven direct.
Where is this mankinde now? who lives to age,
Fit to be made *Methusalem* his page?
Alas, we scarce live long enough to try
Whether a true made clocke run right, or lie. 130
Old Grandsires talke of yesterday with sorrow,
And for our children wee reserve to morrow.
So short is life, that every peasant strives,
In a torne house, or field, to have three lives.
And as in lasting, so in length is man
Contracted to an inch, who was a spanne;
For had a man at first in forrests stray'd,
Or shipwrack'd in the Sea, one would have laid
A wager, that an Elephant, or Whale,
That met him, would not hastily assaile 140
A thing so equall to him: now alas,
The Fairies, and the Pigmies well may passe
As credible; mankinde decayes so soone,

l. 112. *then:* in Old Testament times.

We'are scarce our Fathers shadowes cast at noone:
Onely death addes t'our length: nor are wee growne
In stature to be men, till we are none.
But this were light, did our lesse volume hold
All the old Text; or had wee chang'd to gold
Their silver; or dispos'd into lesse glasse
Spirits of vertue, which then scatter'd was. 150
But 'tis not so: w'are not retir'd, but dampt;
And as our bodies, so our mindes are crampt:
'Tis shrinking, not close weaving that hath thus,
In minde, and body both bedwarfed us.
Wee seeme ambitious, Gods whole worke t'undoe;
Of nothing hee made us, and we strive too,
To bring our selves to nothing backe; and wee
Doe what wee can, to do't so soone as hee.
With new diseases on our selves we warre,
And with new Physicke, a worse Engin farre. 160
Thus man, this worlds Vice-Emperour, in whom
All faculties, all graces are at home;
And if in other creatures they appeare,
They're but mans Ministers, and Legats there,
To worke on their rebellions, and reduce
Them to Civility, and to mans use:
This man, whom God did wooe, and loth t'attend
Till man came up, did downe to man descend,
This man, so great, that all that is, is his,
Oh what a trifle, and poore thing he is! 170
If man were any thing, he's nothing now:
Helpe, or at least some time to wast, allow
T'his other wants, yet when he did depart
With her whom we lament, hee lost his heart.
She, of whom th'Ancients seem'd to prophesie,
When they call'd vertues by the name of *shee;*
Shee in whom vertue was so much refin'd,
That for Allay unto so pure a minde
Shee tooke the weaker Sex; shee that could drive
The poysonous tincture, and the staine of *Eve,* 180
Out of her thoughts, and deeds; and purifie
All, by a true religious Alchymie;

l. 176. *shee:* virtue was given feminine attributes.

Shee, shee is dead; shee's dead: when thou knowest this,
Thou knowest how poore a trifling thing man is.
And learn'st thus much by our Anatomie,
The heart being perish'd, no part can be free.
And that except thou feed (not banquet) on
The supernaturall food, Religion,
Thy better Growth growers withered, and scant;
Be more than man, or thou'rt lesse than an Ant. 190
Then, as mankinde, so is the worlds whole frame
Quite out of joynt, almost created lame:
For, before God had made up all the rest,
Corruption entred, and deprav'd the best:
It seis'd the Angels, and then first of all
The world did in her cradle take a fall,
And turn'd her braines, and tooke a generall maime,
Wronging each joynt of th'universall frame.
The noblest part, man, felt it first; and then
Both beasts and plants, curst in the curse of man. 200
So did the world from the first houre decay,
That evening was beginning of the day,
And now the Springs and Sommers which we see,
Like sonnes of women after fiftie bee.
And new Philosophy calls all in doubt,
The Element of fire is quite put out;
The Sun is lost, and th'earth, and no mans wit
Can well direct him where to looke for it.
And freely men confesse that this world's spent,
When in the Planets, and the Firmament 210
They seeke so many new; then see that this
Is crumbled out againe to his Atomies.
'Tis all in peeces, all cohaerence gone;
All just supply, and all Relation:
Prince, Subject, Father, Sonne, are things forgot,
For every man alone thinkes he hath got

l. 187. *feed (not banquet)*: to Donne, to banquet was to eat lightly; he felt that one had to feed seriously on spiritual things, not merely pick at religious "food."

l. 205. *new Philosophy:* of contemporary astronomers like Galileo.

ll. 216–217. *man . . . Phoenix:* each believes himself to be unique.

To be a Phoenix, and that then can bee
None of that kinde, of which he is, but hee.
This is the worlds condition now, and now
She that should all arts to reunion bow, 220
She that had all Magnetique force alone,
To draw, and fasten sundred parts in one;
She whom wise nature had invented then
When she obser'd that every sort of men
Did in their voyage in this worlds Sea stray,
And needed a new compasse for their way;
She that was best, and first originall
Of all faire copies, and the generall
Steward to Fate; she whose rich eyes, and breast
Guilt the West Indies, and perfum'd the East; 230
Whose having breath'd in this world, did bestow
Spice on those Iles, and bad them still smell so,
And that rich Indie which doth gold interre,
Is but as single money, coyn'd from her:
She to whom this world must it selfe refer,
As Suburbs, or the Microcosme of her,
Shee, shee is dead; shee's dead: when thou knowst this,
Thou knowst how lame a cripple this world is.
And learn'st thus much of our Anatomie,
That this worlds generall sicknesse doth not lie 240
In any humour, or one certaine part;
But as thou sawest it rotten at the heart,
Thou seest a Hectique feaver hath got hold
Of the whole substance, not to be contrould,
And that thou hast but one way, not t'admit
The worlds infection, to be none of it.
For the worlds subtilst immateriall parts
Feele this consuming wound, and ages darts.
For the worlds beauty is decai'd, or gone,
Beauty, that's colour, and proportion. 250
We thinke the heavens enjoy their Sphericall,
Their round proportion embracing all.
But yet their various and perplexed course,
Observ'd in divers ages, doth enforce
Men to finde out so many Eccentrique parts,
Such divers downe-right lines, such overthwarts,

l. 256. *lines . . . overthwarts:* mathematical lines . . . forces.

As disproportion that pure forme: It teares
The Firmament in eight and forty sheires,
And in these Constellations then arise
New starres, and old doe vanish from our eyes: 260
As though heav'n suffered earthquakes, peace or war.
When new Towers rise, and old demolish't are.
They have impal'd within a Zodiake
The free-borne Sun, and keepe twelve Signes awake
To watch his steps; the Goat and Crab controule,
And fright him backe, who else to either Pole
(Did not these Tropiques fetter him) might runne:
For his course is not round; nor can the Sunne
Perfit a Circle, or maintaine his way
One inch direct; but where he rose to-day 270
He comes no more, but with a couzening line,
Steales by that point, and so is Serpentine:
And seeming weary with his reeling thus,
He meanes to sleepe, being now falne nearer us.
So, of the Starres which boast that they doe runne
In Circle still, none ends where he begun.
All their proportion's lame, it sinkes, it swels.
For of Meridians, and Parallels,
Man hath weav'd out a net, and this net throwne
Upon the Heavens, and now they are his owne. 280
Loth to goe up the hill, or labour thus
To goe to heaven, we make heaven come to us.
We spur, we reine the starres, and in their race
They're diversly content t'obey our pace.
But keepes the earth her round proportion still?
Doth not a Tenarif, or higher Hill
Rise so high like a Rocke, that one might thinke
The floating Moone would shipwrack there, and sinke?
Seas are so deepe, that Whales being strooke to day,
Perchance to morrow, scarse at middle way 290
Of their wish'd journies end, the bottome, die.
And men, to sound depths, so much line untie,
As one might justly thinke, that there would rise
At end thereof, one of th'Antipodies:
If under all, a Vault infernall bee,
(Which sure is spacious, except that we
Invent another torment, that there must
Millions into a straight hot roome be thrust)

Then solidnesse, and roundnesse have no place.
Are these but warts, and pock-holes in the face 300
Of th'earth? Thinke so: but yet confesse, in this
The worlds proportion disfigured is;
That those two legges whereon it doth rely,
Reward and punishment are bent awry.
And, Oh, it can no more be questioned,
That beauties best, proportion, is dead,
Since even griefe it selfe, which now alone
Is left us, is without proportion.
Shee by whose lines proportion should bee
Examin'd, measure of all Symmetree, 310
Whom had that Ancient seen, who thought soules made
Of Harmony, he would at next have said
That Harmony was shee, and thence infer,
That soules were but Resultances from her,
And did from her into our bodies goe,
As to our eyes, the formes from objects flow:
Shee, who if those great Doctors truly said
That the Arke to mans proportions was made,
Had been a type for that, as that might be
A type of her in this, that contrary 320
Both Elements, and Passions liv'd at peace
In her, who caus'd all Civill war to cease.
Shee, after whom, what forme soe'r we see,
Is discord, and rude incongruitie;
Shee, shee is dead, shee's dead; when thou knowst this,
Thou knowst how ugly a monster this world is:
And learn'st thus much by our Anatomie,
That here is nothing to enamour thee:
And that, not only faults in inward parts,
Corruptions in our braines, or in our hearts, 330
Poysoning the fountaines, whence our actions spring,
Endanger us: but that if every thing
Be not done fitly'and in proportion,
To satisfie wise, and good lookers on,
(Since most men be such as most thinke they bee)
They're lothsome to, by this Deformitee.
For good, and well, must in our actions meete;

l. 311. *that Ancient:* Pythagoras (?).

Wicked is not much worse than indiscreet.
But beauties other second Element,
Colour, and lustre now, is as neere spent. 340
And had the world his just proportion,
Were it a ring still, yet the stone is gone.
As a compassionate Turcoyse which doth tell
By looking pale, the wearer is not well,
As gold falls sicke being stung with Mercury,
All the worlds parts of such complexion bee.
When nature was most busie, the first weeke,
Swadling the new borne earth, God seem'd to like
That she should sport her selfe sometimes, and play,
To mingle, and vary colours every day: 350
And then, as though shee could not make inow,
Himselfe his various Rainbow did allow.
Sight is the noblest sense of any one,
Yet sight hath only colour to feed on,
And colour is decai'd: summers robe growes
Duskie, and like an oft dyed garment showes.
Our blushing red, which us'd in cheekes to spred,
Is inward sunke, and only our soules are red.
Perchance the world might have recovered,
If she whom we lament had not beene dead: 360
But shee, in whom all white, and red, and blew
(Beauties ingredients) voluntary grew,
As in an unvext Paradise; from whom
Did all things verdure, and their lustre come,
Whose composition was miraculous,
Being all colour, all Diaphanous,
(For Ayre, and Fire but thick grosse bodies were,
And liveliest stones but drowsie, and pale to her,)
Shee, shee, is dead; shee's dead: when thou know'st this,
Thou know'st how wan a Ghost this our world is: 370
And learn'st thus much by our Anatomie,
That it should more affright, than pleasure thee.
And that, since all faire colour then did sinke,
'Tis now but wicked vanitie, to thinke
To colour vicious deeds with good pretence,
Or with bought colors to illude mens sense.
Nor in ought more this worlds decay appears,
Than that her influence the heav'n forbeares,

Or that the Elements doe not feele this,
The father, or the mother barren is. 380
The cloudes conceive not raine, or doe not powre,
In the due birth, downe the balmy showre;
Th'Ayre doth not motherly sit on the earth,
To hatch her seasons, and give all things birth;
Spring-times were common cradles, but are tombes;
And false-conceptions fill the generall wombes;
Th'Ayre showes such Meteors, as none can see,
Not only what they meane, but what they bee;
Earth such new wormes, as would have troubled much
Th'Ægyptian *Mages* to have made more such. 390
What Artist now dares boast that he can bring
Heaven hither, or constellate any thing,
So as the influence of those starres may bee
Imprison'd in an Hearbe, or Charme, or Tree,
And doe by touch, all which those stars could doe?
The art is lost, and correspondence too.
For heaven gives little, and the earth takes lesse,
And man least knowes their trade and purposes.
If this commerce twixt heaven and earth were not
Embarr'd, and all this traffique quite forgot, 400
She, for whose losse we have lamented thus,
Would worke more fully, and pow'rfully on us:
Since herbes, and roots, by dying lose not all,
But they, yea Ashes too, are medicinall,
Death could not quench her vertue so, but that
It would be (if not follow'd) wondred at:
And all the world would be one dying Swan,
To sing her funerall praise, and vanish then.
But as some Serpents poyson hurteth not,
Except it be from the live Serpent shot, 410
So doth her vertue need her here, to fit
That unto us; shee working more than it.
But shee, in whom to such maturity
Vertue was growne, past growth, that it must die;
Shee, from whose influence all Impressions came,
But, by Receivers impotencies, lame,
Who, though she could not transubstantiate
All states to gold, yet guilded every state,

l. 389. *new wormes:* much travel literature describing new reptiles was current in Donne's time.

So that some Princes have some temperance;
Some Counsellers some purpose to advance 420
The common profit; and some people have
Some stay, no more than Kings should give, to crave;
Some women have some taciturnity,
Some nunneries some graines of chastitie.
She that did thus much, and much more could doe,
But that our age was Iron, and rustie too,
Shee, shee is dead; shee's dead; when thou knowst this,
Thou knowst how drie a Cinder this world is.
And learn'st thus much by our Anatomy,
That 'tis in vaine to dew, or mollifie 430
It with thy teares, or sweat, or blood: nothing
Is worth our travaile, griefe, or perishing,
But those rich joyes, which did possesse her heart,
Of which she's now partaker, and a part.
But as in cutting up a man that's dead,
The body will not last out, to have read
On every part, and therefore men direct
Their speech to parts, that are of most effect;
So the worlds carcasse would not last, if I
Were punctuall in this Anatomy; 440
Nor smels it well to hearers, if one tell
Them their disease, who faine would think they're well.
Here therefore be the end: And, blessed maid,
Of whom is meant what ever hath been said,
Or shall be spoken well by any tongue,
Whose name refines course lines, and makes prose song,
Accept this tribute, and his first yeares rent,
Who till his darke short tapers end be spent,
As oft as thy feast sees this widowed earth,
Will yearely celebrate thy second birth, 450
That is, thy death; for though the soule of man
Be got when man is made, 'tis borne but then
When man doth die; our body's as the wombe,
And, as a Mid-wife, death directs it home.
And you her creatures, whom she workes upon,
And have your last, and best concoction
From her example, and her vertue, if you
In reverence to her, do thinke it due,

l. 422. *stay:* ability to control themselves.

That no one should her praises thus rehearse,
As matter fit for Chronicle, not verse; 460
Vouchsafe to call to minde that God did make
A last, and lasting'st peece, a song. He spake
To *Moses* to deliver unto all,
That song, because hee knew they would let fall
The Law, the Prophets, and the History,
But keepe the song still in their memory:
Such an opinion (in due measure) made
Me this great Office boldly to invade:
Nor could incomprehensiblenesse deterre
Mee, from thus trying to emprison her, 470

l. 462. *a song:* the Song of Moses.

FROM HOLY SONNETS

IV

Oh my blacke Soule! now thou art summoned
By sicknesse, deaths herald, and champion;
Thou art like a pilgrim, which abroad hath done
Treason, and durst not turne to whence hee is fled,
Or like a thiefe, which till deaths doome be read,
Wisheth himselfe delivered from prison;
But damn'd and hal'd to execution,
Wisheth that still he might be imprisoned.
Yet grace, if thou repent, thou canst not lacke;
But who shall give thee that grace to beginne? 10
Oh make thy selfe with holy mourning blacke,
And red with blushing, as thou art with sinne;
Or wash thee in Christs blood, which hath this might
That being red, it dyes red soules to white.

X

Death be not proud, though some have called thee
Mighty and dreadfull, for, thou art not soe,

For, those, whom thou think'st, thou dost overthrow,
Die not, poore death, nor yet canst thou kill mee.
From rest and sleepe, which but thy pictures bee,
Much pleasure, then from thee, much more must flow,
And soonest our best men with thee doe goe,
Rest of their bones, and soules deliverie.
Thou art slave to Fate, Chance, kings, and desperate men,
And dost with poyson, warre, and sicknesse dwell, 10
And poppie, or charmes can make us sleepe as well,
And better than thy stroake; why swell'st thou then?
One short sleepe past, wee wake eternally,
And death shall be no more; death, thou shalt die.

l. 11. *poppie:* drugs.
l. 12. *swell'st:* puff with pride.

The Indifferent

I can love both faire and browne,
Her whom abundance melts, and her whom want betraies,
Her who loves lonenesse best, and her who maskes and plaies,
Her whom the country form'd, and whom the town.
Her who beleeves, and her who tries,
Her who still weepes with spungie eyes,
And her who is dry corke, and never cries:
I can love her, and her, and you and you,
I can love any, so she be not true.

Will no other vice content you? 10
Wil it not serve your turn to do, as did your mothers?
Or have you all old vices spent, and now would finde out
others?
Or doth a feare, that men are true, torment you?
Oh we are not, be not you so,
Let mee, and doe you, twenty know.
Rob mee, but binde me not, and let me goe.
Must I, who came to travaile thorow you,
Grow your fixt subject, because you are true?

Venus heard me sigh this song,
And by Loves sweetest Part, Variety, she swore, 20

She heard not this till now; and that it should be so no more.
She went, examin'd, and return'd ere long,
And said, alas, Some two or three
Poore Heretiques in love there bee,
Which thinke to stablish dangerous constancie.
But I have told them, since you will be true,
You shall be true to them, who'are false to you.

Lovers Infinitenesse

If yet I have not all thy love,
Deare, I shall never have it all,
I cannot breath one other sigh, to move,
Nor can intreat one other teare to fall,
And all my treasure, which should purchase thee,
Sighs, teares, and oathes, and letters I have spent.
Yet no more can be due to mee,
Than at the bargaine made was ment,
If then thy gift of love were partiall,
That some to mee, some should to others fall, 10
    Deare, I shall never have Thee All.

Or if then thou gavest mee all,
All was but All, which thou hadst then;
But if in thy heart, since, there be or shall,
New love created bee, by other men,
Which have their stocks intire, and can in teares,
In sighs, in oathes, and letters outbid mee,
This new love may beget new feares,
For, this love was not vowed by thee.
And yet it was, thy gift being generall, 20
The ground, thy heart is mine, what ever shall
    Grow there, deare, I should have it all.

Yet I would not have all yet,
Hee that hath all can have no more,
And since my love doth every day admit
New growth, thou shouldst have new rewards in store;
Thou canst not every day give me thy heart,
If thou canst give it, then thou never gavest it:

Loves riddles are, that though thy heart depart,
It stayes at home, and thou with losing saves it: 30
But wee will have a way more liberall,
Than changing hearts, to joyne them, so wee shall
Be one, and one anothers All.

The Legacie

When I dyed last, and, Deare, I dye
As often as from thee I goe,
Though it be but an houre agoe,
And Lovers houres be full eternity,
I can remember yet, that I
Something did say, and something did bestow;
Though I be dead, which sent mee, I should be
Mine owne executor and Legacie.

I heard mee say, Tell her anon,
That my selfe, (that is you, not I,) 10
Did kill me, and when I felt mee dye,
I bid mee send my heart, when I was gone,
But I alas could there finde none,
When I had ripp'd me, 'and search'd where hearts did lye;
It kill'd mee againe, that I who still was true,
In life, in my last Will should cozen you.

Yet I found something like a heart,
But colours it, and corners had,
It was not good, it was not bad,
It was intire to none, and few had part. 20
As good as could be made by art
It seem'd; and therefore for our losses sad,
I meant to send this heart in stead of mine,
But oh, no man could hold it for twas thine.

l. 16. *cozen:* cheat.

The Message

Send home my long strayd eyes to mee,
Which (Oh) too long have dwelt on thee;

Yet since there they have learn'd such ill,
  Such forc'd fashions,
  And false passions,
    That they be
    Made by thee
Fit for no good sight, keep them still.

Send home my harmlesse heart againe,
Which no unworthy thought could staine; 10
But if it be taught by thine
  To make jestings
  Of protestings,
    And crosse both
    Word and oath,
Keepe it, for then 'tis none of mine.

Yet send me back my heart and eyes,
That I may know, and see thy lyes,
And may laugh and joy, when thou
  Art in anguish 20
  And dost languish
    For some one
    That will none,
Or prove as false as thou art now.

The Extasie

Where, like a pillow on a bed,
  A Pregnant banke swel'd up, to rest
The violets reclining head,
  Sat we two, one anothers best.
Our hands were firmely cimented
  With a fast balme, which thence did spring,
  Our eye-beames twisted, and did thred
  Our eyes, upon one double string;
So to'entergraft our hands, as yet
  Was all the meanes to make us one, 10
And pictures in our eyes to get
  Was all our propagation.

As 'twixt two equall Armies, Fate
  Suspends uncertaine victorie,
Our soules, (which to advance their state,
  Were gone out,) hung 'twixt her, and mee.
And whil'st our soules negotiate there,
  Wee like sepulchrall statues lay;
All day, the same our postures were,
  And wee said nothing, all the day. 20
If any, so by love refin'd,
  That he soules language understood,
And by good love were growen all minde,
  Within convenient distance stood,
He (though he knew not which soul spake,
  Because both meant, both spake the same)
Might thence a new concoction take,
  And part farre purer than he came.
This Extasie doth unperplex
  (We said) and tell us what we love, 30
Wee see by this, it was not sexe,
  Wee see, we saw not what did move:
But as all severall soules containe
  Mixture of things, they know not what,
Love, these mixt soules, doth mixe againe,
  And makes both one, each this and that.
A single violet transplant,
  The strength, the colour, and the size,
(All which before was poore, and scant,)
  Redoubles still, and multiplies. 40
When love, with one another so
  Interinanimates two soules,
That abler soule, which thence doth flow,
  Defects of lonelinesse controules.
Wee then, who are this new soule, know,
  Of what we are compos'd, and made,
For, th'Atomies of which we grow,
  Are soules, whom no change can invade.
But O alas, so long, so farre
  Our bodies why doe wee forbeare? 50

l. 27. *concoction:* attitude.
l. 47. *Atomies:* atoms, the components of a thing.

They'are ours, though they'are not wee, Wee are
  The intelligences, they the spheares.
We owe them thankes, because they thus,
  Did us, to us, at first convay,
Yeelded their forces, sense, to us,
  Nor are drosse to us, but allay.
On man heavens influence workes not so,
  But that it first imprints the ayre,
Soe soule into the soule may flow,
  Though it to body first repaire. 60
As our blood labours to beget
  Spirits, as like soules as it can,
Because such fingers need to knit
  That subtile knot which makes us man:
So must pure lovers soules descend
  T'affections, and to faculties,
Which sense may reach and apprehend,
  Else a great Prince in prison lies.
To'our bodies turne wee then, that so
  Weake men on love reveal'd may looke; 70
Loves mysteries in soules doe grow,
  But yet the body is his booke.
And if some lover, such as wee,
  Have heard this dialogue of one,
Let him still marke us, he shall see
  Small change, when we'are to bodies gone.

l. 56. *allay:* alloy.

The Baite

Come live with mee, and bee my love,
And wee will some new pleasures prove
Of golden sands, and christall brookes,
With silken lines, and silver hookes.

There will the river whispering runne
Warm'd by thy eyes, more than the Sunne.
And there the'inamor'd fish will stay,
Begging themselves they may betray.

l. 2. *prove:* try.

When thou wilt swimme in that live bath,
Each fish, which every channell hath, 10
Will amorously to thee swimme,
Gladder to catch thee, than thou him.

If thou, to be so seene, beest loath,
By Sunne, or Moone, thou darknest both,
And if my selfe have leave to see,
I need not their light, having thee.

Let others freeze with angling reeds,
And cut their legges, with shells and weeds,
Or treacherously poore fish beset,
With strangling snare, or windowie net: 20

Let coarse bold hands, from slimy nest
The bedded fish in banks out-wrest,
Or curious traitors, sleavesilke flies
Bewitch poor fishes wandring eyes.

For thee, thou needst no such deceit,
For thou thy selfe art thine owne bait;
That fish, that is not catch'd thereby,
Alas, is wiser farre than I.

Which when I saw that a strict grave could doe,
I saw not why verse might not do so too. 30
Verse hath a middle nature: heaven keepes Soules,
The Grave keepes bodies, Verse the Fame enroules.

Loves Deitie

I long to talke with some old lovers ghost,
  Who dyed before the god of Love was borne:
I cannot thinke that hee, who then lov'd most,
  Sunke so low, as to love one which did scorne.
But since this god produc'd a destinie,
And that vice-nature, custome, lets it be;
  I must love her, that loves not mee.

Sure, they which made him god, meant not so much,
  Nor he, in his young godhead practis'd it.
But when an even flame two hearts did touch, 10
  His office was indulgently to fit
Actives to passives. Correspondencie
Only his subject was; It cannot bee
  Love, till I love her, that loves mee.

But every moderne god will now extend
  His vast prerogative, as far as Jove.
To rage, to lust, to write to, to commend,
  All is the purlewe of the God of Love.
Oh were wee wak'ned by this Tyrannie
To ungod this child againe, it could not bee 20
  I should love her, who loves not mee.

Rebell and Atheist too, why murmure I,
  As though I felt the worst that love could doe?
Love might make me leave loving, or might trie
  A deeper plague, to make her love mee too,
Which, since she loves before, I'm loth to see;
Falshood is worse than hate; and that must bee,
  If shee whom I love, should love mee.

A Hymne to God the Father

I

Wilt thou forgive that sinne where I begunne,
  Which is my sin, though it were done before?
Wilt thou forgive those sinnes, through which I runne,
  And do run still: though still I do deplore?
    When thou hast done, thou hast not done,
      For, I have more.

II

Wilt thou forgive that sinne by which I'have wonne
  Others to sinne? and, made my sinne their doore?

l. 5. *done . . . done*: note the pun on "Donne."

Wilt thou forgive that sinne which I did shunne
A yeare, or two: but wallowed in, a score? 10
When thou hast done, thou hast not done,
For, I have more.

III

I have a sinne of feare, that when I have spunne
My last thred, I shall perish on the shore;
Sweare by thy selfe, that at my death thy sonne
Shall shine as he shines now, and heretofore;
And, having done that, Thou haste done,
I feare no more.

John Milton

John Milton was born on December 9, 1608 in central London. His father, a scrivener by profession, was a member of the rising urban moneyed class which more and more was gaining political power in the seventeenth century. Acuity in business did not hinder Milton's father from taking an active interest in the arts, and he was an internationally known composer of serious music. Milton was sent at the age of twelve to St. Paul's School, probably the best school in England at that time, for training in the liberal arts. In 1625, he matriculated at Christ's College, Cambridge, where he received his bachelor's degree four years later and his M.A. degree in 1632.

Feeling that his college education had not fully equipped him for the tasks of enlightened citizen and distinguished poet—roles which he had staked out for himself early in life—Milton retired after the Cambridge interlude to his father's estate at Horton, not far from London, where for six years he continued his intellectual preparation. By this time he had been writing poetry for almost a decade and had completed "On the Morning of Christ's Nativity," *Comus*, "Lycidas," and others. Still he felt inadequate for undertaking his mature role; therefore, he decided to take the "Grand Tour" of Europe as the final step in his preliminary education. During 1638–39, he visited Florence, Rome, Geneva, Paris, and other capitals before hurrying home at the outbreak of hostilities between the English and the Scots.

Milton's sympathies did not lie with the English king, Charles I, nor with the Anglican royalists. The poet had for some time been quietly critical of the behavior of many Anglican prelates and of the interference of the Crown in making appointments of bishops. He made his position known in a series of antiprelatical tracts which were published during 1641 and 1642. Alienated from the Church of England, Milton was at this point in his own religious life moving closer to the Presbyterian position.

In 1642, at the age of thirty-four, Milton married a sixteen-year-old girl named Mary Powell, who came from a royalist family. Mary lived with her husband for a few months, then left him abruptly and returned to her family near Oxford in Cavalier territory. Almost immediately the Civil War broke out, and it became impossible for Milton to see his wife on enemy ground, much less to attempt a reconciliation. Nor did the church sanction divorce on grounds of incompatibility. Acutely distressed by this inflexible and, he believed, dishonest position, Milton spent the next two years writing four tracts on divorce to justify and clarify his stand. When their publication met with opposition or indifference from Presbyterian divines, Milton found himself at odds with this new Establishment and moved once again to a more radical religious position with the Independents. As a consequence of his difficulties in publishing tracts not in line with the thought of the Establishment, Milton wrote a spirited defense of freedom to publish which appeared as *Areopagitica* in 1644.

With the imprisonment and later execution of Charles I in 1649 and the coming to power of Oliver Cromwell in the eleven-year Protectorate, the poet came into his own. Milton ignored failing eyesight to become the chief apologist for Cromwell's party, now the government, and was appointed to the office of Latin Secretary to the Council of State, the equivalent of a cabinet post. With the downfall of the regime and the Restoration of the monarchy under Charles II in 1660, Milton's friends feared for his life. But the blind poet escaped punishment, merely losing his position and undergoing a kind of surveillance until his death fourteen years later.

After the Civil War, Milton was reconciled with Mary Powell and lived with her until her death in 1652. He married Katherine Woodcock in 1656. When she died in 1658, Milton married Elizabeth Minshull, who lived until 1727. During this last marriage, Milton published his three greatest poems, *Paradise Lost, Paradise Regained,* and *Samson Agonistes.*

Certainly religion was the most significant single factor in shaping Milton's life and his poetic production. Had he been satisfied with

Anglicanism, as his father was, he would almost surely have become a clergyman, as his friend Edward King of "Lycidas" had planned to do. Instead, his searching examination of his Puritan conscience led him from one extreme religious position to another in his search for truth, and he explained his changes of position in pamphlets and poems. Even his infatuation with Mary Powell had to be examined in *Paradise Lost* under the guise of Adam's relationship to Eve, and had to be studied abstractly in the divorce tracts and elsewhere. Religious strife was responsible for his rise to high place in the government and, indirectly, for his fall at the Restoration. Nor was the path which Milton followed based merely on principle. If his divorce pamphlets had been enthusiastically, or even politely, received by Presbyterian leaders, Milton might not have moved to the more extreme Independent position. Similarly, had the warnings that he sounded in the antiprelatical tracts been acknowledged by authority, he might not have strayed from the Anglican fold. In a discussion of a man whose religion was not merely a personal matter but the heart of his poetry, such considerations are particularly important.

The enormous importance of Milton's early background cannot be overstated. His father's tolerance of the beliefs of others provided the boy with a breadth of understanding unusual in seventeenth-century England. His father's interest in the arts—especially in music—meant that the Milton household was often visited by the outstanding composers and performers of the day. It surely accounts for Milton's interest in Italian music and for the numerous times that he mentions music significantly in his writings. Most important, it must account in part for his sensitivity to the musical tone, rhythm, rhyme, and other melodious sound combinations in his poetry.

Milton's schooling too provided for an intelligent youth the best Renaissance education available. The combination of thorough grounding in Judeao-Christian studies with rigorous training in the Greek and Latin authors is reflected with credit in all his works. Moreover, as Milton pointed out in his "Epistle to Thomas Hartlib" with regard to the education of youth, there was plenty of time during the long school day for training in mathematics and science and in foreign languages beyond the classical. All of these studies Milton utilized to good effect in his writings. His blindness, which became a source of theme and image in his later poetry, has been attributed to his excessive studying by candlelight.

As early as 1629, Milton had decided to be an epic poet and had determined to live his life in a manner befitting such a high calling. Asceticism seemed essential to an epic poet whose role, in Milton's eyes, was to be a priest and prophet chosen by God. As Milton put it:

> These [epic] abilities, wheresoever they be found, are the inspired gift of God, rarely bestowed, but yet to some . . . in every nation; and are of power, beside the office of a pulpit, to imbreed and cherish in a great people the seeds of virtue and public civility, to allay the perturbations of the mind, and set the affections in right tune; to celebrate in glorious and lofty hymns the throne and equipage of God's almightiness, and what He works and what He suffers to be wrought with high providence . . . to deplore the general relapses of kingdoms and states from justice and God's true worship. Lastly, whatsoever in religion is holy and sublime, in virtue amiable or grave, whatsoever hath passion or admiration in all the changes of that which is called fortune from without, or the wily subtleties and reflexes of man's thoughts from within; all these things with a solid and treatable smoothness to paint out and describe.

This pronouncement contains in embryo many of Milton's literary themes. The poet as ascetic, hinted at in "Il Penseroso," is declared. The poet as priest, justifying the ways of God to man, is made explicit. The "Hymn on the Morning of Christ's Nativity" is made a natural product of a poet's work. Most important of all, perhaps, is Milton's statement that the poet as prophet has the duty to "deplore the general relapses of kingdoms and states from justice and God's true worship," for it is on this ground that Milton in his prose works often sanctions rebellion against the "legitimate" monarch, in Milton's view an anti-Christ meriting violent overthrow.

Two further pervasive themes of Milton's work are the interplay of knowledge and chastity (in its broadest sense of purity and virtue) and the interplay of passion and reason. As early as his Masque of *Comus,* Milton had insisted that the chastity of the lady be tried and found not wanting rather than allowing her to live in the pure aloofness of untried innocence. The dignity of the human individual, as well as the religious doctrine of Free Will, was central to Milton's thought. His insistence upon it formed the philosophic base of his opposition to censorship in *Areopagitica.* If the reader is sheltered from alleged evil influences through prior censorship, he argues, that reader can hardly be praised for maintaining his chastity and virtue. A cloistered innocence is no innocence at all. It is, in effect, a weakness which comes from not taking a positive position for or against evil. Thus, even in the catastrophe of Man's Fall in the Garden of Eden, Milton finds a certain satisfaction in that Eve insists upon the right to confront temptation and succumb or conquer.

The interplay of passion and reason also underlies much of Milton's writing, though it is usually treated implicitly. The human mind was to Milton a sacred and wonderful thing. It stood for order and intellect: two of the highest elements in life. As Alexander Pope was to do later, Milton embraced the idea of The Great Chain of Being—a cosmic ordering of the universe in which every particle had its appointed, God-given place. To attempt to change the position of links in the Great Chain was to try to overturn Divine order and was to commit the sin of Pride. Reason would prevent such sin; passion would encourage it. Satan in *Paradise Lost* is pictured as having perverted his reason and having been brought low through passion and pride, while God remains the fountainhead and epitome of reason. Before the Fall in the Garden, reason prevails, but with the eating of the apple passion intrudes. Adam and Eve become as animals, sin, are ashamed, and leave the Garden. In *Paradise Regained* Christ resists the attempts of Satan to appeal to the passions and refutes the Devil's arguments with reason.

Milton followed a fairly predictable path of artistic development. His first works are translations of psalms or youthful college exercises in which the poet argues a position, affirmatively or negatively, on a subject chosen by college authorities. He moved on to short occasional poems in English and to sonnets dealing with his own youthful problems: his tendency to look younger than he was, his feelings of insecurity as he devoted years to study without accomplishing the practical goals that society demands. The elegy "Lycidas" mourns a college friend and expresses the poet's feeling that he is about to emerge from contemplation into an active life. *Comus* dramatizes for the poet as well as for his audience the conflict between indifferent aloofness and active virtuous choice. Finally, the great poems, *Paradise Lost, Paradise Regained,* and *Samson Agonistes,* embodying the several strands woven earlier, present Milton's mature vision of reality on an epic scale.

Thoroughly grounded in classical forms and in English poetic tradition, Milton chose to work within traditional patterns in terms of verse forms, meters [see *Handbook:* meter], rhythms, and the like. But his genius, as John Crowe Ransom has pointed out, could not be entirely submerged in, for instance, a traditional blank-verse pattern.

In "Lycidas," the metrical continuity is broken at a dozen places to show, perhaps, Milton's independence of the form [see *Handbook:* metrical variations]. And in his epic he impressed upon the blank verse of Marlowe and Shakespeare his own solemn, dignified, almost liturgical measures that stamp the poetry as unmistakeably his.

Milton's language and his structure owe as much to his century as they do to his artistic inclinations. Students who are put off by sentences which wind sinuously for thirty lines, by structural inversions which withhold the subject until line 17, by epic similes [see *Handbook:* simile] which appear inexhaustible, and by profuse allusion to the Bible and to classical mythology must remember that these are the devices and the resources of seventeenth-century poets and prose writers.

In his own time, Milton was honored and dishonored more for his role in politics and government than for his production as a poet. It was almost impossible for an impartial judgment to be rendered on his work by human beings who were either on the side of the monarchy or of the Protectorate. Even after Milton was forced into the role of private citizen during the Restoration, criticism of his work was always clouded by the critics' realization of the author's earlier political involvements. It is interesting that the government censor who read *Paradise Lost,* prior to publication, marked those passages that merited censorship even as he allowed the work to pass intact because he recognized in it a work of genius.

Since his own time, Milton's reputation has undergone many alterations. Perhaps the nineteenth century was most lavish in its adulation and in the production of many-volumed biographies. In our own time, T. S. Eliot's characterization of Milton as a bad influence on contemporary poets, who required a different kind of idiom to express twentieth-century ideas, seriously interfered with Milton's popularity. Later, Eliot reinstated Milton as a poet worthy of study even by modern poets. The period of rehabilitation is well advanced, and Milton's work is enjoying a resurgence of critical attention.

BIBLIOGRAPHY

Bush, Douglas. *Paradise Lost in Our Time.* Ithaca, N.Y.: Cornell University Press, 1945.

Hanford, Holly. *A Milton Handbook.* New York: F.S. Crofts, 1946.

Lewis, C. S. *A Preface to Paradise Lost.* Oxford: Oxford University Press, 1942.

Lycidas

In this Monody the Author bewails a learned Friend, unfortunately drown'd in his passage from Chester *on the* Irish Seas, 1637. *And by occasion foretells the ruine of our corrupted Clergie then in their height.*

Yet once more, O ye Laurels, and once more
Ye Myrtles brown, with Ivy never sear,
I com to pluck your Berries harsh and crude,
And with forc'd fingers rude,
Shatter your leaves before the mellowing year.
Bitter constraint, and sad occasion dear,
Compells me to disturb your season due:
For *Lycidas* is dead, dead ere his prime,
Young *Lycidas*, and hath not left his peer:
Who would not sing for *Lycidas*? he knew 10
Himself to sing, and build the lofty rhyme.
He must not flote upon his watry bear
Unwept, and welter to the parching wind,
Without the meed of som melodious tear.
  Begin then, Sisters of the sacred well,
That from beneath the seat of *Jove* doth spring,
Begin, and somewhat loudly sweep the string.
Hence with denial vain, and coy excuse,
So may some gentle Muse
With lucky words favour my destin'd Urn, 20
And as he passes turn,
And bid fair peace be to my sable shrowd,
For we were nurst upon the self-same hill,
Fed the same flock; by fountain, shade, and rill.
  Together both, ere the high Lawns appear'd

a learned Friend: Edward King, an acquaintance of Milton at Cambridge.

ll. 3–7. *I com . . . season due:* the poet is young and unripe for the task of celebrating King.

l. 8. *Lycidas:* classical name for a shepherd.

l. 12. *watry bear:* the bier is watery because King drowned.

l. 15. *Sisters:* the Muses.

Under the opening eye-lids of the morn,
We drove afield, and both together heard
What time the Gray-fly winds her sultry horn,
Batt'ning our flocks with the fresh dews of night,
Oft till the Star that rose, at Ev'ning, bright, 30
Toward Heav'ns descent had slop'd his westering wheel.
Mean while the Rural ditties were not mute,
Temper'd to th' Oaten Flute,
Rough *Satyrs* danc'd, and *Fauns* with clov'n heel,
From the glad sound would not be absent long,
And old *Damætas* lov'd to hear our song.
  But O the heavy change, now thou art gon,
Now thou art gon, and never must return!
Thee Shepherd, thee the Woods, and desert Caves,
With wilde Thyme and the gadding Vine o'regrown, 40
And all their echoes mourn.
The Willows, and the Hazle Copses green,
Shall now no more be seen,
Fanning their joyous Leaves to thy soft layes.
As killing as the Canker to the Rose,
Or Taint-worm to the weanling Herds that graze,
Or Frost to Flowers, that their gay wardrop wear,
When first the White Thorn blows;
Such, *Lycidas,* thy loss to Shepherds ear.
  Where were ye Nymphs when the remorseless deep 50
Clos'd o're the head of your lov'd *Lycidas?*
For neither were ye playing on the steep,
Where your old *Bards,* the famous *Druids,* ly,
Nor on the shaggy top of *Mona* high,
Nor yet where *Deva* spreads her wisard stream:
Ay me, I fondly dream!
Had ye bin there—for what could that have don?
What could the Muse her self that *Orpheus* bore,
The Muse her self for her inchanting son
Whom Universal nature did lament, 60
When by the rout that made the hideous roar,

l. 28. *winds:* blows.
l. 29. *Batt'ning:* feeding.
l. 36. *Damætas:* perhaps a name given to a favorite teacher at Cambridge.
l. 47. *wardrop:* wardrobe.

His goary visage down the stream was sent,
Down the swift *Hebrus* to the *Lesbian* shore.
  Alass! What boots it with incessant care
To tend the homely slighted Shepherds trade,
And strictly meditate the thankless Muse,
Were it not better don as others use,
To sport with *Amaryllis* in the shade,
Or with the tangles of *Neæra's* hair?
Fame is the spur that the clear spirit doth raise   70
(That last infirmity of Noble mind)
To scorn delights, and live laborious dayes;
But the fair Guerdon when we hope to find,
And think to burst out into sudden blaze,
Comes the blind *Fury* with th' abhorred shears,
And slits the thin spun life. But not the praise,
Phœbus repli'd, and touch'd my trembling ears;
Fame is no plant that grows on mortal soil,
Nor in the glistering foil
Set off to th' world, nor in broad rumour lies,   80
But lives and spreds aloft by those pure eyes,
And perfet witnes of all-judging *Jove;*
As he pronounces lastly on each deed,
Of so much fame in Heav'n expect thy meed.
  O Fountain *Arethuse,* and thou honour'd floud,
Smooth-sliding *Mincius,* crown'd with vocal reeds,
That strain I heard was of a higher mood:
But now my Oat proceeds,
And listens to the Herald of the Sea
That came in *Neptune's* plea,   90
He ask'd the Waves, and ask'd the Fellon Winds,
What hard mishap hath doom'd this gentle swain?
And question'd every gust of rugged wings
That blows from off each beaked Promontory;

ll. 58–63. *Orpheus . . . shore:* Orpheus was dismembered and his head hurled into the Hebrus. His mother was the Muse Calliope.
l. 64. *What boots it:* what use is it.
l. 68. *Amaryllis:* classical name for shepherd girl.
l. 73. *Guerdon:* reward.
l. 79. *foil:* setting of a gem.
l. 84. *meed:* reward.
l. 88. *Oat:* song.

They knew not of his story,
And sage *Hippotades* their answer brings,
That not a blast was from his dungeon stray'd,
The Air was calm, and on the level brine,
Sleek *Panope* with all her sisters play'd.
It was that fatal and perfidious Bark 100
Built in th' eclipse, and rigg'd with curses dark,
That sunk so low that sacred head of thine.
Next *Camus* reverend Sire, went footing slow,
His Mantle hairy, and his Bonnet sedge,
Inwrought with figures dim, and on the edge
Like to that sanguine flower inscrib'd with woe.
Ah; Who hath reft (quoth he) my dearest pledge?
Last came, and last did go,
The Pilot of the *Galilean* lake,
Two massy Keyes he bore of metals twain, 110
(The Golden opes, the Iron shuts amain)
He shook his Miter'd locks, and stern bespake,
How well could I have spar'd for thee, young swain,
Anow of such as for their bellies sake,
Creep and intrude, and climb into the fold?
Of other care they little reck'ning make,
Then how to scramble at the shearers feast,
And shove away the worthy bidden guest;
Blind mouthes! that scarce themselves know how to hold
A Sheep-hook, or have learn'd ought els the least 120
That to the faithfull Herdmans art belongs!
What recks it them? What need they? They are sped;
And when they list, their lean and flashy songs
Grate on their scrannel Pipes of wretched straw,

l. 96. *Hippotades*: the god of the winds.
l. 99. *Panope*: water nymph.
l. 103. *Camus:* personification of the river Cam which is the Cambridge river and thus the "Sire" of both King and Milton.
l. 109. *Pilot:* Saint Peter.
l. 119. *Blind mouthes:* the Anglican prelates should be people who over*see*, but they are blind. They should feed their flocks, but instead they are "mouths" anxious for material profit.
l. 122. *sped:* successful in this world.
l. 124. *scrannel:* thin.

The hungry Sheep look up, and are not fed,
But swoln with wind, and the rank mist they draw,
Rot inwardly, and foul contagion spread:
Besides what the grim Woolf with privy paw
Daily devours apace, and nothing sed,
But that two-handed engine at the door, 130
Stands ready to smite once, and smite no more.
Return *Alpheus,* the dread voice is past,
That shrunk thy streams: Return *Sicilian* Muse
And call the Vales, and bid them hither cast
Their Bells, and Flourets of a thousand hues.
Ye valleys low where the milde whispers use,
Of shades and wanton winds, and gushing brooks,
On whose fresh lap the swart Star sparely looks,
Throw hither all your quaint enameld eyes,
That on the green terf suck the honied showres, 140
And purple all the ground with vernal flowres.
Bring the rathe Primrose that forsaken dies,
The tufted Crow-toe, and pale Gessamine,
The white Pink, and the Pansie freakt with jeat,
The glowing Violet.
The Musk-rose, and the well attir'd Woodbine,
With Cowslips wan that hang the pensive head,
And every flower that sad embroidery wears:
Bid *Amarantus* all his beauty shed,
And Daffadillies fill their cups with tears, 150
To strew the Laureat Herse where *Lycid* lies.
For so to interpose a little ease,
Let our frail thoughts dally with false surmise.
Ay me! Whilst thee the shores, and sounding Seas
Wash far away, where ere thy bones are hurl'd,
Whether beyond the stormy *Hebrides*
Where thou perhaps under the whelming tide
Visit'st the bottom of the monstrous world;
Or whether thou to our moist vows deny'd,

l. 128. *Woolf:* the Roman Catholic Church.
l. 130. *two-handed engine:* probably the two houses of Parliament; an engine was an instrument of war or torture.
l. 142. *rathe:* early blooming.
l. 159. *moist vows:* crying prayers.

Sleep'st by the fable of *Bellerus* old, 160
Where the great vision of the guarded Mount
Looks toward *Namancos* and *Bayona's* hold;
Look homeward Angel now, and melt with ruth.
And, O ye *Dolphins,* waft the haples youth.
  Weep no more, woful Shepherds weep no more,
For *Lycidas* your sorrow is not dead,
Sunk though he be beneath the watry floar,
So sinks the day-star in the Ocean bed,
And yet anon repairs his drooping head,
And tricks his beams, and with new spangled Ore, 170
Flames in the forehead of the morning sky:
So *Lycidas* sunk low, but mounted high,
Through the dear might of him that walk'd the waves
Where other groves, and other streams along,
With *Nectar* pure his oozy Lock's he laves,
And hears the unexpressive nuptial Song,
In the blest Kingdoms meek of joy and love.
There entertain him all the Saints above,
In solemn troops, and sweet Societies
That sing, and singing in their glory move, 180
And wipe the tears for ever from his eyes.
Now *Lycidas* the Shepherds weep no more;
Henceforth thou art the Genius of the shore,
In thy large recompense, and shalt be good
To all that wander in that perilous flood.
  Thus sang the uncouth Swain to th' Okes and rills,
While the still morn went out with Sandals gray,
He touch'd the tender stops of various Quills,
With eager thought warbling his *Dorick* lay:
And now the Sun had stretch'd out all the hills, 190
And now was dropt into the Western Bay;
At last he rose, and twitch'd his Mantle blew:
To morrow to fresh Woods, and Pastures new.

[1637]

l. 176. *unexpressive nuptial Song:* the indescribably lovely song of the angels for chaste arrivals in heaven.

l. 183. *Genius:* spirit.

l. 193. *To morrow . . . new:* perhaps Milton's way of saying that he would turn to new kinds of poetic expression after "Lycidas."

Commentary

"Lycidas" is a formal elegy [see *Handbook:* elegy] upon the death of one of Milton's Cambridge acquaintances, Edward King, who was drowned in his youth and thus cut off from a promising career in the Anglican ministry. It is also an attack on King's fellow clergy who survive in greed and corruption, heedless of the needs of their parishioners. But above and beyond these points, it is an extremely personal account of Milton's own position at the time of composition and a projection by the poet of his future.

The analogy between Milton's life and King's was not lost upon the poet. Both were young men in their twenties, both had been students at Cambridge. Both had high ideals of service to their fellow men and to God—King through the ministry, Milton in literature. Because of their dedication to the future, both had studied hard, avoiding the easy sloth and easier morality into which many of the undergraduates fell. Yet death had suddenly overtaken one of the two. King was gone and would never realize on earth the rewards of devotion to work, virtue, chastity, study, and Deity. In King's fate Milton sees his own situation very clearly as he thinks of his "destined Urn."

> Alas! What boots it with uncessant care
> To tend the homely slighted Shepherd's trade,
> And strictly meditate the thankless Muse?

Perhaps there is more advantage in wine, women, and song than in the ascetic, studious life as a preparation for a future that may never present itself.

The resolution of the conflict for himself and King comes to Milton almost in the same breath with the statement of the problem. Though the individual may be cut down before he can enjoy fame on earth, his immortal fame will spread and sustain him in Heaven. Milton had spoken in his *Apology* of his "certain reservedness of natural disposition, and moral discipline, learnt out of the noblest philosophy, [which] was enough to keep me in disdain of far less incontinence than this of the bordello." Earlier, in a letter to his college friend, Charles Diodati, he had confided that he was working hard in anticipation of an "immortality of fame." He had, furthermore, resisted the impulse to publish his poetry—his most important contribution to the world, in his own eyes—until he felt that he was ready for the public view. Only the tragedy that had befallen King, which in a sense was Milton's own potential tragedy, impelled him to forsake his determination to keep silent until he had greater maturity and to agree to contribute "Lycidas" to a memorial volume Cambridge wished to dedicate to King.

Quite possibly, Milton agreed to publication of the poem from two other impulses. He may have sensed that he was indeed ready for examination by literary critics and the intellectual community, and he may have decided that the opportunity to attack the shortcomings of the Anglican clergy in telling poetry would never again present itself so obviously and clearly. Very shortly afterward Milton would begin to write the antiprelatical tracts which show clearly that he had studied the matter intensively and had formed forceful conclusions. King offered the ideal touchstone against which erring prelates might be measured and found wanting.

The form of the poem is the classical pastoral elegy, with the characters in the role of shepherds, especially appropriate here since King was a clergyman and Milton a poet-prophet. Milton follows the traditional pattern of announcing the death of the subject, Lycidas. He then calls on supernatural powers for aid in writing the elegy. There follows an idyllic description of King and Milton as students at Cambridge, metaphorically driving their flocks afield. With conventional concern, Milton connects the unwillingness of nature to encourage growing things to the fact that King is dead and he berates her for not saving Lycidas from drowning. The section dealing with promising youth cut off in its prime, already discussed as central to the poem, is followed by a description of the mourners, biblical, mythological, and the rest, as they pay tribute to the dead man. Into the mouth of one of these, Saint Peter, Milton ironically puts the condemnation of erring clergy, apparently the normal digression called for by the classical elegiac form but in reality no digression at all in the tight context of Milton's argument. The poem ends traditionally with the announcement that King is not dead, that he has been made the spirit of the sea in which he drowned to guide those who come after. Further, his soul in heaven is being rewarded for the chaste life which the body lived on earth. As the poet-narrator leaves the scene, he hints at a new era for himself as well as for King.

The principal interest in "Lycidas" lies not in its conventionality, however, but in the youthful Milton's departure from his pattern in broken lines, failure to maintain rhyme throughout, and other liberties which the poet took in the full knowledge that his work might be judged inferior because of them. John Crowe Ransom argues persuasively that Milton wanted to place his own mark on the elegy, wanted to rebel against the past, but wanted to do both within the general framework of the classical elegy. That he succeeded better than he knew is clear from the fame the poem has enjoyed.

"How soon hath time"

How soon hath time the suttle theef of youth,
Stoln on his wing my three and twentieth yeer!
My hasting dayes flie on with full career,
But my late spring no bud or blossom shew'th.
Perhaps my semblance might deceive the truth,
That I to manhood am arriv'd so near,
And inward ripenes doth much less appear,
That som more timely-happy spirits indu'th.
Yet be it less or more, or soon or slow,
It shall be still in strictest measure eev'n, 10
To that same lot, however mean or high,
Toward which Time leads me, and the will of Heav'n;
All is, if I have grace to use it so,
As ever in my great task Masters eye.

[1632]

"When I consider how my light is spent"

When I consider how my light is spent,
E're half my days, in this dark world and wide,
And that one Talent which is death to hide,
Lodg'd with me useless, though my Soul more bent
To serve therewith my Maker, and present
My true account, least he returning chide,
Doth God exact day-labour, light deny'd,
I fondly ask; But patience to prevent
That murmur, soon replies, God doth not need
Either man's work or his own gifts, who best 10
Bear his milde yoak, they serve him best, his State
Is Kingly. Thousands at his bidding speed
And post o're Land and Ocean without rest:
They also serve who only stand and waite.

[1652?]

On the late Massacher in Piemont

Avenge O Lord thy slaughter'd Saints, whose bones
  Lie scatter'd on the Alpine mountains cold,
  Ev'n them who kept thy truth so pure of old
  When all our Fathers worship't Stocks and Stones,
Forget not: in thy book record their groanes
  Who were thy Sheep and in their antient Fold
  Slayn by the bloody *Piemontese* that roll'd
  Mother with Infant down the Rocks. Their moans
The Vales redoubl'd to the Hills, and they
  To Heav'n. Their martyr'd blood and ashes so   10
  O're all th' *Italian* fields where still doth sway
The triple Tyrant: that from these may grow
  A hunder'd-fold, who having learnt thy way
  Early may fly the *Babylonian* wo.

[*1655*]

Paradise Lost

FROM BOOK I

Of Mans First Disobedience, and the Fruit
Of that Forbidden Tree, whose mortal tast
Brought Death into the World, and all our woe,
With loss of *Eden*, till one greater Man
Restore us, and regain the blissful Seat,
Sing Heav'nly Muse, that on the secret top
Of *Oreb*, or of *Sinai*, didst inspire
That Shepherd, who first taught the chosen Seed,
In the Beginning how the Heav'ns and Earth
Rose out of *Chaos:* or if *Sion* Hill   10
Delight thee more, and *Siloa's* Brook that flow'd
Fast by the Oracle of God; I thence
Invoke thy aid to my adventrous Song,

l. 4. *Man:* Christ.
l. 6. *Muse:* Urania, in the early myths the muse of poetry.
l. 7. *Oreb . . . Sinai:* names for mountain (Horeb) on which Moses received the Commandments.

That with no middle flight intends to soar
Above th' *Aonian* Mount, while it pursues
Things unattempted yet in Prose or Rhime.
And chiefly Thou O Spirit, that dost prefer
Before all Temples th' upright heart and pure,
Instruct me, for Thou know'st; Thou from the first
Wast present, and with mighty wings outspread 20
Dove-like satst brooding on the vast Abyss
And mad'st it pregnant: What in me is dark
Illumin, what is low raise and support;
That to the highth of this great Argument
I may assert Eternal Providence,
And justifie the wayes of God to men.

. . .

Is this the Region, this the Soil, the Clime,
Said then the lost Arch-Angel, this the seat
That we must change for Heav'n, this mournful gloom
For that celestial light? Be it so, since he
Who now is Sovran can dispose and bid
What shall be right: fardest from him is best
Whom reason hath equald, force hath made supream
Above his equals. Farewel happy Fields
Where Joy for ever dwells: Hail horrours, hail
Infernal world, and thou profoundest Hell 10
Receive thy new Possessor: One who brings
A mind not to be chang'd by Place or Time.
The mind is its own place, and in it self
Can make a Heav'n of Hell, a Hell of Heav'n.
What matter where, if I be still the same,
And what I should be, all but less then he
Whom Thunder hath made greater? Here at least
We shall be free; th' Almighty hath not built
Here for his envy, will not drive us hence:
Here we may reign secure, and in my choyce 20
To reign is worth ambition though in Hell:
Better to reign in Hell, then serve in Heav'n.
But wherefore let we then our faithful friends,
Th' associates and copartners of our loss

l. 15. *Aonian Mount:* Mount Helicon in Greece.
l. 17. *Spirit:* the spirit of God.

Lye thus astonisht on th' oblivious Pool,
And call them not to share with us their part
In this unhappy Mansion, or once more
With rallied Arms to try what may be yet
Regaind in Heav'n, or what more lost in Hell?

FROM BOOK III

Hail holy light, ofspring of Heav'n first-born,
Or of th' Eternal Coeternal beam
May I express thee-unblam'd? since God is light,
And never but in unapproached light
Dwelt from Eternitie, dwelt then in thee,
Bright effluence of bright essence increate.
Or hear'st thou rather pure Ethereal stream,
Whose Fountain who shall tell? before the Sun,
Before the Heavens thou wert, and at the voice
Of God, as with a Mantle didst invest 10
The rising world of water dark and deep,
Won from the void and formless infinite.
Thee I re-visit now with bolder wing,
Escap't the *Stygian* Pool, though long detain'd
In that obscure sojourn, while in my flight
Through utter and through middle darkness borne
With other notes then to th' *Orphean* Lyre
I sung of *Chaos* and *Eternal Night,*
Taught by the heav'nly Muse to venture down
The dark descent, and up to reascend, 20
Though hard and rare: thee I revisit safe,
And feel thy sovran vital Lamp; but thou
Revisit'st not these eyes, that rowle in vain
To find thy piercing ray, and find no dawn;
So thick a drop serene hath quencht their Orbs,
Or dim suffusion veild. Yet not the more
Cease I to wander where the Muses haunt

l. 25. *astonisht:* dazed.
oblivious Pool: the lake that makes one forget.
l. 2. *beam:* one view of the origin of light was that it was co-eternal with God rather than created by Him.
l. 3. *express . . . unblam'd:* may I invoke thee without guilt at probing supernatural secrets?
l. 6. *increate:* uncreated.
l. 7. *hear'st:* are you named.

Cleer Spring, or shadie Grove, or Sunnie Hill,
Smit with the love of sacred song; but chief
Thee *Sion* and the flowrie Brooks beneath 30
That wash thy hallowd feet, and warbling flow,
Nightly I visit: nor sometimes forget
Those other two equal'd with me in Fate,
So were I equal'd with them in renown,
Blind *Thamyris* and blind *Mæonides,*
And *Tiresias* and *Phineus* Prophets old.
Then feed on thoughts, that voluntarie move
Harmonious numbers; as the wakeful Bird
Sings darkling, and in shadiest Covert hid
Tunes her nocturnal Note. Thus with the Year 40
Seasons return, but not to me returns
Day, or the sweet approach of Ev'n or Morn,
Or sight of vernal bloom, or Summers Rose,
Or flocks, or herds, or human face divine;
But cloud in stead, and ever-during dark
Surrounds me, from the chearful wayes of men
Cut off, and for the Book of knowledg fair
Presented with a Universal blanc
Of Natures works to mee expung'd and ras'd,
And wisdome at one entrance quite shut out. 50
So much the rather thou Celestial light
Shine inward, and the mind through all her powers
Irradiate, there plant eyes, all mist from thence
Purge and disperse, that I may see and tell
Of things invisible to mortal sight.

FROM BOOK IV

So spake our general Mother, and with eyes
Of conjugal attraction unreprov'd,
And meek surrender, half imbracing leand
On our first Father, half her swelling Breast
Naked met his under the flowing Gold

l. 35. *Thamyris . . . Mæonides:* the former is a blind poet mentioned in the Iliad; the latter is a name for Homer.
l. 38. *numbers:* poetry.
l. 39. *darkling:* in the darkness.
l. 48. *blanc:* blankness (a blind person's view of the world).
l. 1. *general Mother:* Eve.

Of her loose tresses hid: he in delight
Both of her Beauty and submissive Charms
Smil'd with superior Love, as *Jupiter*
On *Juno* smiles, when he impregns the Clouds
That shed *May* Flowers; and press'd her Matron lip 10
With kisses pure: aside the Devil turnd
For envie, yet with jealous leer maligne
Ey'd them askance, and to himself thus plaind.
Sight hateful, sight tormenting! thus these two
Imparadis't in one anothers arms
The happier *Eden,* shall enjoy thir fill
Of bliss on bliss, while I to Hell am thrust,
Where neither joy nor love, but fierce desire,
Among our other torments not the least,
Still unfulfill'd with pain of longing pines; 20
Yet let me not forget what I have gain'd
From thir own mouths; all is not theirs it seems:
One fatal Tree there stands of Knowledge call'd,
Forbidden them to taste: Knowledge forbidd'n?
Suspicious, reasonless. Why should thir Lord
Envie them that? can it be sin to know,
Can it be death? and do they onely stand
By Ignorance, is that thir happie state,
The proof of thir obedience and thir faith?
O fair foundation laid whereon to build 30
Thir ruine! Hence I will excite thir minds
With more desire to know, and to reject
Envious commands, invented with designe
To keep them low whom knowledge might exalt
Equal with Gods; aspiring to be such,
They taste and die: what likelier can ensue?
But first with narrow search I must walk round
This Garden, and no corner leave unspi'd;
A chance but chance may lead where I may meet
Some wandring Spirit of Heav'n, by Fountain side, 40
Or in thick shade retir'd, from him to draw
What further would be learnt. Live while ye may,

l. 9. *impregns:* makes pregnant.
l. 13. *plaind:* complained.
l. 20. *pines:* makes me grieve.

Yet happie pair; enjoy, till I return,
Short pleasures, for long woes are to succeed.

FROM BOOK IX

So saying, her rash hand in evil hour
Forth reaching to the Fruit, she pluck'd, she eat:
Earth felt the wound, and Nature from her seat
Sighing through all her Works gave signs of woe,
That all was lost. Back to the Thicket slunk
The guiltie Serpent, and well might, for *Eve*
Intent now wholly on her taste, naught else
Regarded, such delight till then, as seemd,
In Fruit she never tasted, whether true
Or fansied so, through expectation high 10
Of knowledg, nor was God-head from her thought.
Greedily she ingorg'd without restraint,
And knew not eating death: Satiate at length,
And hight'nd as with Wine, jocond and boon,
Thus to her self she pleasingly began.
O Sovran, vertuous, precious of all Trees
In Paradise, of operation blest
To Sapience, hitherto obscur'd, infam'd,
And thy fair Fruit let hang, as to no end
Created; but henceforth my early care, 20
Not without Song, each Morning, and due praise
Shall tend thee, and the fertil burden ease
Of thy full branches offer'd free to all;
Till dieted by thee I grow mature
In knowledge, as the Gods who all things know;
Though others envie what they cannot give;
For had the gift bin theirs, it had not here
Thus grown. Experience, next to thee I owe,
Best guide; not following thee, I had remaind
In ignorance, thou op'nst Wisdoms way, 30
And giv'st access, though secret she retire.

l. 11. *God-head:* Eve commits the sin of Pride by thinking that she may equal God in knowledge.
l. 13. *eating death:* that she was eating death.
l. 14. *boon:* jolly.
l. 18. *Sapience:* able to bestow wisdom.
infam'd: slandered.
l. 21. *due praise:* Eve considers the tree a deity.

And I perhaps am secret; Heav'n is high,
High and remote to see from thence distinct
Each thing on Earth; and other care perhaps
May have diverted from continual watch
Our great Forbidder, safe with all his Spies
About him. But to *Adam* in what sort
Shall I appeer? shall I to him make known
As yet my change, and give him to partake
Full happiness with mee, or rather not, 40
But keep the odds of Knowledge in my power
Without Copartner? so to add what wants
In Femal Sex, the more to draw his Love,
And render me more equal, and perhaps,
A thing not undesireable, somtime
Superior: for inferior who is free?
This may be well: but what if God have seen,
And Death ensue? then I shall be no more,
And *Adam* wedded to another *Eve,*
Shall live with her enjoying, I extinct; 50
A death to think. Confirm'd then I resolve,
Adam shall share with me in bliss or woe:
So dear I love him, that with him all deaths
I could endure, without him live no life.
So saying, from the Tree her step she turnd,
But first low Reverence don, as to the power
That dwelt within, whose presence had infus'd
Into the plant sciential sap, deriv'd
From Nectar, drink of Gods. *Adam* the while
Waiting desirous her return, had wove 60
Of choicest Flours a Garland to adorne
Her Tresses, and her rural labours crown
As Reapers oft are wont thir Harvest Queen.
Great joy he promis'd to his thoughts, and new
Solace in her return, so long delay'd;
Yet oft his heart, divine of somthing ill,
Misgave him; hee the faultring measure felt;
And forth to meet her went, the way she took
That Morn when first they parted; by the Tree
Of Knowledge he must pass, there he her met, 70

l. 66. *divine:* divining, guessing.
l. 67. *faultring measure:* fluttering heartbeats.

Scarse from the Tree returning; in her hand
A bough of fairest fruit that downie smil'd,
New gatherd, and ambrosial smell diffus'd.
To him she hasted, in her face excuse
Came Prologue, and Apologie to prompt,
Which with bland words at will she thus addrest.
  Hast thou not wonderd, *Adam*, at my stay?
Thee I have misst, and thought it long, depriv'd
Thy presence, agonie of love till now
Not felt, nor shall be twice, for never more 80
Mean I to trie, what rash untri'd I sought,
The paine of absence from thy sight. But strange
Hath bin the cause, and wonderful to heare:
This Tree is not as we are told, a Tree
Of danger tasted, nor to evil unknown
Op'ning the way, but of Divine effect
To open Eyes, and make them Gods who taste;
And hath bin tasted such: the Serpent wise,
Or not restraind as wee, or not obeying,
Hath eat'n of the fruit, and is become, 90
Not dead, as we are threatn'd, but thenceforth
Endu'd with human voice and human sense,
Reasoning to admiration, and with mee
Perswasively hath so prevaild, that I
Have also tasted, and have also found
Th' effects to correspond, opener mine Eyes,
Dimm erst, dilated Spirits, ampler Heart,
And growing up to Godhead; which for thee
Chiefly I sought, without thee can despise.
For bliss, as thou hast part, to me is bliss, 100
Tedious, unshar'd with thee, and odious soon.
Thou therefore also taste, that equal Lot
May joyne us, equal Joy, as equal Love;
Least thou not tasting, different degree
Disjoyne us, and I then too late renounce
Deitie for thee, when Fate will not permit.
  Thus *Eve* with Countnance blithe her storie told;

l. 81. *what . . . sought:* what, untested, I rashly looked for.
l. 88. *tasted such:* discovered to be such, by tasting.
l. 97. *erst:* before, earlier.
l. 105. *Disjoyne:* separate.

But in her Cheek distemper flushing glowd.
On th' other side, *Adam,* soon as he heard
The fatal Trespass done by *Eve,* amaz'd, 110
Astonied stood and Blank, while horror chill
Ran through his veins, and all his joynts relax'd;
From his slack hand the Garland wreath'd for *Eve*
Down drop'd, and all the faded Roses shed:
Speechless he stood and pale, till thus at length
First to himself he inward silence broke.
O fairest of Creation, last and best
Of all Gods Works, Creature in whom excell'd
Whatever can to sight or thought be formd,
Holy, divine, good, amiable, or sweet! 120
How art thou lost, how on a sudden lost,
Defac't, deflourd, and now to Death devote?
Rather how hast thou yeelded to transgress
The strict forbiddance, how to violate
The sacred Fruit forbidd'n! som cursed fraud
Of Enemie hath beguil'd thee, yet unknown,
And mee with thee hath ruind, for with thee
Certain my resolution is to Die;
How can I live without thee, how forgoe
Thy sweet Converse and Love so dearly joyn'd, 130
To live again in these wilde Woods forlorn?
Should God create another *Eve,* and I
Another Rib afford, yet loss of thee
Would never from my heart; no no, I feel
The Link of Nature draw me: Flesh of Flesh,
Bone of my Bone thou art, and from thy State
Mine never shall be parted, bliss or woe.
So having said, as one from sad dismay
Recomforted, and after thoughts disturbd
Submitting to what seemd remediless, 140
Thus in calme mood his Words to *Eve* he turnd.
Bold deed thou hast presum'd, adventrous *Eve,*
And peril great provok't, who thus hath dar'd
Had it bin onely coveting to Eye
That sacred Fruit, sacred to abstinence,

l. 111. *Astonied:* astonished.
l. 122. *devote:* given over.

Much more to taste it under banne to touch.
But past who can recall, or don undoe?
Not God Omnipotent, nor Fate, yet so
Perhaps thou shalt not Die, perhaps the Fact
Is not so hainous now, foretasted Fruit, 150
Profan'd first by the Serpent, by him first
Made common and unhallowd ere our taste;
Nor yet on him found deadly, he yet lives,
Lives, as thou saidst, and gaines to life as Man
Higher degree of Life, inducement strong
To us, as likely tasting to attaine
Proportional ascent, which cannot be
But to be Gods, or Angels Demi-gods.
Nor can I think that God, Creator wise,
Though threatning, will in earnest so destroy 160
Us his prime Creatures, dignifi'd so high,
Set over all his Works, which in our Fall,
For us created, needs with us must faile,
Dependent made; so God shall uncreate,
Be frustrate, do, undo, and labour loose,
Not well conceav'd of God, who though his Power
Creation could repeate, yet would be loath
Us to abolish, least the Adversary
Triumph and say; Fickle their State whom God
Most Favors, who can please him long? Mee first 170
He ruind, now Mankind; whom will he next?
Matter of scorne, not to be given the Foe.
However I with thee have fixt my Lot,
Certain to undergoe like doom, if Death
Consort with thee, Death is to mee as Life;
So forcible within my heart I feel
The Bond of Nature draw me to my owne,
My own in thee, for what thou art is mine;
Our State cannot be severd, we are one,
One Flesh; to loose thee were to loose my self. 180
So *Adam*, and thus *Eve* to him repli'd.
O glorious trial of exceeding Love,
Illustrious evidence, example high!
Ingaging me to emulate, but short

l. 150. *foretasted:* the fruit having already been tasted.

Of thy perfection, how shall I attaine,
Adam, from whose deare side I boast me sprung,
And gladly of our Union heare thee speak,
One Heart, one Soul in both; whereof good prooff
This day affords, declaring thee resolvd,
Rather then Death or aught then Death more dread 190
Shall separate us, linkt in Love so deare,
To undergoe with mee one Guilt, one Crime,
If any be, of tasting this fair Fruit,
Whose vertue, for of good still good proceeds,
Direct, or by occasion hath presented
This happie trial of thy Love, which else
So eminently never had bin known.
Were it I thought Death menac't would ensue
This my attempt, I would sustain alone
The worst, and not perswade thee, rather die 200
Deserted, then oblige thee with a fact
Pernicious to thy Peace, chiefly assur'd
Remarkably so late of thy so true,
So faithful Love unequald; but I feel
Farr otherwise th' event, not Death, but Life
Augmented, op'nd Eyes, new Hopes, new Joyes,
Taste so Divine, that what of sweet before
Hath toucht my sense, flat seems to this, and harsh.
On my experience, *Adam,* freely taste.
And fear of Death deliver to the Windes. 210
 So saying, she embrac'd him, and for joy
Tenderly wept, much won that he his Love
Had so enobl'd, as of choice to incurr
Divine displeasure for her sake, or Death.
In recompence (for such compliance bad
Such recompence best merits) from the bough
She gave him of that fair enticing Fruit
With liberal hand: he scrupl'd not to eat
Against his better knowledge, not deceav'd,
But fondly overcome with Femal charm. 220
Earth trembl'd from her entrails, as again
In pangs, and Nature gave a second groan,
Skie lowr'd and muttering Thunder, som sad drops
Wept at compleating of the mortal Sin
Original; while *Adam* took no thought,

Eating his fill, nor *Eve* to iterate
Her former trespass fear'd, the more to soothe
Him with her lov'd societie, that now
As with new Wine intoxicated both
They swim in mirth, and fansie that they feel 230
Divinitie within them breeding wings
Wherewith to scorn the Earth: but that false Fruit
Farr other operation first displaid,
Carnal desire enflaming, hee on *Eve*
Began to cast lascivious Eyes, she him
As wantonly repaid; in Lust they burne:
Till *Adam* thus 'gan *Eve* to dalliance move.
Eve, now I see thou art exact of taste,
And elegant, of Sapience no small part,
Since to each meaning savour we apply, 240
And Palate call judicious; I the praise
Yeild thee, so well this day thou hast purvey'd.
Much pleasure we have lost, while we abstain'd
From this delightful Fruit, nor known till now
True relish, tasting; if such pleasure be
In things to us forbidden, it might be wish'd,
For this one Tree had bin forbidden ten.
But come, so well refresh't, now let us play,
As meet is, after such delicious Fare;
For never did thy Beautie since the day 250
I saw thee first and wedded thee, adorn'd
With all perfections, so enflame my sense
With ardor to enjoy thee, fairer now
Than ever, bountie of this vertuous Tree.
So said he, and forbore not glance or toy
Of amorous intent, well understood
Of *Eve,* whose Eye darted contagious Fire.
Her hand he seis'd, and to a shadie bank,
Thick overhead with verdant roof imbowr'd
He led her nothing loath; Flours were the Couch, 260
Pansies, and Violets, and Asphodel,
And Hyacinth, Earths freshest softest lap.
There they thir fill of Love and Loves disport

l. 238. *exact:* nice (in the sense of precise and elegant).
l. 249. *meet:* fitting.
l. 263. *disport:* play.

Took largely, of thir mutual guilt the Seale,
The solace of thir sin, till dewie sleep
Oppress'd them, wearied with thir amorous play.
Soon as the force of that fallacious Fruit,
That with exhilerating vapour bland
About thir spirits had plaid, and inmost powers
Made erre, was now exhal'd, and grosser sleep 270
Bred of unkindly fumes, with conscious dreams
Encumberd, now had left them, up they rose
As from unrest, and each the other viewing,
Soon found thir Eyes how op'nd, and thir minds
How dark'nd; innocence, that as a veile
Had shadow'd them from knowing ill, was gon,
Just confidence, and native righteousness,
And honour from about them, naked left
To guiltie shame; hee cover'd, but his Robe
Uncover'd more. So rose the *Danite* strong 280
Herculean Samson from the Harlot-lap
Of *Philistean Dalilah,* and wak'd
Shorn of his strength, They destitute and bare
Of all thir vertue: silent, and in face
Confounded long they sate, as struck'n mute,
Till *Adam,* though not less then *Eve* abasht,
At length gave utterance to these words constraind.
O *Eve,* in evil hour thou didst give eare
To that false Worm, of whomsoever taught
To counterfet Mans voice, true in our Fall, 290
False in our promis'd Rising; since our Eyes
Op'nd we find indeed, and find we know
Both Good and Evil, Good lost, and Evil got,
Bad Fruit of Knowledge, if this be to know,
Which leaves us naked thus, of Honour void,
Of Innocence, of Faith, of Puritie,
Our wonted Ornaments now soild and staind,
And in our Faces evident the signes
Of foul concupiscence; whence evil store;
Even shame, the last of evils; of the first 300
Be sure then. How shall I behold the face
Henceforth of God or Angel, earst with joy

l. 271. *unkindly:* unnatural.
l. 302. *earst:* formerly.

And rapture so oft beheld? those heav'nly shapes
Will dazle now this earthly, with thir blaze
Insufferably bright. O might I here
In solitude live savage, in some glade
Obscur'd, where highest Woods impenetrable
To Starr or Sun-light, spread thir umbrage broad,
And brown as Evening: Cover me ye Pines,
Ye Cedars, with innumerable boughs 310
Hide me, where I may never see them more.
But let us now, as in bad plight, devise
What best may for the present serve to hide
The Parts of each from other, that seem most
To shame obnoxious, and unseemliest seen,
Some Tree whose broad smooth Leaves together sowd,
And girded on our loyns, may cover round
Those middle parts, that this new commer, Shame,
There sit not, and reproach us as unclean.
So counsel'd hee, and both together went 320
Into the thickest Wood, there soon they chose
The Figtree, not that kind for Fruit renown'd,
But such as at this day to *Indians* known
In *Malabar* or *Decan* spreds her Armes
Braunching so broad and long, that in the ground
The bended Twigs take root, and Daughters grow
About the Mother Tree, a Pillard shade
High overarch't, and echoing Walks between;
There oft the *Indian* Herdsman shunning heate
Shelters in coole, and tends his pasturing Herds 330
At Loopholes cut through thickest shade: Those Leaves
They gatherd, broad as *Amazonian* Targe,
And with what skill they had, together sowd,
To gird thir waste, vain Covering if to hide
Thir guilt and dreaded shame; O how unlike
To that first naked Glorie. Such of late
Columbus found th' *American* so girt
With featherd Cincture, naked else and wilde
Among the Trees on Iles and woodie Shores.
Thus fenc't, and as they thought, thir shame in part 340
Coverd, but not at rest or ease of Mind,

l. 324. *Malabar . . . Decan:* sections of India.
l. 332. *Targe:* shield.

They sate them down to weep, nor onely Teares
Raind at thir Eyes, but high Winds worse within
Began to rise, high Passions, Anger, Hate,
Mistrust, Suspicion, Discord, and shook sore
Thir inward State of Mind, calme Region once
And full of Peace, now tost and turbulent:
For Understanding rul'd not, and the Will
Heard not her lore, both in subjection now
To sensual Appetite, who from beneathe 350
Usurping over sovran Reason claimd
Superior sway: From thus distemperd brest,
Adam, estrang'd in look and alterd stile,
Speech intermitted thus to *Eve* renewd.
Would thou hadst heark'nd to my words, and stai'd
With me, as I besought thee, when that strange
Desire of wandring this unhappie Morn,
I know not whence possessd thee; we had then
Remaind still happie, not as now, despoild
Of all our good, sham'd, naked, miserable. 360
Let none henceforth seek needless cause to approve
The Faith they owe; when earnestly they seek
Such proof, conclude, they then begin to faile.
To whom soon mov'd with touch of blame thus *Eve*.
What words have past thy Lips, *Adam* severe,
Imput'st thou that to my default, or will
Of wandering, as thou call'st it, which who knows
But might as ill have happ'nd thou being by,
Or to thy self perhaps: hadst thou bin there,
Or here th' attempt, thou couldst not have discernd 370
Fraud in the Serpent, speaking as he spake;
No ground of enmitie between us known,
Why hee should mean me ill, or seek to harme.
Was I to have never parted from thy side?
As good have grown there still a liveless Rib.
Being as I am, why didst not thou the Head
Command me absolutely not to go,
Going into such danger as thou saidst?
Too facil then thou didst not much gainsay,
Nay, didst permit, approve, and fair dismiss. 380

l. 361. *approve:* test.
l. 362. *owe:* possess.

Hadst thou bin firm and fixt in thy dissent,
Neither had I transgress'd, nor thou with mee.
To whom then first incenst *Adam* repli'd.
Is this the Love, is this the recompence
Of mine to thee, ingrateful *Eve,* exprest
Immutable when thou wert lost, not I,
Who might have liv'd and joyd immortal bliss,
Yet willingly chose rather Death with thee:
And am I now upbraided, as the cause
Of thy trangressing? not enough severe, 390
It seems, in thy restraint: what could I more?
I warn'd thee, I admonish'd thee, foretold
The danger, and the lurking Enemie
That lay in wait; beyond this had bin force,
And force upon free Will hath here no place.
But confidence then bore thee on, secure
Either to meet no danger, or to finde
Matter of glorious trial; and perhaps
I also err'd in overmuch admiring
What seemd in thee so perfet, that I thought 400
No evil durst attempt thee, but I rue
That errour now, which is become my crime,
And thou th' accuser. Thus it shall befall
Him who to worth in Women overtrusting
Lets her Will rule; restraint she will not brook,
And left to her self, if evil thence ensue,
Shee first his weak indulgence will accuse.
Thus they in mutual accusation spent
The fruitless hours, but neither self-condemning,
And of thir vain contest appeer'd no end. 410

FROM BOOK XII

So spake our Mother *Eve,* and *Adam* heard
Well pleas'd, but answer'd not; for now too nigh
Th' Archangel stood, and from the other Hill
To thir fixt Station, all in bright array
The Cherubim descended; on the ground
Gliding meteorous, as Ev'ning Mist
Ris'n from a River o're the marish glides,

ll. 385–386. *exprest Immutable:* displayed as immutable.
l. 7. *marish:* swampy land.

And gathers ground fast at the Labourers heel
Homeward returning. High in Front advanc't,
The brandisht Sword of God before them blaz'd 10
Fierce as a Comet; which with torrid heat,
And vapour as the *Libyan* Air adust,
Began to parch that temperate Clime; whereat
In either hand the hastning Angel caught
Our lingring Parents, and to th' Eastern Gate
Led them direct, and down the Cliff as fast
To the subjected Plaine; then disappeer'd.
They looking back, all th' Eastern side beheld
Of Paradise, so late thir happie seat,
Wav'd over by that flaming Brand, the Gate 20
With dreadful Faces throng'd and fierie Armes:
Som natural tears they drop'd, but wip'd them soon;
The World was all before them, where to choose
Thir place of rest, and Providence thir guide:
They hand in hand with wandring steps and slow,
Through Eden took thir solitarie way.

[*1655?–65*]

l. 9. *advanc't:* held up.
l. 12. *adust:* burned.
l. 17. *subjected:* spread out below.
l. 20. *Brand:* sword.

L'Allegro

Hence loathed Melancholy
Of *Cerberus,* and blackest midnight born,
In *Stygian* Cave forlorn.
'Mongst horrid shapes, and shreiks, and sights unholy,
Find out some uncouth cell,
Where brooding darkness spreads his jealous wings,
And the night-Raven sings;
There under *Ebon* shades, and low-brow'd Rocks,
As ragged as thy Locks,
In dark *Cimmerian* desert ever dwell. 10
But com thou Goddess fair and free,
In Heav'n ycleap'd *Euphrosyne,*
And by men, heart-easing Mirth,

Whom lovely *Venus* at a birth
With two sister Graces more
To Ivy-crowned *Bacchus* bore;
Or whether (as som Sager sing)
The frolick Wind that breathes the Spring,
Zephir with *Aurora* playing,
As he met her once a Maying, 20
There on Beds of Violets blew,
And fresh-blown Roses washt in dew,
Fill'd her with thee a daughter fair,
So bucksom, blith, and debonair.
Haste thee nymph, and bring with thee
Jest and youthful Jollity,
Quips and Cranks, and wanton Wiles,
Nods, and Becks, and Wreathed Smiles
Such as hang on *Hebe's* cheek,
And love to live in dimple sleek; 30
Sport that wrincled Care derides,
And Laughter holding both his sides,
Com, and trip it as you go
On the light fantastick toe,
And in thy right hand lead with thee,
The Mountain Nymph, sweet Liberty;
And if I give thee honour due,
Mirth, admit me of thy crue
To live with her, and live with thee,
In unreproved pleasures free; 40
To hear the Lark begin his flight,
And singing startle the dull night,
From his watch-towre in the skies,
Till the dappled dawn doth rise;
Then to com in spight of sorrow,
And at my window bid good morrow,
Through the Sweet-Briar, or the Vine,
Or the twisted Eglantine,
While the Cock with lively din,
Scatters the rear of darkness thin, 50
And to the stack, or the Barn dore,
Stoutly struts his Dames before,
Oft list'ning how the Hounds and Horn
Chearly rouse the slumbring morn,

From the side of som Hoar Hill,
Through the high wood echoing shrill.
Som time walking not unseen
By Hedge-row Elms, on Hillocks green,
Right against the Eastern gate,
Where the great Sun begins his state, 60
Roab'd in flames, and Amber light,
The clouds in thousand Liveries dight,
While the Plowman neer at hand,
Whistles ore the Furrow'd Land,
And the Milkmaid singeth blithe,
And the Mower whets his sithe,
And every Shepherd tells his tale
Under the Hawthorn in the dale.
Streit mine eye hath caught new pleasures
Whilst the Lantskip round it measures, 70
Russet Lawns, and Fallows Gray,
Where the nibling flocks do stray,
Mountains on whose barren brest
The labouring clouds do often rest:
Meadows trim with Daisies pide,
Shallow Brooks, and Rivers wide.
Towers, and Battlements it sees
Boosom'd high in tufted Trees,
Wher perhaps som beauty lies,
The Cynosure of neighbouring eyes. 80
Hard by, a Cottage chimney smokes,
From betwixt two aged Okes,
Where *Corydon* and *Thyrsis* met,
Are at their savory dinner set
Of Hearbs, and other Country Messes,
Which the neat-handed *Phillis* dresses;
And then in haste her Bowre she leaves,
With *Thestylis* to bind the Sheaves;
Or if the earlier season lead
To the tann'd Haycock in the Mead, 90
Some times with secure delight
The up-land Hamlets will invite,
When the merry Bells ring round,
And the jocond rebecks sound
To many a youth, and many a maid,

Dancing in the Chequer'd shade;
And young and old com forth to play
On a Sunshine Holyday,
Till the live-long day-light fail,
Then to the Spicy Nut-brown Ale, 100
With stories told of many a feat,
How *Faery Mab* the junkets eat,
She was pincht, and pull'd she sed,
And by the Friars Lanthorn led
Tells how the drudging *Goblin* swet,
To ern his Cream-bowle duly set,
When in one night, ere glimps of morn,
His shadowy Flale hath thresh'd the Corn,
That ten day-labourers could not end,
Then lies him down the Lubbar Fend. 110
And stretch'd out all the Chimney's length,
Basks at the fire his hairy strength;
And Crop-full out of dores he flings,
Ere the first Cock his Mattin rings,
Thus done the Tales, to bed they creep,
By whispering Winds soon lull'd asleep.
Towred Cities please us then,
And the busie humm of men,
Where throngs of Knights and Barons bold,
In weeds of Peace high triumphs hold, 120
With store of Ladies, whose bright eies
Rain influence, and judge the prise,
Of Wit, or Arms, while both contend
To win her Grace, whom all commend,
There let *Hymen* oft appear
In Saffron robe, with Taper clear,
And pomp, and feast, and revelry,
With mask, and antique Pageantry,
Such sights as youthful Poets dream
On Summer eeves by haunted stream. 130
Then to the well-trod stage anon,
If *Jonsons* learned Sock be on,
Or sweetest *Shakespear* fancies childe,
Warble his native Wood-notes wilde,
And ever against eating Cares,
Lap me in soft *Lydian* Aires,

Married to immortal verse
Such as the meeting soul may pierce
In notes, with many a winding bout
Of lincked sweetness long drawn out, 140
With wanton heed, and giddy cunning,
The melting voice through mazes running;
Untwisting all the chains that ty
The hidden soul of harmony.
That *Orpheus* self may heave his head
From golden slumber on a bed
Of heapt *Elysian* flowres, and hear
Such streins as would have won the ear
Of *Pluto,* to have quite set free
His half regain'd *Eurydice.* 150
These delights, if thou canst give,
Mirth with thee, I mean to live.

[*1631?*]

Il Penseroso

Hence vain deluding joyes,
The brood of folly without father bred,
How little you bested,
Or fill the fixed mind with all your toyes;
Dwell in some idle brain,
And fancies fond with gaudy shapes possess,
As thick and numberless
As the gay motes that people the Sun Beams,
Or likest hovering dreams
The fickle Pensioners of *Morpheus* train. 10
But hail thou Goddess, sage and holy,
Hail divinest Melancholy,
Whose Saintly visage is too bright
To hit the Sense of human sight;
And therefore to our weaker view,
Ore laid with black staid Wisdoms hue.
Black, but such as in esteem,
Prince *Memnons* sister might beseem,
Or that starr'd *Ethiope* Queen that strove
To set her beauties praise above

The Sea Nymphs, and their powers offended,
Yet thou art higher far descended,
Thee bright-hair'd *Vesta* long of yore,
To solitary *Saturn* bore;
His daughter she (in *Saturns* raign,
Such mixture was not held a stain)
Oft in glimmering Bowres, and glades
He met her, and in secret shades
Of woody *Ida's* inmost grove,
While yet there was no fear of *Jove*. 30
Com pensive Nun, devout and pure,
Sober, stedfast, and demure,
All in a robe of darkest grain,
Flowing with majestick train,
And sable stole of *Cipres* Lawn,
Over thy decent shoulders drawn.
Com, but keep thy wonted state,
With eev'n step, and musing gate,
And looks commercing with the skies,
Thy rapt soul sitting in thine eyes: 40
There held in holy passion still,
Forget thy self to Marble, till
With a sad Leaden downward cast,
Thou fix them on the earth as fast.
And joyn with thee calm Peace, and Quiet,
Spare Fast, that oft with gods doth diet,
And hears the Muses in a ring,
Ay round about *Joves* Altar sing.
And adde to these retired leasure,
That in trim Gardens takes his pleasure; 50
But first, and chiefest, with thee bring,
Him that yon soars on golden wing,
Guiding the fiery-wheeled throne,
The Cherub Contemplation,
And the mute Silence hist along,
'Less *Philomel* will deign a Song,
In her sweetest, saddest plight,
Smoothing the rugged brow of night,
While *Cynthia* checks her Dragon yoke,
Gently o're th' accustom'd Oke; 60
Sweet Bird that shunn'st the noise of folly,

Most musical, most Melancholy!
Thee Chauntress oft the Woods among,
I woo to hear thy Even-Song;
And missing thee, I walk unseen
On the dry smooth-shaven Green,
To behold the wandring Moon,
Riding neer her highest noon,
Like one that had bin led astray
Through the Heav'ns wide pathles way; 70
And oft, as if her head she bow'd,
Stooping through a fleecy cloud.
Oft on a Plat of rising ground,
I hear the far-off *Curfeu* sound,
Over some wide-water'd shoar,
Swinging slow with sullen roar;
Or if the Ayr will not permit,
Som still removed place will fit,
Where glowing Embers through the room
Teach light to counterfeit a gloom, 80
Far from all resort of mirth,
Save the Cricket on the hearth,
Or the Belmans drowsie charm,
To bless the dores from nightly harm:
Or let my Lamp at midnight hour,
Be seen in some high lonely Towr,
Where I may oft out-watch the *Bear,*
With thrice great *Hermes,* or unsphear
The spirit of *Plato* to unfold
What Worlds, or what vast Regions hold 90
The immortal mind that hath forsook
Her mansion in this fleshly nook:
And of those *Dæmons* that are found
In fire, air, flood, or under ground,
Whose power hath a true consent
With Planet, or with Element.
Som time let Gorgeous Tragedy
In Scepter'd Pall com sweeping by,
Presenting *Thebs,* or *Pelops* line,
Or the tale of *Troy* divine. 100
Or what (though rare) of later age,
Ennobled hath the Buskind stage.

But, O sad Virgin, that thy power
Might raise *Musæus* from his bower,
Or bid the soul of *Orpheus* sing
Such notes as warbled to the string,
Drew Iron tears down *Pluto's* cheek,
And made Hell grant what Love did seek.
Or call up him that left half told
The story of *Cambuscan* bold, 110
Of *Camball,* and of *Algarsife,*
And who had *Canace* to wife,
That own'd the vertuous Ring and Glass,
And of the wondrous Hors of Brass,
On which the *Tartar* King did ride;
And if ought els, great *Bards* beside,
In sage and solemn tunes have sung,
Of Turneys and of Trophies hung;
Of Forests, and inchantments drear,
Where more is meant then meets the ear. 120
Thus night oft see me in thy pale career,
Till civil-suited Morn appeer,
Not trickt and frounc't as she was wont,
With the Attick Boy to hunt,
But Cherchef't in a comely Cloud,
While rocking Winds are Piping loud,
Or usher'd with a shower still,
When the gust hath blown his fill,
Ending on the russling Leaves,
With minute drops from off the Eaves. 130
And when the Sun begins to fling
His flaring beams, me Goddess bring
To arched walks of twilight groves,
And shadows brown that *Sylvan* loves
Of Pine, or monumental Oake,
Where the rude Ax with heaved stroke,
Was never heard the Nymphs to daunt,
Or fright them from their hallow'd haunt.
There in close covert by some Brook,
Where no prophaner eye may look, 140
Hide me from Day's garish eie,
While the Bee with Honied thie,
That at her flowry work doth sing,

And the Waters murmuring
With such consort as they keep,
Entice the dewy-feather'd Sleep;
And let som strange mysterious dream,
Wave at his Wings in Airy stream,
Of lively portrature display'd,
Softly on my eye-lids laid. 150
And as I wake, sweet musick breath
Above, about, or underneath,
Sent by som spirit to mortals good,
Or th' unseen Genius of the Wood.
But let my due feet never fail,
To walk the studious Cloysters pale.
And love the high embowed Roof,
With antick Pillars massy proof,
And storied Windows richly dight,
Casting a dimm religious light. 160
There let the pealing Organ blow,
To the full voic'd Quire below,
In Service high, and Anthems cleer,
As may with sweetness, through mine ear,
Dissolve me into extasies,
And bring all Heav'n before mine eyes.
And may at last my weary age
Find out the peacefull hermitage,
The Hairy Gown and Mossy Cell,
Where I may sit and rightly spell 170
Of every Star that heav'n doth shew,
And every Herb that sips the dew;
Till old experience do attain
To something like Prophetic strain.
These pleasures *Melancholy* give,
And I with thee will choose to live.

[*1631?*]

On Shakespear. *1630*

What needs my *Shakespear* for his honour'd Bones,
The labour of an age in piled Stones,
Or that his hallow'd reliques should be hid

Under a Star-ypointing *Pyramid?*
Dear son of memory, great heir of Fame,
What need'st thou such weak witness of thy name!
Thou in our wonder and astonishment
Hast built thy self a live-long Monument.
For whilst to th'shame of slow-endeavouring art,
Thy easie numbers flow, and that each heart 10
Hath from the leaves of thy unvalu'd Book,
Those Delphick lines with deep impression took,
Then thou our fancy of it self bereaving,
Dost make us Marble with too much conceaving;
And so Sepulcher'd in such pomp dost lie,
That Kings for such a Tomb would wish to die.

Alexander Pope

Alexander Pope was born on May 21, 1688 in London, the son of a moderately successful merchant and his good-natured wife. The child was congenitally so deformed that it seemed unlikely he could survive. Dr. Johnson described his dwarfish and hunchbacked frame in this way:

> He [Pope] has . . . compared himself to a spider, . . . His stature was so low that to bring him to a level with common tables, it was necessary to raise his seat. . . . When he rose, he was invested in a bodice made of stiff canvas, being scarce able to hold himself erect till it was laced, and he then put on a flannel waistcoat. One side was contracted. His legs were so slender that he enlarged their bulk with three pairs of stockings, which were drawn on and off by the maid; for he was not able to dress or undress himself, and neither went to bed nor rose without help. . . .

Though his family circumstances were pleasant, his deformity made him lonely much of the time. Moreover, the Roman Catholicism of his parents prevented him from attending the usual public schools available to Anglican children of means and standing, and tended to increase his isolation.

Neither his religion nor his deformity, however, could cloud the brilliance of his mind. At twelve, he wrote a play; at thirteen, an epic poem. His mind early turned to poetry and, as he puts it in the

"Epistle to Dr. Arbuthnot," "I lisped in numbers for the numbers came." His childhood idol was Dryden. Though he loved urban life, removal to Binfield Forest with his parents furnished both inspiration and subject matter for the "Pastorals" he wrote while still in his teens.

At fifteen, Pope prevailed upon his parents to allow him to live in London unsupervised. There the pastoral poems were published in Tonson's *Miscellany* in 1709, without eliciting much attention. There, too, he became acquainted with the elderly writer William Wycherley, who allowed Pope to criticize and even to revise his poetry. Later Wycherley resented Pope's help and became his enemy. This was the first of numerous fallings out that Pope had with important figures in London's literary jungle. In a period when literature was a means of settling personal scores, the *argumentum ad hominem* was carried to vicious lengths both by Pope and his detractors; but Pope's wit and poetic talents normally carried the day against his opponents' reliance upon slighting references to the poet's physical deformity. Pope's "Essay on Criticism," published in 1711, is an example of the young writer's view of his contemporaries.

Pope's physical condition did not prevent him from falling in love, at the age of nineteen, with Martha Blount, who held the poet in esteem and affection but never encouraged his suit. Nor did Pope's enemies let him forget in print that he did not cut a husbandly or romantic figure. Pope's hopeless love for Martha lasted all his life, long after the young girl had lost her beauty and become a noisy, talkative, old woman. Their relationship, except for one strained period, was always pleasant and platonic.

As fame carried Pope along, he became acquainted with the great men of his time: Addison he knew but did not particularly like; Swift was his friend, and Pope was deeply affected by his friend's madness and eventual isolation from society; the Prime Minister, Lord Bolingbroke, was his confidant; the Prince of Wales visited him; Lady Mary Wortley Montagu cultivated him and then heartlessly laughed at him when he pursued her. At his estate at Twickenham, Pope entertained the most distinguished members of society with unceasing generosity. To Swift, for instance, he wrote:

> I could keep you, for I am rich, that is, I have more than I want. I can afford room for yourself and two servants; I have indeed room enough, nothing but myself at home. . . . my house is enlarged, and the gardens extend and flourish. . . . I have more fruit trees and kitchen gardens than you have any thought

> of. . . . for God's sake, why should not you . . . e'en give all you have to the poor of Ireland (for whom you have already done everyting else) so quit the place, and live and die with me?

Pope was indeed rich, for his long-heralded translation of Homer had been published by subscription in 1715 with enormous financial and critical success. Besieged by friends and enemies alike for favors, Pope found wealth and fame not entirely comfortable. There seemed no end of young poets and playwrights who demanded his attention, if not his approval. Publishers fought to bring out his works, his letters, his editions; and if they were unsuccessful in obtaining the right to do so legitimately, they might pirate his work or forge letters never written by the poet. Much of his anger against the pettiness and corruption of this literary and publishing environment Pope turned into poetry in a long and intensely personal poem called "The Dunciad."

By the time his "Essay on Man" appeared in 1732, Pope was a sad, disillusioned man. His alienation from life had been reinforced by the death of his friend, John Gay. His mother was to die in 1733. Martha Blount was old, and Swift was living out his life in madness and exile. At Twickenham, Pope busied himself in writing the later "Dunciad" and other poems. For relaxation, he worked on details of his "grotto," a cavernous retreat constructed on his estate to allow for complete privacy and exotic fancy. After an extremely painful and yet socially and artistically triumphant old age, he died in 1744.

Pope's physical infirmities and his Roman Catholicism were perhaps the most powerful influences on his career. The former meant that his childhood would be spent more in reading and contemplation than might be customary for a robust child. Diversion for the sickly youngster became the writing of verses and experimentation with the technique of poetry. Furthermore, Pope's sense of apartness from his peers, his sense of private destiny, must have sharpened his eye and his pen for the satirical battles with enemies soon to appear on the horizon. Pope's Catholicism reinforced the feeling of separateness which infirmity and deformity had generated. It kept him from attending classes with other children, and even influenced him and his family to leave the joys of urban living for country surroundings. But most of all, it turned him inward to a dependence on his own judgment and taste in literature. Deprived of the standard curriculum for schoolboys, Pope discovered for himself those classical authors most congenial to his needs and the contemporary authors (Chaucer,

Shakespeare, and Milton) who could teach him how to be a poet. Without the necessity to satisfy a teacher, he could concentrate on imitations of the epic, the pastoral, and other forms. In a sense, Pope owed much to the discrimination against him of nature and man.

Pope's early poetic career, largely imitative, gave promise of outstanding poetic talent, but not of the direction which that talent was to take. The pastoral poems are perfect in their manner but have little interest for today's reader apart from their importance as juvenile documents. Even "Windsor Forest," one of the poems that helped establish Pope's literary importance in the eighteenth century, lacks the characteristics that have sustained his reputation.

With "The Rape of the Lock," Pope struck the note that was to become identified with his work: the urbane, sophisticated, citified man observing the pulsing life of the metropolis and commenting wittily and satirically [see *Handbook:* satire] on the foibles of civilized man as a social creature. In beautifully ordered heroic couplets Pope arraigns the disorder in society, the discord man has struck out of universal harmony, the apparent badness in this best of all possible worlds. Reason and good humor are his prescriptions for the ills he noted everywhere, though in his more burning quarrels with other literary men, as dramatized in "The Dunciad," he sometimes forsakes both.

Like most of his contemporaries, Pope was also addicted to the didactic [see *Handbook:* didactic poetry] and the moralistic, turning poetry to the service of education by composing long treatises in endless heroic couplets. But Pope was usually able to combine the didactic with the truly poetic—to stress the correctness of his moral, ethical, religious, or historical position more through the beauty of his poetry than through the strength of his intellectual formulations. Though he was shocked to be accused by his enemies of expressing Deist doctrine in his "Essay on Man," he had to admit the accusation. Nonetheless, the poem remains the most memorably poetic statement of a familiar eighteenth-century view of man's place in the universe. Pope represents the ultimate in versifying "what oft was thought but ne'er so well expressed."

Probably no other major poet put all his poetic eggs in one stanzaic basket as Pope did. Using as his basic tool two lines of iambic pentameter rhymed [see *Handbook:* rhyme], he worked infinitely subtle variations on the basic pattern as he explained a poet ought to do in his youthful "Essay on Criticism." It is not illogical that this child of the Age of Reason should have constrained his talents within narrow bounds, for, assuming the heroic couplet to be the ideal form [see *Handbook:* form] for contemporary poets—affording room for invention within fixed boundaries—why should the poet seek to deviate from the reasonable and critically approved norm? When he set out to translate Homer, Pope found it just as logical to render the work of that more robust and less predictable poet in stately heroic couplets.

From his earliest publications, the literary set and the wider reading public delighted in Pope's verbal talents. His "Rape of the Lock" went into several editions almost immediately, and the most reputable publishers of the time wrote to him asking for the privilege of bringing out his works. That such acclaim is overshadowed in our memory of Pope by the petty feuds in which he participated with Addison, Dennis, and the Grub Street variety of hack is explained by the temper of the times: Pope's London was a place of fierce invective, brutal verbal attacks on public figures, intrigues which often found their way into print and thus were dignified and perpetuated long after the emotions had cooled. Apart from all the backbiting, however, Pope's reputation with the public was never in any danger, though it did suffer after his death in the general Romantic disapproval of Neoclassical poetry and its practitioners. In our own time, much of Pope's difficult allusive poetry is read only by specialists, but his more general works, such as "The Rape of the Lock," receive the attention and praise they deserve.

BIBLIOGRAPHY

Root, R. K. *The Poetical Career of Alexander Pope*. Princeton, N.J.: Princeton University Press, 1938.

Sherburn, George. *The Early Career of Alexander Pope*. Oxford: Oxford University Press, 1934.

Tillotson, Geoffrey. *On the Poetry of Pope*. Oxford: Oxford University Press, 1938.

Epistle to Miss Teresa Blount, On Her Leaving the Town After the Coronation

As some fond virgin, whom her mother's care
Drags from the town to wholesome country air,
Just when she learns to roll a melting eye,
And hear a spark, yet think no danger nigh;
From the dear man unwilling she must sever,
Yet takes one kiss before she parts forever:
Thus from the world fair Zephalinda flew,
Saw others happy, and with sighs withdrew;
Not that their pleasures caused her discontent,
She sighed not that they stayed, but that she went. 10
  She went to plain work, and to purling brooks,
Old-fashioned halls, dull aunts, and croaking rooks;
She went from opera, park, assembly, play,
To morning walks, and prayers three hours a day;
To part her time 'twixt reading and bohea,
To muse, and spill her solitary tea,
Or o'er cold coffee trifle with the spoon,
Count the slow clock, and dine exact at noon;
Divert her eyes with pictures in the fire,
Hum half a tune, tell stories to the squire; 20
Up to her godly garret after seven,
Then starve and pray, for that's the way to Heaven.
  Some squire, perhaps, you take delight to rack,
Whose game is whisk, whose treat a toast in sack;
Who visits with a gun, presents you birds,
Then gives a smacking buss, and cries—"No words!"
Or with his hounds comes hallowing from the stable,
Makes love with nods and knees beneath a table:
Whose laughs are hearty, tho' his jests are coarse,
And loves you best of all things—but his horse. 30
  In some fair evening, on your elbow laid,
You dream of triumphs in the rural shade;
In pensive thought recall the fancied scene,

See coronations rise on every green;
Before you pass the imaginary sights
Of lords, and earls, and dukes, and gartered knights,
While the spread fan o'ershades your closing eyes;
Then give one flirt, and all the vision flies.
Thus vanish scepters, coronets, and balls,
And leave you in lone woods or empty walls. 40
So when your slave, at some dear idle time,
(Not plagued with headaches, or the want of rhyme)
Stands in the streets, abstracted from the crew,
And while he seems to study, thinks of you;
Just when his fancy points your sprightly eyes,
Or sees the blush of soft Parthenia rise,
Gay pats my shoulder, and you vanish quite;
Streets, chairs, and coxcombs rush upon my sight;
Vexed to be still in town, I knit my brow,
Look sour, and hum a tune—as you may now. 50

[*1714?*]

Commentary

This short, early poem, written about 1714 and published in 1717, contains the germ of much of Pope's later work. The "meaning" of the poem is too obvious to need more than restatement: the poet records the sadness of an eligible young lady forced to leave London and its glittering society for the less exciting, though perhaps morally superior, environment of the countryside. Her absence bothers the poet, as his may her, until the diversions of city life impinge to divert his mind.

Though this specific theme is not pervasive in Pope's work, the materials with which Pope deals here are to become his principal stock in trade. A celebrator of urban life more enthusiastically than any English poet before him, Pope here deserts the traditional eulogy of the pastoral scene earlier forced upon him by his models in classical verse to concentrate on the area of his major interest—the vibrant social scene of London's fashionable set, with its "spread fan," its "scepters, coronets, and balls," its "streets, chairs, and coxcombs." And though he may speak of the "wholesome country air," it is obvious to the reader that Pope's heart lies with the city.

Likewise in this gentle satire, the emphasis is on amorous interplay, as it was to be in "The Rape of the Lock." Using the flirtations of his friends Teresa and Martha Blount (whom he calls Zephalinda and Parthenia in the traditional fanciful manner), the poet focuses on the minutiae of relationships between men and women in the brittle leisure society of the eighteenth century. Unconcerned with depth psychology or economic factors or a serious probing of the emotions, Pope keeps his distance, preferring to examine superficially the paraphernalia of relationship. As in "The Rape," he is concerned with coquettishness, the wink of the eye, the dropped fan, the love note, the gossip of bystanders, and the exhilaration of the chase. His attitude is perhaps inevitable from two points of view: as a cripple and a male deprived of the opportunity for normal marital or extramarital love, he maintains in his poetry a flippant and standoffish tone that often reflects a "sour grapes" approach. He can watch others play the game and dissect their every move and motive with a precision and a detachment not found in participants. Secondarily, Pope's attitude is most probably shaped by his time's concern for cataloging the mass rather than for intensive analysis of the singular love affair or the aberrant couple. The Misses Blount become Every-flirt and the enforced departure from London of Zephalinda becomes generalized into the fate of many women. The reader is looking at society, not at specific people, though Pope may identify the persons of the drama to give private piquancy to his verses.

The poem offers few difficulties of comprehension. The names of the two women derive from a series of playfully amorous letters in which the sisters identified themselves by the pseudonyms. In line 15, "bohea" is a kind of tea. "Rack," in line 23, means "submit to torture." In the next line, "whisk" stands for "whist," a rural and crude diversion as compared to the elegant game of cards played by society in "The Rape." "Sack" in the same line, refers to a favorite English wine. In line 26, "buss" is a kiss. In line 41, "your slave" is the writer of the poem. The "Gay" of line 48 is Pope's old friend John Gay.

Many of Pope's stylistic devices are admirably adumbrated in this early poem. First in importance is his (and, indeed, most writers' of the eighteenth century) use of antithesis as the foundation of the poem as well as in structuring individual lines within the poem. Behind the story of the young lady, Pope deals more fundamentally with the contrast of city and country. Milton had chosen to deal with the same subject in two companion poems. Here in shorter space and narrower focus Pope puts the case for both ways of life. Within the poem too, the poet sprinkles his antitheses: "She sighed not that they stayed, but that she went" or "Thus vanish scepters, coronets, and balls, / And leave you in lone woods or empty walls." [See *Handbook:* end-stopped.]

The poem illustrates also other devices which Pope was later to perfect. His use of comic deflation is apparent in "And loves you best of all things—but his horse." The first ten lines of the poem are in the form of a long epic simile reduced to the ridiculous by the insignificance of the subject matter. The entire spirit of his later masterpiece, "The Rape of the Lock," is in these lines with their hint of the mock-epic. The dull-witted squire who "gives a smacking buss, and cries—'No words!' " seems related to Sir Plume of "The Rape."

Even in this early poem, Pope's skill with rhythms and sounds is masterful. In "Thus vanish scepters, coronets, and balls, / And leave you in lone woods or empty walls" Pope alternates a line full of the excitement and bustle of high society life in London with a slower, more plaintive line echoing the more peaceful noises of the country. The dullness and plainness of the line beginning "Old-fashioned halls, dull aunts" is deliberately followed by the sharp, ugly sounds in "and croaking rooks." Or, when Pope wishes to convey the fast, vibrant pattern of city life, he combines the noise and speed of "Streets, chairs, and coxcombs rush upon my sight" to give the feeling as well as the idea of what he has in mind.

The Rape of the Lock

AN HEROI-COMICAL POEM

Nolueram, Belinda, tuos violare capillos;
Sed juvat, hoc precibus me tribuisse tuis.
MARTIAL [*Epigr.* XII. 84.]

To Mrs. Arabella Fermor

MADAM,

It will be in vain to deny that I have some regard for this piece, since I dedicate it to You. Yet you may bear me witness, it was intended only to divert a few young Ladies, who have good sense and good humour enough to laugh not only at their sex's little unguarded follies, but at their own. But as it was communicated with the air of a Secret, it soon found its way into the world. An imperfect copy having been offer'd to a Bookseller, you had the good-nature for my sake to consent to the publication of one more correct: This I was forc'd to, before I had executed half my design, for the Machinery was entirely wanting to compleat it.

The Machinery, Madam, is a term invented by the Critics, to signify that part which the Deities, Angels, or Dæmons are made to act in a Poem: For the ancient Poets are in one respect like many modern Ladies: let an action be never so trivial in itself, they always make it appear of the utmost importance. These Machines I determined to raise on a very new and odd foundation, the Rosicrucian doctrine of Spirits.

I know how disagreeable it is to make use of hard words before a Lady; but 't is so much the concern of a Poet to have his works understood, and particularly by your Sex, that you must give me leave to explain two or three difficult terms.

The Rosicrucians are a people I must bring you acquainted with. The best account I know of them is in a French book call'd *Le Comte de Gabalis,* which both in its title and size is so like a Novel, that many of the Fair Sex have read it for one by mistake. According to

Nolueram . . . tuis: I was unwilling, Belinda, to violate your curls, but it pleases me to have offered up this to your entreaties.

these Gentlemen, the four Elements are inhabited by Spirits, which they call Sylphs, Gnomes, Nymphs, and Salamanders. The Gnomes or Dæmons of Earth delight in mischief; but the Sylphs, whose habitation is in the Air, are the best condition'd creatures imaginable. For they say, any mortals may enjoy the most intimate familiarities with these gentle Spirits, upon a condition very easy to all true Adepts, an inviolate preservation of Chastity.

As to the following Cantos, all the passages of them are as fabulous, as the Vision at the beginning, or the Transformation at the end; (except the loss of your Hair, which I always mention with reverence). The Human persons are as fictitious as the airy ones; and the character of Belinda, as it is now manag'd, resembles you in nothing but in Beauty.

If this Poem had as many Graces as there are in your Person, or in your Mind, yet I could never hope it should pass thro' the world half so Uncensur'd as You have done. But let its fortune be what it will, mine is happy enough, to have given me this occasion of assuring you that I am, with the truest esteem, MADAM,

Your most obedient, Humble Servant,

A. POPE.

Canto I

What dire offence from am'rous causes springs,
What mighty contests rise from trivial things,
I sing—This verse to *Caryl,* Muse! is due:
This, ev'n Belinda may vouchsafe to view:
Slight is the subject, but not so the praise,
If She inspire, and He approve my lays.
Say what strange motive, Goddess! could compel
A well-bred Lord t' assault a gentle Belle?
O say what stranger cause, yet unexplor'd,
Could make a gentle Belle reject a Lord? 10
In tasks so bold, can little men engage,
And in soft bosoms dwells such mighty Rage?
Sol thro' white curtains shot a tim'rous ray,
And oped those eyes that must eclipse the day:
Now lap-dogs give themselves the rousing shake,

l. 3. *Caryl:* John Caryll was a friend of Pope who suggested that he write a poem to soften the rift between the Fermor and the Petre families.

And sleepless lovers, just at twelve, awake:
Thrice rung the bell, the slipper knock'd the ground,
And the press'd watch return'd a silver sound.
Belinda still her downy pillow prest
Her guardian *Sylph* prolong'd the balmy rest: 20
'T was He had summon'd to her silent bed
The morning-dream that hover'd o'er her head;
A Youth more glitt'ring than a Birth-night Beau,
(That ev'n in slumber caus'd her cheek to glow)
Seem'd to her ear his winning lips to lay,
And thus in whsipers said, or seem'd to say.
"Fairest of mortals, thou distinguish'd care
Of thousand bright Inhabitants of Air!
If e'er one vision touch'd thy infant thought,
Of all the Nurse and all the Priest have taught; 30
Of airy Elves by moonlight shadows seen,
The silver token, and the circled green,
Or virgins visited by Angel-pow'rs,
With golden crowns and wreaths of heav'nly flow'rs;
Hear and believe! thy own importance know,
Nor bound thy narrow views to things below,
Some secret truths, from learned pride conceal'd,
To Maids alone and Children are reveal'd:
What tho' no credit doubting Wits may give?
The Fair and Innocent shall still believe. 40
Know, then, unnumber'd Spirits round thee fly,
The light Militia of the lower sky:
These, tho' unseen, are ever on the wing,
Hang o'er the Box, and hover round the Ring.
Think what an equipage thou hast in Air,
And view with scorn two Pages and a Chair.
As now your own, our beings were of old,
And once enclos'd in Woman's beauteous mould;
Thence, by a soft transition, we repair
From earthly Vehicles to these of air. 50
Think not, when Woman's transient breath is fled

l. 18. *press'd watch:* time piece that would chime the hour when pressed.
l. 44. *Box . . . Ring:* the Box refers to seats at the theater; the Ring was a fashionable circular drive in Hyde Park.
l. 46. *Chair:* sedan chair borne by two pages.

That all her vanities at once are dead;
Succeeding vanities she still regards,
And tho' she plays no more, o'erlooks the cards.
Her joy in gilded Chariots, when alive,
And love of Ombre, after death survive.
For when the Fair in all their pride expire,
To their first Elements their Souls retire:
The Sprites of fiery Termagants in Flame
Mount up, and take a Salamander's name. 60
Soft yielding minds to Water glide away,
And sip, with Nymphs, their elemental Tea.
The graver Prude sinks downward to a Gnome,
In search of mischief still on Earth to roam.
The light Coquettes in Sylphs aloft repair,
And sport and flutter in the fields of Air.
"Know further yet; whoever fair and chaste
Rejects mankind, is by some Sylph embrac'd:
For Spirits, freed from mortal laws, with ease
Assume what sexes and what shapes they please. 70
What guards the purity of melting Maids,
In courtly balls, and midnight masquerades,
Safe from the treach'rous friend, the daring spark,
The glance by day, the whisper in the dark,
When kind occasion prompts their warm desires,
When music softens, and when dancing fires?
'T is but their Sylph, the wise Celestials know,
Tho' Honour is the word with Men below.
"Some nymphs there are, too conscious of their face
For life predestin'd to the Gnomes' embrace. 80
These swell their prospects and exalt their pride,
When offers are disdain'd, and love deny'd:
Then gay Ideas crowd the vacant brain,
While Peers, and Dukes, and all their sweeping train,
And Garters, Stars, and Coronets appear,
And in soft sounds, 'Your Grace' salutes their ear.
'T is these that early taint the female soul,
Instruct the eyes of young Coquettes to roll,
Teach Infant-cheeks a bidden blush to know,
And little hearts to flutter at a Beau. 90

l. 56. *Ombre:* a fashionable card game.

"Oft, when the world imagine women stray,
The Sylphs thro' mystic mazes guide their way,
Thro' all the giddy circle they pursue,
And old impertinence expel by new.
What tender maid but must a victim fall
To one man's treat, but for another's ball?
When Florio speaks what virgin could withstand,
If gentle Damon did not squeeze her hand?
With varying vanities, from ev'ry part,
They shift the moving Toyshop of their heart; 100
Where wigs with wigs, with sword-knots sword-knots strive,
Beaux banish beaux, and coaches coaches drive.
This erring mortals Levity may call;
Oh blind to truth! the Sylphs contrive it all.
"Of these am I, who thy protection claim,
A watchful sprite, and Ariel is my name.
Late, as I rang'd the crystal wilds of air,
In the clear Mirror of thy ruling Star
I saw, alas! some dread event impend,
Ere to the main this morning sun descend, 110
But heav'n reveals not what, or how, or where:
Warn'd by the Sylph, oh pious maid, beware!
This to disclose is all thy guardian can:
Beward of all, but most beware of Man!"
He said; when Shock, who thought she slept too long,
Leap'd up, and wak'd his mistress with his tongue.
'T was then, Belinda, if report say true,
Thy eyes first open'd on a Billet-doux;
Wounds, Charms, and Ardors were no sooner read,
But all the Vision vanish'd from thy head, 120
And now, unveil'd, the Toilet stands display'd,
Each silver Vase in mystic order laid.
First, rob'd in white, the Nymph intent adores,
With head uncover'd, the Cosmetic pow'rs.
A heav'nly image in the glass appears,
To that she bends, to that her eyes she rears;
Th' inferior Priestess, at her altar's side,
Trembling begins the sacred rites of Pride.

l. 118. *Billet-doux:* love note.
l. 127. *inferior Priestess:* Belinda's lady's maid.

Unnumber'd treasures ope at once, and here
The various off'rings of the world appear; 130
From each she nicely culls with curious toil,
And decks the Goddess with the glitt'ring spoil.
This casket India's glowing gems unlocks,
And all Arabia breathes from yonder box.
The Tortoise here and Elephant unite,
Transform'd to combs, the speckled, and the white.
Here files of pins extend their shining rows,
Puffs, Powders, Patches, Bibles, Billet-doux.
Now awful Beauty puts on all its arms;
The fair each moment rises in her charms, 140
Repairs her smiles, awakens ev'ry grace,
And calls forth all the wonders of her face;
Sees by degrees a purer blush arise,
And keener lightnings quicken in her eyes.
The busy Sylphs surround their darling care,
These set the head, and those divide the hair,
Some fold the sleeve, whilst others plait the gown;
And Betty's prais'd for labours not her own.

Canto II

Not with more glories, in th' etherial plain,
The Sun first rises o'er the purpled main,
Than, issuing forth, the rival of his beams
Launch'd on the bosom of the silver Thames.
Fair Nymphs, and well-drest Youths around her shone,
But ev'ry eye was fix'd on her alone.
On her white breast a sparkling Cross she wore,
Which Jews might kiss, and Infidels adore.
Her lively looks a sprightly mind disclose,
Quick as her eyes, and as unfix'd as those: 10
Favours to none, to all she smiles extends;
Oft she rejects, but never once offends.
Bright as the sun, her eyes the gazers strike,
And, like the sun, they shine on all alike.
Yet graceful ease, and sweetness void of pride,
Might hide her faults, if Belles had faults to hide:
If to her share some female errors fall,

l. 143. *purer blush:* provided by cosmetics such as rouge.

Look on her face, and you 'll forget 'em all.
  This Nymph, to the destruction of mankind,
Nourish'd two Locks, which graceful hung behind 20
In equal curls, and well conspir'd to deck
With shining ringlets the smooth iv'ry neck.
Love in these labyrinths his slaves detains,
And mighty hearts are held in slender chains.
With hairy springes we the birds betray,
Slight lines of hair surprise the finny prey,
Fair tresses man's imperial race ensnare,
And beauty draws us with a single hair.
  Th' advent'rous Baron the bright locks admir'd;
He saw, he wish'd, and to the prize aspir'd. 30
Resolv'd to win, he meditates the way,
By force to ravish, or by fraud betray;
For when success a Lover's toil attends,
Few ask, if fraud or force attain'd his ends.
  For this, ere Phœbus rose, he had implor'd
Propitious heav'n, and ev'ry pow'r ador'd,
But chiefly Love—to Love an Altar built,
Of twelve vast French Romances, neatly gilt.
There lay three garters, half a pair of gloves;
And all the trophies of his former loves; 40
With tender Billet-doux he lights the pyre,
And breathes three am'rous sighs to raise the fire.
Then prostrate falls, and begs with ardent eyes
Soon to obtain, and long possess the prize:
The pow'rs gave ear, and granted half his pray'r,
The rest, the winds dispers'd in empty air.
  But now secure the painted vessel glides,
The sun-beams trembling on the floating tides:
While melting music steals upon the sky,
And soften'd sounds along the waters die; 50
Smooth flow the waves, the Zephyrs gently play,
Belinda smil'd, and all the world was gay.
All but the Sylph—with careful thoughts opprest,
Th' inpending woe sat heavy on his breast.
He summons strait his Denizens of air;
The lucid squadrons round the sails repair:

l. 25. *springes:* nets.

Soft o'er the shrouds aerial whispers breathe,
That seem'd but Zephyrs to the train beneath.
Some to the sun their insect-wings unfold,
Waft on the breeze, or sink in clouds of gold; 60
Transparent forms, too fine for mortal sight,
Their fluid bodies half dissolv'd in light,
Loose to the wind their airy garments flew,
Thin glitt'ring textures of the filmy dew,
Dipt in the richest tincture of the skies,
Where light disports in ever-mingling dyes,
While ev'ry beam new transient colours flings,
Colours that change whene'er they wave their wings.
Amid the circle, on the gilded mast,
Superior by the head, was Ariel plac'd; 70
His purple pinions op'ning to the sun,
He rais'd his azure wand, and thus begun.
"Ye Sylphs and Sylphids, to your chief give ear!
Fays, Fairies, Genii, Elves, and Dæmons, hear!
Ye know the spheres and various tasks assign'd
By laws eternal to th' aerial kind.
Some in the fields of purest Æther play,
And bask and whiten in the blaze of day.
Some guide the course of wand'ring orbs on high,
Or roll the planets thro' the boundless sky. 80
Some less refin'd, beneath the moon's pale light
Pursue the stars that shoot athwart the night,
Or suck the mists in grosser air below,
Or dip their pinions in the painted bow,
Or brew fierce tempests on the wintry main,
Or o'er the glebe distil the kindly rain.
Others on earth o'er human race preside,
Watch all their ways, and all their actions guide:
Of these the chief the care of Nations own,
And guard with Arms divine the British Throne. 90
"Our humbler province is to tend the Fair,
Not a less pleasing, tho' less glorious care;
To save the powder from too rude a gale,
Nor let th' imprison'd essences exhale;
To draw fresh colours from the vernal flow'rs;

l. 86. *glebe:* land.

To steal from rainbows e'er they drop in show'rs
A brighter wash; to curl their waving hairs,
Assist their blushes, and inspire their airs;
Nay oft, in dreams, invention we bestow,
To change a Flounce, or add a Furbelow. 100
"This day, black Omens threat the brightest Fair,
That e'er deserv'd a watchful spirit's care;
Some dire disaster, or by force, or slight;
But what, or where, the fates have wrapt in night.
Whether the nymph shall break Diana's law,
Or some frail China jar receive a flaw;
Or stain her honour or her new brocade;
Forget her pray'rs, or miss a masquerade;
Or lose her heart, or necklace, at a ball;
Or whether Heav'n has doom'd that Shock must fall. 110
Haste, then, ye spirits! to your charge repair:
The flutt'ring fan be Zephyretta's care;
The drops to thee, Brillante, we consign;
And, Momentilla, let the watch be thine;
Do thou, Crispissa, tend her fav'rite Lock;
Ariel himself shall be the guard of Shock.
"To fifty chosen Sylphs, of special note,
We trust th' important charge, the Petticoat:
Oft have we known that seven-fold fence to fail,
Tho' stiff with hoops, and arm'd with ribs of whale; 120
Form a strong line about the silver bound,
And guard the wide circumference around.
"Whatever spirit, careless of his charge,
His post neglects, or leaves the fair at large,
Shall feel sharp vengeance soon o'ertake his sins,
Be stopp'd in vials, or transfix'd with pins;
Or plung'd in lakes of bitter washes lie,
Or wedg'd whole ages in a bodkin's eye:
Gums and Pomatums shall his flight restrain,
While clogg'd he beats his silken wings in vain; 130
Or Alum styptics with contracting pow'r
Shrink his thin essence like a rivel'd flow'r:
Or, as Ixion fix'd, the wretch shall feel

l. 105. *Diana's law:* Diana is goddess of chastity.
l. 128. *bodkin's eye:* the eye of the hatpin.
l. 133. *Ixion:* mythical character who was punished by being chained eternally to a wheel in motion.

The giddy motion of the whirling Mill,
In fumes of burning Chocolate shall glow,
And tremble at the sea that froths below!"
He spoke; the spirits from the sails descend;
Some, orb in orb, around the nymph extend;
Some thrid the mazy ringlets of her hair;
Some hang upon the pendants of her ear: 140
With beating hearts the dire event they wait,
Anxious, and trembling for the birth of Fate.

Canto III

Close by those meads, for ever crown'd with flow'rs,
Where Thames with pride surveys his rising tow'rs,
There stands a structure of majestic frame,
Which from the neighb'ring Hampton takes its name.
Here Britain's statesmen oft the fall foredoom
Of foreign Tyrants and of Nymphs at home;
Here thou, great *Anna!* whom three realms obey,
Dost sometimes counsel take—and sometimes Tea.
Hither the heroes and the nymphs resort,
To taste awhile the pleasures of a Court; 10
In various talk th' instructive hours they past,
Who gave the ball, or paid the visit last;
One speaks the glory of the British Queen,
And one describes a charming Indian screen;
A third interprets motions, looks, and eyes;
At ev'ry word a reputation dies.
Snuff, or the fan, supply each pause of chat,
With singing, laughing, ogling, *and all that.*
Meanwhile, declining from the noon of day,
The sun obliquely shoots his burning ray; 20
The hungry Judges soon the sentence sign,
And wretches hang that jury-men may dine;
The merchant from th' Exchange returns in peace,
And the long labours of the Toilet cease.
Belinda now, whom thirst of fame invites,
Burns to encounter two advent'rous Knights,
At Ombre singly to decide their doom;
And swells her breast with conquests yet to come.
Straight the three bands prepare in arms to join,

l. 7. *Anna:* Queen Anne.

Each band the number of the sacred nine. 30
Soon as she spreads her hand, th' aerial guard
Descend, and sit on each important card:
First Ariel perch'd upon a Matadore,
Then each, according to the rank they bore;
For Sylphs, yet mindful of their ancient race,
Are, as when women, wondrous fond of place.
Behold, four Kings in majesty rever'd,
With hoary whiskers and a forky beard;
And four fair Queens whose hands sustain a flow'r,
Th' expressive emblem of their softer pow'r; 40
Four Knaves in garbs succinct, a trusty band,
Caps on their heads, and halberts in their hand;
And particolour'd troops, a shining train,
Draw forth to combat on the velvet plain.
The skilful Nymph reviews her force with care:
"Let Spades be trumps!" she said, and trumps they were.
Now move to war her sable Matadores,
In show like leaders of the swarthy Moors.
Spadillio first, unconquerable Lord!
Led off two captive trumps, and swept the board. 50
As many more Manillio forc'd to yield,
And march'd a victor from the verdant field.
Him Basto follow'd, but his fate more hard
Gain'd but one trump and one Plebian card.
With his broad sabre next, a chief in years,
The hoary Majesty of Spades appears,
Puts forth one manly leg, to sight reveal'd,
The rest, his many-colour'd robe conceal'd.
The rebel Knave, who dares his prince engage,
Proves the just victim of his royal rage. 60
Ev'n mighty Pam, that Kings and Queens o'erthrew
And mow'd down armies in the fights of Lu,
Sad chance of war! now destitute of aid,
Falls undistinguish'd by the victor Spade!
Thus far both armies to Belinda yield;
Now to the Baron fate inclines the field.
His warlike Amazon her host invades,
Th' imperial consort of the crown of Spades.

l. 33. *Matadore:* this and the proper names that follow through line 62 refer to cards in the game of Ombre.

The Club's black Tyrant first her victim dy'd,
Spite of his haughty mien, and barb'rous pride: 70
What boots the regal circle on his head,
His giant limbs, in state unwieldy spread;
That long behind he trails his pompous robe,
And, of all monarch's, only grasps the globe?
The Baron now his Diamonds pours apace;
Th' embroider'd King who shows but half his face,
And his refulgent Queen, with pow'rs combin'd
Of broken troops an easy conquest find.
Clubs, Diamonds, Hearts, in wild disorder seen,
With throngs promiscuous strew the level green. 80
Thus when dispers'd a routed army runs,
Of Asia's troops, and Afric's sable sons,
With like confusion different nations fly,
Of various habit, and of various dye,
The pierc'd battalions disunited fall,
In heaps on heaps; one fate o'erwhelms them all.
The Knave of Diamonds tries his wily arts,
And wins (oh shameful chance!) the Queen of Hearts.
At this, the blood the virgin's cheek forsook,
A livid paleness spreads o'er all her look; 90
She sees, and trembles at th' approaching ill,
Just in the jaws of ruin, and Codille.
And now (as oft in some distemper'd State)
On one nice Trick depends the gen'ral fate.
An Ace of Hearts steps forth: The King unseen
Lurk'd in her hand, and mourn'd his captive Queen:
He springs to Vengeance with an eager pace,
And falls like thunder on the prostrate Ace.
The nymph exulting fills with shouts the sky;
The walls, the woods, and long canals reply. 100
Oh thoughtless mortals! ever blind to fate,
Too soon dejected, and too soon elate.
Sudden, these honours shall be snatch'd away,
And curs'd for ever this victorious day.
For lo! the board with cups and spoons is crown'd,
The berries crackle, and the mill turns round;
On shining Altars of Japan they raise

l. 92. *Codille:* failure to make one's bid.
l. 106. *mill:* coffee mill for use of the guests.

The silver lamp; the fiery spirits blaze:
From silver spouts the grateful liquors glide,
While China's earth receives the smoking tide: 110
At once they gratify their scent and taste,
And frequent cups prolong the rich repast.
Straight hover round the Fair her airy band;
Some, as she sipp'd the fuming liquor fann'd,
Some o'er her lap their careful plumes display'd,
Trembling, and conscious of the rich brocade.
Coffee, (which makes the politician wise,
And see thro' all things with his half-shut eyes)
Sent up in vapours to the Baron's brain
New Stratagems, the radiant Lock to gain. 120
Ah cease, rash youth! desist ere 't is too late,
Fear the just Gods, and think of Scylla's Fate!
Chang'd to a bird, and sent to flit in air,
She dearly pays for Nisus' injur'd hair!
But when to mischief mortals bend their will,
How soon they find fit instruments of ill!
Just then, Clarissa drew with tempting grace
A two-edg'd weapon from her shining case:
So Ladies in Romance assist their Knight,
Present the spear, and arm him for the fight. 130
He takes the gift with rev'rence, and extends
The little engine on his fingers' ends;
This just behind Belinda's neck he spread,
As o'er the fragrant steams she bends her head.
Swift to the Lock a thousand Sprites repair,
A thousand wings, by turns, blow back the hair;
And thrice they twitch'd the diamond in her ear;
Thrice she look'd back, and thrice the foe drew near.
Just in that instant, anxious Ariel sought
The close recesses of the Virgin's thought; 140
As on the nosegay in her breast reclin'd,
He watch'd th' Ideas rising in her mind,
Sudden he view'd, in spite of all her art,
An earthly Lover lurking at her heart.

l. 122. *Scylla's Fate*: when the kingdom of Nisus, her father, was besieged, she betrayed him by tearing out his magical hair, which had hitherto kept the kingdom from harm. Nisus turned into an eagle, she into a small bird, and he pursues her everlastingly.

Amaz'd, confus'd, he found his pow'r expir'd,
Resign'd to fate, and with a sigh retir'd.
The Peer now spreads the glitt'ring Forfex wide,
T' inclose the Lock; now joins it, to divide.
Ev'n then, before the fatal engine clos'd,
A wretched Sylph too fondly interpos'd; 150
Fate urg'd the shears, and cut the Sylph in twain,
(But airy substance soon unites again)
The meeting points the sacred hair dissever
From the fair head, for ever, and for ever!
Then flash'd the living lightning from her eyes,
And screams of horror rend th' affrighted skies.
Not louder shrieks to pitying heav'n are cast,
When husbands, or when lap-dogs breathe their last;
Or when rich China vessels fall'n from high,
In glitt'ring dust and painted fragments lie! 160
"Let wreaths of triumph now my temples twine
(The victor cry'd) the glorious Prize is mine!
While fish in streams, or birds delight in air
Or in a coach and six the British Fair,
As long as Atalantis shall be read,
Or the small pillow grace a Lady's bed,
While visits shall be paid on solemn days,
When num'rous wax-lights in bright order blaze,
While nymphs take treats, or assignations give,
So long my honour, name, and praise shall live!" 170
What Time would spare, from Steel receives its date,
And monuments, like men, submit to fate!
Steel could the labour of the Gods destroy,
And strike to dust th' imperial tow'rs of Troy;
Steel could the works of mortal pride confound,
And hew triumphal arches to the ground.
What wonder then, fair nymph! thy hairs should feel,
The conqu'ring force of unresisted steel?

Canto IV

But anxious cares the pensive nymph oppress'd,
And secret passions labour'd in her breast.
Not youthful kings in battle seiz'd alive,

l. 147. *Forfex:* shears.
l. 165. *Atalantis:* a risqué work of fiction.

Not scornful virgins who their charms survive,
Not ardent lovers robb'd of all their bliss,
Not ancient ladies when refus'd a kiss,
Not tyrants fierce that unrepenting die,
Not Cynthia when her manteau 's pinn'd awry,
E'er felt such rage, resentment, and despair,
As thou, sad Virgin! for thy ravish'd Hair. 10
For, that sad moment, when the Sylphs withdrew
And Ariel weeping from Belinda flew,
Umbriel, a dusky, melancholy sprite,
As ever sully'd the fair face of light,
Down to the central earth, his proper scene,
Repair'd to search the gloomy Cave of Spleen.
Swift on his sooty pinions flits the Gnome,
And in a vapour reach'd the dismal dome.
No cheerful breeze this sullen region knows,
The dreaded East is all the wind that blows. 20
Here in a grotto, shelter'd close from air,
And screen'd in shades from day's detested glare,
She sighs for ever on her pensive bed,
Pain at her side, and Megrim at her head.
Two handmaids wait the throne: alike in place,
But diff'ring far in figure and in face.
Here stood Ill-nature like an ancient maid,
Her wrinkled form in black and white array'd;
With store of pray'rs, for mornings, nights, and noons,
Her hand is fill'd; her bosom with lampoons. 30
There Affectation, with a sickly mien,
Shows in her cheek the roses of eighteen,
Practis'd to lisp, and hang the head aside,
Faints into airs, and languishes with pride,
On the rich quilt sinks with becoming woe,
Wrapt in a gown, for sickness, and for show.
The fair ones feel such maladies as these,
When each new night-dress gives a new disease.
A constant Vapour o'er the palace flies;
Strange phantoms rising as the mists arise; 40
Dreadful, as hermit's dreams in haunted shades,

l. 16. *Spleen:* name applied to neurotic tendencies.
l. 24. *Megrim:* migraine.

Or bright, as visions of expiring maids.
Now glaring fiends, and snakes on rolling spires,
Pale spectres, gaping tombs, and purple fires:
Now lakes of liquid gold, Elysian scenes,
And crystal domes, and angels in machines.
  Unnumber'd throngs on every side are seen,
Of bodies chang'd to various forms by Spleen.
Here living Tea-pots stand, one arm held out,
One bent; the handle this, and that the spout: 50
A Pipkin there, like Homer's Tripod walks;
Here sighs a Jar, and there a Goose-pie talks;
Men prove with child, as pow'rful fancy works,
And maids turn'd bottles, call aloud for corks.
  Safe past the Gnome thro' this fantastic band,
A branch of healing Spleenwort in his hand.
Then thus address'd the pow'r: "Hail, wayward Queen!
Who rule the sex to fifty from fifteen:
Parent of vapours and of female wit,
Who give th' hysteric, or poetic fit, 60
On various tempers act by various ways,
Make some take physic, others scribble plays;
Who cause the proud their visits to delay,
And send the godly in a pet to pray.
A nymph there is, that all thy pow'r disdains,
And thousands more in equal mirth maintains.
But oh! if e'er thy Gnome could spoil a grace,
Or raise a pimple on a beauteous face,
Like Citron-waters matrons' cheeks inflame,
Or change complexions at a losing game; 70
If e'er with airy horns I planted heads,
Or rumpled petticoats, or tumbled beds,
Or caus'd suspicion when no soul was rude,
Or discompos'd the head-dress of a Prude,
Or e'er to costive lap-dog gave disease,
Which not the tears of brightest eyes could ease:
Hear me, and touch Belinda with chagrin,
That single act gives half the world the spleen."
  The Goddess with a discontented air

l. 69. *Citron-waters:* brandy and lemon peel, considered beneficial to the complexion.

l. 71. *airy horns:* the horns of a cuckold.

Seems to reject him, tho' she grants his pray'r. 80
A wond'rous Bag with both her hands she binds,
Like that where once Ulysses held the winds;
There she collects the force of female lungs,
Sighs, sobs, and passions, and the war of tongues.
A Vial next she fills with fainting fears,
Soft sorrows, melting griefs, and flowing tears.
The Gnome rejoicing bears her gifts away,
Spreads his black wings, and slowly mounts to day.
Sunk in Thalestris' arms the nymph he found,
Her eyes dejected and her hair unbound. 90
Full o'er their heads the swelling bag he rent,
And all the Furies issu'd at the vent.
Belinda burns with more than mortal ire,
And fierce Thalestris fans the rising fire.
"O wretched maid!" she spread her hands, and cry'd,
(While Hampton's echoes, "Wretched maid!" reply'd)
"Was it for this you took such constant care
The bodkin, comb, and essence to prepare?
For this your locks in paper durance bound,
For this with tort'ring irons wreath'd around? 100
For this with fillets strained your tender head,
And bravely bore the double loads of lead?
Gods! shall the ravisher display your hair,
While the Fops envy, and the Ladies stare!
Honour forbid! at whose unrivall'd shrine
Ease, pleasure, virtue, all our sex resign.
Methinks already I your tears survey,
Already hear the horrid things they say,
Already see you a degraded toast,
And all your honour in a whisper lost! 110
How shall I, then, your helpless fame defend?
'T will then be infamy to seem your friend!
And shall this prize, th' inestimable prize,
Expos'd thro' crystal to the gazing eyes,
And heighten'd by the diamond's circling rays,
On that rapacious hand for ever blaze?
Sooner shall grass in Hyde-park Circus grow,

l. 89. *Thalestris:* an Amazon queen.
l. 99. *paper durance:* hair curlers.

And wits take lodgings in the sound of Bow;
Sooner let earth, air, sea, to Chaos fall,
Men, monkeys, lap-dogs, parrots, perish all!" 120
She said; then raging to Sir Plume repairs,
And bids her Beau demand the precious hairs:
(Sir Plume of amber snuff-box justly vain,
And the nice conduct of a clouded cane)
With earnest eyes, and round unthinking face,
He first the snuff-box open'd, then the case,
And thus broke out—"My Lord, why, what the devil?
Z—ds! damn the lock! 'fore Gad, you must be civil!
Plague on 't! 't is past a jest—nay prithee, pox!
Give her the hair"—he spoke, and rapp'd his box. 130
"It grieves me much" (reply'd the Peer again)
"Who speaks so well should ever speak in vain.
But by this Lock, this sacred Lock I swear,
(Which never more shall join its parted hair;
Which never more its honours shall renew,
Clipp'd from the lovely head where late it grew)
That while my nostrils draw the vital air,
This hand, which won it, shall for ever wear."
He spoke, and speaking, in proud triumph spread
The long-contended honours of her head. 140
But Umbriel, hateful Gnome! forbears not so;
He breaks the Vial whence the sorrows flow.
Then see! the nymph in beauteous grief appears,
Her eyes half-languishing, half-drown'd in tears;
On her heav'd bosom hung her drooping head,
Which, with a sigh, she rais'd; and thus she said.
"For ever curs'd be this detested day,
Which snatch'd my best, my fav'rite curl away!
Happy! ah ten times happy had I been,
If Hampton-Court these eyes had never seen! 150
Yet am not I the first mistaken maid,
By love of Courts to num'rous ills betray'd.
Oh had I rather un-admir'd remain'd
In some lone isle, or distant Northern land;
Where the gilt Chariot never marks the way,
Where none learn Ombre, none e'er taste Bohea!
There kept my charms conceal'd from mortal eye,
Like roses, that in deserts bloom and die.

What mov'd my mind with youthful Lords to roam?
Oh had I stay'd, and said my pray'rs at home! 160
'T was this, the morning omens seem'd to tell,
Thrice from my trembling hand the patch-box fell;
The tott'ring China shook without a wind,
Nay, Poll sat mute, and Shock was most unkind!
A Sylph too warn'd me of the threats of fate,
In mystic visions, now believ'd too late!
See the poor remnants of these slighted hairs!
My hands shall rend what ev'n thy rapine spares:
These in two sable ringlets taught to break,
Once gave new beauties to the snowy neck; 170
The sister-lock now sits uncouth, alone,
And in its fellow's fate foresees its own;
Uncurl'd it hangs, the fatal shears demands,
And tempts once more thy sacrilegious hands.
Oh hadst thou, cruel! been content to seize
Hairs less in sight, or any hairs but these!"

Canto V

She said: the pitying audience melt in tears.
But Fate and Jove had stopp'd the Baron's ears.
In vain Thalestris with reproach assails,
For who can move when fair Belinda fails?
Not half so fix'd the Trojan could remain,
While Anna begg'd and Dido rag'd in vain.
Then grave Clarissa graceful wav'd her fan;
Silence ensu'd, and thus the nymph began.
"Say why are Beauties prais'd and honour'd most,
The wise man's passion, and the vain man's toast? 10
Why deck'd with all that land and sea afford,
Why Angels call'd, and Angel-like ador'd?
Why round our coaches crowd the white-glov'd Beaux,
Why bows the side-box from its inmost rows;
How vain are all these glories, all our pains,
Unless good sense preserve what beauty gains:
That men may say, when we the front-box grace:
'Behold the first in virtue as in face!'

l. 6. *Anna . . . Dido:* in the *Aeneid,* Dido and her sister beg Aeneas not to leave Carthage.

Oh! if to dance all night, and dress all day,
Charm'd the small-pox, or chas'd old-age away; 20
Who would not scorn what housewife's cares produce,
Or who would learn one earthly thing of use?
To patch, nay ogle, might become a Saint,
Nor could it sure be such a sin to paint.
But since, alas! frail beauty must decay,
Curl'd or uncurl'd, since Locks will turn to grey;
Since painted, or not painted, all shall fade,
And she who scorns a man, must die a maid;
What then remains but well our pow'r to use,
And keep good-humour still whate'er we lose? 30
And trust me, dear! good-humour can prevail,
When airs, and flights, and screams, and scolding fail.
Beauties in vain their pretty eyes may roll;
Charms strike the sight, but merit wins the soul."
So spoke the Dame, but no applause ensu'd;
Belinda frown'd, Thalestris call'd her Prude.
"To arms, to arms!" the fierce Virago cries,
And swift as lightning to the combat flies.
All side in parties, and begin th' attack;
Fans clap, silks rustle, and tough whalebones crack; 40
Heroes' and Heroines' shouts confus'dly rise,
And bass, and treble voices strike the skies.
No common weapons in their hands are found,
Like Gods they fight, nor dread a mortal wound.
So when bold Homer makes the Gods engage,
And heav'nly breasts with human passions rage;
'Gainst Pallas, Mars; Latona, Hermes arms;
And all Olympus rings with loud alarms:
Jove's thunder roars, heav'n trembles all around,
Blue Neptune storms, the bellowing deeps resound: 50
Earth shakes her nodding tow'rs, the ground gives way,
And the pale ghosts start at the flash of day!
Triumphant Umbriel on a sconce's height
Clapp'd his glad wings, and sate to view the fight:
Propp'd on their bodkin spears, the Sprites survey
The growing combat, or assist the fray.
While thro' the press enrag'd Thalestris flies,
And scatters death around from both her eyes,
A Beau and Witling perish'd in the throng,

One died in metaphor, and one in song. 60
"O cruel nymph! a living death I bear,"
Cry'd Dapperwit, and sunk beside his chair.
A mournful glance Sir Fopling upwards cast,
"Those eyes are made so killing"—was his last.
Thus on Mæander's flow'ry margin lies
Th' expiring Swan, and as he sings he dies.
  When bold Sir Plume had drawn Clarissa down,
Chloe stepp'd in, and kill'd him with a frown;
She smil'd to see the doughty hero slain,
But, at her smile, the Beau reviv'd again. 70
  Now Jove suspends his golden scales in air,
Weighs the Men's wits against the Lady's hair;
The doubtful beam long nods from side to side;
At length the wits mount up, the hairs subside.
  See, fierce Belinda on the Baron flies,
With more than usual lightning in her eyes:
Nor fear'd the Chief th' unequal fight to try,
Who sought no more than on his foe to die.
But this bold Lord with manly strength endu'd,
She with one finger and a thumb subdu'd: 80
Just where the breath of life his nostrils drew,
A charge of Snuff the wily virgin threw;
The Gnomes direct, to ev'ry atom just,
The pungent grains of titillating dust.
Sudden, with starting tears each eye o'erflows,
And the high dome re-echoes to his nose.
  "Now meet thy fate," incens'd Belinda cry'd,
And drew a deadly bodkin from her side.
(The same, his ancient personage to deck,
Her great great grandsire wore about his neck, 90
In three seal-rings; which after, melted down,
Form'd a vast buckle for his widow's gown:
Her infant grandame's whistle next it grew,
The bells she jingled, and the whistle blew;
Then in a bodkin grac'd her mother's hairs,
Which long she wore, and now Belinda wears.)
  "Boast not my fall" (he cry'd) "insulting foe!
Thou by some other shalt be laid as low,
Nor think, to die dejects my lofty mind:
All that I dread is leaving you behind! 100
Rather than so, ah let me still survive,

And burn in Cupid's flames—but burn alive."
"Restore the Lock!" she cries; and all around
"Restore the Lock!" the vaulted roofs rebound.
Not fierce Othello in so loud a strain
Roar'd for the handkerchief that caus'd his pain.
But see how oft ambitious aims are cross'd,
And chiefs contend 'till all the prize is lost!
The Lock, obtain'd with guilt, and keep with pain,
In ev'ry place is sought, but sought in vain: 110
With such a prize no mortal must be blest,
So heav'n decrees! with heav'n who can contest?
Some thought it mounted to the Lunar sphere,
Since all things lost on earth are treasur'd there.
There Heros' wits are kept in pond'rous vases,
And beaux', in snuff-boxes and tweezer-cases.
There broken vows and death-bed alms are found,
And lovers' hearts with ends of riband bound,
The courtier's promises, and sick man's pray'rs,
The smiles of harlots, and the tears of heirs, 120
Cages for gnats, and chains to yoke a flea,
Dry'd butterflies, and tomes of casuistry.
But trust the Muse—she saw it upward rise,
Tho' mark'd by none but quick, poetic eyes:
(So Rome's great founder to the heav'ns withdrew,
To Proculus alone confess'd in view)
A sudden Star, it shot thro' liquid air,
And drew behind a radiant trail of hair.
Not Berenice's Locks first rose so bright,
The heav'ns bespangling with dishevell'd light. 130
The Sylphs behold it kindling as it flies,
And pleas'd pursue its progress thro' the skies.
This the Beau monde shall from the Mall survey,
And hail with music its propitious ray.
This the blest Lover shall for Venus take,
And send up vows from Rosamonda's lake.
This Partridge soon shall view in cloudless skies,

l. 125. *Rome's great founder:* Romulus rose to heaven before the eyes of Proculus.

l. 129. *Berenice's Locks:* this wife of Ptolemy II offered her hair to insure her husband's safety in war. The hair became a constellation.

l. 137. *Partridge:* a prophet and writer of seventeenth-century almanacs.

When next he looks thro' Galileo's eyes;
And hence th' egregious wizard shall foredoom
The fate of Louis, and the fall of Rome. 140
  Then cease, bright Nymph! to mourn thy ravish'd hair,
Which adds new glory to the shining sphere!
Not all the tresses that fair head can boast,
Shall draw such envy as the Lock you lost.
For, after all the murders of your eye,
When after millions slain, yourself shall die:
When those fair suns shall set, as set they must,
And all those tresses shall be laid in dust,
This Lock, the Muse shall consecrate to fame,
And 'midst the stars inscribe Belinda's name. 150

[*1711*]

l. 138. *Galileo's eyes:* the telescope.
l. 140. *Louis:* Louis XIV.

An Essay on Man

TO

H. ST. JOHN LORD BOLINGBROKE

Argument of Epistle I

OF THE NATURE AND STATE OF MAN, WITH RESPECT TO THE UNIVERSE

Of Man in the abstract. I. That we can judge only with regard to our own system, being ignorant of the relations of systems and things, v. 17, &c. II. That Man is not to be deemed imperfect, but a Being suited to his place and rank in the creation, agreeable to the general Order of things, and conformable to Ends and Relations to him unknown, v. 35, &c. III. That it is partly upon his ignorance of future events, and partly upon the hope of a future state, that all his happiness in the present depends, v. 77, &c. IV. The pride of aiming at more knowledge, and pretending to more Perfection, the cause of Man's error and misery. The impiety of putting himself in the place of God, and judging of the fitness or unfitness, perfection or imperfection, justice or injustice of his dispensations, v. 113, &c. V. The absurdity of conceiting himself the final cause of the creation, or expecting that perfection in the moral world, which is not in the natural, v. 131, &c. VI. The unreasonableness of his complaints against Providence, while on the one hand he demands the Perfections of the Angels, and on the other the bodily qualifications of the Brutes; though, to possess any of the sensitive faculties in a higher degree, would render him miserable, v. 173, &c. VII. That throughout the whole visible world, an universal order and gradation in the sensual and mental faculties is observed, which causes a subordination of creature to creature, and of all creatures to Man. The gradations of sense, instinct, thought, reflection, reason; that Reason alone countervails all the other faculties, v. 207. VIII. How much further this order and subordination of living creatures may extend, above and below us; were any part of which broken, not that part only, but the whole connected creation must be destroyed, v. 233. IX. The extravagance, madness, and pride of such a desire, v. 259.

Bolingbroke: prominent statesman, prime minister, and friend of Pope.

X. The consequence of all, the absolute submission due to Providence, both as to our present and future state, v. 281, &c, to the end.

Epistle I

Awake, my *St. John!* leave all meaner things
To low ambition, and the pride of Kings.
Let us (since Life can little more supply
Than just to look about us and to die)
Expatiate free o'er all this scene of Man;
A mighty maze! but not without a plan;
A Wild, where weeds and flow'rs promiscuous shoot;
Or Garden, tempting with forbidden fruit.
Together let us beat this ample field,
Try what the open, what the covert yield; 10
The latent tracts, the giddy heights, explore
Of all who blindly creep, or sightless soar;
Eye Nature's walks, shoot Folly as it flies,
And catch the Manners living as they rise;
Laugh where we must, be candid where we can;
But vindicate the ways of God to Man.
I. Say first, of God above, or Man below,
What can we reason, but from what we know?
Of Man, what see we but his station here,
From which to reason, or to which refer? 20
Thro' worlds unnumber'd tho' the God be known,
'Tis ours to trace him only in our own.
He, who thro' vast immensity can pierce,
See worlds on worlds compose one universe,
Observe how system into system runs,
What other planets circle other suns,
What vary'd Being peoples ev'ry star,
May tell why Heav'n has made us as we are.
But of this frame the bearings, and the ties,
The strong connexions, nice dependencies, 30
Gradations just, has thy pervading soul
Look'd thro'? or can a part contain the whole?
Is the great chain, that draws all to agree,

l. 33. *the great chain*: the philosophical idea, current in the seventeenth and eighteenth centuries, that everything in the universe has its appointed place on a divinely conceived

And drawn supports, upheld by God, or thee?
  II. Presumptuous Man! the reason wouldst thou find,
Why form'd so weak, so little, and so blind?
First, if thou canst, the harder reason guess,
Why form'd no weaker, blinder, and no less?
Ask of thy mother earth, why oaks are made
Taller or stronger than the weeds they shade? 40
Or ask of yonder argent fields above,
Why *Jove's* satellites are less than *Jove?*
  Of Systems possible, if 't is confest
That Wisdom infinite must form the best,
Where all must full or not coherent be,
And all that rises, rise in due degree;
Then, in the scale of reas'ning life, 't is plain,
There must be, somewhere, such a rank as Man:
And all the question (wrangle e'er so long)
Is only this, if God has plac'd him wrong? 50
  Respecting Man, whatever wrong we call,
May, must be right, as relative to all.
In human works, tho' labour'd on with pain,
A thousand movements scarce one purpose gain;
In God's, one single can its end produce;
Yet serves to second too some other use.
So Man, who here seems principal alone,
Perhaps acts second to some sphere unknown,
Touches some wheel, or verges to some goal;
'Tis but a part we see, and not a whole. 60
  When the proud steed shall know why Man restrains
His fiery course, or drives him o'er the plains:
When the dull Ox, why now he breaks the clod,
Is now a victim, and now Ægypt's God:
Then shall Man's pride and dulness comprehend
His actions', passions', being's, use and end;
Why doing, suff'ring, check'd, impell'd; and why
This hour a slave, the next a deity.
  Then say not Man's imperfect, Heav'n in fault;
Say rather, Man's as perfect as he ought: 70
His knowledge measur'd to his state and place;

Great Chain of Being which ordered the world. To try to change one's position in the Chain was to commit the paramount sin of Pride.

His time a moment, and a point his space.
If to be perfect in a certain sphere,
What matter, soon or late, or here or there?
The blest today is as completely so,
As who began a thousand years ago.
III. Heav'n from all creatures hides the book of Fate,
All but the page prescrib'd, their present state:
From brutes what men, from men what spirits know:
Or who could suffer Being here below? 80
The lamb thy riot dooms to bleed today,
Had he thy Reason, would he skip and play?
Pleas'd to the last, he crops the flow'ry food,
And licks the hand just rais'd to shed his blood.
Oh blindness to the future! kindly giv'n,
That each may fill the circle mark'd by Heav'n:
Who sees with equal eye, as God of all,
A hero perish, or a sparrow fall,
Atoms or systems into ruin hurl'd,
And now a bubble burst, and now a world. 90
Hope humbly then; with trembling pinions soar;
Wait the great teacher Death; and God adore.
What future bliss, he gives not thee to know,
But gives that Hope to be thy blessing now.
Hope springs eternal in the human breast:
Man never Is, but always To be blest:
The soul, uneasy and confin'd from home,
Rests and expatiates in a life to come.
Lo, the poor Indian! whose untutor'd mind
Sees God in clouds, or hears him in the wind: 100
His soul, proud Science never taught to stray
Far as the solar walk, or milky way;
Yet simple Nature to his hope has giv'n,
Behind the cloud-topt hill, an humbler heav'n;
Some safer world in depth of woods embrac'd,
Some happier island in the watry waste,
Where slaves once more their native land behold,
No fiends torment, no Christians thirst for gold.
To Be, contents his natural desire,
He asks no Angel's wing, no Seraph's fire; 110
But thinks, admitted to that equal sky,
His faithful dog shall bear him company.

IV. Go, wiser thou! and, in thy scale of sense,
Weigh thy Opinion against Providence;
Call imperfection what thou fancy'st such,
Say, here he gives too little, there too much:
Destroy all Creatures for thy sport or gust,
Yet cry, If Man's unhappy, God's unjust;
If Man alone engross not Heav'n's high care,
Alone made perfect here, immortal there: 120
Snatch from his hand the balance and the rod,
Re-judge his justice, be the GOD of GOD.
In Pride, in reas'ning Pride, our error lies;
All quit their sphere, and rush into the skies.
Pride still is aiming at the blest abodes,
Men would be Angels, Angels would be Gods.
Aspiring to be Gods, if Angels fell,
Aspiring to be Angels, Men rebel:
And who but wishes to invert the laws
Of *Order*, sins against th' Eternal Cause.   130
V. Ask for what end the heav'nly bodies shine,
Earth for whose use? Pride answers, " 'T is for mine:
For me kind Nature wakes her genial Pow'r,
Suckles each herb, and spreads out ev'ry flow'r;
Annual for me, the grape, the rose renew
The juice nectareous, and the balmy dew;
For me, the mine a thousand treasures brings;
For me, health gushes from a thousand springs;
Seas roll to waft me, suns to light me rise;
My foot-stool earth, my canopy the skies."   140
But errs not Nature from this gracious end,
From burning suns when livid deaths descend,
When earthquakes swallow, or when tempests sweep
Towns to one grave, whole nations to the deep?
"No, ('t is reply'd) the first Almighty Cause
Acts not by partial, but by gen'ral laws;
Th' exceptions few; some change since all began:
And what created perfect?"—Why then Man?
If the great end be human Happiness,
Then Nature deviates; and can Man do less?   150
As much that end a constant course requires

l. 117. *gust:* taste.

Of show'rs and sun-shine, as of Man's desires;
As much eternal springs and cloudless skies,
As Men for ever temp'rate, calm, and wise.
If plagues or earthquakes break not Heav'n's design,
Why then a Borgia, or a Catiline?
Who knows but he, whose hand the lightning forms,
Who heaves old Ocean, and who wings the storms;
Pours fierce Ambition in a Cæsar's mind,
Or turns young Ammon loose to scourge mankind? 160
From pride, from pride, our very reas'ning springs;
Account for moral, as for nat'ral things:
Why charge we Heav'n in those, in these acquit?
In both, to reason right is to submit.
  Better for us, perhaps, it might appear,
Were there all harmony, all virtue here;
That never air or ocean felt the wind;
That never passion discompos'd the mind.
But *all* subsists by elemental strife;
And Passions are the elements of Life. 170
The gen'ral *Order*, since the whole began,
Is kept in Nature, and is kept in Man.
  VI. What would this Man? Now upward will he soar,
And little less than Angel, would be more;
Now looking downwards, just as griev'd appears
To want the strength of bulls, the fur of bears.
Made for his use all creatures if he call,
Say what their use, had he the pow'rs of all?
Nature to these, without profusion, kind,
The proper organs, proper pow'rs assign'd; 180
Each seeming want compensated of course,
Here with degrees of swiftness, there of force;
All in exact proportion to the state;
Nothing to add, and nothing to abate.
Each beast, each insect, happy in its own:
Is Heav'n unkind to Man, and Man alone?
Shall he alone, whom rational we call,
Be pleas'd with nothing, if not bless'd with all?
  The bliss of Man (could Pride that blessing find)
Is not to act or think beyond mankind; 190

l. 160. *Ammon:* a name for Alexander.

No pow'rs of body or of soul to share,
But what his nature and his state can bear.
Why has not Man a microscopic eye?
For this plain reason, Man is not a Fly.
Say what the use, were finer optics giv'n,
T' inspect a mite, not comprehend the heav'n?
Or touch, if tremblingly alive all o'er,
To smart and agonize at every pore?
Or quick effluvia darting thro' the brain,
Die of a rose in aromatic pain? 200
If nature thunder'd in his op'ning ears,
And stunn'd him with the music of the spheres,
How would he wish that Heav'n had left him still
The whisp'ring Zephyr, and the purling rill?
Who finds not Providence all good and wise,
Alike in what it gives, and what denies?
VII. Far as Creation's ample range extends,
The scale of sensual, mental pow'rs ascends:
Mark how it mounts, to Man's imperial race,
From the green myriads in the peopled grass: 210
What modes of sight betwixt each wide extreme,
The mole's dim curtain, and the lynx's beam:
Of smell, the headlong lioness between,
And hound sagacious on the tainted green:
Of hearing, from the life that fills the Flood,
To that which warbles thro' the vernal wood:
The spider's touch, how exquisitely fine!
Feels at each thread, and lives along the line:
In the nice bee, what sense so subtly true
From pois'nous herbs extracts the healing dew? 220
How Instinct varies in the grov'ling swine,
Compar'd, half-reas'ning elephant, with thine!
'Twixt that, and Reason, what a nice barrier,
For ever sep'rate, yet for ever near!
Remembrance and Reflection how allied;
What thin partitions Sense from Thought divide:
And middle natures, how they long to join,
Yet never pass th' insuperable line!
Without this just gradation, could they be
Subjected, these to those, or all to thee? 230
The pow'rs of all subdu'd by thee alone,

Is not thy Reason all these pow'rs in one?
VIII. See, thro' this air, this ocean, and this earth,
All matter quick, and bursting into birth.
Above, how high, progressive life may go!
Around, how wide! how deep extend below!
Vast chain of Being! which from God began,
Natures ethereal, human, angel, man,
Beast, bird, fish, insect, what no eye can see,
No glass can reach; from Infinite to thee, 240
From thee to Nothing.—On superior pow'rs
Were we to press, inferior might on ours;
Or in the full creation leave a void,
Where, one step broken, the great scale's destroy'd:
From Nature's chain whatever link you strike,
Tenth or ten thousandth, breaks the chain alike.
And, if each system in gradation roll
Alike essential to th' amazing Whole,
The least confusion but in one, not all
That system only, but the Whole must fall. 250
Let Earth unbalanc'd from her orbit fly,
Planets and Suns run lawless thro' the sky;
Let ruling angels from their spheres be hurl'd,
Being on being wreck'd, and world on world;
Heav'n's whole foundations to their center nod,
And Nature tremble to the throne of God.
All this dread *Order* break—for whom? for thee?
Vile worm!—Oh Madness! Pride! Impiety!
IX. What if the foot, ordain'd the dust to tread,
Or hand, to toil, aspir'd to be the head? 260
What if the head, the eye, or ear repin'd
To serve mere engines to the ruling Mind?
Just as absurd for any part to claim
To be another, in this gen'ral frame:
Just as absurd, to mourn the tasks or pains,
The great directing *Mind of All* ordains.
All are but parts of one stupendous whole,
Whose body Nature is, and God the soul;
That, chang'd thro' all, and yet in all the same;
Great in the earth, as in th' ethereal frame; 270
Warms in the sun, refreshes in the breeze,
Glows in the stars, and blossoms in the trees,

Lives thro' all life, extends thro' all extent,
Spreads undivided, operates unspent;
Breathes in our soul, informs our mortal part,
As full, as perfect, in a hair as heart:
As full, as perfect, in vile Man that mourns,
As the rapt Seraph that adores and burns:
To him no high, no low, no great, no small;
He fills, he bounds, connects, and equals all. 280
X. Cease then, nor *Order* Imperfection name:
Our proper bliss depends on what we blame.
Know thy own point: This kind, this due degree
Of blindness, weakness, Heav'n bestows on thee.
Submit.—In this, or any other sphere,
Secure to be as blest as thou canst bear:
Safe in the hand of one disposing Pow'r,
Or in the natal, or the mortal hour.
All Nature is but Art, unknown to thee;
All Chance, Direction, which thou canst not see; 290
All Discord, Harmony not understood;
All partial Evil, universal Good:
And, spite of Pride, in erring Reason's spite,
One truth is clear, *Whatever is, is right.*

[1732–34?]

William Wordsworth

William Wordsworth, the chief poet of the English Romantic Movement, was born on April 7, 1770 in the wild and rugged Cumberland country of England. Wild and undisciplined himself, he gained little from his stay at Anne Birkett's infant school at Penrith, for he preferred truancy in the fields to study. His mother died when he was eight and his father died when he was thirteen. From this time on, the moody boy was brought up by his uncles. At fifteen he was writing verses. At seventeen he entered Cambridge, where he distinguished himself for brilliance if not for diligence.

Wordsworth's experiences on the Continent during the years 1790–92, were extremely important. On a walking tour through Switzerland and France with his friend, Robert Jones, he first came into contact with the grandeur of the Alps, an event which he describes as "sublime." At the same time, the idealistic youth was brought face to face with the French Revolution. Its emotionally moving and high-minded aspects so impressed him that he considered becoming an active revolutionary leader. And, finally, he met and fell in love with Annette Vallon, who presented him with a daughter on December 15, 1792.

Wordsworth's almost hysterical excitement and his sense of personal involvement in great events were tempered by the practical problems that 1793 brought. He left France for England as soon as his daughter Caroline was born. Very soon afterward, in 1793, England declared war on the French revolutionary government. This action brought Wordsworth to the point of a physical and psychological breakdown for two reasons: ideologically, he was torn between his sentiments as a loyal Englishman and his equally strong inclination to support what he took to be the forces of right, struggling for liberty in France. Personally, he was troubled by his abandonment of the unwed Annette and his child, especially since the outbreak of war between England and the revolutionaries made his return to France impossible.

There followed a period of restless and seemingly aimless activity in England while Wordsworth tried to get his bearings. He lived for a time with his sister Dorothy. He tried his hand at editing a magazine. He met Coleridge, and he published some of his poems under the title of *Descriptive Sketches.* By 1797, he and Coleridge were planning the *Lyrical Ballads.* In 1799, Wordsworth traveled to Germany, where some of the autobiographical *Prelude* and the "Lucy" poems were written. The year's end found him back in England, at Grasmere, living with his sister, Dorothy, in Dove Cottage where he remained until 1808. During this period, he spent at least a month visiting Annette and his daughter in France. He also married Mary Hutchinson, by whom he had several children in the years that followed.

By 1810, the fiery revolutionary had become the conservative citizen. Though he was unusually productive at this time, his reputation as a poet had reached a low point. His poetry was attacked vigorously in the *Edinburgh Review,* and Byron was to ridicule "The Excursion." Wordsworth's conservatism was formalized by his successful application for a government sinecure and his appointment in 1813 as Stamp-Distributor for Westmorland. With attainment of this office, he moved into Rydal Mount, where he spent the remaining half of his long life.

Wordsworth continued to turn out poetry prolifically, but the outpouring of this later period does not rank with the work done before 1810. In spite of this falling off of poetic inspiration, Wordsworth's popularity increased measurably shortly before 1820. On his numerous travels he was honored both in England and abroad. The British government bestowed upon him a Civil List pension of 300 pounds per year in 1842. In the following year, Wordsworth accepted the Laureateship, which he held until his death, at the age of eighty, on April 23, 1850.

The principal forces which shaped Wordsworth's life were his affinity for nature, his commitment to, and eventual shrinking from, the French Revolution, and his affair with Annette Vallon.

Wordsworth's love of nature was not at all a literary convenience. From earliest childhood, he preferred the solace of the countryside to association with people. His trip to the Alps reinforced his belief that the beauty of nature required the presence in it of a supernatural Being—that, indeed, God was immanent in the trees, the hills, the streams. This pantheistic belief, expounded at length in such poems as "Tintern Abbey," sustained the poet during those times when he had to be away from his natural haunts. To him, nature exerted not only a religious influence, but a moral force as well, accounting for many of the finer instincts of man's character. Without the healing and soothing effect of nature, perhaps, Wordsworth could not have withstood the assault on his spirit of the fiasco of the Revolution and of the Annette Vallon affair.

The chart of Wordsworth's emotional involvement in the French Revolution is revealing. Totally committed at the beginning, he detected the march of liberty and the dawn of a new era in the relationships of freemen to their governors. He wanted to be part of that movement and may, in fact, have worked actively with the revolutionists for a short time. But as the idealism of the French revolutionaries of 1789 gave way in succeeding years to The Terror and The Directorate, Wordsworth's confidence in his earlier position suffered a severe jolt. Prudence and caution replaced eager impetuosity as his guide to conduct. The result was twofold: Wordsworth became a conservative politically, and he appeared to lose the strain of poetic inspiration that gave the earlier work its brilliance. Burned once by involvement in new, vital experience, the poet apparently was reluctant to experiment again with the untried and the threatening. His sister and his wife joined in the effort to preserve a calm balance in his daily life. But without fresh experience, even so great a poet as Wordsworth must find the well of poetic inspiration drying up. Perhaps this circumstance accounts for the deadness and dullness of the hundreds of technically blameless poems that Wordsworth wrote in the final decades of his career.

Intimately involved with his mixed feelings regarding the French Revolution were his equally distressed emotions toward Annette and his daughter. Wordsworth obviously did not fancy the idea of deserting the mother of his child almost as soon as the infant was born, and he relished even less his inability to return to them. Furthermore, an attachment which had been wholly based on passion could hardly be sustained by correspondence alone. Thus the poet found himself in the position, as time went by, of not wishing especially to resume the relationship. But his essential uprightness gave him a heavy burden of guilt at his failure. Some critics believe that Wordsworth, in his own mind, transferred his cooling feelings for Annette to his waning enthusiasm for the Revolution and thus was able to function with less sense of private guilt.

Few poets have revealed themselves so publically as Wordsworth in the themes that run through their poems. Nature in itself and in its relationship to man dominated his verse from the beginning to the end of his career. His ambitious autobiographical poem, *The Prelude,* which runs to over one hundred double-columned pages, is almost a pantheistic hymn. And in "Tintern Abbey," "Michael," the "Ode on Intimations of Immortality," and scores of other, shorter poems, he describes and praises nature's benevolent influence. Like a child psychologist, almost, he discusses specifically the stages in one's appreciation of nature, from babyhood, through boyhood, to adolescence, young manhood, and maturity, analyzing the relationship of the individual to nature at each period: nature as pure sensation, as a dramatic background, as a moral force, as a religious sacrament, and as a philosophical consolation in old age.

Only during the exciting early days of the French Revolution did nature, as Wordsworth himself admitted, take second place to man in his affections and his mind. Then the poet's thoughts turned to heroes who had suffered for freedom, and he celebrated them in his poems. The vigor with which he espoused freedom and the new order and the events in France that were to make it possible rendered the disillusion, when it came, all the more shattering. Surely, the "Ode to Duty" is one of the saddest poems in the English language. In it, Wordsworth rationalizes his conduct in France, admits his failure of judgment, and embraces duty as henceforth his guardian. The poem announces his retirement (at the age of thirty-five) from active involvement in the new and untried:

> Me this unchartered freedom tires;
> I feel the weight of chance-desires:
> My hopes no more must change their name,
> I long for a repose that ever is the same.

In this decision lies the seed of his decline as a major poet.

In the technical sense, however, Wordsworth never declined.

Very early in his career, he grew surfeited with the artificial diction and fixed verse forms of such predecessors as Dryden and Pope. His "Preface" to the *Lyrical Ballads* states a Romantic preference, which never altered, for the simplicity and innocence of the countryside and its unsophisticated inhabitants over the more contrived, elaborate, and guileful life of the city. "A poet," said Wordsworth, "is a man talking to men," and he tried to approximate the simplicity of common speech in his verse. The "modest mansion" and "unmelodious moan" of eighteenth-century verse became the "cottage" and the "grunting of pigs" in Wordsworth's poetry. And the confining, often monotonous reiteration of heroic couplet after heroic couplet, sometimes for twenty thousand consecutive lines, gave way in his poetry to a variety of forms: the sonnet, the ode, the ballad [see *Handbook:* ode; ballad; ballad meter], and the distinctively free and adaptable blank-verse poem. To come to Wordsworth after reading Pope is to enter a wild woodland scene as one leaves the angular paths of a French formal garden.

Today, Wordsworth's place in English literary history seems assured. He is certainly the father of the Romantic Movement; yet his work as an innovator is firm, mature, the most distinguished example of its type. In his criticism, moreover, Wordsworth was able to define his role historically and artistically and to evaluate the contribution of Coleridge and himself to the new trend. That he failed to sustain the high poetic excellence of his early poetry is less important than that he did contribute a considerable body of imaginative literature.

More important even than his poetry to students of literary history is Wordsworth's role as the embodiment of the Romantic Movement. Though the glimmerings of a new way of life and thought are to be found as early as Thomas Gray and William Blake, the full force of the Romantic idea is felt in the poetry of Wordsworth's young manhood. It is interesting that the French Revolution, which questioned violently the eighteenth-century dogma that "Whatever is, is right," came when the poet was an impressionable nineteen years old. Questioning of the primacy of reason over human impulse, of tradition and civilization over unsophisticated emotion, was implicit in the Revolution and explicit in the works of the poet. The heart was to rule the head. Rigid discipline—in government, in gardening, in verse forms, in architecture—was to give way to a psychological discipline, perhaps, but one which took into account the unpredictable and volatile in the human personality and in his art. No longer was the emphasis in literature to be, if Wordsworth and his circle had their way, on the conformity of human beings in the society of the "here and the now." The world beyond, in time and space, became fit subject for literature. The supernatural vied for superiority with the natural in philosophy and art. Far away places (Arabia, the Orient) and distant times (the Middle Ages was a favorite period for Romantic writers) replaced interest in London society belles and court gossip. Wildly imaginative works were more in demand than restatements of "What oft was thought, but ne'er so well expressed." In short, Wordsworth, with his friend Coleridge, brought to fruition a revolution in English poetry as meaningful as the debacle in France.

BIBLIOGRAPHY

Coleridge, Samuel Taylor. *Biographia Literaria,* ed. John Shawcross. Oxford: Oxford University Press, 1907.

Meyer, George W. *Wordsworth's Formative Years.* Ann Arbor: University of Michigan Press, 1943.

Lines Composed a Few Miles Above Tintern Abbey, on Revisiting the Banks of the Wye During a Tour. July 13, 1798

Five years have past; five summers, with the length
Of five long winters! and again I hear
These waters, rolling from their mountain-springs
With a soft inland murmur.—Once again
Do I behold these steep and lofty cliffs,
That on a wild secluded scene impress
Thoughts of more deep seclusion; and connect
The landscape with the quiet of the sky.
The day is come when I again repose
Here, under this dark sycamore, and view 10
These plots of cottage-ground, these orchard-tufts,
Which at this season, with their unripe fruits,
Are clad in one green hue, and lose themselves
'Mid groves and copses. Once again I see
These hedge-rows, hardly hedge-rows, little lines
Of sportive wood run wild: these pastoral farms,
Green to the very door; and wreaths of smoke
Sent up, in silence, from among the trees!
With some uncertain notice, as might seem
Of vagrant dwellers in the houseless woods, 20
Or of some Hermit's cave, where by his fire
The Hermit sits alone.
These beauteous forms,
Through a long absence, have not been to me
As is a landscape to blind man's eye:
But oft, in lonely rooms, and 'mid the din
Of towns and cities, I have owed to them
In hours of weariness, sensations sweet,
Felt in the blood, and felt along the heart;
And passing even into my purer mind,
With tranquil restoration:—feelings too 30
Of unremembered pleasure: such, perhaps,

As have no slight or trivial influence
On that best portion of a good man's life,
His little, nameless, unremembered, acts
Of kindness and of love. Nor less, I trust,
To them I may have owed another gift,
Of aspect more sublime; that blessed mood,
In which the burthen of the mystery,
In which the heavy and the weary weight
Of all this unintelligible world, 40
Is lightened:—that serene and blessed mood,
In which the affections gently lead us on,—
Until, the breath of this corporeal frame
And even the motion of our human blood
Almost suspended, we are laid asleep
In body, and become a living soul:
While with an eye made quiet by the power
Of harmony, and the deep power of joy,
We see into the life of things.
If this
Be but a vain belief, yet, oh! how oft— 50
In darkness and amid the many shapes
Of joyless daylight; when the fretful stir
Unprofitable, and the fever of the world,
Have hung upon the beatings of my heart—
How oft, in spirit, have I turned to thee,
O sylvan Wye! thou wanderer thro' the woods,
How often has my spirit turned to thee!
And now, with gleams of half-extinguished thought,
With many recognitions dim and faint,
And somewhat of a sad perplexity, 60
The picture of the mind revives again:
While here I stand, not only with the sense
Of present pleasure, but with pleasing thoughts
That in this moment there is life and food
For future years. And so I dare to hope,
Though changed, no doubt, from what I was when first
I came among these hills; when like a roe
I bounded o'er the mountains, by the sides
Of the deep rivers, and the lonely streams,
Wherever nature led: more like a man 70
Flying from something that he dreads than one
Who sought the thing he loved. For nature then

(The coarser pleasures of my boyish days,
And their glad animal movements all gone by)
To me was all in all.—I cannot paint
What then I was. The sounding cataract
Haunted me like a passion: the tall rock,
The mountain, and the deep and gloomy wood,
Their colours and their forms, were then to me
An appetite; a feeling and a love, 80
That had no need of a remoter charm,
By thought supplied, nor any interest
Unborrowed from the eye.—That time is past,
And all its aching joys are now no more,
And all its dizzy raptures. Not for this
Faint I, nor mourn nor murmur; other gifts
Have followed; for such loss, I would believe,
Abundant recompense. For I have learned
To look on nature, not as in the hour
Of thoughtless youth; but hearing oftentimes 90
The still, sad music of humanity,
Nor harsh nor grating, though of ample power
To chasten and subdue. And I have felt
A presence that disturbs me with the joy
Of elevated thoughts; a sense sublime
Of something far more deeply interfused,
Whose dwelling is the light of setting suns,
And the round ocean and the living air,
And the blue sky, and in the mind of man;
A motion and a spirit, that impels 100
All thinking things, all objects of all thought,
And rolls through all things. Therefore am I still
A lover of the meadows and the woods,
And mountains; and of all that we behold
From this green earth; of all the mighty world
Of eye, and ear,—both what they half create,
And what perceive; well pleased to recognise
In nature and the language of the sense
The anchor of my purest thoughts, the nurse,
The guide, the guardian of my heart, and soul 110
Of all my moral being.

Nor perchance,
If I were not thus taught, should I the more
Suffer my genial spirits to decay:

For thou art with me here upon the banks
Of this fair river; thou my dearest Friend,
My dear, dear Friend; and in thy voice I catch
The language of my former heart, and read
My former pleasures in the shooting lights
Of thy wild eyes. Oh! yet a little while
May I behold in thee what I was once, 120
My dear, dear Sister! and this prayer I make,
Knowing that Nature never did betray
The heart that loved her; 'tis her privilege,
Through all the years of this our life, to lead
From joy to joy: for she can so inform
The mind that is within us, so impress
With quietness and beauty, and so feed
With lofty thoughts, that neither evil tongues,
Rash judgments, nor the sneers of selfish men,
Nor greetings where no kindness is, nor all 130
The dreary intercourse of daily life,
Shall e'er prevail against us, or disturb
Our cheerful faith, that all which we behold
Is full of blessings. Therefore let the moon
Shine on thee in thy solitary walk;
And let the misty mountain-winds be free
To blow against thee: and, in after years,
When these wild ecstasies shall be matured
Into a sober pleasure; when thy mind
Shall be a mansion for all lovely forms, 140
Thy memory be as a dwelling-place
For all sweet sounds and harmonies; oh! then,
If solitude, or fear, or pain, or grief,
Should be thy portion, with what healing thoughts
Of tender joy wilt thou remember me,
And these my exhortations! Nor, perchance—
If I should be where I no more can hear
Thy voice, nor catch from thy wild eyes these gleams
Of past existence—wilt thou then forget
That on the banks of this delightful stream 150
We stood together; and that I, so long
A worshipper of Nature, hither came
Unwearied in that service: rather say
With warmer love—oh! with far deeper zeal
Of holier love. Nor wilt thou then forget,

That after many wanderings, many years
Of absence, these steep woods and lofty cliffs,
And this green pastoral landscape, were to me
More dear, both for themselves and for thy sake!
[1798]

Commentary

In "Tintern Abbey," Wordsworth defines the relationship of nature to man at specific stages in the life of the human being. He wants to show his sister in the poem—and all readers through the poem—the abounding satisfactions of natural beauty at every period of existence. The result is an autobiographical document which states succinctly what Wordsworth said in profuse detail in *The Prelude* and in the great bulk of his canon: nature remains constant; man comes to it at different times for different gifts and is never disappointed.

Wordsworth's view of nature, at whatever period, is always the Romantic view; never does he present the orderly, "methodized" nature of Pope and the earlier century. There are cliffs in his landscape, "steep and lofty." The scene is "wild" and "secluded," and even the hedges are "little lines of sportive wood run wild."

The poem presents few difficulties that a careful reading cannot handle. The poet after an absence of five years, stands with his sister viewing the Wye River as it flows down the mountain. Lines 2–22 describe the scene, objectifying Wordsworth's idea of natural beauty. Line 22 begins his philosophical analysis of the influence of such beauty on the human psyche. Line 29—"felt in the blood" means "felt intuitively." In line 39, "burthen" means "burden" or "significance." In line 44, note that "corporeal frame" is a throwback to eighteenth-century diction and means simply "body." In line 54, "the fretful stir" found in cities is the bustle of business which Wordsworth condemns in "The world is too much with us. . . . Getting and spending we lay waste our powers." To the Romantics, God made the country and man made the town. Wordsworth preferred the creation of the Deity. The "presence" in line 96 refers ostensibly to a spiritual force immanent in nature. In line 103, "All thinking things, all objects of all thought" shows that Wordsworth feels that both animate and inanimate objects are governed by this presence in nature. "Suffer my genial spirits to decay," in line 116 may be paraphrased as "Allow my good mood to change." The "dearest Friend" of line 118 is his sister Dorothy. In lines 151–152 "these gleams / Of past existence" refer to the remnants of immortal knowledge which children bring into this world at birth and which they lose as they grow up. (See Wordsworth's "Ode on Intimations of Immortality.")

After the initial description of the scene which spreads out before the poet and his sister, Wordsworth proceeds to outline his relationship to nature, but he approaches it unchronologically. The proper order would be as follows:

lines 74–76—The sensual pleasure that a baby or young boy would derive from nature.

lines 67–85—The excitement of boyhood in the colors and forms of nature and in the physical contact with it.

lines 23–67
and 90–end—Man's love of nature for its ability to satisfy the aesthetic sense even when absent, through images of remembered loveliness; respect for nature as a moral force leading man to virtuous acts; veneration of nature in its spiritual aspect and for its ability to communicate to man intuitively the meaning of life; and, finally, appreciation of nature as a philosophic fountainhead and a guide to life in maturity.

Dramatically, it is effective that the poet speaks the lines to his sister, several years younger than he, and consequently at an earlier stage of development with respect to nature. Furthermore, though Wordsworth declares himself a pantheist in this poem, his reliance on a fellow human being reduces the cosmic sentiments to the personal level and makes them more meaningful in the context of a life. In a sense, Wordsworth is here combining his belief in the primacy of nature and his earlier revolutionary predilection for the supremacy of man in a practical pattern of human response to life.

In this poem, as elsewhere, the poet protests vigorously that time has not spoiled his world, that the sobering experiences in France, personal and political, have not broken him. His enthusiasm may be tempered and his boyish responses tamed, but a religious communion with nature and a philosophic attitude toward it are ample recompense. The protests here and in the "Intimations" are intellectually credible, but the reader may question whether Wordsworth had fully come to terms with his role as elderly philosopher—at the age of twenty-eight. Almost, some critics believe, he protests too much.

Strange Fits of Passion Have I Known

Strange fits of passion have I known:
And I will dare to tell,
But in the Lover's ear alone,
What once to me befell.

When she I loved looked every day
Fresh as a rose in June,
I to her cottage bent my way,
Beneath an evening-moon.

Upon the moon I fixed my eye,
All over the wide lea; 10
With quickening pace my horse drew nigh
Those paths so dear to me.

And now we reached the orchard-plot;
And, as we climbed the hill,
The sinking moon to Lucy's cot
Came near, and nearer still.

In one of those sweet dreams I slept,
Kind Nature's gentlest boon!
And all the while my eyes I kept
On the descending moon. 20

My horse moved on; hoof after hoof
He raised, and never stopped:
When down behind the cottage roof,
At once, the bright moon dropped.

What fond and wayward thoughts will slide
Into a Lover's head!
"O mercy!" to myself I cried,
"If Lucy should be dead!"

[*1799*]

London, 1802

Milton! thou should'st be living at this hour:
England hath need of thee: she is a fen
Of stagnant waters: altar, sword, and pen,
Fireside, the heroic wealth of hall and bower,
Have forfeited their ancient English dower
Of inward happiness. We are selfish men;
Oh! raise us up, return to us again;
And give us manners, virtue, freedom, power.
Thy soul was like a Star, and dwelt apart;
Thou hadst a voice whose sound was like the sea: 10
Pure as the naked heavens, majestic, free,
So didst thou travel on life's common way,
In cheerful godliness; and yet thy heart
The lowliest duties on herself did lay.

It Is a Beauteous Evening, Calm and Free

It is a beauteous evening, calm and free,
The holy time is quiet as a Nun
Breathless with adoration; the broad sun
Is sinking down in its tranquillity;
The gentleness of heaven broods o'er the Sea:
Listen! the mighty Being is awake,
And doth with his eternal motion make
A sound like thunder—everlastingly.
Dear Child! dear Girl! that walkest with me here,
If thou appear untouched by solemn thought, 10
Thy nature is not therefore less divine:
Thou liest in Abraham's bosom all the year;
And worshipp'st at the Temple's inner shrine,
God being with thee when we know it not.

[1802]

l. 9. *dear Girl:* the daughter of Wordsworth and Annette.
l. 12. *Abraham's bosom:* pure souls mount to this place before reaching Heaven.

Ode
Intimations of Immortality from Recollections of Early Childhood

I

There was a time when meadow, grove, and stream,
The earth, and every common sight,
To me did seem
Apparelled in celestial light,
The glory and the freshness of a dream.
It is not now as it hath been of yore;—
Turn wheresoe'er I may,
By night or day,
The things which I have seen I now can see no more.

II

The Rainbow comes and goes, 10
And lovely is the Rose,
The Moon doth with delight
Look round her when the heavens are bare;
Waters on a starry night
Are beautiful and fair;
The sunshine is a glorious birth;
But yet I know, where'er I go,
That there hath past away a glory from the earth.

III

Now, while the birds thus sing a joyous song,
And while the young lambs bound 20
As to the tabor's sound,
To me alone there came a thought of grief:
A timely utterance gave that thought relief,
And I again am strong:
The cataracts blow their trumpets from the steep;

In some editions, the poem is preceded by three lines from Wordsworth's "My Heart Leaps Up": The child is father of the man / And I could wish my days to be / Bound each to each by natural piety.

l. 21. *tabor*: a small drum.

No more shall grief of mine the season wrong;
I hear the Echoes through the mountains throng,
The Winds come to me from the fields of sleep,
And all the earth is gay;
Land and sea 30
Give themselves up to jollity,
And with the heart of May
Doth every Beast keep holiday;—
Thou Child of Joy,
Shout round me, let me hear thy shouts, thou happy Shep-
herd-boy!

IV

Ye blessèd Creatures, I have heard the call
Ye to each other make; I see
The heavens laugh with you in your jubilee;
My heart is at your festival,
My head hath its coronal, 40
The fulness of your bliss, I feel—I feel it all.
Oh evil day! if I were sullen
While Earth herself is adorning,
This sweet May-morning,
And the Children are culling
On every side,
In a thousand valleys far and wide,
Fresh flowers; while the sun shines warm,
And the Babe leaps up on his Mother's arm:—
I hear, I hear, with joy I hear! 50
—But there's a Tree, of many, one,
A single Field which I have looked upon,
Both of them speak of something that is gone:
The Pansy at my feet
Doth the same tale repeat:
Whither is fled the visionary gleam?
Where is it now, the glory and the dream?

V

Our birth is but a sleep and a forgetting:
The Soul that rises with us, our life's Star,
Hath had elsewhere its setting, 60
And cometh from afar:

Not in entire forgetfulness,
And not in utter nakedness,
But trailing clouds of glory do we come
From God, who is our home:
Heaven lies about us in our infancy!
Shades of the prison-house begin to close
Upon the growing Boy,
But He
Beholds the light, and whence it flows, 70
He sees it in his joy;
The Youth, who daily farther from the east
Must travel, still is Nature's Priest,
And by the vision splendid
Is on his way attended;
At length the Man perceives it die away,
And fade into the light of common day.

VI

Earth fills her lap with pleasures of her own;
Yearnings she hath in her own natural kind,
And, even with something of a Mother's mind, 80
And no unworthy aim,
The homely Nurse doth all she can
To make her Foster-child, her Inmate Man,
Forget the glories he hath known,
And that imperial palace whence he came.

VII

Behold the Child among his new-born blisses,
A six years' Darling of a pigmy size!
See, where 'mid work of his own hand he lies,
Frettied by sallies of his mothers' kisses,
With light upon him from his father's eyes! 90
See, at his feet, some little plan or chart,
Some fragment from his dream of human life,
Shaped by himself with newly-learned art;
A wedding or a festival,
A mourning or a funeral;
And this hath now his heart,
And unto this he frames his song:
Then will he fit his tongue

To dialogues of business, love, or strife;
 But it will not be long 100
 Ere this be thrown aside,
 And with new joy and pride
The little Actor cons another part;
Filling from time to time his "humourous stage"
With all the Persons, down to palsied Age,
That Life brings with her in her equipage;
 As if his whole vocation
 Were endless imitation.

VIII

Thou, whose exterior semblance doth belie
 Thy Soul's immensity; 110
Thou best Philosopher, who yet dost keep
Thy heritage, thou Eye among the blind,
That, deaf and silent, read'st the eternal deep,
Haunted for ever by the eternal mind,—
 Mighty Prophet! Seer blest!
 On whom those truths do rest,
Which we are toiling all our lives to find,
In darkness lost, the darkness of the grave;
Thou over whom thy Immortality
Broods like the Day, a Master o'er a Slave, 120
A Presence which is not to be put by;
Thou little Child, yet glorious in the might
Of heaven-born freedom on thy being's height,
Why with such earnest pains dost thou provoke
The years to bring the inevitable yoke,
Thus blindly with thy blessedness at strife?
Full soon thy Soul shall have her earthly freight,
And custom lie upon thee with a weight,
Heavy as frost, and deep almost as life!

IX

 O joy! that in our embers 130
 Is something that doth live,
 That nature yet remembers
 What was so fugitive!
The thought of our past years in me doth breed
Perpetual benediction: not indeed

For that which is most worthy to be blest;
Delight and liberty, the simple creed
Of Childhood, whether busy or at rest,
With new-fledged hope still fluttering in his breast:—
Not for these I raise 140
The song of thanks and praise;
But for those obstinate questionings
Of sense and outward things,
Fallings from us, vanishings;
Blank misgivings of a Creature
Moving about in worlds not realised,
High instincts before which our mortal Nature
Did tremble like a guilty thing surprised:
But for those first affections,
Those shadowy recollections, 150
Which, be they what they may,
Are yet the fountain light of all our day,
Are yet a master light of all our seeing;
Uphold us, cherish, and have power to make
Our noisy years seem moments in the being
Of the eternal Silence: truths that wake,
To perish never;
Which neither listlessness, nor mad endeavour,
Nor Man nor Boy,
Nor all that is at enmity with joy, 160
Can utterly abolish or destroy!
Hence in a season of calm weather
Though inland far we be,
Our Souls have sight of that immortal sea
Which brought us hither,
Can in a moment travel thither,
And see the Children sport upon the shore,
And hear the mighty waters rolling evermore.

X

Then sing, ye Birds, sing, sing a joyous song!
And let the young Lambs bound 170
As to the tabor's sound!
We in thought will join your throng,
Ye that pipe and ye that play,
Ye that through your hearts to-day

Feel the gladness of the May!
What though the radiance which was once so bright
Be now for ever taken from my sight,
Though nothing can bring back the hour
Of splendour in the grass, of glory in the flower;
We will grieve not, rather find 180
Strength in what remains behind;
In the primal sympathy
Which having been must ever be;
In the soothing thoughts that spring
Out of human suffering;
In the faith that looks through death,
In years that bring the philosophic mind.

XI

And O, ye Fountains, Meadows, Hills, and Groves,
Forebode not any severing of our loves!
Yet in my heart of hearts I feel your might; 190
I only have relinquished one delight
To live beneath your more habitual sway.
I love the Brooks which down your channels fret,
Even more than when I tripped lightly as they;
The innocent brightness of a new-born Day
Is lovely yet;
The Clouds that gather round the setting sun
Do take a sober colouring from an eye
That hath kept watch o'er man's mortality;
Another race hath been, and other palms are won. 200
Thanks to the human heart by which we live,
Thanks to its tenderness, its joys, and fears,
To me the meanest flower that blows can give
Thoughts that do often lie too deep for tears.

[*1802–4*]

The Old Cumberland Beggar

I saw an aged Beggar in my walk;
And he was seated, by the highway side,
On a low structure of rude masonry
Built at the foot of a huge hill, that they

Who lead their horses down the steep rough road
May thence remount at ease. The aged Man
Had placed his staff across the broad smooth stone
That overlays the pile; and, from a bag
All white with flour, the dole of village dames,
He drew his scraps and fragments, one by one; 10
And scanned them with a fixed and serious look
Of idle computation. In the sun,
Upon the second step of that small pile,
Surrounded by those wild unpeopled hills,
He sat, and ate his food in solitude:
And ever, scattered from his palsied hand,
That, still attempting to prevent the waste,
Was baffled still, the crumbs in little showers
Fell on the ground; and the small mountain birds,
Not venturing yet to peck their destined meal, 20
Approached within the length of half his staff.

Him from my childhood have I known; and then
He was so old, he seems not older now;
He travels on, a solitary Man,
So helpless in appearance, that for him
The sauntering Horseman throws not with a slack
And careless hand his alms upon the ground,
But stops,—that he may safely lodge the coin
Within the old Man's hat; nor quits him so,
But still, when he has given his horse the rein, 30
Watches the aged Beggar with a look
Sidelong, and half-reverted. She who tends
The toll-gate, when in summer at her door
She turns her wheel, if on the road she sees
The aged beggar coming, quits her work,
And lifts the latch for him that he may pass.
The post-boy, when his rattling wheels o'ertake
The aged Beggar in the woody lane,
Shouts to him from behind; and, if thus warned,
The old man does not change his course, the boy 40
Turns with less noisy wheels to the roadside,
And passes gently by, without a curse
Upon his lips, or anger at his heart.

He travels on, a solitary Man;
His age has no companion. On the ground

His eyes are turned, and, as he moves along,
They move along the ground; and, evermore,
Instead of common and habitual sight
Of fields with rural works, of hill and dale,
And the blue sky, one little span of earth 50
Is all his prospect. Thus, from day to day.
Bow-bent, his eyes for ever on the ground,
He plies his weary journey; seeing still,
And seldom knowing that he sees, some straw,
Some scattered leaf, or marks which, in one track,
The nails of cart or chariot-wheel have left
Impressed on the white road,—in the same line,
At distance still the same. Poor Traveller!
His staff trails with him; scarcely do his feet
Disturb the summer dust; he is so still 60
In look and motion, that the cottage curs,
Ere he has passed the door, will turn away,
Weary of barking at him. Boys and girls,
The vacant and the busy, maids and youths,
And urchins newly breeched—all pass him by:
Him even the slow-paced waggon leaves behind.
But deem not this Man useless—Statesmen! ye
Who are so restless in your wisdom, ye
Who have a broom still ready in your hands
To rid the world of nuisances; ye proud, 70
Heart-swoln, while in your pride ye contemplate
Your talents, power, or wisdom, deem him not
A burthen of the earth! 'Tis Nature's law
That none, the meanest of created things,
Of forms created the most vile and brute,
The dullest or most noxious, should exist
Divorced from good—a spirit and pulse of good,
A life and soul, to every mode of being
Inseparably linked. Then be assured
That least of all can aught—that ever owned 80
The heaven-regarding eye and front sublime
Which man is born to—sink, howe'er depressed,
So low as to be scorned without a sin;
Without offence to God cast out of view;
Like the dry remnant of a garden-flower
Whose seeds are shed, or as an implement

Worn out and worthless. While from door to door,
This old Man creeps, the villagers in him
Behold a record which together binds
Past deeds and offices of charity 90
Else unremembered, and so keeps alive
The kindly mood in hearts which lapse of years,
And that half-wisdom half-experience gives,
Make slow to feel, and by sure steps resign
To selfishness and cold oblivious cares.
Among the farms and solitary huts,
Hamlets and thinly-scattered villages,
Where'er the aged Beggar takes his rounds,
The mild necessity of use compels
To acts of love; and habit does the work 100
Of reason; yet prepares that after-joy
Which reason cherishes. And thus the soul,
By that sweet taste of pleasure unpursued,
Doth find herself insensibly disposed
To virtue and true goodness. Some there are
By their good works exalted, lofty minds
And meditative, authors of delight
And happiness, which to the end of time
Will live, and spread, and kindle: even such minds
In childhood, from this solitary Being, 110
Or from like wanderer, haply have received
(A thing more precious far than all that books
Or the solicitudes of love can do!)
That first mild touch of sympathy and thought,
In which they found their kindred with a world
Where want and sorrow were. The easy man
Who sits at his own door,—and, like the pear
That overhangs his head from the green wall,
Feeds in the sunshine; the robust and young,
The prosperous and unthinking, they who live 120
Sheltered, and flourish in a little grove
Of their own kindred;—all behold in him
A silent monitor, which on their minds
Must needs impress a transitory thought
Of self-congratulation, to the heart
Of each recalling his peculiar boons,
His charters and exemptions; and, perchance,

Though he to no one give the fortitude
And circumspection needful to preserve
His present blessings, and to husband up 130
The respite of the season, he, at least,
And 't is no vulgar service, makes them felt.
Yet further.—Many, I believe, there are
Who live a life of virtuous decency,
Men who can hear the Decalogue and feel
No self-reproach; who of the moral law
Established in the land where they abide
Are strict observers; and not negligent
In acts of love to those with whom they dwell,
Their kindred, and the children of their blood. 140
Praise be to such, and to their slumbers peace!
—But of the poor man, ask the abject poor;
Go, and demand of him, if there be here
In this cold abstinence from evil deeds,
And these inevitable charities,
Wherewith to satisfy the human soul?
No—man is dear to man; the poorest poor
Long for some moments in a weary life
When they can know and feel that they have been,
Themselves, the fathers and the dealers-out 150
Of some small blessings; have been kind to such
As needed kindness, for this single cause,
That we have all of us one human heart.
—Such pleasure is to one kind Being known,
My neighbour, when with punctual care, each week
Duly as Friday comes, though pressed herself
By her own wants, she from her store of meal
Takes one unsparing handful for the scrip
Of this old Mendicant, and, from her door
Returning with exhilarated heart, 160
Sits by her fire, and builds her hope in heaven.
Then let him pass, a blessing on his head!
And while in that vast solitude to which
The tide of things has borne him, he appears
To breathe and live but for himself alone,
Unblamed, uninjured, let him bear about

l. 158. *scrip:* bag.

The good which the benignant law of Heaven
Has hung around him: and, while life is his,
Still let him prompt the unlettered villagers
To tender offices and pensive thoughts. 170
—Then let him pass, a blessing on his head!
And, long as he can wander, let him breathe
The freshness of the valleys; let his blood
Struggle with frosty air and winter snows;
And let the chartered wind that sweeps the heath
Beat his grey locks against his withered face.
Reverence the hope whose vital anxiousness
Gives the last human interest to his heart.
May never *House,* misnamed of *Industry,*
Make him a captive!—for that pent-up din, 180
Those life-consuming sounds that clog the air,
Be his the natural silence of old age!
Let him be free of mountain solitudes;
And have around him, whether heard or not,
The pleasant melody of woodland birds.
Few are his pleasures: if his eyes have now
Been doomed so long to settle upon earth
That not without some effort they behold
The countenance of the horizontal sun,
Rising or setting, let the light at least 190
Find a free entrance to their languid orbs.
And let him, *where* and *when* he will, sit down
Beneath the trees, or on a grassy bank
Of highway side, and with the little birds
Share his chance-gathered meal; and, finally,
As in the eye of Nature he has lived,
So in the eye of Nature let him die!

[1797]

l. 179. *House:* poorhouse.

Expostulation and Reply

"Why, William, on that old grey stone,
Thus for the length of half a day,

Why, William, sit you thus alone,
And dream your time away?

"Where are your books?—that light bequeathed
To Beings else forlorn and blind!
Up! up! and drink the spirit breathed
From dead men to their kind.

"You look round on your Mother Earth,
As if she for no purpose bore you; 10
As if you were her first-born birth,
And none had lived before you!"

One morning thus, by Esthwaite lake,
When life was sweet, I knew not why,
To me my good friend Matthew spake,
And thus I made reply:

"The eye—it cannot choose but see;
We cannot bid the ear be still;
Our bodies feel, where'er they be,
Against or with our will. 20

"Nor less I deem that there are Powers
Which of themselves our minds impress;
That we can feed this mind of ours
In a wise passiveness.

"Think you, 'mid all this mighty sum
Of things for ever speaking,
That nothing of itself will come,
But we must still be seeking?

"—Then ask not wherefore, here, alone,
Conversing as I may, 30
I sit upon this old grey stone,
And dream my time away."

[1798]

l. 15. *Matthew*: William Taylor, a schoolmaster of the poet.

Resolution and Independence

I

There was a roaring in the wind all night;
The rain came heavily and fell in floods;
But now the sun is rising calm and bright;
The birds are singing in the distant woods;
Over his own sweet voice the Stock-dove broods;
The Jay makes answer as the Magpie chatters;
And all the air is filled with pleasant noise of waters.

II

All things that love the sun are out of doors;
The sky rejoices in the morning's birth;
The grass is bright with rain-drops;—on the moors 10
The hare is running races in her mirth;
And with her feet she from the plashy earth
Raises a mist; that, glittering in the sun,
Runs with her all the way, wherever she doth run.

III

I was a Traveller then upon the moor;
I saw the hare that raced about with joy;
I heard the woods and distant waters roar;
Or heard them not, as happy as a boy:
The pleasant season did my heart employ:
My old remembrances went from me wholly; 20
And all the ways of men, so vain and melancholy.

IV

But, as it sometimes chanceth, from the might
Of joy in minds that can no further go,
As high as we have mounted in delight
In our dejection do we sink as low;
To me that morning did it happen so;
And fears and fancies thick upon me came;
Dim sadness—and blind thoughts, I knew not, nor could
name.

V

I heard the sky-lark warbling in the sky;
And I bethought me of the playful hare: 30
Even such a happy Child of earth am I;
Even as these blissful creatures do I fare;
Far from the world I walk, and from all care;
But there may come another day to me—
Solitude, pain of heart, distress, and poverty.

VI

My whole life I have lived in pleasant thought,
As if life's business were a summer mood;
As if all needful things would come unsought
To genial faith, still rich in genial good;
But how can He expect that others should 40
Build for him, sow for him, and at his call
Love him, who for himself will take no heed at all?

VII

I thought of Chatterton, the marvellous Boy,
The sleepless Soul that perished in his pride;
Of Him who walked in glory and in joy
Following his plough, along the mountainside:
By our own spirits are we deified:
We Poets in our youth begin in gladness;
But thereof come in the end despondency and madness.

VIII

Now, whether it were by peculiar grace, 50
A leading from above, a something given,
Yet it befell that, in this lonely place,
When I with these untoward thoughts had striven,
Beside a pool bare to the eye of heaven
I saw a Man before me unawares:
The oldest man he seemed that ever wore grey hairs.

IX

As a huge stone is sometimes seen to lie
Couched on the bald top of an eminence;

l. 43. *Chatterton:* Thomas Chatteron, a talented young English poet who killed himself at the age of seventeen.

Wonder to all who do the same espy,
By what means it could thither come, and whence; 60
So that it seems a thing endued with sense:
Like a sea-beast crawled forth, that on a shelf
Of rock or sand reposeth, there to sun itself;

X

Such seemed this Man, not all alive nor dead,
Nor all asleep—in his extreme old age:
His body was bent double, feet and head
Coming together in life's pilgrimage;
As if some dire constraint of pain, or rage
Of sickness felt by him in times long past,
A more than human weight upon his frame had cast. 70

XI

Himself he propped, limbs, body, and pale face,
Upon a long grey staff of shaven wood:
And, still as I drew near with gentle pace,
Upon the margin of that moorish flood
Motionless as a cloud the old Man stood,
That heareth not the loud winds when they call;
And moveth all together, if it move at all.

XII

At length, himself unsettling, he the pond
Stirred with his staff, and fixedly did look
Upon the muddy water, which he conned, 80
As if he had been reading in a book:
And now a stranger's privilege I took;
And, drawing to his side, to him did say,
"This morning gives us promise of a glorious day."

XIII

A gentle answer did the old Man make,
In courteous speech which forth he slowly drew:
And him with further words I thus bespake,
"What occupation do you there pursue?
This is a lonesome place for one like you."
Ere he replied, a flash of mild surprise 90
Broke from the sable orbs of his yet-vivid eyes,

XIV

His words came feebly, from a feeble chest,
But each in solemn order followed each,
With something of a lofty utterance drest—
Choice word and measured phrase, above the reach
Of ordinary men; a stately speech;
Such as grave Livers do in Scotland use,
Religious men, who give to God and man their dues.

XV

He told, that to these waters he had come
To gather leeches, being old and poor: 100
Employment hazardous and wearisome!
And he had many hardships to endure:
From pond to pond he roamed, from moor to moor;
Housing, with God's good help, by choice or chance;
And in this way he gained an honest maintenance.

XVI

The old Man still stood talking by my side;
But now his voice to me was like a stream
Scarce heard; nor word from word could I divide;
And the whole body of the Man did seem
Like one whom I had met with in a dream; 110
Or like a man from some far region sent,
To give me human strength, by apt admonishment.

XVII

My former thoughts returned: the fear that kills;
And hope that is unwilling to be fed;
Cold, pain, and labour, and all fleshly ills;
And mighty Poets in their misery dead.
—Perplexed, and longing to be comforted,
My question eagerly did I renew,
"How is it that you live, and what is it you do?"

XVIII

He with a smile did then his words repeat; 120
And said that, gathering leeches, far and wide
He travelled; stirring thus above his feet

The waters of the pools where they abide.
"Once I could meet with them on every side;
But they have dwindled long by slow decay;
Yet still I persevere, and find them where I may."

XIX

While he was talking thus, the lonely place,
The old Man's shape, and speech—all troubled me:
In my mind's eye I seemed to see him pace
About the weary moors continually, 130
Wandering about alone and silently.
While I these thoughts within myself pursued,
He, having made a pause, the same discourse renewed.

XX

And soon with this he other matter blended,
Cheerfully uttered, with demeanour kind,
But stately in the main; and when he ended,
I could have laughed myself to scorn to find
In that decrepit Man so firm a mind.
"God," said I, "be my help and stay secure;
I'll think of the Leech-gatherer on the lonely moor!" 140

[*1802*]

Nuns Fret Not at Their Convent's Narrow Room

Nuns fret not at their convent's narrow room;
And hermits are contented with their cells;
And students with their pensive citadels;
Maids at the wheel, the weaver at his loom,
Sit blithe and happy; bees that soar for bloom,
High as the highest Peak of Furness-fells,
Will murmur by the hour in foxglove bells:
In truth the prison, into which we doom
Ourselves, no prison is: and hence for me,
In sundry moods, 'twas pastime to be bound 10
Within the Sonnet's scanty plot of ground;
Pleased if some Souls (for such there needs must be)

Who have felt the weight of too much liberty,
Should find brief solace there, as I have found.

[1804]

Composed upon Westminster Bridge

SEPTEMBER 3, 1802

Earth has not anything to show more fair:
Dull would he be of soul who could pass by
A sight so touching in its majesty:
This City now doth, like a garment, wear
The beauty of the morning; silent, bare,
Ships, towers, domes, theaters, and temples lie
Open unto the fields, and to the sky;
All bright and glittering in the smokeless air.
Never did sun more beautifully steep
In his first splendour, valley, rock, or hill; 10
Ne'er saw I, never felt, a calm so deep!
The river glideth at his own sweet will:
Dear God! the very houses seem asleep;
And all that mighty heart is lying still!

Ode to Duty

Stern Daughter of the Voice of God!
O Duty! if that name thou love
Who art a light to guide, a rod
To check the erring, and reprove;
Thou, who art victory and law
When empty terrors overawe;
From vain temptations dost set free;
And calm'st the weary strife of frail humanity!

There are who ask not if thine eye
Be on them; who, in love and truth, 10
Where no misgiving is, rely
Upon the genial sense of youth;
Glad Hearts! without reproach or blot;

Who do thy work, and know it not:
Oh! if through confidence misplaced
They fail, thy saving arms, dread Power! around them cast.

Serene will be our days and bright,
And happy will our nature be,
When love is an unerring light,
And joy its own security. 20
And they a blissful course may hold
Even now, who, not unwisely bold,
Live in the spirit of this creed;
Yet seek thy firm support, according to their need.

I, loving freedom, and untried;
No sport of every random gust,
Yet being to myself a guide,
Too blindly have reposed my trust:
And oft, when in my heart was heard
Thy timely mandate, I deferred 30
The task, in smoother walks to stray;
But thee I now would serve more strictly, if I may.

Through no disturbance of my soul,
Or strong compunction in me wrought,
I supplicate for thy control;
But in the quietness of thought:
Me this unchartered freedom tires;
I feel the weight of chance-desires:
My hopes no more must change their name,
I long for a repose that ever is the same. 40

Stern Lawgiver! yet thou dost wear
The Godhead's most benignant grace;
Nor know we anything so fair
As is the smile upon thy face:
Flowers laugh before thee on their beds
And fragrance in thy footing treads;
Thou dost preserve the stars from wrong;

l. 37. *freedom tires:* Wordsworth shows his disillusionment with the direction the French Revolution has taken.

And the most ancient heavens, through Thee, are fresh and
strong.

To humbler functions, awful Power!
I call thee: I myself commend 50
Unto thy guidance from this hour;
Oh, let my weakness have an end!
Give unto me, made lowly wise,
The spirit of self-sacrifice;
The confidence of reason give;
And in the light of truth thy Bondman let me live!

[1804]

The World Is Too Much with Us; Late and Soon

The world is too much with us; late and soon,
Getting and spending, we lay waste our powers:
Little we see in Nature that is ours;
We have given our hearts away, a sordid boon!
This Sea that bares her bosom to the moon;
The winds that will be howling at all hours,
And are up-gathered now like sleeping flowers;
For this, for everything, we are out of tune;
It moves us not.—Great God! I'd rather be
A Pagan suckled in a creed outworn; 10
So might I, standing on this pleasant lea,
Have glimpses that would make me less forlorn;
Have sight of Proteus rising from the sea;
Or hear old Triton blow his wreathèd horn.

[1804]

John Keats

John Keats was born in 1795, the eldest son of a livery stable proprietor and his wife, Frances. His father died (by a fall from a horse) when the poet was nine years old; his mother, after an unfortunate second marriage, died of tuberculosis in 1810. At this point Keats' spirited and athletic childhood ended when his guardian apprenticed him for five years to a surgeon who practiced medicine at Edmonton. It is clear that the young man accepted the indenture solely as a practical means of earning a livelihood, for he showed much greater interest in literary pursuits, especially in ancient mythology, than in the details of his profession. At eighteen he read Edmund Spenser and, in his own words, "forgot all surgery." A disagreement with his master in 1814 led to the premature ending of his apprenticeship. In that year, he went to London to continue his studies at Guy's and St. Thomas' hospitals. Successful in his examinations, he was apathetic in hospital work and spent all his spare time writing poetry.

By 1816, the circle of his friends was almost exclusively a literary one, including John Hamilton Reynolds, Charles Dilke, Charles Brown, and others. In that year he met Leigh Hunt, the liberal writer whose release from prison in 1815 had been the occasion of a sonnet by Keats. The friendship was immediate and significant and was to provoke the enmity of the conservatives toward the younger man. These associations confirmed in Keats his determination to be a poet and led to the publication of his first volume of poems in 1817. Living with his brothers in a house in Hampstead, Keats finished "Endymion" and wrote articles on the theater.

The next year was a fateful one in the poet's life. His brother died of consumption, giving Keats a preview of what was in store for him. In the summer of that year, Keats went on a walking tour of the English lakes and Scotland which seriously undermined his health. To make matters worse, he returned to England on doctor's orders in time to read the vicious reviews of "Endymion" in the conservative London quarterlies, *Blackwood's Magazine* and the *Quarterly*. Finally, and most important, he met Fanny Brawne and was fascinated by the pretty, sixteen-year-old flirt.

Keats' attraction to Fanny inspired much of his best poetry. Shortly after their meeting, he wrote "The Eve of St. Agnes" and "The Eve of St. Mark." The pair became engaged. Keats, to show that he could earn a living, returned to London to seek work in journalism, but his love for Fanny and his failing health soon brought him back home.

By the beginning of 1820, Keats knew that he was doomed. His lungs were subject to hemorrhage. He was too weak to remain alone. A letter from Shelley invited him to spend the winter in Italy, but Keats declined. It was decided, however, that he would go abroad with his friend, Joseph Severn. They landed in Naples and then went to Rome where they took lodgings adjoining the Spanish Stairs. Here the twenty-five-year-old poet died after a long and painful illness on February 23, 1821. He is buried in the Protestant Cemetery in Rome beneath a tombstone which bears his own epitaph: "Here lies one whose name was writ in water."

The principal influences on Keats' career were his love for Fanny Brawne and his knowledge that consumption would cut short his life. These two factors worked together upon him to intensify his horror and dismay. Keats had always shied away from involvements with women, owing to an inferiority complex which made him sure that they would scorn him for his lack of manly stature—especially for his shortness. To find, therefore, that Fanny, the one woman he had ever seriously desired, wanted him too, filled him with incredulous joy. Yet by close contact with her in love and marriage he risked infecting her with his disease. Even worse, marriage was out of the question unless Keats were able to support a wife; yet the progress of his malady made employment impossible.

The frustration occasioned by this state of affairs became one of the cornerstones of Keats' poetry. Keats could see clearly the beauty of the ideal relationship with Fanny, and in such poems as "The Eve of St. Agnes" he indulged in wish fulfillment as he allows Porphyro to overcome all obstacles to win the love of his lady. In more sober moments, Keats knew that such an outcome was not for him. The "Ode on a Grecian Urn" seeks to halt the process of aging and decay —to arrest love at its most vibrant moment. And in the "Ode to a Nightingale," after resorting to one escape after another (drugs, wine, poetry), the poet seeks the consolation of death and the immortality of the singer when joys of this world fail.

Beauty and pain seem always joined in Keats' work as they were in his life. At every point of his mature life, the pattern held. The joy of creating poetry was chilled by the necessity to work at an unromantic and unrewarding hospital job. The thrill of publication was marred by the harsh invective of the reviewers arrayed against him. The ecstasy of finding Fanny ran parallel to the discovery of his sickness. That Keats was aware of the relationship between pain of imminent death and a quickened sense of physical beauties is evident in his poems as it is in letters like this:

> When I have been, or supposed myself in health, I have had my share of . . . [haunting and deformed thoughts and feelings], especially within the last year [1819–20]. I may say that for six months before I was taken ill I had not passed a tranquil day. Either that gloom overspread me, or I was suffering under some passionate feeling, or if I turned to versify, that acerbated the poison of either sensation. The beauties of Nature had lost their power over me. How astonishingly (here I must premise that illness, as far as I can judge in so short a time, has relieved my mind of a load of deceptive thoughts and images, and makes me perceive things in a truer light)—how astonishingly does the chance of leaving the world impress a sense of its natural beauties upon us! Like poor Falstaff, though I do not "babble," I think of green fields; I muse with the greatest affection on every flower I have known from my infancy—their shapes and colours are as new to me as if I had just created them with a superhuman fancy. . . .

This heightened sensitivity to things in nature resulted in poetry of unparalleled sensuousness. Keats saw in the world what other poets had seen, but he described it with greater vividness and intensity—as though each impingement upon his senses might be his last. In "The Eve of St. Agnes," the heroine must wear "warmed jewels"; her "boddice" must be "fragrant"; and she must drift into "the poppied warmth of sleep." In this "azure-lidded sleep / In blanched linen, smooth and lavender'd," she must remain till wakened by Porphyro's feast

> Of candied apple, quince, and plum and gourd;
> With jellies soother than the creamy curd,
> And lucent syrops, tinct with cinnamon;
> Manna and dates, in argosy transferr'd
> From Fez; and spiced dainties, every one,
> From silken Samarcand to cedar'd Lebanon.

Nor does this passage represent an extreme example of Keats' subject matter, tone, and technique. Rather, it seems typical.

Keats was a published poet for only about four years of his life: his first volume was issued in 1817 and he died at the beginning of 1821. It is therefore unfair, perhaps, to speak of his literary reputation in his own time. Yet so virulent were the attacks on his poetry and his person in the conservative journals that both Byron and Shelley blamed the bitingly unfavorable reviews for his early death. Like Tennyson, Keats had to contend not only with legitimate criticism of his poetry but with politically inspired enmity that would have found an outlet regardless of the quality of his work. He had to contend with guilt by association, paying the penalty in reputation for consorting with "dangerous" liberals like Leigh Hunt. Shortly after his death, many who had been his friends responded with belligerent over-praise, seeking too early to rank him with the immortals. Now a more objective century has established Keats as one of the great lyricists of the English language.

With Byron and Shelley, Keats was a second-generation Romantic poet, following in the path blazed by Wordsworth and Coleridge. For him there was no need of manifestoes, for the Romantic Movement was thoroughly entrenched and its doctrines were part of English cultural life. His Romanticism is, therefore, much more taken for granted than that of his predecessors. Like that of the other Romantics, Keats' poetry emphasizes the emotions; in fact, most of Keats' poems deal with love as a realized or an about-to-be-realized experience. Logic plays little part in the poetry, most of which take place in a dream state, in reverie, or in fantasy. The supernatural dominates such poems as "La Belle Dame Sans Merci" and "The Eve of St. Agnes," and both poems have a medieval setting. Nature is as important to Keats as it is to Wordsworth, though in a different way.

In one sense, Keats never outgrew the boyish reaction to nature as a realm of sensuous delight, which the famous Odes present. Nature as a presence never became for the later poet the spiritual guide and solace it had been for the earlier one. In a sense, however, Keats' use of Romantic nature is more sophisticated than Wordsworth's, for he is able to objectify his own situation by embodying it in specific natural symbols [see *Handbook:* symbol], the most famous being the nightingale. "Thou was not born for death, Immortal Bird," becomes the pitiful cry of awareness of his own fate as contrasted to that of nature's woodland singer. The shift from Wordsworth to Keats is a subtle one, but very important: the new Romantics no longer stand in awe of nature as an abstraction; rather, they identify with specific manifestations of nature to bring nature and man together in intimate rapport.

BIBLIOGRAPHY

Bowra, C. M. *The Romantic Imagination.* Cambridge, Mass.: Harvard University Press, 1949.

Murry, John Middleton. *Keats.* New York: Noonday Press, 1955.

Rollins, Hyder, ed. *The Letters of John Keats, 1814–1821.* Cambridge, Mass.: Harvard University Press, 1958.

Ode on Melancholy

I

No, no, go not to Lethe, neither twist 2 ems
Wolf's-bane, tight-rooted, for its poisonous wine;
Nor suffer thy pale forehead to be kiss'd
By nightshade, ruby grape of Proserpine;
Make not your rosary of yew-berries,
Nor let the beetle nor the death-moth be
Your mournful Psyche, nor the downy owl
A partner in your sorrow's mysteries;
For shade to shade will come too drowsily,
And drown the wakeful anguish of the soul. 10

II

But when the melancholy fit shall fall
Sudden from heaven like a weeping cloud,
That fosters the droop-headed flowers all,
And hides the green hill in an April shroud;
Then glut thy sorrow on a morning rose,
Or on the rainbow of the salt sand-wave,
Or on the wealth of globed peonies;
Or if thy mistress some rich anger shows,
Emprison her soft hand, and let her rave,
And feed deep, deep upon her peerless eyes. 20

III

She dwells with Beauty—Beauty that must die;
And Joy, whose hand is ever at his lips
Bidding adieu; and aching Pleasure nigh,
Turning to Poison while the bee-mouth sips:
Ay, in the very temple of Delight
Veil'd Melancholy has her sovran shrine,
Though seen of none save him whose strenuous tongue
Can burst Joy's grape against his palate fine:
His soul shall taste the sadness of her might,
And be among her cloudy trophies hung. 30

[1819]

Commentary

The poem explains Keats' belief that pain and melancholy are inextricably bound up with joy and beauty. The poet exhorts the reader to avoid the approach of numbed senses that imminent death brings because such a blurred state of consciousness prevents the keen apprehension of the coexistence of joy and melancholy. When the melancholy condition does prevail, however, Keats counsels submerging one's sadness in the perception of beauty, whether in flowers or in a lovely woman. Melancholy, he concludes, goes hand in hand with beauty and joy, though only one who can enjoy pleasure fully can see its intimate connection with melancholy. Such a person—the poet, very likely—will be a victim to her strength.

The paradox that, at the very moment of supreme culmination (whether of joy, passion, beauty, pleasure), melancholy stands ready to attack became a cornerstone of Keats' philosophy. The place of this theme in the poet's life has been explored in the introduction. Keats found it necessary to salvage something from the certainty of a life of perpetual illness and frustration, and his belief that the experiences of beauty and joy were necessarily allied with the condition of melancholy must have made his own wretched state easier to endure.

The first stanza of the poem is difficult. Lethe, in line 1, is one of the rivers of the Underworld, whose waters induced forgetfulness. Wolf's-bane, in the next line, is a poisonous yellow-blossomed plant. In line 4, nightshade is another poisonous plant, source of the drug belladonna. Proserpine, in the same line, is the wife of the ruler of the Underworld, Pluto. The "beetle" and the "death-moth" in line 6 are symbols of death as contrasted with "Psyche" in line 7, which stands for the soul and is traditionally represented as a butterfly. Keats is here warning the reader not to take symbols of death as the mark of the soul. The final two lines of the stanza give warning that the shadows of death and sadness creep up to numb the victim and prevent his sharp awareness of his true condition.

Stanza two assumes the onset of melancholy and the approach of death, suggesting an antidote, or at least a palliative for the event. The images are funereal: the cloud of line 12 is "weeping"; the flowers are "droop-headed"; and there is a symbolic "April shroud." "Glut," in line 15, means "feed" or "nourish."

The final stanza begins on a deliberately ambiguous note, for the "She" of line 21 ought refer to melancholy personified, but grammatically it refers to "mistress" in the preceding sentence. Since both the mistress and Melancholy dwell with beauty, and since to Keats both the woman and the melancholy state from which he suffered were often fused in his mind, the ambiguity seems planned. Notice that Pleasure is described as "aching" in Keats' usual effort to blend pain and joy. The "bee-mouth" in line 24 keeps us the insect imagery resorted to in "beetle . . . death-moth" earlier, and reinforces Psyche as butterfly. "Sovran" in line 26 is an obsolete spelling of "sovereign." To "burst Joy's grape" in line 28 is to taste sensuous pleasure to the full. And in the last line, the trophies of Melancholy are "cloudy" because She has her abode in Heaven, but also because these trophies are obscure, hidden from normal view.

Keats deals cleverly with his theme. Rather than putting the stress on his own situation and perhaps sinking into sentimentality and pathos, the poet addresses his exhortation to a fellow mortal, telling him what to expect from the onset of melancholy. This allows for the detachment the theme needs and yet permits the narrator to be interested in his disinterestedness.

The first stanza advises fierce opposition to death and melancholy, which are treated as one and the same. The biographical background is obviously relevant here, for this poem was published in 1820, when Keats knew the seriousness of his illness but was still strong enough to fight it. In the next stanza, indeed, the melancholy "fit" may be melancholy or may be death itself. If it is melancholy, it is presented, as has been pointed out, in funeral dress through the use of imagery of shrouds, weeping, and drooping.

Characteristically, Keats' answer to the onset of melancholy and death is immersion in sensuous beauty, in nature or woman. But Keats could not entirely convince even himself that momentary diversion in beauty and joy negates the horror of melancholy death. In a letter to George Keats in 1819, he had written: "While we are laughing, the seed of some trouble is put into the wide arable land of events—While we are laughing, it sprouts, it grows, and suddenly bears a poison fruit which we must pluck." He knew, as one whose "strenuous tongue / Can burst Joy's grape against his palate fine," that death and melancholy would be victorious. Yet the presence of the poem itself, the "Ode on Melancholy," is articulate testimony that the beauty which the melancholy approach of death aroused in him does in a sense take the measure of death and assert Keats' victory.

The poem shows that Keats is an accomplished poet, an excellent lyricist, and yet a youthful and inexperienced writer. The choice of the ode shows a willingness to look back to the Neoclassical period, though Wordsworth and Coleridge had certainly done so too. Keats' poem is replete with ancient mythological references, and rather trite ones at that: Lethe, Proserpine, Psyche. Personifications [see *Handbook:* personification] abound: Melancholy, Beauty, Joy. Even the outmoded poetic diction of Pope and Dryden crops up in "sovran shrine" and "April shroud." Keats' taste for poetic inversion, as in "palate fine" also seems a throwback to the past. What rescues the short poem from inundation by the language is the patent sincerity and intensity of the wholly poetic idea. Though the narrator pretends to teach, this is no didactic poem in the eighteenth-century manner. Keats' poetic personality and his involvement in the poem keep it distinctly fresh and romantically his own.

The Eve of St. Agnes

I

St. Agnes' Eve—Ah, bitter chill it was!
The owl, for all his feathers, was a-cold;
The hare limp'd trembling through the frozen grass,
And silent was the flock in woolly fold:
Numb were the Beadsman's fingers, while he told
His rosary, and while his frosted breath,
Like pious incense from a censer old,
Seem'd taking flight for heaven, without a death,
Past the sweet Virgin's picture, while his prayer he saith.

II

His prayer he saith, this patient, holy man; 10
Then takes his lamp, and riseth from his knees,
And back returneth, meagre, barefoot, wan,
Along the chapel aisle by slow degrees:
The sculptur'd dead, on each side, seem to freeze,
Emprison'd in black, purgatorial rails:
Knights, ladies, praying in dumb orat'ries,
He passeth by; and his weak spirit fails
To think how they may ache in icy hoods and mails.

III

Northward he turneth through a little door,
And scarce three steps, ere Music's golden tongue 20
Flatter'd to tears this aged man and poor;
But no—already had his deathbell rung:
The joys of all his life were said and sung:
His was harsh penance on St. Agnes' Eve:
Another way he went, and soon among
Rough ashes sat he for his soul's reprieve,
And all night kept awake, for sinners' sake to grieve.

l. 5. *Beadsman:* a man who says prayers for the souls of those to whom he is indebted.

IV

That ancient Beadsman heard the prelude soft;
And so it chanc'd, for many a door was wide,
From hurry to and fro. Soon, up aloft, 30
The silver, snarling trumpets 'gan to chide:
The level chambers, ready with their pride,
Were glowing to receive a thousand guests:
The carved angels, ever eager-eyed,
Star'd, where upon their heads the cornice rests,
With hair blown back, and wings put cross-wise on their breasts.

V

At length burst in the argent revelry,
With plume, tiara, and all rich array,
Numerous as shadows haunting faerily
The brain, new-stuff'd, in youth, with triumphs gay 40
Of old romance. These let us wish away,
And turn, sole-thoughted, to one Lady there,
Whose heart had brooded, all that wintry day,
On love, and wing'd St. Agnes' saintly care,
As she had heard old dames full many times declare.

VI

They told her how, upon St. Agnes' Eve,
Young virgins might have visions of delight,
And soft adorings from their loves receive
Upon the honey'd middle of the night,
If ceremonies due they did aright; 50
As, supperless to bed they must retire,
And couch supine their beauties, lily white;
Nor look behind, nor sideways, but require
Of Heaven with upward eyes for all that they desire.

VII

Full of this whim was thoughtful Madeline:
The music, yearning like a God in pain,
She scarcely heard: her maiden eyes divine,
Fix'd on the floor, saw many a sweeping train
Pass by—she heeded not at all: in vain
Came many a tiptoe, amorous cavalier, 60

And back retir'd; not cool'd by high disdain,
But she saw not: her heart was otherwhere:
She sigh'd for Agnes' dreams, the sweetest of the year.

VIII

She danc'd along with vague, regardless eyes,
Anxious her lips, her breathing quick and short:
The hallow'd hour was near at hand: she sighs
Amid the timbrels, and the throng'd resort
Of whisperers in anger, or in sport;
'Mid looks of love, defiance, hate, and scorn,
Hoodwink'd with faery fancy; all amort, 70
Save to St. Agnes and her lambs unshorn,
And all the bliss to be before to-morrow morn.

IX

So, purposing each moment to retire,
She linger'd still. Meantime, across the moors,
Had come young Porphyro, with heart on fire
For Madeline. Beside the portal doors,
Buttress'd from moonlight, stands he, and implores
All saints to give him sight of Madeline,
But for one moment in the tedious hours,
That he might gaze and worship all unseen; 80
Perchance speak, kneel, touch, kiss—in sooth such things have been.

X

He ventures in: let no buzz'd whisper tell:
All eyes be muffled, or a hundred swords
Will storm his heart, Love's fev'rous citadel:
For him, those chambers held barbarian hordes,
Hyena foemen, and hot-blooded lords,
Whose very dogs would execrations howl
Against his lineage: not one breast affords
Him any mercy, in that mansion foul,
Save one old beldame, weak in body and in soul. 90

l. 70. *amort:* unheeding or dead.
l. 71. *lambs unshorn:* two lambs were traditionally shorn during mass on St. Agnes' Day, January 22; the wool was then spun and woven by nuns (see stanza XIII).
l. 90. *beldame:* crone, old woman.

XI

Ah, happy chance! the aged creature came,
Shuffling along with ivory-headed wand,
To where he stood, hid from the torch's flame,
Behind a broad hall-pillar, far beyond
The sound of merriment and chorus bland:
He startled her; but soon she knew his face,
And grasp'd his fingers in her palsied hand,
Saying, "Mercy, Porphyro! hie thee from this place:
They are all here to-night, the whole blood-thirsty race!

XII

"Get hence! get hence! there's dwarfish Hildebrand; 100
He had a fever late, and in the fit
He cursed thee and thine, both house and land:
Then there's that old Lord Maurice, not a whit
More tame for his gray hairs—Alas me! flit!
Flit like a ghost away."—"Ah, Gossip dear,
We're safe enough; here in this arm-chair sit,
And tell me how"—"Good saints! not here, not here;
Follow me, child, or else these stones will be thy bier."

XIII

He follow'd through a lowly arched way,
Brushing the cobwebs with his lofty plume; 110
And as she mutter'd "Well-a—well-a-day!"
He found him in a little moonlight room,
Pale, latticed, chill, and silent as a tomb.
"Now tell me where is Madeline," said he,
"O tell me, Angela, by the holy loom
Which none but secret sisterhood may see,
When they St. Agnes' wool are weaving piously."

XIV

"St. Agnes! Ah! it is St. Agnes' Eve—
Yet men will murder upon holy days:
Thou must hold water in a witch's sieve, 120
And be liege-lord of all the Elves and Fays,
To venture so: it fills me with amaze
To see thee, Porphyro!—St. Agnes' Eve!

God's help! my lady fair the conjuror plays
This very night: good angels her deceive!
But let me laugh awhile, I've mickle time to grieve."

XV

Feebly she laugheth in the languid moon,
While Porphyro upon her face doth look,
Like puzzled urchin on an aged crone
Who keepeth clos'd a wond'rous riddle-book, 130
As spectacled she sits in chimney nook.
But soon his eyes grew brilliant, when she told
His lady's purpose; and he scarce could brook
Tears, at the thought of those enchantments cold,
And Madeline asleep in lap of legends old.

XVI

Sudden a thought came like a full-blown rose,
Flushing his brow, and in his pained heart
Made purple riot: then doth he propose
A stratagem, that makes the beldame start:
"A cruel man and impious thou art: 140
Sweet lady, let her pray, and sleep, and dream
Alone with her good angels, far apart
From wicked men like thee. Go, go!—I deem
Thou canst not surely be the same that thou didst seem."

XVII

"I will not harm her, by all saints I swear,"
Quoth Porphyro: "O may I ne'er find grace
When my weak voice shall whisper its last prayer,
If one of her soft ringlets I displace,
Or look with ruffian passion in her face:
Good Angela, believe me by these tears; 150
Or I will, even in a moment's space,
Awake, with horrid shout, my foemen's ears,
And beard them, though they be more fang'd than wolves and bears."

XVIII

"Ah! why wilt thou affright a feeble soul?
A poor, weak, palsy-stricken, churchyard thing,

l. 126. *mickle:* much.

Whose passing-bell may ere the midnight toll;
Whose prayers for thee, each morn and evening,
Were never miss'd,"—Thus plaining, doth she bring
A gentler speech from burning Porphyro;
So woeful, and of such deep sorrowing, 160
That Angela gives promise she will do
Whatever he shall wish, betide her weal or woe.

XIX

Which was, to lead him, in close secrecy,
Even to Madeline's chamber, and there hide
Him in a closet, of such privacy
That he might see her beauty unespied,
And win perhaps that night a peerless bride,
While legion'd faeries pac'd the coverlet,
And pale enchantment held her sleepy-eyed.
Never on such a night have lovers met, 170
Since Merlin paid his Demon all the monstrous debt.

XX

"It shall be as thou wishest," said the Dame:
"All cates and dainties shall be stored there
Quickly on this feast-night: by the tambour frame
Her own lute thou wilt see: no time to spare,
For I am slow and feeble, and scarce dare
On such a catering trust my dizzy head.
Wait here, my child, with patience, kneel in prayer
The while: Ah! thou must needs the lady wed,
Or may I never leave my grave among the dead." 180

XXI

So saying she hobbled off with busy fear.
The lover's endless minutes slowly pass'd;
The dame return'd, and whisper'd in his ear
To follow her; with aged eyes aghast
From fright of dim espial. Safe at last
Through many a dusky gallery, they gain
The maiden's chamber, silken, hush'd, and chaste;

l. 171. *Merlin:* Arthur's magician who committed crimes to satisfy a demon to whom he was indebted for his life.
l. 173. *cates:* special delicacies.

Where Porphyro took covert, pleas'd amain.
His poor guide hurried back with agues in her brain.

XXII

Her faltering hand upon the balustrade, 190
Old Angela was feeling for the stair,
When Madeline, St. Agnes' charmed maid,
Rose, like a mission'd spirit, unaware:
With silver taper's light, and pious care,
She turn'd and down the aged gossip led
To a safe level matting. Now prepare,
Young Porphyro, for gazing on that bed;
She comes, she comes again, like ring-dove fray'd and fled.

XXIII

Out went the taper as she hurried in;
Its little smoke, in pallid moonshine, died: 200
She closed the door, she panted, all akin
To spirits of the air, and visions wide:
No utter'd syllable, or, woe betide!
But to her heart, her heart was voluble,
Paining with eloquence her balmy side;
As though a tongueless nightingale should swell
Her throat in vain, and die, heart-stifled, in her dell.

XXIV

A casement high and triple-arch'd there was,
All garlanded with carven imag'ries,
Of fruits, and flowers, and bunches of knot-grass, 210
And diamonded with panes of quaint device,
Innumerable of stains and splendid dyes,
As are the tiger-moth's deep-damask'd wings;
And in the midst, 'mong thousand heraldries,
And twilight saints, and dim emblazonings,
A shielded scutcheon blush'd with blood of queens and kings.

XXV

Full on this casement shone the wintry moon,
And threw warm gules on Madeline's fair breast,

l. 218. *gules:* the heraldic name for red.

As down she knelt for heaven's grace and boon;
Rose-bloom fell on her hands, together prest, 220
And on her silver cross soft amethyst,
And on her hair a glory, like a saint:
She seem'd a splendid angel, newly drest,
Save wings, for heaven:—Porphyro grew faint:
She knelt, so pure a thing, so free from mortal taint.

XXVI

Anon his heart revives: her vespers done,
Of all its wreathed pearls her hair she frees;
Unclasps her warmed jewels one by one;
Loosens her fragrant boddice; by degrees
Her rich attire creeps rustling to her knees: 230
Half-hidden, like a mermaid in sea-weed,
Pensive awhile she dreams awake, and sees,
In fancy, fair St. Agnes in her bed,
But dares not look behind, or all the charm is fled.

XXVII

Soon, trembling in her soft and chilly nest,
In sort of wakeful swoon, perplex'd she lay,
Until the poppied warmth of sleep oppress'd
Her soothed limbs, and soul fatigued away;
Flown, like a thought, until the morrow-day;
Blissfully haven'd both from joy and pain; 240
Clasp'd like a missal where swart Paynims pray;
Blinded alike from sunshine and from rain,
As though a rose should shut, and be a bud again.

XXVIII

Stol'n to this paradise, and so entranced,
Porphyro gazed upon her empty dress,
And listen'd to her breathing, if it chanced
To wake into a slumberous tenderness;
Which when he heard, that minute did he bless,
And breath'd himself: then from the closet crept,
Noiseless as fear in a wide wilderness, 250
And over the hush'd carpet, silent, stept,
And 'tween the curtains peep'd, where, lo!—how fast she slept.

XXIX

Then by the bed-side, where the faded moon
Made a dim, silver twilight, soft he set
A table, and, half anguish'd, threw thereon
A cloth of woven crimson, gold, and jet:—
O for some drowsy Morphean amulet!
The boisterous, midnight, festive clarion,
The kettle-drum, and far-heard clarionet,
Affray his ears, though but in dying tone:— 260
The hall door shuts again, and all the noise is gone.

XXX

And still she slept an azure-lidded sleep,
In blanched linen, smooth, and lavender'd,
While he from forth the closet brought a heap
Of candied apple, quince, and plum, and gourd;
With jellies soother than the creamy curd,
And lucent syrops, tinct with cinnamon;
Manna and dates, in argosy transferr'd
From Fez; and spiced dainties, every one,
From silken Samarcand to cedar'd Lebanon. 270

XXXI

These delicates he heap'd with glowing hand
On golden dishes and in baskets bright
Of wreathed silver: sumptuous they stand
In the retired quiet of the night,
Filling the chilly room with perfume light.—
"And now, my love, my seraph fair, awake!
Thou art my heaven, and I thine eremite:
Open thine eyes, for meek St. Agnes' sake,
Or I shall drowse beside thee, so my soul doth ache."

XXXII

Thus whispering, his warm, unnerved arm 280
Sank in her pillow. Shaded was her dream
By the dusk curtains:—'twas a midnight charm
Impossible to melt as iced stream:

l. 257. *Morphean:* from Morpheus, the god of sleep.
l. 277. *eremite:* a religious recluse.

The lustrous salvers in the moonlight gleam;
Broad golden fringe upon the carpet lies:
It seem'd he never, never could redeem
From such a stedfast spell his lady's eyes;
So mus'd, awhile, entoil'd in woofed phantasies.

XXXIII

Awakening up, he took her hollow lute,—
Tumultuous,—and, in chords that tenderest be, 290
He play'd an ancient ditty, long since mute,
In Provence call'd, "La belle dame sans mercy":
Close to her ear touching the melody;—
Wherewith disturb'd, she utter'd a soft moan:
He ceased—she panted quick—and suddenly
Her blue affrayed eyes wide open shone:
Upon his knees he sank, pale as smooth-sculptured stone.

XXXIV

Her eyes were open, but she still beheld,
Now wide awake, the vision of her sleep:
There was a painful change, that nigh expell'd 300
The blisses of her dream so pure and deep
At which fair Madeline began to weep,
And moan forth witless words with many a sigh;
While still her gaze on Porphyro would keep;
Who knelt, with joined hands and piteous eye,
Fearing to move or speak, she look'd so dreamingly.

XXXV

"Ah, Porphyro!" said she, "but even now
Thy voice was at sweet tremble in mine ear,
Made tunable with every sweetest vow;
And those sad eyes were spiritual and clear: 310
How changed thou art: how pallid, chill, and drear!
Give me that voice again, my Porphyro,
Those looks immortal, those complainings dear!
Oh leave me not in this eternal woe,
For if thou diest, my Love, I know not where to go."

l. 292. *La belle dame sans mercy:* the beautiful lady without mercy.

XXXVI

Beyond a mortal man impassion'd far
At these voluptuous accents, he arose,
Ethereal, flush'd, and like a throbbing star
Seen 'mid the sapphire heaven's deep repose;
Into her dream he melted, as the rose 320
Blendeth its odour and the violet,—
Solution sweet: meantime the frost-wind blows
Like Love's alarum, pattering the sharp sleet
Against the window-panes; St. Agnes' moon hath set.

XXXVII

'Tis dark: quick pattereth the flaw-blown sleet.
"This is no dream, my bride, my Madeline!"
'Tis dark: the iced gusts still rave and beat:
"No dream, alas! alas! and woe is mine!
Porphyro will leave me here to fade and pine.—
Cruel! what traitor could thee hither bring? 330
I curse not, for my heart is lost in thine,
Though thou forsakest a deceived thing;—
A dove forlorn and lost with sick unpruned wing."

XXXVIII

"My Madeline! sweet dreamer! lovely bride!
Say, may I be for aye thy vassal blest?
Thy beauty's shield, heart-shap'd and vermeil dyed?
Ah, silver shrine, here will I take my rest
After so many hours of toil and quest,
A famish'd pilgrim,—sav'd by miracle.
Though I have found, I will not rob thy nest 340
Saving of thy sweet self; if thou think'st well
To trust, fair Madeline, to no rude infidel.

XXXIX

"Hark! 'tis an elfin-storm from faery land,
Of haggard seeming, but a boon indeed:
Arise—arise! the morning is at hand;—
The bloated wassaillers will never heed:—
Let us away, my love, with happy speed;

There are no ears to hear, or eyes to see,—
Drown'd all in Rhenish and the sleepy mead:
Awake! arise! my love, and fearless be, 350
For o'er the southern moors I have a home for thee."

XL

She hurried at his words, beset with fears,
For there were sleeping dragons all around,
At glaring watch, perhaps, with ready spears—
Down the wide stairs a darkling way they found.—
In all the house was heard no human sound.
A chain-dropp'd lamp was flickering by each door;
The arras, rich with horseman, hawk, and hound,
Flutter'd in the besieging wind's uproar;
And the long carpets rose along the gusty floor. 360

XLI

They glide, like phantoms, into the wide hall;
Like phantoms, to the iron porch, they glide;
Where lay the Porter, in uneasy sprawl,
With a huge empty flaggon by his side:
The wakeful bloodhound rose, and shook his hide,
But his sagacious eye an inmate owns:
By one, and one, the bolts full easy slide:—
The chains lie silent on the footworn stones;—
The key turns, and the door upon its hinges groans.

XLII

And they are gone: aye, ages long ago 370
These lovers fled away into the storm.
That night the Baron dreamt of many a woe,
And all his warrior-guests, with shade and form
Of witch, and demon, and large coffin-worm,
Were long be-nightmar'd. Angela the old
Died palsy-twitch'd, with meagre face deform;
The Beadsman, after thousand aves told,
For aye unsought for slept among his ashes cold.

[*1819*]

l. 349. *Rhenish:* wine.

Ode to a Nightingale

I

My heart aches, and a drowsy numbness pains
  My sense, as though of hemlock I had drunk,
Or emptied some dull opiate to the drains
  One minute past, and Lethe-wards had sunk:
'Tis not through envy of thy happy lot,
  But being too happy in thy happiness,—
    That thou, light-winged Dryad of the trees,
        In some melodious plot
  Of beechen green, and shadows numberless,
    Singest of summer in full-throated ease. 10

II

O for a draught of vintage! that hath been
  Cool'd a long age in the deep-delved earth,
Tasting of Flora and the country-green,
  Dance, and Provençal song, and sun-burnt mirth!
O for a beaker full of the warm South,
  Full of the true, the blushful Hippocrene,
    With beaded bubbles winking at the brim,
        And purple-stained mouth;
  That I might drink, and leave the world unseen,
    And with thee fade away into the forest dim: 20

III

Fade far away, dissolve, and quite forget
  What thou among the leaves hast never known,
The weariness, the fever, and the fret
  Here, where men sit and hear each other groan;
Where palsy shakes a few, sad, last gray hairs,
  Where youth grows pale, and spectre-thin, and dies;
    Where but to think is to be full of sorrow
        And leaden-eyed despairs;
  Where Beauty cannot keep her lustrous eyes,
    Or new Love pine at them beyond to-morrow. 30

l. 7. *Dryad:* tree nymph.
l. 13. *Flora:* deity who presided over flowers.
l. 16. *Hyppocrene:* classical fountain whose waters inspired poets.

IV

Away! away! for I will fly to thee,
  Not charioted by Bacchus and his pards,
But on the viewless wings of Poesy,
  Though the dull brain perplexes and retards:
Already with thee! tender is the night,
  And haply the Queen-Moon is on her throne,
    Cluster'd around by all her starry Fays;
        But here there is no light,
  Save what from heaven is with the breezes blown.
    Through verdurous glooms and winding mossy ways. 40

V

I cannot see what flowers are at my feet,
  Nor what soft incense hangs upon the boughs,
But, in embalmed darkness, guess each sweet
  Wherewith the seasonable month endows
The grass, the thicket, and the fruit-tree wild;
  White hawthorn, and the pastoral eglantine;
    Fast-fading violets cover'd up in leaves;
        And mid-May's eldest child,
  The coming musk-rose, full of dewy wine,
    The murmurous haunt of flies on summer eves. 50

VI

Darkling I listen; and for many a time
  I have been half in love with easeful Death,
Call'd him soft names in many a mused rhyme,
  To take into the air my quiet breath;
Now more than ever seems it rich to die,
  To cease upon the midnight with no pain,
    While thou art pouring forth thy soul abroad
        In such an ecstasy!
  Still wouldst thou sing, and I have ears in vain—
    To thy high requiem become a sod. 60

VII

Thou wast not born for death, immortal Bird!
  No hungry generations tread thee down;

l. 51. *Darkling:* hidden in darkness.

The voice I hear this passing night was heard
In ancient days by emperor and clown:
Perhaps the self-same song that found a path
Through the sad heart of Ruth, when, sick for home,
She stood in tears amid the alien corn;
The same that oft-times hath
Charm'd magic casements, opening on the foam
Of perilous seas, in faery lands forlorn. 70

VIII

Forlorn! the very word is like a bell
To toll me back from thee to my sole self!
Adieu! the fancy cannot cheat so well
As she is fam'd to do, deceiving elf.
Adieu! adieu! thy plaintive anthem fades
Past the near meadows, over the still stream,
Up the hill-side; and now 'tis buried deep
In the next valley-glades:
Was it a vision, or a waking dream?
Fled is that music:—Do I wake or sleep? 80

[*1819*]

l. 66. *Ruth:* see Old Testament, *Book of Ruth,* II, 1–23.

Ode on a Grecian Urn

I

Thou still unravish'd bride of quietness!
Thou foster-child of silence and slow time,
Sylvan historian, who canst thus express
A flowery tale more sweetly than our rhyme:
What leaf-fringed legend haunts about thy shape
Of deities or mortals, or of both,
In Tempe or the dales of Arcady?
What men or gods are these? What maidens loath?
What mad pursuit? What struggle to escape?
What pipes and timbrels? What wild ecstasy? 10

l. 7. *Tempe . . . Arcady:* districts in Greece.

II

Heard melodies are sweet, but those unheard
Are sweeter; therefore, ye soft pipes, play on;
Not to the sensual ear, but, more endear'd,
Pipe to the spirit ditties of no tone:
Fair youth, beneath the trees, thou canst not leave
Thy song, nor ever can those trees be bare;
Bold Lover, never, never canst thou kiss,
Though winning near the goal—yet, do not grieve;
She cannot fade, though thou hast not thy bliss,
For ever wilt thou love, and she be fair! 20

III

Ah, happy, happy boughs! that cannot shed
Your leaves, nor ever bid the Spring adieu;
And, happy melodist, unwearied,
For ever piping songs for ever new;
More happy love! more happy, happy love!
For ever warm and still to be enjoy'd,
For ever panting and for ever young;
All breathing human passion far above,
That leaves a heart high sorrowful and cloy'd,
A burning forehead, and a parching tongue. 30

IV

Who are these coming to the sacrifice?
To what green altar, O mysterious priest,
Lead'st thou that heifer lowing at the skies,
And all her silken flanks with garlands drest?
What little town by river or sea-shore,
Or mountain-built with peaceful citadel,
Is emptied of its folk, this pious morn?
And, little town, thy streets for evermore
Will silent be; and not a soul to tell
Why thou art desolate, can e'er return. 40

V

O Attic shape! Fair attitude! with brede

l. 41. *Attic:* of Attica (in Greece).
brede: embroidered pattern.

Of marble men and maidens overwrought,
With forest branches and the trodden weed;
Thou, silent form! dost tease us out of thought
As doth eternity: Cold Pastoral!
When old age shall this generation waste,
Thou shalt remain, in midst of other woe
Than ours, a friend to man, to whom thou say'st,
"Beauty is truth, truth beauty,"—that is all
Ye know on earth, and all ye need to know. 50

[*1819*]

La Belle Dame Sans Merci

I

O what can ail thee, knight-at-arms,
Alone and palely loitering?
The sedge is wither'd from the lake,
And no birds sing.

II

O what can ail thee, knight-at-arms,
So haggard and so woe-begone?
The squirrel's granary is full,
And the harvest's done.

III

I see a lily on thy brow
With anguish moist and fever dew; 10
And on thy cheek a fading rose
Fast withereth too.

IV

I met a lady in the meads,
Full beautiful—a faery's child,
Her hair was long, her foot was light,
And her eyes were wild.

V

I made a garland for her head,
And bracelets too, and fragrant zone;

She look'd at me as she did love,
  And made sweet moan. 20

VI

I set her on my pacing steed,
  And nothing else saw all day long,
For sideways would she lean, and sing
  A faery's song.

VII

She found me roots of relish sweet,
  And honey wild, and manna dew;
And sure in language strange she said—
  "I love thee true!"

VIII

She took me to her elfin grot,
  And there she gazed and sigh'd full sore, 30
And there I shut her wild wild eyes
  With kisses four.

IX

And there she lulled me asleep,
  And there I dream'd—ah! woe betide!
The latest dream I ever dream'd
  On the cold hill side.

X

I saw pale kings and princes too,
  Pale warriors, death-pale were they all;
Who cried—"La Belle Dame sans merci
  Hath thee in thrall!" 40

XI

I saw their starv'd lips in the gloam,
  With horrid warning gaped wide,
And I awoke, and found me here,
  On the cold hill side.

XII

And this is why I sojourn here,
  Alone and palely loitering,

Though the sedge is wither'd from the lake,
And no birds sing.

[*1819*]

Endymion

FROM BOOK I

A thing of beauty is a joy for ever:
Its loveliness increases; it will never
Pass into nothingness; but still will keep
A bower quiet of us, and a sleep
Full of sweet dreams, and health, and quiet breathing.
Therefore, on every morrow, are we wreathing
A flowery band to bind us to the earth,
Spite of despondence, of the inhuman dearth
Of noble natures, of the gloomy days,
Of all the unhealthy and o'er-darkened ways 10
Made for our searching: yes, in spite of all,
Some shape of beauty moves away the pall
From our dark spirits. Such the sun, the moon,
Trees old and young, sprouting a shady boon
For simple sheep; and such are daffodils
With the green world they live in; and clear rills
That for themselves a cooling covert make
'Gainst the hot season; the mid-forest brake,
Rich with a sprinkling of fair musk-rose blooms:
And such too is the grandeur of the dooms 20
We have imagined for the mighty dead;
All lovely tales that we have heard or read:
An endless fountain of immortal drink,
Pouring unto us from the heaven's brink.

[*1817–18*]

On First Looking into Chapman's Homer

Much have I travell'd in the realms of gold,
And many goodly states and kingdoms seen;

Chapman's Homer: George Chapman was an early seventeenth-century translator of the *Iliad* and *Odyssey*.

Round many western islands have I been
Which bards in fealty to Apollo hold.
Oft of one wide expanse had I been told
That deep-brow'd Homer ruled as his demesne:
Yet did I never breathe its pure serene
Till I heard Chapman speak out loud and bold:
Then felt I like some watcher of the skies
When a new planet swims into his ken; 10
Or like stout Cortez when with eagle eyes
He star'd at the Pacific—and all his men
Look'd at each other with a wild surmise—
Silent, upon a peak in Darien.

[*1816*]

l. 6. *demesne:* realm; it is pronounced "demain."
l. 11. *Cortez:* Keats is wrong; Balboa discovered the Pacific.

On Seeing the Elgin Marbles

My spirit is too weak—mortality
Weighs heavily on me like unwilling sleep,
And each imagin'd pinnacle and steep
Of godlike hardship, tells me I must die
Like a sick Eagle looking at the sky.
Yet 'tis a gentle luxury to weep,
That I have not the cloudy winds to keep,
Fresh for the opening of the morning's eye.
Such dim-conceived glories of the brain
Bring round the heart an indescribable feud; 10
So do these wonders a most dizzy pain,
That mingles Grecian grandeur with the rude
Wasting of old Time—with a billowy main—
A sun—a shadow of a magnitude.

[*1817*]

Elgin Marbles: Greek sculptures in the British Museum.

Ode to Psyche

O Goddess! hear these tuneless numbers, wrung
By sweet enforcement and remembrance dear,

Psyche: mortal lover of Cupid who was later given immortality.

And pardon that thy secrets should be sung
Even into thine own soft-conched ear:
Surely I dreamt to-day, or did I see
The winged Psyche with awaken'd eyes?
I wander'd in a forest thoughtlessly,
And, on the sudden, fainting with surprise,
Saw two fair creatures, couched side by side
In deepest grass, beneath the whisp'ring roof 10
Of leaves and trembled blossoms, where there ran
A brooklet, scarce espied:

'Mid hush'd, cool-rooted flowers, fragrant-eyed,
Blue, silver-white, and budded Tyrian,
They lay calm-breathing on the bedded grass;
Their arms embraced, and their pinions too:
Their lips touch'd not, but had not bade adieu,
As if disjoined by soft-handed slumber,
And ready still past kisses to outnumber
At tender eye-dawn of aurorean love: 20
The winged boy I knew;
But who wast thou, O happy, happy dove?
His Psyche true!

O latest born and loveliest vision far
Of all Olympus' faded hierarchy!
Fairer than Phoebe's sapphire-region'd star,
Or Vesper, amorous glow-worm of the sky;
Fairer than these, though temple thou hast none,
Nor altar heap'd with flowers;
Nor virgin-choir to make delicious moan 30
Upon the midnight hours;
No voice, no lute, no pipe, no incense sweet
From chain-swung censer teeming;
No shrine, no grove, no oracle, no heat
Of pale-mouth'd prophet dreaming.

O brightest! though too late for antique vows,
Too, too late for the fond believing lyre,
When holy were the haunted forest boughs,

l. 14. *Tyrian:* purple.
l. 26. *Phoebe's . . . star:* the moon.

Holy the air, the water, and the fire;
Yet even in these days so far retir'd 40
From happy pieties, thy lucent fans,
Fluttering among the faint Olympians,
I see, and sing, by my own eyes inspir'd.
So let me be thy choir, and make a moan
Upon the midnight hours;
Thy voice, thy lute, thy pipe, thy incense sweet
From swinged censer teeming;
Thy shrine, thy grove, thy oracle, thy heat
Of pale-mouth'd prophet dreaming.

Yes, I will be thy priest, and build a fane 50
In some untrodden region of my mind,
Where branched thoughts, new grown with pleasant pain,
Instead of pines shall murmur in the wind:
Far, far around shall those dark-cluster'd trees
Fledge the wild-ridged mountains steep by steep;
And there by zephyrs, streams, and birds, and bees,
The moss-lain Dryads shall be lull'd to sleep;
And in the midst of this wide quietness
A rosy sanctuary will I dress
With the wreath'd trellis of a working brain, 60
With buds, and bells, and stars without a name.
With all the gardener Fancy e'er could feign,
Who breeding flowers, will never breed the same:
And there shall be for thee all soft delight
That shadowy thought can win,
A bright torch, and a casement ope at night,
To let the warm Love in!

[*1819*]

l. 50. *fane*: temple.

To Autumn

I

Season of mists and mellow fruitfulness!
Close bosom-friend of the maturing sun;

Conspiring with him how to load and bless
  With fruit the vines that round the thatch-eves run;
To bend with apples the moss'd cottage-trees,
And fill all fruit with ripeness to the core;
    To swell the gourd, and plump the hazel shells
  With a sweet kernel; to set budding more,
And still more, later flowers for the bees,
Until they think warm days will never cease, 10
    For Summer has o'er-brimm'd their clammy cells.

II

Who hath not seen thee oft amid thy store?
  Sometimes whoever seeks abroad may find
Thee sitting careless on a granary floor,
  Thy hair soft-lifted by the winnowing wind;
Or on a half-reap'd furrow sound asleep,
  Drowsed with the fumes of poppies, while thy hook
    Spares the next swath and all its twined flowers:
And sometimes like a gleaner thou dost keep
  Steady thy laden head across a brook; 20
  Or by a cyder-press, with patient look,
    Thou watchest the last oozings hours by hours.

III

Where are the songs of Spring? Ay, where are they?
  Think not of them, thou hast thy music too,—
While barred clouds bloom the soft-dying day,
  And touch the stubble-plains with rosy hue;
Then in a wailful choir the small gnats mourn
  Among the river sallows, borne aloft
    Or sinking as the light wind lives or dies;
And full-grown lambs loud bleat from hilly bourn; 30
  Hedge-crickets sing; and now with treble soft
  The red-breast whistles from a garden-croft;
    And gathering swallows twitter in the skies.

[1819]

l. 28. *sallows:* willows.
l. 32. *garden-croft:* a fenced-in garden.

Ode on Indolence

"They toil not, neither do they spin."

I

One morn before me were three figures seen,
  With bowed necks, and joined hands, side-faced;
And one behind the other stepp'd serene,
  In placid sandals, and in white robes graced;
    They pass'd, like figures on a marble urn,
  When shifted round to see the other side;
They came again; as when the urn once more
    Is shifted round, the first seen shades return;
  And they were strange to me, as may betide
With vases, to one deep in Phidian lore. 10

II

How is it, Shadows! that I knew ye not?
  How came ye muffled in so hush a mask?
Was it a silent deep-disguised plot
  To steal away, and leave without a task
    My idle days? Ripe was the drowsy hour;
  The blissful cloud of summer-indolence
Benumb'd my eyes; my pulse grew less and less;
    Pain had no sting, and pleasure's wreath no flower:
  Oh, why did ye not melt, and leave my sense
Unhaunted quite of all but—nothingness? 20

III

A third time pass'd they by, and, passing, turn'd
  Each one the face a moment whiles to me;
Then faded, and to follow them I burn'd
  And ach'd for wings, because I knew the three;
    The first was a fair Maid, and Love her name;
  The second was Ambition, pale of cheek,
And ever watchful with fatigued eye;
    The last, whom I love more, the more of blame

l. 10. *Phidian lore:* sculpture, after the famous Greek sculptor Phidias.

Is heap'd upon her, maiden most unmeek,—
I knew to be my demon Poesy. 30

IV

They faded, and, forsooth! I wanted wings:
O folly! What is Love? and where is it?
And for that poor Ambition! it springs
From a man's little heart's short fever-fit;
For Poesy!—no,—she has not a joy,—
At least for me,—so sweet as drowsy noons,
And evenings steep'd in honied indolence;
O, for an age so shelter'd from annoy,
That I may never know how change the moons,
Or hear the voice of busy common-sense! 40

V

And once more came they by;—alas! wherefore?
My sleep had been embroider'd with dim dreams;
My soul had been a lawn besprinkled o'er
With flowers, and stirring shades, and baffled beams:
The morn was clouded, but no shower fell,
Tho' in her lids hung the sweet tears of May;
The open casement press'd a new-leav'd vine,
Let in the budding warmth and throstle's lay;
O Shadows! 'twas a time to bid farewell!
Upon your skirts had fallen no tears of mine. 50

VI

So, ye three Ghosts, adieu! Ye cannot raise
My head cool-bedded in the flowery grass;
For I would not be dieted with praise,
A pet-lamb in a sentimental farce!
Fade softly from my eyes, and be once more
In masque-like figures on the dreamy urn;
Farewell! I yet have visions for the night,
And for the day faint visions there is store;
Vanish, ye Phantoms! from my idle spright,
Into the clouds, and never more return! 60

[*1819*]

l. 59. *spright:* spirit, mood.

Alfred Tennyson

Alfred Tennyson was born in Somersby, England, in 1809. His father, George Tennyson, apparently exerted a greater influence upon the poet's life than did his timid, gentle mother. The Reverend George Tennyson was an elder son who had been disinherited in favor of his younger brother and had thereby been forced by economic circumstances into an uncongenial clerical role. His frustration and sadness at the blow life had dealt him showed in spells of acute depression and a generally gloomy, sharp, mournful attitude toward life.

Alfred Tennyson's schooling in the grammar school at Louth was a very unhappy time, for he was lonesome, unathletic, and bookish. His significant education came from the books in his father's library. At twelve, the poet was a prodigy, who could write to his aunt: "Going into the library this morning, I picked up 'Sampson [sic] Agonistes' . . . on which I shall send you my remarks." At seventeen, he published with his brother a volume of poems called *Poems by Two Brothers*.

Tennyson entered Cambridge in 1828. There the ungainly country boy found himself largely alienated from the sophisticated and wealthy young men who set the tone of the place. Tennyson complained of a "want of love" and he rejected angrily the condescending attitude of his Cambridge associates toward him. Out of spite, almost, he made up his mind: "I mean to be famous." But his university experience was not entirely negative. At Cambridge he met Arthur

Henry Hallam, whose death he was to lament at length in "In Memoriam." Here too he was elected to the circle of The Apostles in 1830 and became their official "poet," putting their doctrines of idealistic world reform into verse with youthful enthusiasm. When his father died in 1831 Tennyson left college without taking his degree—a fact he did not regret, since he had never excelled academically.

From his Cambridge days came the poems which filled the volumes of 1830 and 1832. These books were the signal for a bitter attack on Tennyson by conservative reviewers of the influential quarterlies, notably Christopher North and John Lockhart. In part, their animosity was directed against the pathos and sentimentality of the poetry; but in part it was politically inspired as a reaction to the excessive praise lavished on Tennyson's work by Hallam and The Apostles. Whatever the motivation, the result of the attacks was to make Tennyson renounce publication for an entire decade (from 1832 to 1842) while he took stock, revised his verses, and licked his wounds.

The events of this silent decade were important. In 1833, Hallam, now engaged to Tennyson's sister Emily, died suddenly on a trip to the Continent. Tennyson, shocked and unnerved by the sudden tragedy which had robbed him of his friend and idol, felt his faith in divine providence ebbing. His elegy for Hallam, "In Memoriam," is partly an attempt to come to terms with the death and with its meaning in the Grand Design. Four years later, the poet became engaged to Emily Sellwood—an unimpulsive arrangement that lasted for thirteen years, survived a rift in 1840, and eventually culminated in a satisfactory marriage. During the latter half of the decade, Tennyson lived near London and became a friend and associate of Carlyle, Thackeray, Landor, Dickens, and other literary men. During that period, too, Tennyson, with uncharacteristic abandon, invested his money unwisely, lost it, and suffered a nervous breakdown.

The poems of 1842 restored Tennyson to public favor and set him on the path to the Laureateship. Fame and public favor healed his youthful wounds but just as surely they marred his personality. Tennyson became cautious and prim, neurotic, inefficient, and selfish. A hypochondriac, he allowed others to support him. He accepted a pension of two hundred pounds a year from the government, a sum which allowed him to travel. Though earlier he had been responsive to intelligent criticism of his works, he now wished to hear only favorable notices. He regarded himself as an inspired reader of his own works and would cry openly, overcome by the beauty of passages he had written. By 1850, he had invested himself as a kind of saint and encouraged public and critics to speak of his "mission" as poetic prophet of England.

Tennyson became Poet Laureate in 1850. "In Memoriam" was published in 1851, although it had been almost a score of years in preparation. These two events confirmed Tennyson as the most representative writer of the Victorian age. His "safe" works found favor with rich and poor alike. Not to appreciate him was heresy. The Queen herself cried over his poems and valued the personal friendship of the poet. Offered a peerage in 1883, Tennyson hesitated but accepted it in the following year. He developed a mania for privacy in his last years, rejecting biography and suppressing letters and documents that offered too intimate a view of his former activities. Utterly depressed by the state of England as it was about to enter the twentieth century, he died in 1892.

There is little mystery as to the forces that shaped Tennyson's life and work. His lonely childhood in a country rectory and under the chill influence of his gloomy father turned him into an insecure young man whose poems stress aloneness, alienation, and the frightened cry of the child in the night. Typically, Tennyson found his reception by the Cambridge students cold and distant very likely because he had himself lost the ability to relate warmly to other people. His visitors reported that even in old age he appeared to erect a barrier between himself and the guest, making conversation formidable and conviviality unthinkable.

His association with Hallam and The Apostles was an exception to the general current of rejection, and its effect on his life was considerable. The young college student was delighted to be taken into the warm fellowship of this charming, witty, and talented group. He was stirred by their intellectual attacks on political, social, and moral evils. That they recognized his poetic gifts excited him. He placed himself at their disposal to versify their position on any matter. And, too uncritically, he accepted their belief that his gift lay in didactic exposition of a political, social, or cultural position. He gave too little thought to the relative thinness of his ability to handle such public matters and apparently ignored, as they did, his obvious gift as a lyric poet and singer. Nor did the avid championing of Tennyson by Hallam and The Apostles in any literary controversy impress him as anything but just and deserved. Thus, the poet came to hold a false opinion of his own role as prophet and his *metier* as artist through excess admiration.

According to biographers, Tennyson's wife was guilty of the same well-meaning deception of the poet with regard to his role and his abilities. Unwilling to see him hurt, worried about his morbid reaction to adverse criticism, Emily Tennyson devoted herself to perpetuating the myth of infallibility of taste, of judgment, of conception, and of artistic execution in which her husband believed. With all his work being of equal merit in her eyes, Tennyson became unable to distinguish between the silly and insincere pieces that he contributed to Victorian "Ladybooks," eagerly read by young girls, and the serious literary works on which his reputation is based. Moreover, his wife confirmed the mistaken judgment of The Apostles that he was destined to be a prophetic ethical force rather than a lyric poet—and Tennyson trusted her judgment. This accounts, perhaps, for his apparent frustration in the last two decades of the nineteenth century when the world was proceeding on paths never dreamed of by his Victorian imagination.

Tennyson handled a myriad of themes in the seventy years of his productive career, but they are capable of classification, as his chief biographer, Harold Nicolson, has pointed out, under the categories of love, politics, and religion. The poet's conception of love was clearly restricted by the Victorian reticence toward sex and by the need to appear at all times the guardian of conventional morality. Almost exclusively Tennyson's poems deal with *married* love, the sanctioned caress of the husband and wife, preferably while the children sleep contentedly in the room next door. And even on the few occasions when he did treat of infidelity, as in the *Idylls of the King,* or of bigamy, as in *Enoch Arden,* the public was aroused by the suggestion of immorality. Queen Victoria herself questioned Tennyson concerning the propriety of the latter poem. Passion was ruled out by the preference of Victorians for the comfortable. Nor did the public demand for the depiction of emotional insipidity run counter to Tennyson's inclinations, for in his own emotional relationships he appears invariably to have favored cautious warmth to passionate involvement.

Tennyson's political views, as we have said, scarcely bear repeating, for they differ not at all from the convictions of most middle-class Victorian Englishmen. Intensely patriotic, the Laureate dutifully recorded in verse the exploits of English military men. He was convinced of the superiority of his nation over all others and wished to maintain England's isolation from other peoples. A reactionary from his youth, his principal concern was that progress be orderly, well behaved, and based in tradition. It is significant that he did not raise his voice against the excesses of the Industrial Revolution except to recommend charity for the poor and a cheerful bearing of one's lot. What bothered him most was to see the cracks appearing in the Victorian edifice: the appearance of Zolaism in England, the brutal frankness of the French Symbolists, the naturalist works of George Moore, and the ever-widening base of political power which he felt would vulgarize and weaken his country.

Perhaps Tennyson's most memorable theme is the struggle for religious belief. Its strength in his poetry is testimony to the sincerity of his own fight to reconcile the teachings of science and the faith of his childhood. Superficial in many areas of thought and emotion, Tennyson was deeply committed to working out his spiritual destiny. He would have undergone the agony if he had not been a poet; being one allowed him to verbalize the conflict for himself and others. Characteristically, Tennyson found the resolution of this conflict in compromise. He rejected his natural flair for mysticism and a mystic solution, since Victorianism did not allow for it. And his scientific study did not encourage belief in the God of his fathers. His compromise was simple: "It is hard to believe in God, but it is harder not to believe. I believe in God, not from what I see in nature, but from what I find in man." And if this solution eludes logic, it did allow Tennyson to write many of his finest poems.

Tennyson appeared on the literary stage in England more than a generation after Wordsworth had enunciated and exemplified the dogmas of Romanticism. By about 1840, though the Romantic strain was still strong in terms of theme (the wanderer's return in *Enoch Arden;* the knights of the Middle Ages in *Idylls of the King*) and in terms of the emphasis on nature ("The Lotus-Eaters," "Maud"), the purity of the strain was undergoing adulteration. In Tennyson's works, this Victorian brand of "tamed" Romanticism may be clearly observed. Pure lyrics on nature are balanced by poems in which nature is examined *intellectually* and deplored for its wildness. There is almost a longing for Pope's "Nature methodized." The requirements of the wild-eyed nonconformist are to be subordinated in a land of "settled government" which relies not on impulsive genius, but on "precedent." There is little room for the noble savage in Tennyson's later poetry—for untoward references may hurt Queen Victoria and retard sales. If the pendulum has not swung back from emphasis on heart to emphasis on mind, at least the consideration of the heart must be safe, proper, and confined within Victorian limits. The process of degeneration had already begun for the Romantic view, but it would not become critical until the end of the century.

BIBLIOGRAPHY

Baum, Paul F. *Tennyson Sixty Years After*. Chapel Hill: University of North Carolina Press, 1948.

Buckley, Jerome. *The Victorian Temper*. Cambridge, Mass.: Harvard University Press, 1951.

Nicolson, Harold. *Tennyson: Aspects of His Life, Character and Poetry*. London: Constable, 1923.

Ulysses

It little profits that an idle king,
By this still hearth, among these barren crags,
Match'd with an aged wife, I mete and dole
Unequal laws unto a savage race,
That hoard, and sleep, and feed, and know not me.
I cannot rest from travel; I will drink
Life to the lees. All times I have enjoy'd
Greatly, have suffer'd greatly, both with those
That loved me, and alone; on shore, and when
Thro' scudding drifts the rainy Hyades 10
Vext the dim sea. I am become a name;
For always roaming with a hungry heart
Much have I seen and known,—cities of men
And manners, climates, councils, governments,
Myself not least, but honor'd of them all,—
And drunk delight of battle with my peers,
Far on the ringing plains of windy Troy.
I am a part of all that I have met;
Yet all experience is an arch wherethro'
Gleams that untravell'd world whose margin fades 20
For ever and for ever when I move.
How dull it is to pause, to make an end,
To rust unburnish'd, not to shine in use!
As tho' to breathe were life! Life piled on life
Were all too little, and of one to me
Little remains; but every hour is saved
From that eternal silence, something more,
A bringer of new things; and vile it were
For some three suns to store and hoard myself,
And this gray spirit yearning in desire 30
To follow knowledge like a sinking star,
Beyond the utmost bound of human thought.
  This is my son, mine own Telemachus,
To whom I leave the sceptre and the isle,—
Well-loved of me, discerning to fulfil
This labor, by slow prudence to make mild

A rugged people, and thro' soft degrees
Subdue them to the useful and the good.
Most blameless is he, centred in the sphere
Of common duties, decent not to fail 40
In offices of tenderness, and pay
Meet adoration to my household gods,
When I am gone. He works his work, I mine.
 There lies the port; the vessel puffs her sail;
There gloom the dark, broad seas. My mariners,
Souls that have toil'd, and wrought, and thought with me,—
That ever with a frolic welcome took
The thunder and the sunshine, and opposed
Free hearts, free foreheads,—you and I are old;
Old age hath yet his honor and his toil. 50
Death closes all; but something ere the end,
Some work of noble note, may yet be done,
Not unbecoming men that strove with Gods.
The lights begin to twinkle from the rocks;
The long day wanes; the slow moon climbs; the deep
Moans round with many voices. Come, my friends,
'Tis not too late to seek a newer world.
Push off, and sitting well in order smite
The sounding furrows; for my purpose holds
To sail beyond the sunset, and the baths 60
Of all the western stars, until I die.
It may be that the gulfs will wash us down;
It may be we shall touch the Happy Isles,
And see the great Achilles, whom we knew.
Tho' much is taken, much abides; and tho'
We are not now that strength which in old days
Moved earth and heaven, that which we are, we are,—
One equal temper of heroic hearts,
Made weak by time and fate, but strong in will
To strive, to seek, to find, and not to yield. 70

[*1842*]

Commentary

The central theme of the poem is the need, on the part of certain men, constantly to resist the comfort of the known and to progress toward distant horizons. This theme is a natural corollary to the Victorian fetish of progress, though the poem's rejection of home and family is at variance with Tennyson's customary position. Like most Victorians, Tennyson had a deep faith that civilization—especially the civilization of England—was on the move toward a better day. To be part of this forward movement of history was regarded as an unquestioned desideratum by enterprising citizens. Matthew Arnold in "Hebraism and Hellenism," first questioned the blind urge to advance without the sure knowledge that the path led where England ought to go. Browning, however, implicitly sided with Tennyson, insisting that "A man's reach should exceed his grasp or what's a heaven for."

The immediate impetus for the writing of "Ulysses," however, probably came from Tennyson's disturbed condition after the death of Hallam. For a long while after the tragedy, the poet regarded the future with numbed shock. The value of forging ahead, of experience for its own sake and the sake of one's role in life seemed negligible. But as the months and years went by, a reaffirmation of the value of struggle became a poetic necessity. Furthermore, if the narrator of the poem is speaking for the artist, then the poem becomes a declaration of independence by the poet of all the routine drudgery of everyday existence. It becomes a plea for the widest experience and the most extensive world view in the shaping of a man of letters. The fact that Telemachus is excluded from the necessity of embarking on the quest for experience indicates that Tennyson's strictures about seeking "a newer world" are not addressed to all men.

Little needs be said of the text of the poem. The title identifies the narrator as the Greek hero, but the story shows that Tennyson had in mind Dante's version of Odysseus rather than Homer's. Homer depicted his hero as overjoyed to reach Ithaca and delighted to stay there. Dante altered the plot to indicate Ulysses' insistent wanderlust and his need to leave his homeland for further adventures into the unknown. In line 10, "Hyades" refers to stars whose rising in the sky ordinarily heralds rainy weather. In lines 19–21, the "arch wherethro' / Gleams that untravell'd world whose margin fades / For ever and for ever when I move" is analogous to the optical illusion of the converging railroad tracks which remain always unconverging as the traveler approaches. Telemachus, in line 33, is the son of Ulysses. "Meet" in line 42 is a synonym for "deserved."

The theme too needs little clarification, for the poem proceeds by statement rather than by indirection. Noteworthy are the Victorian sentiments that pervade the poem.

How dull it is to pause, to make an end,
To rust unburnish'd, not to shine in use!

is typical of the practical, homely philosophy of the nineteenth century. Also in character is the task which the poet assigns to Telemachus: "by slow prudence to make mild / A rugged people, and thro' soft degrees / Subdue them to the useful and the good." And the final lines combine the proper proportions of bravado, patriotism, and fortitude of the noble English spirit:

One equal temper of heroic hearts,
Made weak by time and fate, but strong in will
To strive, to seek, to find, and not to yield.

The impact of Hallam's death on Tennyson may be adduced from the narrator's statement that he has "suffer'd greatly, both with those / that loved me, and alone." Death is very final, but "something ere the end, / Some work of noble note, may yet be done." In spite of the tragedy, " 'Tis not too late to seek a newer world," for "Tho' much is taken, much abides." The poem may thus be read as Tennyson's return to active life after his breakdown and drifting following his friend's death.

Much may be said for interpretation of the poem as a call to the artist to immerse himself in the active, adventurous life—the creation of "a newer world." Tennyson himself insisted: ". . . there is more about myself in 'Ulysses,' which was written under the sense of loss and that all had gone by, but that still life must be fought out to the end. It was more written with the feeling of his loss upon me than many poems in 'In Memoriam.' " But Tennyson was speaking partly as a man, partly as a poet whose creative life depends upon a constant renewal of reservoirs of imagery, symbolism, narrative patterns, and the like. Rejecting the life of indolence that he had earlier pictured in "The Lotus-Eaters," the poet here declares for action and change, not for all men but for the chosen.

The style of the poem is stark and simple, the words almost pedestrian and conversational, perhaps as a way of reinforcing the sincerity of the content. The narrator's restiveness is indicated by the jaggedness of the lines [see *Handbook:* enjambement] of blank verse, almost all of which are broken with sharp pauses [see *Handbook:* caesura] at several points: "And manners, climates, councils, governments," and "That hoard, and sleep, and feed, and know not me."

Once the narrator has resolved his conflict and is off to sea again, his calm is restored and the lines flow smoothly:

> for my purpose holds
> To sail beyond the sunset, and the baths
> Of all the western stars, until I die.
> It may be that the gulfs will wash us down;
> It may be we shall touch the Happy Isles,
> And see the great Achilles, whom we knew.

The Lotos-Eaters

"Courage!" he said, and pointed toward the land,
"This mounting wave will roll us shoreward soon."
In the afternoon they came unto a land
In which it seemed always afternoon.
All round the coast the languid air did swoon,
Breathing like one that hath a weary dream.
Full-faced above the valley stood the moon;
And, like a downward smoke, the slender stream
Along the cliff to fall and pause and fall did seem.

A land of streams! some, like a downward smoke, 10
Slow-dropping veils of thinnest lawn, did go;
And some thro' wavering lights and shadows broke,
Rolling a slumbrous sheet of foam below.
They saw the gleaming river seaward flow
From the inner land; far off, three mountain-tops,
Three silent pinnacles of aged snow,
Stood sunset-flush'd; and, dew'd with showery drops,
Up-clomb the shadowy pine above the woven copse.

The charmed sunset linger'd low adown
In the red West; thro' mountain clefts the dale 20
Was seen far inland, and the yellow down
Border'd with palm, and many a winding vale
And meadow, set with slender galingale;
A land where all things always seem'd the same!
And round about the keel with faces pale,
Dark faces pale against that rosy flame,
The mild-eyed melancholy Lotos-eaters came.

Branches they bore of that enchanted stem,
Laden with flower and fruit, whereof they gave
To each, but whoso did receive of them 30

l. 1. *he:* Odysseus; this poem is a companion piece to "Ulysses."
l. 23. *galingale:* an aromatic plant.

And taste, to him the gushing of the wave
Far far away did seem to mourn and rave
On alien shores; and if his fellow spake,
His voice was thin, as voices from the grave;
And deep-asleep he seem'd, yet all awake,
And music in his ears his beating heart did make.

They sat them down upon the yellow sand,
Between the sun and moon upon the shore;
And sweet it was to dream of Fatherland,
Of child, and wife, and slave; but evermore 40
Most weary seem'd the sea, weary the oar,
Weary the wandering fields of barren foam.
Then some one said, "We will return no more;"
And all at once they sang, "Our island home
Is far beyond the wave; we will no longer roam."

Choric Song

I

There is sweet music here that softer falls
Than petals from blown roses on the grass,
Or night-dews on still waters between walls
Of shadowy granite, in a gleaming pass;
Music that gentlier on the spirit lies,
Than tired eyelids upon tired eyes;
Music that brings sweet sleep down from the blissful skies.
Here are cool mosses deep,
And thro' the moss the ivies creep,
And in the stream the long-leaved flowers weep, 10
And from the craggy ledge the poppy hangs in sleep.

II

Why are we weigh'd upon with heaviness,
And utterly consumed with sharp distress,
While all things else have rest from weariness?
All things have rest: why should we toil alone,
We only toil, who are the first of things,
And make perpetual moan,
Still from one sorrow to another thrown;
Nor ever fold our wings,

And cease from wanderings, 20
Nor steep our brows in slumber's holy balm;
Nor harken what the inner spirit sings,
"There is no joy but calm!"—
Why should we only toil, the roof and crown of things?

III

Lo! in the middle of the wood,
The folded leaf is woo'd from out the bud
With winds upon the branch, and there
Grows green and broad, and takes no care,
Sun-steep'd at noon, and in the moon
Nightly dew-fed; and turning yellow 30
Falls, and floats adown the air.
Lo! sweeten'd with the summer light,
The full-juiced apple, waxing over-mellow,
Drops in a silent autumn night.
All its allotted length of days
The flower ripens in its place,
Ripens and fades, and falls, and hath no toil,
Fast-rooted in the fruitful soil.

IV

Hateful is the dark-blue sky,
Vaulted o'er the dark-blue sea. 40
Death is the end of life; ah, why
Should life all labor be?
Let us alone. Time driveth onward fast,
And in a little while our lips are dumb.
Let us alone. What is it that will last?
All things are taken from us, and become
Portions and parcels of the dreadful past.
Let us alone. What pleasure can we have
To war with evil? Is there any peace
In ever climbing up the climbing wave? 50
All things have rest, and ripen toward the grave
In silence—ripen, fall, and cease:
Give us long rest or death, dark death, or dreamful ease.

V

How sweet it were, hearing the downward stream,
With half-shut eyes ever to seem

Falling asleep in a half-dream!
To dream and dream, like yonder amber light,
Which will not leave the myrrh-bush on the height;
To hear each other's whisper'd speech;
Eating the Lotos day by day, 60
To watch the crisping ripples on the beach,
And tender curving lines of creamy spray;
To lend our hearts and spirits wholly
To the influence of mild-minded melancholy;
To muse and brood and live again in memory,
With those old faces of our infancy
Heap'd over with a mound of grass,
Two handfuls of white dust, shut in an urn of brass!

VI

Dear is the memory of our wedded lives,
And dear the last embraces of our wives 70
And their warm tears; but all hath suffer'd change;
For surely now our household hearths are cold,
Our sons inherit us, our looks are strange,
And we should come like ghosts to trouble joy.
Or else the island princes over-bold
Have eat our substance, and the minstrel sings
Before them of the ten years' war in Troy,
And our great deeds, as half-forgotten things.
Is there confusion in the little isle?
Let what is broken so remain. 80
The Gods are hard to reconcile;
'Tis hard to settle order once again.
There *is* confusion worse than death,
Trouble on trouble, pain on pain,
Long labor unto aged breath,
Sore tasks to hearts worn out by many wars
And eyes grown dim with gazing on the pilot-stars.

VII

But, propt on beds of amaranth and moly,
How sweet—while warm airs lull us, blowing lowly—
With half-dropt eyelid still, 90
Beneath a heaven dark and holy,

l. 88. *amaranth and moly:* fabled plants; the former was thought to be undying, the latter to have magical powers.

To watch the long bright river drawing slowly
His waters from the purple hill—
To hear the dewy echoes calling
From cave to cave thro' the thick-twined vine—
To watch the emerald-color'd water falling
Thro' many a woven acanthus-wreath divine!
Only to hear and see the far-off sparkling brine,
Only to hear were sweet, stretch'd out beneath the pine.

VIII

The Lotos blooms below the barren peak, 100
The Lotos blows by every winding creek;
All day the wind breathes low with mellower tone;
Thro' every hollow cave and alley lone
Round and round the spicy downs the yellow Lotos-dust is blown.
We have had enough of action, and of motion we,
Roll'd to starboard, roll'd to larboard, when the surge was seething free,
Where the wallowing monster spouted his foam-fountains in the sea.
Let us swear an oath, and keep it with an equal mind,
In the hollow Lotos-land to live and lie reclined
On the hills like Gods together, careless of mankind. 110
For they lie beside their nectar, and the bolts are hurl'd
Far below them in the valleys, and the clouds are lightly curl'd
Round their golden houses, girdled with the gleaming world;
Where they smile in secret, looking over wasted lands,
Blight and famine, plague and earthquake, roaring deeps and fiery sands,
Clanging fights, and flaming towns, and sinking ships, and praying hands.
But they smile, they find a music centred in a doleful song
Steaming up, a lamentation and an ancient tale of wrong,
Like a tale of little meaning tho' the words are strong;
Chanted from an ill-used race of men that cleave the soil, 120
Sow the seed, and reap the harvest with enduring toil,
Storing yearly little dues of wheat, and wine and oil;
Till they perish and they suffer—some, 'tis whisper'd—down in hell
Suffer endless anguish, others in Elysian valleys dwell,

Resting weary limbs at last on beds of asphodel.
Surely, surely, slumber is more sweet than toil, the shore
Than labor in the deep mid-ocean, wind and wave and oar;
O, rest ye, brother mariners, we will not wander more.

[1853]

Locksley Hall

Comrades, leave me here a little, while as yet 'tis early morn;
Leave me here, and when you want me, sound upon the bugle-
horn.

'Tis the place, and all around it, as of old, the curlews call,
Dreary gleams about the moorland flying over Locksley Hall;

Locksley Hall, that in the distance overlooks the sandy tracts,
And the hollow ocean-ridges roaring into cataracts.

Many a night from yonder ivied casement, ere I went to rest,
Did I look on great Orion sloping slowly to the west.

Many a night I saw the Pleiads, rising thro' the mellow shade,
Glitter like a swarm of fireflies tangled in a silver braid. 10

Here about the beach I wander'd, nourishing a youth sublime
With the fairy tales of science, and the long result of time;

When the centuries behind me like a fruitful land reposed;
When I clung to all the present for the promise that it closed;

When I dipt into the future far as human eye could see,
Saw the vision of the world and all the wonder that would
be.—

In the spring a fuller crimson comes upon the robin's breast;
In the spring the wanton lapwing gets himself another crest;

In the spring a livelier iris changes on the burnish'd dove;
In the spring a young man's fancy lightly turns to thoughts of
love. 20

Then her cheek was pale and thinner than should be for one so young,
And her eyes on all my motions with a mute observance hung.

And I said, "My cousin Amy, speak, and speak the truth to me,
Trust me, cousin, all the current of my being sets to thee."

On her pallid cheek and forehead came a color and a light,
As I have seen the rosy red flushing in the northern night.

And she turn'd—her bosom shaken with a sudden storm of sighs—
All the spirit deeply dawning in the dark of hazel eyes—

Saying, "I have hid my feelings, fearing they should do me wrong;"
Saying, "Dost thou love me, cousin?" weeping, "I have loved thee long." 30

Love took up the glass of Time, and turn'd it in his glowing hands;
Every moment, lightly shaken, ran itself in golden sands.

Love took up the harp of Life, and smote on all the chords with might;
Smote the chord of Self, that, trembling, past in music out of sight.

Many a morning on the moorland did we hear the copses ring,
And her whisper throng'd my pulses with the fulness of the spring.

Many an evening by the waters did we watch the stately ships,
And our spirits rush'd together at the touching of the lips.

O my cousin, shallow-hearted! O my Amy, mine no more!
O the dreary, dreary moorland! O the barren, barren shore! 40

Falser than all fancy fathoms, falser than all songs have sung,
Puppet to a father's threat, and servile to a shrewish tongue!

Is it well to wish thee happy?—having known me—to decline
On a range of lower feelings and narrower heart than mine!

Yet it shall be; thou shalt lower to his level day by day,
What is fine within thee growing coarse to sympathize with clay.

As the husband is, the wife is; thou art mated with a clown,
And the grossness of his nature will have weight to drag thee down.

He will hold thee, when his passion shall have spent its novel force,
Something better than his dog, a little dearer than his horse. 50

What is this? his eyes are heavy; think not they are glazed with wine.
Go to him, it is thy duty; kiss him, take his hand in thine.

It may be my lord is weary, that his brain is overwrought;
Soothe him with thy finer fancies, touch him with thy lighter thought.

He will answer to the purpose, easy things to understand—
Better thou wert dead before me, tho' I slew thee with my hand!

Better thou and I were lying, hidden from the heart's disgrace,
Roll'd in one another's arms, and silent in a last embrace.

Cursed be the social wants that sin against the strength of youth!
Cursed be the social lies that warp us from the living truth! 60

Cursed be the sickly forms that err from honest Nature's rule!
Cursed be the gold that gilds the straiten'd forehead of the fool!

Well—'t is well that I should bluster!—Hadst thou less unworthy proved—
Would to God—for I had loved thee more than ever wife was loved.

Am I mad, that I should cherish that which bears but bitter fruit?
I will pluck it from my bosom, tho' my heart be at the root.

Never, tho' my mortal summers to such length of years should come
As the many-winter'd crow that leads the clanging rookery home.

Where is comfort? in division of the records of the mind?
Can I part her from herself, and love her, as I knew her, kind? 70

I remember one that perish'd; sweetly did she speak and move;
Such a one do I remember, whom to look at was to love.

Can I think of her as dead, and love her for the love she bore?
No—she never loved me truly; love is love for evermore.

Comfort? comfort scorn'd of devils! this is truth the poet sings,
That a sorrow's crown of sorrow is remembering happier things.

Drug thy memories, lest thou learn it, lest thy heart be put to proof,
In the dead unhappy night, and when the rain is on the roof.

Like a dog, he hunts in dreams, and thou art staring at the wall,
Where the dying night-lamp flickers, and the shadows rise and fall. 80

Then a hand shall pass before thee, pointing to his drunken sleep,
To thy widow'd marriage-pillows, to the tears that thou wilt weep.

Thou shalt hear the "Never, never," whisper'd by the phantom years,
And a song from out the distance in the ringing of thine ears;

And an eye shall vex thee, looking ancient kindness on thy pain.
Turn thee, turn thee on thy pillow; get thee to thy rest again.

l. 75. *the poet:* Dante.

Nay, but Nature brings thee solace; for a tender voice will cry.
'Tis a purer life than thine, a lip to drain thy trouble dry.

Baby lips will laugh me down; my latest rival brings thee rest.
Baby fingers, waxen touches, press me from the mother's breast. 90

O, the child too clothes the father with a dearness not his due.
Half is thine and half is his; it will be worthy of the two.

O, I see thee old and formal, fitted to thy petty part,
With a little hoard of maxims preaching down a daughter's heart.

"They were dangerous guides the feelings—she herself was not exempt—
Truly, she herself had suffer'd"—Perish in thy self-contempt!

Overlive it—lower yet—be happy! wherefore should I care?
I myself must mix with action, lest I wither by despair.

What is that which I should turn to, lighting upon days like these?
Every door is barr'd with gold, and opens but to golden keys. 100

Every gate is throng'd with suitors, all the markets overflow.
I have but an angry fancy; what is that which I should do?

I had been content to perish, falling on the foeman's ground,
When the ranks are roll'd in vapor, and the winds are laid with sound.

But the jingling of the guinea helps the hurt that Honor feels,
And the nations do but murmur, snarling at each other's heels.

Can I but relive in sadness? I will turn that earlier page.
Hide me from my deep emotion, O thou wondrous Mother-Age!

Make me feel the wild pulsation that I felt before the strife,
When I heard my days before me, and the tumult of my life; 110

Yearning for the large excitement that the coming years would
yield,
Eager-hearted as a boy when first he leaves his father's field,

And at night along the dusky highway near and nearer drawn,
Sees in heaven the light of London flaring like a dreary dawn;

And his spirit leaps within him to be gone before him then,
Underneath the light he looks at, in among the throngs of men;

Men, my brothers, men the workers, ever reaping something
new;
That which they have done but earnest of the things that they
shall do.

For I dipt into the future, far as human eye could see,
Saw the Vision of the world, and all the wonder that would be; 120

Saw the heavens fill with commerce, argosies of magic sails,
Pilots of the purple twilight, dropping down with costly bales;

Heard the heavens fill with shouting, and there rain'd a ghastly
dew
From the nations' airy navies grappling in the central blue;

Far along the world-wide whisper of the south-wind rushing
warm,
With the standards of the peoples plunging thro' the thunder-
storm;

Till the war-drum throbb'd no longer, and the battle-flags were
furl'd
In the Parliament of man, the Federation of the world.

There the common sense of most shall hold a fretful realm in
awe,
And the kindly earth shall slumber, lapt in universal law. 130

So I triumph'd ere my passion sweeping thro' me left me dry,
Left me with the palsied heart, and left me with the jaundiced
eye;

Eye, to which all order festers, all things here are out of joint.
Science moves, but slowly, slowly, creeping on from point to
point;

Slowly comes a hungry people, as a lion, creeping nigher,
Glares at one that nods and winks behind a slowly-dying fire.

Yet I doubt not thro' the ages one increasing purpose runs,
And the thoughts of men are widen'd with the process of the
suns.

What is that to him that reaps not harvest of his youthful joys,
Tho' the deep heart of existence beat for ever like a boy's? 140

Knowledge comes, but wisdom lingers, and I linger on the
shore,
And the individual withers, and the world is more and more.

Knowledge comes, but wisdom lingers, and he bears a laden
breast,
Full of sad experience, moving toward the stillness of his rest.

Hark, my merry comrades call me, sounding on the bugle-horn,
They to whom my foolish passion were a target for their scorn.

Shall it not be scorn to me to harp on such a moulder'd string?
I am shamed thro' all my nature to have loved so slight a thing.

Weakness to be wroth with weakness! woman's pleasure, woman's pain—
Nature made them blinder motions bounded in a shallower
brain. 150

Woman is the lesser man, and all thy passions, match'd with
mine,
Are as moonlight unto sunlight, and as water unto wine—

Here at least, where nature sickens, nothing. Ah, for some retreat
Deep in yonder shining Orient, where my life began to beat,

Where in wild Mahratta-battle fell my father evil-starr'd;—
I was left a trampled orphan, and a selfish uncle's ward.

Or to burst all links of habit—there to wander far away,
On from island unto island at the gateways of the day.

Larger constellations burning, mellow moons and happy skies,
Breadths of tropic shade and palms in cluster, knots of Paradise. 160

Never comes the trader, never floats an European flag,
Slides the bird o'er lustrous woodland, swings the trailer from the crag;

Droops the heavy-blossom'd bower, hangs the heavy-fruited tree—
Summer isles of Eden lying in dark-purple spheres of sea.

There methinks would be enjoyment more than in this march of mind,
In the steamship, in the railway, in the thoughts that shake mankind.

There the passions cramp'd no longer shall have scope and breathing space;
I will take some savage woman, she shall rear my dusky race.

Iron-jointed, supple-sinew'd, they shall dive, and they shall run,
Catch the wild goat by the hair, and hurl their lances in the sun; 170

Whistle back the parrot's call, and leap the rainbows of the brooks,
Not with blinded eyesight poring over miserable books—

Fool, again the dream, the fancy! but I *know* my words are wild,
But I count the gray barbarian lower than the Christian child.

I, to herd with narrow foreheads, vacant of our glorious gains,
Like a beast with lower pleasures, like a beast with lower pains!

l. 155. *Mahratta-battle:* the British occasionally fought the Indian Mahratta.

Mated with a squalid savage—what to me were sun or clime?
I the heir of all the ages, in the foremost files of time—

I that rather held it better men should perish one by one,
Than that earth should stand at gaze like Joshua's moon in
Ajalon! 180

Not in vain the distance beacons. Forward, forward let us range,
Let the great world spin for ever down the ringing grooves of
change.

Thro' the shadow of the globe we sweep into the younger day;
Better fifty years of Europe than a cycle of Cathay.

Mother-Age,—for mine I knew not,—help me as when life
begun;
Rift the hills, and roll the waters, flash the lightnings, weigh the
sun.

O, I see the crescent promise of my spirit hath not set.
Ancient founts of inspiration well thro' all my fancy yet.

Howsoever these things be, a long farewell to Locksley Hall!
Now for me the woods may wither, now for me the roof-tree
fall. 190

Comes a vapor from the margin, blackening over heath and holt,
Cramming all the blast before it, in its breast a thunderbolt.

Let it fall on Locksley Hall, with rain or hail, or fire or snow;
For the mighty wind arises, roaring seaward, and I go.

[*1835–42*]

l. 180. *Joshua's moon:* Joshua called on sun and moon not to move so that the Israelites might have longer daylight in which to defeat their enemies. See Joshua: X, 12–15.

FROM *In Memoriam A.H.H.*

XXVII

I envy not in any moods
  The captive void of noble rage,
  The linnet born within the cage,
That never knew the summer woods;

I envy not the beast that takes
  His license in the field of time,
  Unfetter'd by the sense of crime,
To whom a conscience never wakes;

Nor, what may count itself as blest,
  The heart that never plighted troth   10
  But stagnates in the weeds of sloth;
Nor any want-begotten rest.

I hold it true, whate'er befall;
  I feel it when I sorrow most;
  'Tis better to have loved and lost
Than never to have loved at all.

LIV

O, yet we trust that somehow good
  Will be the final goal of ill,
  To pangs of nature, sins of will,
Defects of doubt, and taints of blood;

That nothing walks with aimless feet;
  That not one life shall be destroy'd,
  Or cast as rubbish to the void,
When God hath made the pile complete;

That not a worm is cloven in vain;
  That not a moth with vain desire   10
  Is shrivell'd in a fruitless fire,
Or but subserves another's gain.

In Memoriam: for discussion of In Memoriam stanza see *Handbook.*
A. H. H.: Arthur Henry Hallam; see bottom p. 219 to p. 221.

Behold, we know not anything;
  I can but trust that good shall fall
  At last—far off—at last, to all,
And every winter change to spring.

So runs my dream; but what am I?
  An infant crying in the night;
  An infant crying for the light,
And with no language but a cry. 20

LV

The wish, that of the living whole
  No life may fail beyond the grave,
  Derives it not from what we have
The likest God within the soul?

Are God and Nature then at strife,
  That Nature lends such evil dreams?
  So careful of the type she seems,
So careless of the single life,

That I, considering everywhere
  Her secret meaning in her deeds, 10
  And finding that of fifty seeds
She often brings but one to bear,

I falter where I firmly trod,
  And falling with my weight of cares
  Upon the great world's altar-stairs
That slope thro' darkness up to God,

I stretch lame hands of faith, and grope,
  And gather dust and chaff, and call
  To what I feel is Lord of all,
And faintly trust the larger hope. 20

LVI

"So careful of the type?" but no.
  From scarped cliff and quarried stone

l. 20. *the larger hope:* the hope that a purified mankind will be saved at last.

l. 2. *scarped:* eroded.

She cries, "A thousand types are gone;
I care for nothing, all shall go.

"Thou makest thine appeal to me:
I bring to life, I bring to death;
The spirit does but mean the breath:
I know no more." And he, shall he,

Man, her last work, who seem'd so fair,
Such splendid purpose in his eyes, 10
Who roll'd the psalm to wintry skies,
Who built him fanes of fruitless prayer,

Who trusted God was love indeed
And love Creation's final law—
Tho' Nature, red in tooth and claw
With ravine, shriek'd against his creed—

Who loved, who suffer'd countless ills,
Who battled for the True, the Just,
Be blown about the desert dust,
Or seal'd within the iron hills? 20

No more? A monster then, a dream,
A discord. Dragons of the prime,
That tare each other in their slime,
Were mellow music match'd with him.

O life as futile, then, as frail!
O for thy voice to soothe and bless!
What hope of answer, or redress?
Behind the veil, behind the veil.

LVII

Peace; come away: the song of woe
Is after all an earthly song.

l. 23. *tare:* tear.
l. 26. *thy:* Hallam's. The poem is an elegy on the death of Tennyson's college friend, Arthur Hallam.

Peace; come away: we do him wrong
To sing so wildly: let us go.

Come; let us go: your cheeks are pale;
But half my life I leave behind.
Methinks my friend is richly shrined;
But I shall pass, my work will fail.

Yet in these ears, till hearing dies,
One set slow bell will seem to toll 10
The passing of the sweetest soul
That ever look'd with human eyes.

I hear it now, and o'er and o'er,
Eternal greetings to the dead;
And "Ave, Ave, Ave," said,
"Adieu, adieu," for evermore.

CVI

Ring out, wild bells, to the wild sky,
The flying cloud, the frosty light:
The year is dying in the night;
Ring out, wild bells, and let him die.

Ring out the old, ring in the new,
Ring, happy bells, across the snow:
The year is going, let him go;
Ring out the false, ring in the true.

Ring out the grief that saps the mind,
For those that here we see no more; 10
Ring out the feud of rich and poor,
Ring in redress to all mankind.

Ring out a slowly dying cause,
And ancient forms of party strife;
Ring in the nobler modes of life,
With sweeter manners, purer laws.

Ring out the want, the care, the sin,
The faithless coldness of the times;

Ring out, ring out my mournful rhymes,
But ring the fuller minstrel in. 20

Ring out false pride in place and blood,
The civic slander and the spite;
Ring in the love of truth and right,
Ring in the common love of good.

Ring out old shapes of foul disease;
Ring out the narrowing lust of gold;
Ring out the thousand wars of old,
Ring in the thousand years of peace.

Ring in the valiant man and free,
The larger heart, the kindlier hand; 30
Ring out the darkness of the land,
Ring in the Christ that is to be.

[*published 1850*]

Crossing the Bar

Sunset and evening star,
And one clear call for me!
And may there be no moaning of the bar,
When I put out to sea,

But such a tide as moving seems asleep,
Too full for sound and foam,
When that which drew from out the boundless deep
Turns again home.

Twilight and evening bell,
And after that the dark! 10
And may there be no sadness of farewell,
When I embark;

For tho' from out our bourne of Time and Place
The flood may bear me far,
I hope to see my Pilot face to face
When I have crost the bar.

[*1889; published 1889*]

The Lady of Shalott

Part I

On either side the river lie
Long fields of barley and of rye,
That clothe the wold and meet the sky;
And thro' the field the road runs by
        To many-tower'd Camelot;
And up and down the people go,
Gazing where the lilies blow
Round an island there below,
        The island of Shalott.

Willows whiten, aspens quiver, 10
Little breezes dusk and shiver
Thro' the wave that runs for ever
By the island in the river
        Flowing down to Camelot.
Four gray walls, and four gray towers,
Overlook a space of flowers,
And the silent isle imbowers
        The Lady of Shalott.

By the margin, willow-veil'd,
Slide the heavy barges trail'd 20
By slow horses; and unhail'd
The shallop flitteth silken-sail'd
        Skimming down to Camelot:
But who hath seen her wave her hand?
Or at the casement seen her stand?
Or is she known in all the land,
        The Lady of Shalott?

Only reapers, reaping early
In among the bearded barley,
Hear a song that echoes cheerly 30
From the river winding clearly,
        Down to tower'd Camelot;

l. 3. *wold:* an upland plain.
l. 5. *Camelot:* the place where King Arthur had his court of the Round Table.

And by the moon the reaper weary,
Piling sheaves in uplands airy,
Listening, whispers " 'Tis the fairy
Lady of Shalott."

Part II

There she weaves by night and day
A magic web with colors gay.
She has heard a whisper say,
A curse is on her if she stay
To look down to Camelot.
She knows not what the curse may be,
And so she weaveth steadily,
And little other care hath she,
The Lady of Shalott.

And moving thro' a mirror clear 10
That hangs before her all the year,
Shadows of the world appear.
There she sees the highway near
Winding down to Camelot;
There the river eddy whirls,
And there the surly village-churls,
And the red cloaks of market girls,
Pass onward from Shalott.

Sometimes a troop of damsels glad,
An abbot on an ambling pad, 20
Sometimes a curly shepherd-lad,
Or long-hair'd page in crimson clad,
Goes by to tower'd Camelot;
And sometimes thro' the mirror blue
The knights come riding two and two:
She hath no loyal knight and true,
The Lady of Shalott.

But in her web she still delights
To weave the mirror's magic sights,
For often thro' the silent nights 30

l. 20. *pad:* horse.

A funeral, with plumes and lights
        And music, went to Camelot;
Or when the moon was overhead,
Came two young lovers lately wed:
"I am half sick of shadows," said
        The Lady of Shalott.

Part III

A bow-shot from her bower-eaves,
He rode between the barley-sheaves,
The sun came dazzling thro' the leaves,
And flamed upon the brazen greaves
        Of bold Sir Lancelot.
A red-cross knight for ever kneel'd
To a lady in his shield,
That sparkled on the yellow field,
        Beside remote Shalott.

The gemmy bridle glitter'd free, 10
Like to some branch of stars we see
Hung in the golden Galaxy.
The bridle bells rang merrily
        As he rode down to Camelot;
And from his blazon'd baldric slung
A mighty silver bugle hung,
And as he rode his armor rung,
        Beside remote Shalott.

All in the blue unclouded weather
Thick-jewell'd shone the saddle-leather, 20
The helmet and the helmet-feather
Burn'd like one burning flame together,
        As he rode down to Camelot;
As often thro' the purple night,
Below the starry clusters bright,
Some bearded meteor, trailing light,
        Moves over still Shalott.

l. 4. *brazen greaves:* bronze leg armor.
l. 15. *baldric:* belt, often ornamented ("blazon'd"), slung from the shoulder to the opposite hip.

His broad clear brow in sunlight glow'd;
On burnish'd hooves his war-horse trode;
From underneath his helmet flow'd 30
His coal-black curls as on he rode,
As he rode down to Camelot.
From the bank and from the river
He flash'd into the crystal mirror,
"Tirra lirra," by the river
Sang Sir Lancelot.

She left the web, she left the loom,
She made three paces thro' the room,
She saw the water-lily bloom,
She saw the helmet and the plume, 40
She look'd down to Camelot.
Out flew the web and floated wide;
The mirror crack'd from side to side;
"The curse is come upon me," cried
The Lady of Shalott.

Part IV

In the stormy east-wind straining,
The pale yellow woods were waning,
The broad stream in his banks complaining,
Heavily the low sky raining
Over tower'd Camelot;
Down she came and found a boat
Beneath a willow left afloat,
And round about the prow she wrote
The Lady of Shalott.

And down the river's dim expanse— 10
Like some bold seër in a trance,
Seeing all his own mischance—
With a glassy countenance
Did she look to Camelot.
And at the closing of the day
She loosed the chain, and down she lay;
The broad stream bore her far away,
The Lady of Shalott.

Lying, robed in snowy white
That loosely flew to left and right— 20
The leaves upon her falling light—
Thro' the noises of the night
She floated down to Camelot;
And as the boat-head wound along
The willowy hills and fields among,
They heard her singing her last song,
The Lady of Shalott.

Heard a carol, mournful, holy,
Chanted loudly, chanted lowly,
Till her blood was frozen slowly, 30
And her eyes were darken'd wholly,
Turn'd to tower'd Camelot.
For ere she reach'd upon the tide
The first house by the water-side,
Singing in her song she died,
The Lady of Shalott.

Under tower and balcony,
By garden-wall and gallery,
A gleaming shape she floated by,
Dead-pale between the houses high, 40
Silent into Camelot.
Out upon the wharfs they came,
Knight and burgher, lord and dame,
And round the prow they read her name,
The Lady of Shalott.

Who is this? and what is here?
And in the lighted palace near
Died the sound of royal cheer;
And they cross'd themselves for fear,
All the knights at Camelot: 50
But Lancelot mused a little space;
He said, "She has a lovely face;
God in his mercy lend her grace,
The Lady of Shalott."

[*published 1832, 1842*]

Tithonus

The woods decay, the woods decay and fall,
The vapors weep their burthen to the ground,
Man comes and tills the field and lies beneath,
And after many a summer dies the swan.
Me only cruel immortality
Consumes; I wither slowly in thine arms,
Here at the quiet limit of the world,
A white-hair'd shadow roaming like a dream
The ever-silent spaces of the East,
Far-folded mists, and gleaming halls of morn. 10
Alas! for this gray shadow, once a man—
So glorious in his beauty and thy choice,
Who madest him thy chosen, that he seem'd
To his great heart none other than a God!
I ask'd thee, "Give me immortality."
Then didst thou grant mine asking with a smile,
Like wealthy men who care not how they give.
But thy strong Hours indignant work'd their wills,
And beat me down and marr'd and wasted me,
And tho' they could not end me, left me maim'd 20
To dwell in presence of immortal youth,
Immortal age beside immortal youth,
And all I was in ashes. Can thy love,
Thy beauty, make amends, tho' even now,
Close over us, the silver star, thy guide,
Shines in those tremulous eyes that fill with tears
To hear me? Let me go; take back thy gift.
Why should a man desire in any way
To vary from the kindly race of men,
Or pass beyond the goal of ordinance 30
Where all should pause, as is most meet for all?
A soft air fans the cloud apart; there comes
A glimpse of that dark world where I was born.
Once more the old mysterious glimmer steals
From thy pure brows, and from thy shoulders pure,

Tithonus: Eos, the goddess of the morning, won the gift of eternal life from Zeus for her mortal lover Tithonus, but neglected to ask also for eternal youth.

And bosom beating with a heart renew'd.
Thy cheek begins to redden thro' the gloom,
Thy sweet eyes brighten slowly close to mine,
Ere yet they blind the stars, and the wild team
Which love thee, yearning for thy yoke, arise, 40
And shake the darkness from their loosen'd manes,
And beat the twilight into flakes of fire.
  Lo! ever thus thou growst beautiful
In silence, then before thine answer given
Departest, and thy tears are on my cheek.
  Why wilt thou ever scare me with thy tears,
And make me tremble lest a saying learnt,
In days far-off, on that dark earth, be true?
"The Gods themselves cannot recall their gifts."
  Ay me! ay me! with what another heart 50
In days far-off, and with what other eyes
I used to watch—if I be he that watch'd—
The lucid outline forming round thee; saw
The dim curls kindle into sunny rings;
Changed with thy mystic change, and felt my blood
Glow with the glow that slowly crimson'd all
Thy presence and thy portals, while I lay,
Mouth, forehead, eyelids, growing dewy-warm
With kisses balmier than half-opening buds
Of April, and could hear the lips that kiss'd 60
Whispering I knew not what of wild and sweet,
Like that strange song I heard Apollo sing,
While Ilion like a mist rose into towers.
  Yet hold me not for ever in thine East;
How can my nature longer mix with thine?
Coldly thy rosy shadows bathe me, cold
Are all thy lights, and cold my wrinkled feet
Upon thy glimmering thresholds, when the steam
Floats up from those dim fields about the homes
Of happy men that have the power to die, 70
And grassy barrows of the happier dead.
Release me, and restore me to the ground.
Thou seest all things, thou wilt see my grave;
Thou wilt renew thy beauty morn by morn,
I earth in earth forget these empty courts,
And thee returning on thy silver wheels.

[*1833–34; final version 1859*]

Rizpah

17—

I

Wailing, wailing, wailing, the wind over land and sea—
And Willy's voice in the wind, "O mother, come out to me!"
Why should he call me to-night, when he knows that I cannot
go?
For the downs are as bright as day, and the full moon stares at
the snow.

II

We should be seen, my dear; they would spy us out of the town.
The loud black nights for us, and the storm rushing over the
down,
When I cannot see my own hand, but am led by the creak of
the chain,
And grovel and grope for my son till I find myself drenched with
the rain.

III

Anything fallen again? nay—what was there left to fall?
I have taken them home, I have number'd the bones, I have
hidden them all. 10
What am I saying? and what are *you*? do you come as a spy?
Falls? what falls? who knows? As the tree falls so must it lie.

IV

Who let her in? how long has she been? you—what have you
heard?
Why did you sit so quiet? you never have spoken a word.
O—to pray with me—yes—a lady—none of their spies—
But the night has crept into my heart, and begun to darken my
eyes.

V

Ah—you, that have lived so soft, what should *you* know of the
night,

The blast and the burning shame and the bitter frost and the
fright?
I have done it, while you were asleep—you were only made for
the day.
I have gather'd my baby together—and now you may go your
way. 20

VI

Nay—for it's kind of you, madam, to sit by an old dying wife.
But say nothing hard of my boy, I have only an hour of life.
I kiss'd my boy in the prison, before he went out to die.
"They dared me to do it," he said, and he never has told me a
lie.
I whipt him for robbing an orchard once when he was but a
child—
"The farmer dared me to do it," he said; he was always so wild—
And idle—and couldn't be idle—my Willy—he never could
rest.
The King should have made him a soldier, he would have been
one of his best.

VII

But he lived with a lot of wild mates, and they never would let
him be good;
They swore that he dare not rob the mail, and he swore that he
would; 30
And he took no life, but he took one purse, and when all was
done
He flung it among his fellows—"I'll none of it," said my son.

VIII

I came into court to the judge and the lawyers. I told them my
tale,
God's own truth—but they kill'd him, they kill'd him for robbing
the mail.
They hang'd him in chains for a show—we had always borne a
good name—
To be hang'd for a thief—and then put away—isn't that enough
shame?
Dust to dust—low down—let us hide! but they set him so high
That all the ships of the world could stare at him, passing by.

God'ill pardon the hell-black raven and horrible fowls of the air,
But not the black heart of the lawyer who kill'd him and hang'd
him there. 40

IX

And the jailer forced me away. I had bid him my last good-bye;
They had fasten'd the door of his cell. "O mother!" I heard him
cry.
I couldn't get back tho' I tried, he had something further to say,
And now I never shall know it. The jailer forced me away.

X

Then since I couldn't but hear that cry of my boy that was dead,
They seized me and shut me up: they fasten'd me down on my
bed.
"Mother, O mother!"—he call'd in the dark to me year after
year—
They beat me for that, they beat me—you know that I couldn't
but hear;
And then at the last they found I had grown so stupid and still
They let me abroad again—but the creatures had worked their
will. 50

XI

Flesh of my flesh was gone, but bone of my bone was left—
I stole them all from the lawyers—and you, will you call it a
theft?—
My baby, the bones that had suck'd me, the bones that had
laughed and had cried—
Theirs? O, no! they are mine—not theirs—they had moved in
my side.

XII

Do you think I was scared by the bones? I kiss'd 'em, I buried
'em all—
I can't dig deep, I am old—in the night by the churchyard wall.
My Willy 'ill rise up whole when the trumpet of judgment 'ill
sound,
But I charge you never to say that I laid him in holy ground.

XIII

They would scratch him up—they would hang him again on the cursed tree.
Sin? O, yes, we are sinners, I know—let all that be, 60
And read me a Bible verse of the Lord's goodwill toward men—
"Full of compassion and mercy, the Lord"—let me hear it again;
"Full of compassion and mercy—long-suffering." Yes, O, yes!
For the lawyer is born but to murder—the Saviour lives but to bless.
He'll never put on the black cap except for the worst of the worst.
And the first may be last—I have heard it in church—and the last may be first.
Suffering—O, long-suffering—yes, as the Lord must know.
Year after year in the mist and the wind and the shower and the snow.

XIV

Heard, have you? what? they have told you he never repented his sin.
How do they know it? are *they* his mother? are *you* of his kin? 70
Heard! have you ever heard, when the storm on the downs began,
The wind that 'ill wail like a child and the sea that 'ill moan like a man?

XV

Election, Election, and Reprobation—it's all very well.
But I go to-night to my boy, and I shall not find him in hell.
For I cared so much for my boy that the Lord has look'd into my care,
And He means me I'm sure to be happy with Willy, I know not where.

XVI

And if *he* be lost—but to save *my* soul, that is all your desire—
Do you think that I care for *my* soul if my boy be gone to the fire?
I have been with God in the dark—go, go, you may leave me alone—

You never have borne a child—you are just as hard as a stone. 80

XVII

Madam, I beg your pardon, I think that you mean to be kind,
But I cannot hear what you say for my Willy's voice in the wind—
The snow and the sky so bright—he used but to call in the dark,
And he calls to me now from the church and not from the gibbet—for hark!
Nay—you can hear it yourself—it is coming—shaking the walls—
Willy—the moon's in a cloud——Good-night. I am going. He calls.

[*published 1880*]

Robert Browning

Robert Browning was born in Camberwell, a suburb of London, in 1812. His father was a submissive, sweet-tempered person, a clerk in the Bank of England. His mother, who dominated the household and the life of her son, was a determined, earnestly religious woman. Both parents lived for their son, pampering him physically and deferring to his wishes in trivial or important matters. When Robert rejected formal schooling, they undertook to educate him at home. There, in the warmth of his father's large and curious library, he read widely in history and art. At great financial sacrifice his father allowed him to attend the University of London, and, with equal openness of heart, permitted him to withdraw when Robert disliked the masculine, competitive atmosphere of the place.

Browning had toyed with the idea of becoming a poet from the age of fourteen after reading and being awed by Shelley's poems. His emulation of that poet extended to embracing Shelley's atheism and his vegetarianism, but Browning's mother was eventually able to win him back from atheism. His decision to devote his life to poetry raised many problems for his parents. Bank clerks, who at the best earned less than 300 pounds in Victorian England, are hardly in a position to subsidize poets, and Browning did not show the slightest interest in supporting himself while he wrote. However, both parents decided to sacrifice whatever was necessary to make their son a poet. The sacrifice involved their supporting their son until he was in his middle thirties and able to use the money his marriage brought to him.

Browning's youthful publications left the reviewers cold. His first major effort, *Pauline,* published in 1833, was almost uniformly attacked as obscure (which it was) and unreadable. John Stuart Mill concurred in the general opinion, but did recognize that the poem was a "psychological history" of its author which showed an "intense morbid self-consciousness." Seven years later, another obscure narrative, *Sordello,* appeared to end the poet's hope of fame. *Paracelsus* had fared slightly better in 1835, giving Browning entry into literary society. His dramatic efforts of the decade that began in 1837 were wholly unsuccessful.

In the mid-1840s Browning's life underwent a significant change as a result of his courtship of and marriage to Elizabeth Barrett, a frail, semi-invalided poetess whose works were much more in demand than his own. Several years older than Browning and unwilling to saddle him with a sick wife, she resisted for a time his entreaties that they marry. Eventually she was convinced of his serious devotion to her and, to avoid her father's opposition, they were secretly married in September, 1846, and left almost immediately for Italy. At Pisa, physically inseparable, they lived and wrote in isolation. Their calm was disturbed by two events: the birth of a son after two miscarriages and the death of Browning's mother, which plunged the poet into deep depression.

After five years of life in Italy, the Brownings began a round of travels that ended with the death of Elizabeth. In 1851 they were back in England but found proximity to their old haunts depressing. They tried living in Paris, where Mrs. Browning acquired a passion for the monarchy and a disgust for republicanism. The attraction of Italy took them to Rome, where, at the insistence of his wife, Browning investigated the claims of spiritualism but remained skeptical. With the great success of his wife's *Aurora Leigh* and the financial failure of his own *Men and Women* in 1855, Browning decided to advance his wife's career at the expense of his own dubious future. But Elizabeth became seriously ill by 1858, and an invalid by 1860. Upon her death in 1861, he returned to England with his son to begin a new life.

Browning's popularity with the English critics and public dates from this period. By 1863, his peculiar genius was recognized. He was encouraged sufficiently by the change to begin work on the long "epic" narrative of *The Ring and the Book,* executed from 1864 to 1868. Though his creative inspiration flagged during the final twenty years of his life, he was lionized by elderly devotees. His conservatism grew as his public success mounted. In 1889, he returned to visit Asolo in Italy, with its memories of his life with Elizabeth. From there he went to Venice to visit his son, now married and a painter. There Browning became ill and died in December, 1889.

The major influence in Browning's life was his mother. From her he got the basic training in religion and morality which was to remain with him permanently, affecting all the adult relationships of his career. His intellect was acute and often at odds with his acquired opinions. But, after the early period of rebellion into atheism and vegetarianism, the poet invariably deferred to the pressure of maternal instruction. Indeed, biographers attribute the obscurity of his early autobiographical poems to the tension between intellect, on the one hand, and his mother's moral preachments, on the other. Even beyond matters of morality and religion, Browning submitted completely and gladly. He accepted the tender care of his parents far into mature life. His mother packed his bags when he traveled. The goodnight kiss was a daily ritual. His mother's pains were felt sympathetically in his own body. The result in his life was inability to maintain a relationship with a young woman except on a nonsexual basis. His meaningful involvements were with women like Elizabeth Barrett—women older than himself, who needed to be cared for in brotherly fashion. He had, in fact, offered to be in marriage with her "no more than one of your brothers." His works reflect this attitude toward marriage and man–woman relationships.

Browning's marriage to Elizabeth Barrett was undoubtedly the other significant involvement in his life. In a practical sense, and undoubtedly without his realizing the fact, it involved trading the security and love that his mother had offered for the security and love of an older, maternal woman. His parents ceased to support him, but Elizabeth's financial resources became his own. The goodnight kiss that he had tendered to his mother for thirty-three years was now given to his wife. And his need to be needed, to hover over, and to be solicitous, was satisfied by his wife's semi-invalidism. The patterns remained unchanged in other ways too. Just as his mother had made most practical decisions for Browning in his premarital days, now his wife assumed the role of decision-maker. She discovered early in the marriage that she was the stronger, and, though not necessarily through choice, became the dominant voice in the household. Browning apparently wanted it this way, but, in spite of this, the arrangement apparently depressed and frustrated him—especially when, emerging from invalidism and seclusion, Elizabeth displayed a lack of good sense in interpreting the world around her. It was too late, however, to change the pattern. The poet's only means of compensating was to live more and more a bachelor existence away from his wife as she grew physically more feeble.

One theory holds that Browning was too much a man of intellect not to have realized that he was repudiating reason in both relationships. The compartmentalization of his moral, emotional nature and his intellectual nature made frustration inevitable, no matter how thoroughly he appeared to have surrendered the latter to the former. His intermittent and neurotic repudiations of Shelley in youth and again in old age as immoral and antireligious must have caused him qualms. His dabbling in spiritualism, which his skeptical mind rejected, and his acquiescence in raising his son in effeminate softness, could not have happened without Browning's being aware of his compromise with his own intellect. This knowledge of his own duplicity accounts, some say, for his extravagant interest in depicting characters who are frauds, mediums, hypocrites, and double-dealers in many of his poems—"Mr. Sludge, 'the Medium,'" "My Last Duchess," "The Bishop Orders His Tomb," "Fra Lippo Lippi," "Soliloquy of the Spanish Cloister," and "Andrea del Sarto." In this last poem, the dominating female figure of his wife is both the joy and the frustration of the artist.

Love between man and woman—especially in the married state—became one of Browning's most persistent themes, and he tried to analyze minutely the elements of the love relationship. Apparently he believed, as did Tennyson, that the highest human relationship was compatible marriage. He had, moreover, the example of his own marriage to celebrate in verse in poems such as "At the Fireside." But, probably more often than he realized, the jarring notes of incompatibility and dissatisfaction intruded. Jealous wives and husbands and mismated couples account for much of Browning's most memorable poetry.

Browning was further concerned to define the role of the artist with respect to his God and to his fellow men. "Fra Lippo Lippi" points out, for example, that the artist has the right, even the obligation, to depict human beings as he accually finds them on this earth. There is no need to "spiritualize" the portrait or to soften the harsh features. If the artist does his work properly, God's artistry will shine through the realistic depiction. Thus, the sensual monk in the poem defends his penchant for verisimilitude not as opposed to the will of the Deity, but rather as a glorification of His work. Going further,

Browning establishes the poet as a surrogate of God on earth, observing human beings, probing their motives and actions, and rendering an account for judgment. In "How It Strikes a Contemporary," Browning puts it this way:

> He [the artist] took such cognizance of men and things,
> If any beat a horse, you felt he saw;
> If any cursed a woman, he took note;
> Yet stared at nobody—you stared at him,
> And found, less to your pleasure than surprise,
> He seemed to know you and expect as much.
> So, next time that a neighbor's tongue was loosed,
> It marked the shameful and notorious fact,
> We had among us, not so much a spy,
> As a recording chief-inquisitor,
> The town's true master if the town but knew!
> We merely kept a Governor for form,
> While this man walked about and took account
> Of all thought, said, and acted, then went home,
> And wrote it fully to our Lord the King. . . .

To succeed in this ambitious poetic enterprise, Browning needed a technique that would allow for intimate contact between the characters he was interpreting and the reader. He found this technique in the dramatic monologue. By allowing the character to verbalize his thoughts in a dramatic soliloquy or to speak them directly to another person or persons, without the seeming intervention of the author, Browning could offer maximum exposure of the mind of his protagonist. Through this "stream-of-consciousness" method, he could project the personality of the character directly, and, by a judicious choice of thoughts, allow the reader to gain insights into the character quite at variance with the impression the character is striving to present. The result is a psychological *tour de force*.

For the reader in the mid-nineteenth century, this method of dramatic monologue had the disadvantage of obscurity. There were no helpful authorial asides to guide the reader. The stage directions were suggested rather than elaborated. With the bishop in "The Bishop Orders His Tomb," for instance, the reader must follow the mystifying twists and turns of a mind in delirium as it shifts without warning from the present to the past to the future, from the imagined to the real. That his audience was able and willing in the last decades of Browning's life to make the effort necessary to appreciate the poems is a tribute to his enormous skill in creating and sustaining a characterization.

BIBLIOGRAPHY

DeVane, William Clyde. *A Browning Handbook*. New York: Appleton-Century-Crofts, 1955.

Duckworth, F. G. R. *Browning, Background and Conflict*. London: E. Benn, 1931.

Miller, Betty. *Robert Browning: A Portrait*. New York: Charles Scribner's Sons, 1952.

My Last Duchess

Ferrara

That's my last Duchess painted on the wall,
Looking as if she were alive. I call
That piece a wonder, now: Frà Pandolf's hands
Worked busily a day, and there she stands.
Will't please you sit and look at her? I said
"Frà Pandolf" by design, for never read
Strangers like you that pictured countenance,
The depth and passion of its earnest glance,
But to myself they turned (since none puts by
The curtain I have drawn for you, but I) 10
And seemed as they would ask me, if they durst,
How such a glance came there; so, not the first
Are you to turn and ask thus. Sir, 'twas not
Her husband's presence only, called that spot
Of joy into the Duchess' cheek: perhaps
Frà Pandolf chanced to say "Her mantle laps
Over my Lady's wrist too much," or "Paint
Must never hope to reproduce the faint
Half-flush that dies along her throat;" such stuff
Was courtesy, she thought, and cause enough 20
For calling up that spot of joy. She had
A heart—how shall I say?—too soon made glad,
Too easily impressed; she liked whate'er
She looked on, and her looks went everywhere.
Sir, 'twas all one! My favour at her breast,
The dropping of the daylight in the West,
The bough of cherries some officious fool
Broke in the orchard for her, the white mule
She rode with round the terrace—all and each
Would draw from her alike the approving speech, 30
Or blush, at least. She thanked men,—good! but thanked
Somehow—I know not how—as if she ranked
My gift of a nine-hundred-years-old name
With anybody's gift. Who'd stoop to blame
This sort of trifling? Even had you skill

In speech—(which I have not)—to make your will
Quite clear to such an one, and say "Just this
Or that in you disgusts me; here you miss,
Or there exceed the mark"—and if she let
Herself be lessoned so, nor plainly set 40
Her wits to yours, forsooth, and made excuse,
—E'en then would be some stooping, and I choose
Never to stoop. Oh, sir, she smiled, no doubt,
Whene'er I passed her; but who passed without
Much the same smile? This grew; I gave commands;
Then all smiles stopped together. There she stands
As if alive. Will't please you rise? We'll meet
The company below, then. I repeat,
The Count your Master's known munificence
Is ample warrant that no just pretence 50
Of mine for dowry will be disallowed;
Though his fair daughter's self, as I avowed
At starting, is my object. Nay, we'll go
Together down, sir. Notice Neptune, though,
Taming a sea-horse, thought a rarity,
Which Claus of Innsbruck cast in bronze for me.

[*1842*]

Commentary

The poem is a character study of the Duke of Ferrara in one of Browning's most famous dramatic monologues. The story is simple: the Duchess has died at an early age, and the Duke is negotiating with the emissary of another nobleman for the hand of his daughter in a new marriage. The Duke recalls the character of his former Duchess—her openness, her innocence, her childlike delight with compliments and harmless diversions, her sunny nature. But in his cruel, suspicious eyes these inoffensive qualities condemn her as an unworthy, perhaps unfaithful, wife who had to be gotten rid of. Though the Duke views himself as blameless and truly noble, while condemning his wife in every respect, the reader forms the opposite opinion, as Browning intended.

The dramatic monologue bears many of Browning's trademarks as thinker and poet. It deals with the delicate balance of psychological tensions that marks the marriage of man and woman: the jealousies and misinterpretations and individual quirks of character that can mar the ideal relationship. It deals with Renaissance Italy, the favorite time and place of Browning's poetic settings. The protagonist is once more a witting or unwitting hypocrite, seeking to present himself in a light to which his true nature is almost diametrically opposed. In the last ten lines of the poem the Duke exposes himself as a lying charlatan greedy for a dowry. It seems unnecessary to rehearse the factors in the poet's life that may have led to his interest in presenting a husband of this kind.

The poem presents few verbal difficulties. "Frà" Pandolf in line 3 indicates that the artist was a monk. In line 40, "lessoned" means "taught." "Warrant" in line 50 means "guarantee." Frà Pandolf and Claus of Innsbruck are imaginary artists.

An intensive explication of the meaning of the poem is not justified, since its content is obvious. However, it is profitable to examine the poem as a model of the dramatic monologue technique. Though the Duke is the only character with a speaking role, the reader learns something about the envoy to whom the protagonist speaks and a great deal about the last Duchess, represented only by her portrait.

The Duke indicts himself by his display of overweening vanity. He had as little consideration for his former wife as he has for the painting in which she appears. She was important to him, it becomes clear, not for herself, but because she *belonged* to him as the painting does now. In fact, having completed his monologue on the portrait, he can turn casually from it to a sculpture of Neptune whose attraction for him is that it was "cast in bronze for me." Significantly, this outburst of egocentricity is witnessed by the man who is conducting financial negotiations for the "sale" of the next Duchess to the Duke. For both wives, the idea of love is submerged beneath the Duke's self-interest in a "nine-hundred-years-old name," dowries, and the jealous retention of private property, whether human or inanimate. And when the merchandise fails to give satisfaction, the Duke has no qualms about casting aside his former asset.

Yet the "stage directions" show that, heartless though he may be, the Duke hypocritically maintains a surface of nobility, grace, and politeness. The tension between the animal brutality beneath and the civilized suavity of his manner makes the horror more pronounced. "Will 't please you sit and look at her?" may be a command, but it is couched in civil language, as is his "Will 't please you rise?" which signals the abrupt end of his revelations concerning his wife's fate. Finally, when, apparently in deference to his host's rank, the envoy stands aside to allow the Duke to precede him down the staircase, the gentlemanly wretch offers a magnanimous "Nay, we'll go / Together down, sir." By such touches as these is the monologue made theatrically dramatic with a word or gesture.

The style of the poetry is distinctively Browning's. Though the lines are actually rhyming couplets, so explosive is the language and so scattered and unexpected the pauses indicating the divisions of thought groups that the reader is ordinarily unaware that the rhyme exists. The Duke speaks bombastically and with gusto as do many of Browning's protagonists. The sentences are liberally sprinkled with asides and parenthetical expressions—"Even had you skill / In speech—(which I have not)—to make your will / Quite clear. . . ." There are homey turns of expression: "She had / A heart—how shall I say?—too soon made glad, / Too easily impressed. . . ." The intellectual context of the verse is simple, but the vagaries of sentence structure are occasionally puzzling.

Only during the last twenty years of Browning's life did his Victorian audience consider his verse worth the effort of deciphering. In 1881 Browning Societies were formed throughout England for the purpose of reading his poetry and explicating the puzzling stanzas. But in these last decades his poetry became ever more comprehensible as, perhaps, maturity and acclaim made less essential the need to cloak himself from the public gaze in obscure allusions.

The Bishop Orders His Tomb at Saint Praxed's Church

[ROME, 15—]

Vanity, saith the preacher, vanity!
Draw round my bed: is Anselm keeping back?
Nephews—sons mine . . . ah God, I know not! Well—
She, men would have to be your mother once,
Old Gandolf envied me, so fair she was!
What's done is done, and she is dead beside,
Dead long ago, and I am Bishop since,
And as she died so must we die ourselves,
And thence ye may perceive the world's a dream.
Life, how and what is it? As here I lie 10
In this state-chamber, dying by degrees,
Hours and long hours in the dead night, I ask
"Do I live, am I dead?" Peace, peace seems all.
Saint Praxed's ever was the church for peace;
And so, about this tomb of mine. I fought
With tooth and nail to save my niche, ye know:
—Old Gandolf cozened me, despite my care;
Shrewd was that snatch from out the corner South
He graced his carrion with, God curse the same!
Yet still my niche is not so cramped but thence 20
One sees the pulpit o' the epistle-side,
And somewhat of the choir, those silent seats,
And up into the aery dome where live
The angels, and a sunbeam's sure to lurk:
And I shall fill my slab of basalt there,
And 'neath my tabernacle take my rest,
With those nine columns round me, two and two,
The odd one at my feet where Anselm stands:
Peach-blossom marble all, the rare, the ripe
As fresh-poured red wine of a mighty pulse. 30

l. 1. *vanity:* the text is from *Ecclesiastes.*
l. 17. *cozened:* cheated.
l. 21. *epistle-side:* to the right of the altar.

—Old Gandolf with his paltry onion-stone,
Put me where I may look at him! True peach,
Rosy and flawless: how I earned the prize!
Draw close: that conflagration of my church
—What then? So much was saved if aught were missed!
My sons, ye would not be my death? Go dig
The white-grape vineyard where the oil-press stood,
Drop water gently till the surface sinks,
And if ye find . . . Ah, God I know not, I! . . .
Bedded in store of rotten figleaves soft, 40
And corded up in a tight olive-frail,
Some lump, ah God, of *lapis lazuli,*
Big as a Jew's head cut off at the nape,
Blue as a vein o'er the Madonna's breast . . .
Sons, all have I bequeathed you, villas, all,
That brave Frascati villa with its bath,
So, let the blue lump poise between my knees,
Like God the Father's globe on both His hands
Ye worship in the Jesu Church so gay,
For Gandolf shall not choose but see and burst! 50
Swift as a weaver's shuttle fleet our years:
Man goeth to the grave, and where is he?
Did I say basalt for my slab, sons? Black—
'Twas ever antique-black I meant! How else
Shall ye contrast my frieze to come beneath?
The bas-relief in bronze ye promised me,
Those Pans and Nymphs ye wot of, and perchance
Some tripod, thyrsus, with a vase or so,
The Saviour at his sermon on the mount,
Saint Praxed in a glory, and one Pan 60
Ready to twitch the Nymph's last garment off,
And Moses with the tables . . . but I know
Ye mark me not! What do they whisper thee,
Child of my bowels, Anselm? Ah, ye hope
To revel down my villas while I gasp
Bricked o'er with beggar's mouldy travertine
Which Gandolf from his tomb-top chuckles at!
Nay, boys, ye love me—all of jasper, then!

l. 41. *olive-frail:* a basket to hold olives.
l. 58. *tripod, thyrsus:* the former is a stool, the latter a pagan staff.

'Tis jasper ye stand pledged to, lest I grieve.
My bath must needs be left behind, alas! 70
One block, pure green as a pistachio-nut,
There's plenty jasper somewhere in the world—
And have I not Saint Praxed's ear to pray
Horses for ye, and brown Greek manuscripts,
And mistresses with great smooth marbly limbs?
—That's if ye carve my epitaph aright,
Choice Latin, picked phrase, Tully's every word,
No gaudy ware like Gandolf's second line—
Tully, my masters? Ulpian serves his need!
And then how I shall lie through centuries, 80
And hear the blessed mutter of the mass,
And see God made and eaten all day long,
And feel the steady candle-flame, and taste
Good strong thick stupefying incense-smoke!
For as I lie here, hours of the dead night,
Dying in state and by such slow degrees,
I fold my arms as if they clasped a crook,
And stretch my feet forth straight as stone can point,
And let the bedclothes for a mortcloth drop
Into great laps and folds of sculptor's-work: 90
And as yon tapers dwindle, and strange thoughts
Grow, with a certain humming in my ears,
About the life before I lived this life,
And this life too, Popes, Cardinals and Priests,
Saint Praxed at his sermon on the mount,
Your tall pale mother with her talking eyes,
And new-found agate urns as fresh as day,
And marble's language, Latin pure, discreet,
—Aha, *elucescebat* quoth our friend?
No Tully, said I, Ulpian at the best! 100
Evil and brief hath been my pilgrimage.
All *lapis*, all, sons! Else I give the Pope
My villas: will ye ever eat my heart?

l. 79. *Ulpian:* a late Latin writer whose style was decadent.
l. 82. *God made and eaten*: refers to the Eucharist; communion with the body and blood of Christ.
l. 89. *mortcloth:* a kind of shroud.
l. 95. *Saint Praxed . . . mount:* the bishop's mind is wandering.
l. 99. *elucescebat:* he was famous.

Ever your eyes were as a lizard's quick,
They glitter like your mother's for my soul,
Or ye would heighten my impoverished frieze,
Piece out its starved design, and fill my vase
With grapes, and add a vizor and a Term,
And to the tripod ye would tie a lynx
That in his struggle throws the thyrsus down, 110
To comfort me on my entablature
Whereon I am to lie till I must ask
"Do I live, am I dead?" There, leave me, there!
For ye have stabbed me with ingratitude
To death—ye wish it—God, ye wish it! Stone—
Gritstone, a-crumble! Clammy squares which sweat
As if the corpse they keep were oozing through—
And no more *lapis* to delight the world!
Well, go! I bless ye. Fewer tapers there,
But in a row: and, going, turn your backs 120
—Ay, like departing altar-ministrants,
And leave me in my church, the church for peace,
That I may watch at leisure if he leers—
Old Gandolf, at me, from his onion-stone,
As still he envied me, so fair she was!

[*1845?*]

l. 108. *vizor and a Term:* a face-covering and a sculpted bust.

Home-Thoughts, from Abroad

I

Oh, to be in England
Now that April's there,
And whoever wakes in England
Sees, some morning, unaware,
That the lowest boughs and the brushwood sheaf
Round the elm-tree bole are in tiny leaf,
While the chaffinch sings on the orchard bough
In England—now!

II

And after April, when May follows,
And the whitethroat builds, and all the swallows! 10

Hark, where my blossomed pear-tree in the hedge
Leans to the field and scatters on the clover
Blossoms and dewdrops—at the bent spray's edge—
That's the wise thrush; he sings each song twice over,
Lest you should think he never could recapture
The first fine careless rapture!
And though the fields look rough with hoary dew,
All will be gay when noontide wakes anew
The buttercups, the little children's dower
—Far brighter than this gaudy melon-flower! 20

[*1845*]

Andrea Del Sarto

(CALLED "The Faultless Painter")

But do not let us quarrel any more,
No, my Lucrezia; bear with me for once:
Sit down and all shall happen as you wish.
You turn your face, but does it bring your heart?
I'll work then for your friend's friend, never fear,
Treat his own subject after his own way,
Fix his own time, accept too his own price,
And shut the money into this small hand
When next it takes mine. Will it? tenderly?
Oh, I'll content him,—but to-morrow, Love! 10
I often am much wearier than you think,
This evening more than usual, and it seems
As if—forgive now—should you let me sit
Here by the window with your hand in mine
And look a half hour forth on Fiesole,
Both of one mind, as married people use,
Quietly, quietly, the evening through,
I might get up to-morrow to my work
Cheerful and fresh as ever. Let us try.
To-morrow how you shall be glad for this! 20

Andrea del Sarto: sixteenth-century painter of technical excellence whose unfortunate choice of wife spoiled his career and led him into difficulties.

l. 5. *friend's friend:* a friend of Lucrezia's lover.

Your soft hand is a woman of itself,
And mine the man's bared breast she curls inside.
Don't count the time lost, either; you must serve
For each of the five pictures we require—
It saves a model. So! keep looking so—
My serpentining beauty, rounds on rounds!
—How could you ever prick those perfect ears,
Even to put the pearl there! oh, so sweet—
My face, my moon, my everybody's moon,
Which everybody looks on and calls his, 30
And, I suppose, is looked on by in turn,
While she looks—no one's: very dear, no less!
You smile? why, there's my picture ready made,
There's what we painters call our harmony!
A common greyness silvers everything,—
All in a twilight, you and I alike
—You, at the point of your first pride in me
(That's gone you know),—but I, at every point;
My youth, my hope, my art, being all toned down
To yonder sober pleasant Fiesole. 40
There's the bell clinking from the chapel-top;
That length of convent-wall across the way
Holds the trees safer, huddled more inside;
The last monk leaves the garden; days decrease
And autumn grows, autumn in everything.
Eh? the whole seems to fall into a shape
As if I saw alike my work and self
And all that I was born to be and do,
A twilight-piece. Love, we are in God's hand.
How strange now looks the life He makes us lead! 50
So free we seem, so fettered fast we are!
I feel He laid the fetter: let it lie!
This chamber for example—turn your head—
All that's behind us! you don't understand
Nor care to understand about my art,
But you can hear at least when people speak;
And that cartoon, the second from the door
—It is the thing, Love! so such things should be—
Behold Madonna! I am bold to say.

l. 57. *cartoon:* rough sketch.

I can do with my pencil what I know, 60
What I see, what at bottom of my heart
I wish for, if I ever wish so deep—
Do easily, too—when I say perfectly
I do not boast, perhaps: yourself are judge
Who listened to the Legate's talk last week,
And just as much they used to say in France.
At any rate 'tis easy, all of it,
No sketches first, no studies, that's long past—
I do what many dream of all their lives
—Dream? strive to do, and agonise to do, 70
And fail in doing. I could count twenty such
On twice your fingers, and not leave this town,
Who strive—you don't know how the others strive
To paint a little thing like that you smeared
Carelessly passing with your robes afloat,—
Yet do much less, so much less, Someone says,
(I know his name, no matter)—so much less!
Well, less is more, Lucrezia! I am judged.
There burns a truer light of God in them,
In their vexed, beating, stuffed and stopped-up brain, 80
Heart, or whate'er else, than goes on to prompt
This low-pulsed forthright craftsman's hand of mine.
Their works drop groundward, but themselves, I know,
Reach many a time a heaven that's shut to me,
Enter and take their place there sure enough,
Though they come back and cannot tell the world.
My works are nearer heaven, but I sit here.
The sudden blood of these men! at a word—
Praise them, it boils, or blame them, it boils too.
I, painting from myself and to myself, 90
Know what I do, am unmoved by men's blame
Or their praise either. Somebody remarks
Morello's outline there is wrongly traced,
His hue mistaken—what of that? or else,
Rightly traced and well ordered—what of that?
Speak as they please, what does the mountain care?
Ah, but a man's reach should exceed his grasp,

l. 76. *Someone*: Michelangelo.
l. 93. *Morello:* an Italian mountain.

Or what's a Heaven for? all is silver-grey
Placid and perfect with my art—the worse!
I know both what I want and what might gain— 100
And yet how profitless to know, to sigh
"Had I been two, another and myself,
Our head would have o'erlooked the world!" No doubt.
Yonder's a work, now, of that famous youth
The Urbinate who died five years ago.
('Tis copied, George Vasari sent it me.)
Well, I can fancy how he did it all,
Pouring his soul, with kings and popes to see,
Reaching, that Heaven might so replenish him,
Above and through his art—for it gives way; 110
That arm is wrongly put—and there again—
A fault to pardon in the drawing's lines,
Its body, so to speak: its soul is right,
He means right—that, a child may understand.
Still, what an arm! and I could alter it.
But all the play, the insight and the stretch—
Out of me! out of me! And wherefore out?
Had you enjoined them on me, given me soul,
We might have risen to Rafael, I and you.
Nay, Love, you did give all I asked, I think— 120
More than I merit, yes, by many times.
But had you—oh, with the same perfect brow,
And perfect eyes, and more than perfect mouth,
And the low voice my soul hears, as a bird
The fowler's pipe, and follows to the snare—
Had you, with these the same, but brought a mind!
Some women do so. Had the mouth there urged
"God and the glory! never care for gain.
The Present by the Future, what is that?
Live for fame, side by side with Angelo— 130
Rafael is waiting. Up to God all three!"
I might have done it for you. So it seems—
Perhaps not. All is as God over-rules.
Beside, incentives come from the soul's self;

l. 105. *The Urbinate:* Raphael.
l. 106. *George Vasari:* biographer of del Sarto in *Lives of the Painters,* the work which is the basis of Browning's facts in the poem.

The rest avail not. Why do I need you?
What wife had Rafael, or has Angelo?
In this world, who can do a thing, will not—
And who would do it, cannot, I perceive:
Yet the will's somewhat—somewhat, too, the power—
And thus we half-men struggle. At the end, 140
God, I conclude, compensates, punishes.
'Tis safer for me, if the award be strict,
That I am something underrated here,
Poor this long while, despised, to speak the truth.
I dared not, do you know, leave home all day,
For fear of chancing on the Paris lords.
The best is when they pass and look aside;
But they speak sometimes; I must bear it all.
Well may they speak! That Francis, that first time,
And that long festal year at Fontainebleau! 150
I surely then could sometimes leave the ground,
Put on the glory, Rafael's daily wear,
In that humane great monarch's golden look,—
One finger in his beard or twisted curl
Over his mouth's good mark that made the smile,
One arm about my shoulder, round my neck,
The jingle of his gold chain in my ear,
I painting proudly with his breath on me,
All his court round him, seeing with his eyes,
Such frank French eyes, and such a fire of souls 160
Profuse, my hand kept plying by those hearts,—
And, best of all, this, this, this face beyond,
This in the background, waiting on my work,
To crown the issue with a last reward!
A good time, was it not, my kingly days?
And had you not grown restless—but I know—
'Tis done and past; 'twas right, my instinct said;
Too live the life grew, golden and not grey,
And I'm the weak-eyed bat no sun should tempt
Out of the grange whose four walls make his world. 170
How could it end in any other way?
You called me, and I came home to your heart.
The triumph was, to have ended there; then if
I reached it ere the triumph, what is lost?
Let my hands frame your face in your hair's gold,

You beautiful Lucrezia that are mine!
"Rafael did this, Andrea painted that—
The Roman's is the better when you pray,
But still the other's Virgin was his wife—"
Men will excuse me. I am glad to judge 180
Both pictures in your presence; clearer grows
My better fortune, I resolve to think.
For, do you know, Lucrezia, as God lives,
Said one day Angelo, his very self,
To Rafael . . . I have known it all these years . . .
(When the young man was flaming out his thoughts
Upon a palace-wall for Rome to see,
Too lifted up in heart because of it)
"Friend, there's a certain sorry little scrub
Goes up and down our Florence, none cares how, 190
Who, were he set to plan and execute
As you are, pricked on by your popes and kings,
Would bring the sweat into that brow of yours!"
To Rafael's!—And indeed the arm is wrong.
I hardly dare—yet, only you to see,
Give the chalk here—quick, thus the line should go!
Ay, but the soul! he's Rafael! rub it out!
Still, all I care for, if he spoke the truth,
(What he? why, who but Michael Angelo?
Do you forget already words like those?) 200
If really there was such a chance, so lost,—
Is, whether you're—not grateful—but more pleased.
Well, let me think so. And you smile indeed!
This hour has been an hour! Another smile?
If you would sit thus by me every night
I should work better, do you comprehend?
I mean that I should earn more, give you more.
See, it is settled dusk now; there's a star;
Morello's gone, the watch-lights show the wall,
The cue-owls speak the name we call them by. 210
Come from the window, Love,—come in, at last,
Inside the melancholy little house
We built to be so gay with. God is just.
King Francis may forgive me. Oft at nights
When I look up from painting, eyes tired out,
The walls become illumined, brick from brick

Distinct, instead of mortar, fierce bright gold,
That gold of his I did cement them with!
Let us but love each other. Must you go?
That Cousin here again? he waits outside? 220
Must see you—you, and not with me? Those loans?
More gaming debts to pay? you smiled for that?
Well, let smiles buy me! have you more to spend?
While hand and eye and something of a heart
Are left me, work's my ware, and what's it worth?
I'll pay my fancy. Only let me sit
The grey remainder of the evening out,
Idle, you call it, and muse perfectly
How I could paint, were I but back in France,
One picture, just one more—the Virgin's face, 230
Not your's this time! I want you at my side
To hear them—that is, Michael Angelo—
Judge all I do and tell you of its worth.
Will you? To-morrow, satisfy your friend.
I take the subjects for his corridor,
Finish the portrait out of hand—there, there,
And throw him in another thing or two
If he demurs; the whole should prove enough
To pay for this same Cousin's freak. Beside,
What's better and what's all I care about, 240
Get you the thirteen scudi for the ruff.
Love, does that please you? Ah, but what does he,
The Cousin! what does he to please you more?
 I am grown peaceful as old age to-night.
I regret little, I would change still less.
Since there my past life lies, why alter it?
The very wrong to Francis!—it is true
I took his coin, was tempted and complied,
And built this house and sinned, and all is said.
My father and my mother died of want. 250
Well, had I riches of my own? you see
How one gets rich! Let each one bear his lot.
They were born poor, lived poor, and poor they died:
And I have laboured somewhat in my time

l. 241. *Get you . . . ruff:* use some of the money we earn by selling paintings to your lover to buy a ruff for yourself.

And not been paid profusely. Some good son
Paint my two hundred pictures—let him try!
No doubt, there's something strikes a balance. Yes,
You loved me quite enough, it seems to-night.
This must suffice me here. What would one have?
In Heaven, perhaps, new chances, one more chance— 260
Four great walls in the New Jerusalem
Meted on each side by the angel's reed,
For Leonard, Rafael, Angelo and me
To cover—the three first without a wife,
While I have mine! So—still they overcome
Because there's still Lucrezia,—as I choose.

Again the Cousin's whistle! Go, my Love.

[*1853*]

l. 262. *Meted . . . reed:* measured by the angel's measuring stick.

Prospice

Fear death?—to feel the fog in my throat,
  The mist in my face,
When the snows begin, and the blasts denote
  I am nearing the place,
The power of the night, the press of the storm,
  The post of the foe;
Where he stands, the Arch Fear in a visible form,
  Yet the strong man must go:
For the journey is done and the summit attained,
  And the barriers fall, 10
Though a battle's to fight ere the guerdon be gained,
  The reward of it all.
I was ever a fighter, so—one fight more,
  The best and the last!
I would hate that death bandaged my eyes, and forbore,
  And bade me creep past.
No! let me taste the whole of it, fare like my peers
  The heroes of old,
Bear the brunt, in a minute pay glad life's arrears

l. 11. *guerdon:* reward.

Of pain, darkness and cold. 20
For sudden the worst turns the best to the brave,
The black minute's at end,
And the element's rage, the fiend-voices that rave,
Shall dwindle, shall blend,
Shall change, shall become first a peace, out of pain,
Then a light, then thy breast,
O thou soul of my soul! I shall clasp thee again,
And with God be the rest!

[*1861?*]

Soliloquy of the Spanish Cloister

I

Gr-r-r—there go, my heart's abhorrence!
Water your damned flower-pots, do!
If hate killed men, Brother Lawrence,
God's blood, would not mine kill you!
What? your myrtle-bush wants trimming?
Oh, that rose has prior claims—
Needs its leaden vase filled brimming?
Hell dry you up with its flames!

II

At the meal we sit together:
Salve tibi! I must hear 10
Wise talk of the kind of weather,
Sort of season, time of year:
Not a plenteous cork-crop: scarcely
Dare we hope oak-galls, I doubt:
What's the Latin name for "parsley"?
What's the Greek name for Swine's Snout?

III

Whew! We'll have our platter burnished,
Laid with care on our own shelf!

l. 10. *Salve tibi:* Greetings to you.

With a fire-new spoon we're furnished,
And a goblet for ourself, 20
Rinsed like something sacrificial
Ere 'tis fit to touch our chaps—
Marked with L. for our initial!
(He-he! There his lily snaps!)

IV

Saint, forsooth! While brown Dolores
Squats outside the Convent bank,
With Sanchicha, telling stories,
Steeping tresses in the tank,
Blue-black, lustrous, thick like horse-hairs,
—Can't I see his dead eye glow, 30
Bright as 'twere a Barbary corsair's?
(That is, if he'd let it show!)

V

When he finishes refection,
Knife and fork he never lays
Cross-wise, to my recollection,
As do I, in Jesu's praise.
I, the Trinity illustrate,
Drinking watered orange-pulp—
In three sips the Arian frustrate;
While he drains his at one gulp! 40

VI

Oh, those melons! If he's able
We're to have a feast; so nice!
One goes to the Abbot's table,
All of us get each a slice.
How go on your flowers? None double?
Not one fruit-sort can you spy?
Strange!—And I, too, at such trouble,
Keep them close-nipped on the sly!

l. 39. *Arian:* followers of Arius, a heretic who insisted that Christ and God were not equal, and denied the Trinity.

VII

There's a great text in Galatians,
Once you trip on it, entails 50
Twenty-nine distinct damnations,
One sure, if another fails:
If I trip him just a-dying,
Sure of Heaven as sure as can be,
Spin him round and send him flying
Off to Hell, a Manichee?

VIII

Or, my scrofulous French novel
On grey paper with blunt type!
Simply glance at it, you grovel
Hand and foot in Belial's gripe: 60
If I double down its pages
At the woeful sixteenth print,
When he gathers his greengages,
Ope a sieve and slip it in't?

IX

Or, there's Satan!—one might venture
Pledge one's soul to him, yet leave
Such a flaw in the indenture
As he'd miss till, past retrieve,
Blasted lay that rose-acacia
We're so proud of! *Hy, Zy, Hine* . . . 70
'St, there's Vespers! *Plena gratiâ*
Ave, Virgo! Gr-r-r—you swine!

[*1842*]

l. 49. *Galatians:* New Testament book which sets forth a large number of sins to avoid committing.
l. 56. *Manichee:* a heretic who believes that the world is a stage for the contending forces of evil and good.
l. 60. *Belial:* one of the devils in Hell.
l. 70. *Hy, Zy, Hine:* mysterious words in the poem, perhaps meant to cast an evil spell, perhaps merely the verbal equivalent (Ein, Zwei, Drei) of the sound of the chapel bell tolling.
ll. 71–72. *Plena gratiâ Ave, Virgo:* Hail, Virgin, full of grace.

Fra Lippo Lippi

I am poor brother Lippo, by your leave!
You need not clap your torches to my face.
Zooks, what's to blame? you think you see a monk!
What, it's past midnight, and you go the rounds,
And here you catch me at an alley's end
Where sportive ladies leave their doors ajar?
The Carmine's my cloister: hunt it up,
Do,—harry out, if you must show your zeal,
Whatever rat, there, haps on his wrong hole,
And nip each softling of a wee white mouse, 10
Weke, weke, that's crept to keep him company!
Aha, you know your betters? Then, you'll take
Your hand away that's fiddling on my throat,
And please to know me likewise. Who am I?
Why, one, sir, who is lodging with a friend
Three streets off—he's a certain . . . how d'ye call?
Master—a . . . Cosimo of the Medici,
In the house that caps the corner. Boh! you were best!
Remember and tell me, the day you're hanged,
How you affected such a gullet's-gripe! 20
But you, sir, it concerns you that your knaves
Pick up a manner nor discredit you.
Zooks, are we pilchards, that they sweep the streets
And count fair prize what comes into their net?
He's Judas to a tittle, that man is!
Just such a face! why, sir, you make amends.
Lord, I'm not angry! Bid your hangdogs go
Drink out this quarter-florin to the health
Of the munificent House that harbours me
(And many more beside, lads! more beside!) 30
And all's come square again. I'd like his face—
His, elbowing on his comrade in the door
With the pike and lantern,—for the slave that holds
John Baptist's head a-dangle by the hair
With one hand ("look you, now," as who should say)

Fra Lippo Lippi: born in 1412, he was placed as a child in a monastery, but left it later to become a painter.
l. 23. *pilchards:* small fish.

And his weapon in the other, yet unwiped!
It's not your chance to have a bit of chalk,
A wood-coal or the like? or you should see!
Yes, I'm the painter, since you style me so.
What, brother Lippo's doings, up and down, 40
You know them and they take you? like enough!
I saw the proper twinkle in your eye—
'Tell you, I liked your looks at very first.
Let's sit and set things straight now, hip to haunch.
Here's spring come, and the nights one makes up bands
To roam the town and sing out carnival,
And I've been three weeks shut within my mew,
A-painting for the great man, saints and saints
And saints again. I could not paint all night—
Ouf! I leaned out of window for fresh air. 50
There came a hurry of feet and little feet,
A sweep of lute-strings, laughs, and whifts of song,—
Flower o' the broom,
Take away love, and our earth is a tomb!
Flower o' the quince,
I let Lisa go, and what good's in life since?
Flower o' the thyme—and so on. Round they went.
Scarce had they turned the corner when a titter
Like the skipping of rabbits by moonlight,—three slim shapes—
And a face that looked up . . . zooks, sir, flesh and blood, 60
That's all I'm made of! Into shreds it went,
Curtain and counterpane and coverlet,
All the bed-furniture—a dozen knots,
There was a ladder! down I let myself,
Hands and feet, scrambling somehow, and so dropped,
And after them. I came up with the fun
Hard by Saint Laurence, hail fellow, well met,—
Flower o' the rose,
If I've been merry, what matter who knows? 70
And so as I was stealing back again
To get to bed and have a bit of sleep
Ere I rise up to-morrow and go work
On Jerome knocking at his poor old breast

l. 41. *take:* interest.
l. 67. *Saint Laurence:* the Church of San Lorenzo.
l. 74. *Jerome:* Saint Jerome.

With his great round stone to subdue the flesh,
You snap me of the sudden. Ah, I see!
Though your eye twinkles still, you shake your head—
Mine's shaved,—a monk, you say—the sting's in that!
If Master Cosimo announced himself,
Mum's the word naturally; but a monk! 80
Come, what am I a beast for? tell us, now!
I was a baby when my mother died
And father died and left me in the street.
I starved there, God knows how, a year or two
On fig skins, melon-parings, rinds and shucks,
Refuse and rubbish. One fine frosty day
My stomach being empty as your hat,
The wind doubled me up and down I went.
Old Aunt Lapaccia trussed me with one hand,
(Its fellow was a stinger as I knew) 90
And so along the wall, over the bridge,
By the straight cut to the convent. Six words, there,
While I stood munching my first bread that month:
"So, boy, you're minded," quoth the good fat father
Wiping his own mouth, 'twas refection-time,—
"To quit this very miserable world?
"Will you renounce" . . . "the mouthful of bread?" thought I;
By no means! Brief, they made a monk of me;
I did renounce the world, its pride and greed,
Palace, farm, villa, shop and banking-house, 100
Trash, such as these poor devils of Medici
Have given their hearts to—all at eight years old.
Well, sir, I found in time, you may be sure,
'Twas not for nothing—the good bellyful,
The warm serge and the rope that goes all round,
And day-long blessed idleness beside!
"Let's see what the urchin's fit for"—that came next.
Not overmuch their way, I must confess.
Such a to-do! they tried me with their books.
Lord, they'd have taught me Latin in pure waste! 110
Flower o' the clove,
All the Latin I construe is "amo," I love!
But, mind you, when a boy starves in the streets
Eight years together, as my fortune was,
Watching folk's faces to know who will fling

The bit of half-stripped grape-bunch he desires,
And who will curse or kick him for his pains—
Which gentleman processional and fine,
Holding a candle to the Sacrament
Will wink and let him lift a plate and catch 120
The droppings of the wax to sell again,
Or holla for the Eight and have him whipped,—
How say I?—nay, which dog bites, which lets drop
His bone from the heap of offal in the street,—
Why, soul and sense of him grow sharp alike,
He learns the look of things, and none the less
For admonition from the hunger-pinch.
I had a store of such remarks, be sure,
Which, after I found leisure, turned to use:
I drew men's faces on my copy-books, 130
Scrawled them within the antiphonary's marge,
Joined legs and arms to the long music-notes,
Found nose and eyes and chin for As and Bs,
And made a string of pictures of the world
Betwixt the ins and outs of verb and noun,
On the wall, the bench, the door. The monks looked black.
"Nay," quoth the Prior, "turn him out, d'ye say?
In no wise. Lose a crow and catch a lark.
What if at last we get our man of parts,
We Carmelites, like those Camaldolese 140
And Preaching Friars, to do our church up fine
And put the front on it that ought to be!"
And hereupon they bade me daub away.
Thank you! my head being crammed, their walls a blank,
Never was such prompt disemburdening.
First, every sort of monk, the black and white,
I drew them, fat and lean: then, folks at church,
From good old gossips waiting to confess
Their cribs of barrel-droppings, candle-ends,—
To the breathless fellow at the altar-foot, 150
Fresh from his murder, safe and sitting there
With the little children round him in a row
Of admiration, half for his beard and half

l. 122. *the Eight:* the judges of Florence.
l. 131. *antiphonary's marge:* choir book's margin.

For that white anger of his victim's son
Shaking a fist at him with one fierce arm,
Signing himself with the other because of Christ
(Whose sad face on the cross sees only this
After the passion of a thousand years)
Till some poor girl, her apron o'er her head
Which the intense eyes looked through, came at eve   160
On tip-toe, said a word, dropped in a loaf,
Her pair of earrings and a bunch of flowers
The brute took growling, prayed, and then was gone.
I painted all, then cried " 'tis ask and have—
Choose, for more's ready!"—laid the ladder flat,
And showed my covered bit of cloister-wall.
The monks closed in a circle and praised loud
Till checked,—taught what to see and not to see,
Being simple bodies,—"that's the very man!
Look at the boy who stoops to pat the dog!   170
That woman's like the Prior's niece who comes
To care about his asthma: it's the life!"
But there my triumph's straw-fire flared and funked—
Their betters took their turn to see and say:
The Prior and the learned pulled a face
And stopped all that in no time. "How? what's here?
Quite from the mark of painting, bless us all!
Faces, arms, legs and bodies like the true
As much as pea and pea! it's devil's-game!
Your business is not to catch men with show,   180
With homage to the perishable clay,
But lift them over it, ignore it all,
Make them forget there's such a thing as flesh.
Your business is to paint the souls of men—
Man's soul, and it's a fire, smoke . . . no it's not . . .
It's vapour done up like a new-born babe—
(In that shape when you die it leaves your mouth)
It's . . . well, what matters talking, it's the soul!
Give us no more of body than shows soul!
Here's Giotto, with his Saint a-praising God,   190
That sets you praising,—why not stop with him?
Why put all thoughts of praise out of our heads
With wonder at lines, colours, and what not?
Paint the soul, never mind the legs and arms!

Rub all out, try at it a second time.
Oh, that white smallish female with the breasts,
She's just my niece . . . Herodias, I would say,—
Who went and danced and got men's heads cut off—
Have it all out!" Now, is this sense, I ask?
A fine way to paint soul, by painting body 200
So ill, the eye can't stop there, must go further
And can't fare worse! Thus, yellow does for white
When what you put for yellow's simply black,
And any sort of meaning looks intense
When all beside itself means and looks nought.
Why can't a painter lift each foot in turn,
Left foot and right foot, go a double step,
Make his flesh liker and his soul more like.
Both in their order? Take the prettiest face,
The Prior's niece . . . patron-saint—is it so pretty 210
You can't discover if it means hope, fear,
Sorrow or joy? won't beauty go with these?
Suppose I've made her eyes all right and blue,
Can't I take breath and try to add life's flash,
And then add soul and heighten them threefold?
Or say there's beauty with no soul at all—
(I never saw it—put the case the same—)
If you get simple beauty and nought else,
You get about the best thing God invents,—
That's somewhat. And you'll find the soul you have missed, 220
Within yourself when you return Him thanks.
"Rub all out!" Well, well, there's my life in short.
And so the thing has gone on ever since.
I'm grown a man no doubt, I've broken bounds—
You should not take a fellow eight years old
And make him swear to never kiss the girls.
I'm my own master, paint now as I please—
Having a friend, you see, in the Corner-house!
Lord, it's fast holding by the rings in front—
Those great rings serve more purposes than just 230
To plant a flag in, or tie up a horse!
And yet the old schooling sticks, the old grave eyes

l. 197. *Herodias*: the poet is being ironic, since in the Bible her uncle, Herod, married Herodias. It was Herodias' daughter, Salome, who "went and danced and got men's [Saint John the Baptist's] heads cut off."

Are peeping o'er my shoulder as I work,
The heads shake still—"It's Art's decline, my son!
You're not of the true painters, great and old;
Brother Angelico's the man, you'll find;
Brother Lorenzo stands his single peer:
Fag on at flesh, you'll never make the third!"
Flower o' the pine,
You keep your mistr . . . manners, and I'll stick to mine! 240
I'm not the third, then: bless us, they must know!
Don't you think they're the likeliest to know,
They with their Latin? so, I swallow my rage,
Clench my teeth, suck my lips in tight, and paint
To please them—sometimes do, and sometimes don't,
For, doing most, there's pretty sure to come
A turn, some warm eve finds me at my saints—
A laugh, a cry, the business of the world—
(*Flower o' the peach,*
Death for us all, and his own life for each!) 250
And my whole soul revolves, the cup runs over,
The world and life's too big to pass for a dream,
And I do these wild things in sheer despite,
And play the fooleries you catch me at,
In pure rage! the old mill-horse, out at grass
After hard years, throws up his stiff heels so,
Although the miller does not preach to him
The only good of grass is to make chaff.
What would men have? Do they like grass or no—
May they or mayn't they? all I want's the thing 260
Settled for ever one way: as it is,
You tell too many lies and hurt yourself.
You don't like what you only like too much,
You do like what, if given you at your word,
You find abundantly detestable.
For me, I think I speak as I was taught—
I always see the Garden and God there
A-making man's wife—and, my lesson learned,
The value and significance of flesh,
I can't unlearn ten minutes afterwards. 270

You understand me: I'm a beast, I know.
But see, now—why, I see as certainly

As that the morning-star's about to shine,
What will hap some day. We've a youngster here
Comes to our convent, studies what I do,
Slouches and stares and lets no atom drop—
His name is Guidi—he'll not mind the monks—
They call him Hulking Tom, he let's them talk—
He picks my practice up—he'll paint apace,
I hope so—though I never live so long, 280
I know what's sure to follow. You be judge!
You speak no Latin more than I, belike—
However, you're my man, you've seen the world
—The beauty and the wonder and the power,
The shapes of things, their colours, lights and shades,
Changes, surprises,—and God made it all!
—For what? do you feel thankful, ay or no,
For this fair town's face, yonder river's line,
The mountain round it and the sky above,
Much more the figures of man, woman, child, 290
These are the frame to? What's it all about?
To be passed over, despised? or dwelt upon,
Wondered at? oh, this last of course!—you say.
But why not do as well as say,—paint these
Just as they are, careless what comes of it?
God's works—paint anyone, and count it crime
To let a truth slip. Don't object, "His works
Are here already—nature is complete:
Suppose you reproduce her—(which you can't)
There's no advantage! you must beat her, then." 300
For, don't you mark, we're made so that we love
First when we see them painted, things we have passed
Perhaps a hundred times nor cared to see;
And so they are better, painted—better to us,
Which is the same thing. Art was given for that—
God uses us to help each other so,
Lending our minds out. Have you noticed, now,
Your cullion's hanging face? A bit of chalk,
And trust me but you should, though! How much more,
If I drew higher things with the same truth! 310
That were to take the Prior's pulpit-place,

l. 278. *Tom:* the painter Masaccio.

Interpret God to all of you! oh, oh,
It makes me mad to see what men shall do
And we in our graves! This world's no blot for us,
Nor blank—it means intensely, and means good:
To find its meaning is my meat and drink.
"Ay, but you don't so instigate to prayer!"
Strikes in the Prior: "when your meaning's plain
It does not say to folks—remember matins,
Or, mind you fast next Friday." Why, for this 320
What need of art at all? A skull and bones,
Two bits of stick nailed cross-wise, or, what's best,
A bell to chime the hour with, does as well.
I painted a Saint Laurence six months since
At Prato, splashed the fresco in fine style:
"How looks my painting, now the scaffold's down?"
I ask a brother: "Hugely," he returns—
"Already not one phiz of your three slaves
That turn the Deacon off his toasted side,
But's scratched and prodded to our heart's content, 330
The pious people have so eased their own
When coming to say prayers there in a rage:
We get on fast to see the bricks beneath.
Expect another job this time next year,
For pity and religion grow i' the crowd—
Your painting serves its purpose!" Hang the fools!

—That is—you'll not mistake an idle word
Spoke in a huff by a poor monk, God wot,
Tasting the air this spicy night which turns
The unaccustomed head like Chianti wine! 340
Oh, the church knows! don't misreport me, now!
It's natural a poor monk out of bounds
Should have his apt word to excuse himself:
And hearken how I plot to make amends.
I have bethought me: I shall paint a piece
. . . There's for you! Give me six months, then go, see
Something in Sant' Ambrogio's! Bless the nuns!
They want a cast of my office. I shall paint
God in the midst, Madonna and her babe,

l. 328. *phiz:* visage.

Ringed by a bowery, flowery angel-brood, 350
Lilies and vestments and white faces, sweet
As puff on puff of grated orris-root
When ladies crowd to church at mid-summer.
And then in the front, of course a saint or two—
Saint John, because he saves the Florentines,
Saint Ambrose, who puts down in black and white
The convent's friends and gives them a long day,
And Job, I must have him there past mistake,
The man of Uz, (and Us without the z,
Painters who need his patience.) Well, all these 360
Secured at their devotions, up shall come
Out of a corner when you least expect,
As one by a dark stair into a great light,
Music and talking, who but Lippo! I!—
Mazed, motionless and moon-struck—I'm the man!
Back I shrink—what is this I see and hear?
I, caught up with my monk's things by mistake,
My old serge gown and rope that goes all round,
I, in this presence, this pure company!
Where's a hole, where's a corner for escape? 370
Then steps a sweet angelic slip of a thing
Forward, puts out a soft palm—"Not so fast!"
—Addresses the celestial presence, "nay—
He made you and devised you, after all,
Though he's none of you! Could Saint John there draw—
His camel-hair make up a painting-brush?
We come to brother Lippo for all that,
Iste perfecit opus!" So, all smile—
I shuffle sideways with my blushing face
Under the cover of a hundred wings 380
Thrown like a spread of kirtles when you're gay
And play hot cockles, all the doors being shut,
Till, wholly unexpected, in there pops
The hothead husband! Thus I scuttle off
To some safe bench behind, not letting go
The palm of her, the little lily thing
That spoke the good word for me in the nick,

l. 352. *orris-root:* used as a perfume or powder.
l. 378. *Iste perfecit opus:* this fellow completes the work.
l. 381. *kirtles:* robes.

Like the Prior's niece . . . Saint Lucy, I would say.
And so all's saved for me, and for the church
A pretty picture gained. Go, six months hence! 390
Your hand, sir, and good-bye: no lights, no lights!
The street's hushed, and I know my own way back,
Don't fear me! There's the grey beginning. Zooks!

[1853]

How It Strikes a Contemporary

I only knew one poet in my life:
And this, or something like it, was his way.

You saw go up and down Valladolid,
A man of mark, to know next time you saw.
His very serviceable suit of black
Was courtly once and conscientious still
And many might have worn it, though none did:
The cloak, that somewhat shone and showed the threads,
Had purpose, and the ruff, significance.
He walked and tapped the pavement with his cane, 10
Scenting the world, looking it full in face,
An old dog, bald and blindish, at his heels.
They turned up, now, the alley by the church,
That leads no whither; now, they breathed themselves
On the main promenade just at the wrong time:
You'd come upon his scrutinizing hat,
Making a peaked shade blacker than itself
Against the single window spared some house
Intact yet with its mouldered Moorish work,—
Or else surprise the ferule of his stick 20
Trying the mortar's temper 'tween the chinks
Of some new shop a-building, French and fine.
He stood and watched the cobbler at his trade,
The man who slices lemons into drink,
The coffee-roaster's brasier, and the boys
That volunteer to help him turn its winch.
He glanced o'er books on stalls with half an eye,
And fly-leaf ballads on the vendor's string,

And broad-edge bold-print posters by the wall.
He took such cognisance of men and things, 30
If any beat a horse, you felt he saw;
If any cursed a woman, he took note;
Yet stared at nobody,—they stared at him,
And found, less to their pleasure than surprise,
He seemed to know them and expect as much.
So, next time that a neighbour's tongue was loosed,
It marked the shameful and notorious fact,
We had among us, not so much a spy,
As a recording chief-inquisitor,
The town's true master if the town but knew! 40
We merely kept a Governor for form,
While this man walked about and took account
Of all thought, said and acted, then went home,
And wrote it fully to our Lord the King
Who has an itch to know things, He knows why,
And reads them in His bedroom of a night.
Oh, you might smile! there wanted not a touch,
A tang of . . . well, it was not wholly ease
As back into your mind the man's look came—
Stricken in years a little,—such a brow 50
His eyes had to live under!—clear as flint
On either side the formidable nose
Curved, cut, and coloured like an eagle's claw.
Had he to do with A's surprising fate?
When altogether old B disappeared
And young C got his mistress,—was 't our friend,
His letter to the King, that did it all?
What paid the bloodless man for so much pains?
Our Lord the King has favourites manifold,
And shifts His ministry some once a month; 60
Our city gets new Governors at whiles,—
But never word or sign, that I could hear,
Notified to this man about the streets
The King's approval of those letters conned
The last thing duly at the dead of night.
Did the man love his office? Frowned our Lord,
Exhorting when none heard—"Beseech Me not!
Too far above My people,—beneath Me!
I set the watch,—how should the people know?

Forget them, keep Me all the more in mind!" 70
Was some such understanding 'twixt the two?

I found no truth in one report at least—
That if you tracked him to his home, down lanes
Beyond the Jewry, and as clean to pace,
You found he ate his supper in a room
Blazing with lights, four Titians on the wall,
And twenty naked girls to change his plate!
Poor man, he lived another kind of life
In that new, stuccoed, third house by the bridge,
Fresh-painted, rather smart than otherwise! 80
The whole street might o'erlook him as he sat,
Leg crossing leg, one foot on the dog's back,
Playing a decent cribbage with his maid
(Jacynth, you're sure her name was) o'er the cheese
And fruit, three red halves of starved winter-pears,
Or treat of radishes in April! nine,
Ten, struck the church clock, straight to bed went he.

My father, like the man of sense he was,
Would point him out to me a dozen times;
"St—St," he'd whisper, "the Corregidor!" 90
I had been used to think that personage
Was one with lacquered breeches, lustrous belt,
And feathers like a forest in his hat,
Who blew a trumpet and proclaimed the news,
Announced the bull-fights, gave each church its turn,
And memorized the miracle in vogue!
He had a great observance from us boys;
We were in error; that was not the man.

I'd like now, yet had haply been afraid,
To have just looked, when this man came to die, 100
And seen who lined the clean gay garret's sides
And stood about the neat low truckle-bed,
With the heavenly manner of relieving guard.
Here had been, mark, the general-in-chief,

l. 74. *the Jewry:* the Jewish quarter.
l. 90. *the Corregidor:* the chief magistrate.

Thro' a whole campaign of the world's life and death,
Doing the King's work all the dim day long,
In his old coat and up to his knees in mud,
Smoked like a herring, dining on a crust,—
And, now the day was won, relieved at once!
No further show or need for that old coat, 110
You are sure, for one thing! Bless us, all the while
How sprucely we are dressed out, you and I!
A second, and the angels alter that.
Well, I could never write a verse,—could you?
Let's to the Prado and make the most of time.

[*1852?*]

l. 115. *the Prado:* the fashionable avenue.

Gerard Manley Hopkins

Gerard Manley Hopkins was born in 1844 to upper-middle-class parents. One of eight children, he grew up in an environment that encouraged literary, artistic, and musical exploration. His father was a diplomat and an author of sorts, and his mother studied philosophy.

After a successful career in prep school, Hopkins entered Oxford in 1863 at a time when the university was in ferment over the doctrines of the Oxford Movement. Here he came under the influence of John Ruskin and William Pusey. He was taught by Walter Pater and made friends with fellow student Robert Bridges, who was later to edit his poetry. Assailed by doubts of the truth of Anglicanism, the religion of his parents, he read theological arguments and was impressed by Cardinal Newman's *Difficulties of Anglicans.* Newman received him kindly when Hopkins sought an interview; in 1866 Hopkins became a member of the Roman Catholic Church.

The poet decided to become a priest two years later. He was ordained in 1877. Part of the nine years of his novitiate was spent in study in Wales. Once a priest, Hopkins was assigned by his order, the Society of Jesus, to teaching duties in slum districts of one gloomy industrial city after another—Bedford Leigh, Liverpool, Glasgow. In 1884, he became an instructor in Classics at University College in Dublin and Fellow at the Royal University.

The prestige of his new assignment did not entirely compensate for Hopkins' growing personal difficulties. A poet by inclination and temperament, he had given up writing for about seven years after becoming a Jesuit. By 1875, he was writing again, but he confined his audience to himself, his God, and two publishing poets, Robert Bridges and R. W. Dixon. To publish his own poems might be to seek personal fame, and Hopkins could not square this act with the Jesuits' injunction against committing the sin of pride. Moreover, Hopkins' frail constitution could not easily endure the hardships of Irish weather or the long hours spent in meticulously grading hundreds of examination papers. As a result, Hopkins suffered a physical and psychological breakdown from which he never recovered. During the final five years of his life (1885–89), he wrote much of his best poetry, though he did not recognize its great merit.

That Hopkins was early headed for a career as a priest—and, perhaps, a Jesuit—is clear, through hindsight, from scrutiny of his childhood. At school, he often mortified his flesh, partly as a lark but partly as a means of imposing discipline upon the body. He would give up all salt for a long period or refuse to drink any liquids whatever until he collapsed and had to be put to bed by school authorities. His drift toward Catholicism at Oxford seems further proof of his desire for rigorous discipline and personal restraint. And when it came time for him to select the order in which he wished to serve, he passed up the Benedictines and others in favor of the strict Jesuits. His early notebooks contain entries like this one:

> For Lent. No puddings on Sundays. No tea except if to keep me awake and then without sugar. No verses in Passion week or on Fridays. Not to sit in armchair except can work no other way. . . .

At the same time, Hopkins reveled throughout his life in the beauty of the physical world. As a child he was sickened by ugly sounds and driven to tears by a blemished face. In young manhood, his interest was in poetry and in music. He played the violin and the piano; he composed music. He found nature a source of ecstatic pleasure for its colors, its shapes, its odors, and its sounds. The reconciliation of Hopkins' tendency toward restraint of the physical with his love of the manifest world came through his experience as a Jesuit priest. His studies in the novitiate taught him the sacramental view of nature.

That view became one of the most pervasive motifs of his poetry. Before he entered the order, most of Hopkins' poems were pretty but insipid exercises in Keatsian sensuousness, without depth or sinew:

> The zenith melted to a rose of air;
> The waves were rosy-lipp'd; the crimson glare
> Shower'd the cliffs and every fret and spire
> With garnet wreaths and blooms of rosy-budded fire.

Once he embraced the Jesuit discipline, Hopkins' poems began to display firmness and direction. Even in recording his everyday life as a priest, as in "Felix Randal," or "Spring and Fall: to a Young Child," they go beyond the occasional to affirm a universal truth. The beauty of this world is seen as a consequence of other-worldly beauty and may be enjoyed in the comfortable assurance that God is immanent in the Epiphany.

But submission to Jesuit discipline brought to Hopkins more problems than it solved. The physical burden of being a cog in the Jesuit education machine was a recurrent theme in his letters. They document his poor health; his feeling of frustration as a teacher of classics in damp, cold, dreary buildings; and his wrestlings with his conscience as he strove to be fair to his students in grading their uninspired papers. His poems record the horror of those days in sharp, pained strokes. Hopkins' most memorable theme, the realization of his "dark night of the soul," when God seems absent from the tortured sufferer, informs the aptly named "terrible" sonnets such as "No worst, there is none. . . ." and "I wake and feel the fell of dark, not day." The concentrated anguish, despair, resignation, and love, once tasted by the reader, are not likely to be forgotten.

The theme of spiritual crisis and of personal, private woe was intense during the 1880s. Hopkins felt keenly an aridity, a barrenness in his life—as man, as poet, as Catholic soul. Unable to write poetry for publication, he had for years been unable to enter the literary community except through correspondence. As a priest, he was in a sense out of the mainstream of Victorian events. As a teacher, he had to keep his distance from the students. All this Hopkins was able to endure. But feeling at odds with his God was the ultimate trial. In sonnet after sonnet, Hopkins uses images of struggle. He "wrestles" with the Deity. God subdues him in combat and stands over him like a lion over his fallen prey. Worse, God sometimes gets so far away from Hopkins that the poet feels out of touch with Him. This spiritual crisis, moreover, forced a literary crisis, for in these days of turbulent questionings, Hopkins' creative power slackened and he could not write.

Yet it is in the expression of this conflict that Hopkins excelled.

His involvement as poet in crisis was largely responsible for the technical development of his distinctive style—his so-called "modernity." Hopkins used conventional forms for his poetry—ballad, sonnet, ode, and the like—but a new system of metrics and unusual poetic devices of explosive force that broke out of the boundaries. Anticipating his successors, he filled his lines with excess rhyme, with half rhyme [see *Handbook:* near rhyme], with outlandish rhymes [see *Handbook:* broken rhyme] (he rhymed "portholes" with "mortals" in a serious, indeed, solemn, stanza). In Hopkins' poems alliteration becomes a necessary structural device. Incremental repetition abounds. Syntax seems bizarre, though grammatical analysis usually proves that Hopkins knew what he was doing with his language.

Hopkins' departure from conventional versification gives his poetry what he himself called its queerness [see *Handbook:* inscape and instress]. He named the metrical scheme "Sprung Rhythm" [see *Handbook*]. As every student of English poetry knows, traditional meters (iambic, trochaic, dactylic, and anapestic [see *Handbook* for description of these meters]) divide a line of poetry into measurable units called "feet [see *Handbook:* foot]." With these meters, each foot contains either two or three syllables arranged in a specific order according to the requirement of the meter selected by the poet for the poem in question. "Sprung Rhythm" adds to this traditional scheme the monosyllabic and the quadrisyllabic foot. It also allows for the use of *mixed* meters [see *Handbook: logaoedic*] within a line or stanza. As Hopkins explains his arrangement in a preface:

> Sprung Rhythm . . . is measured by feet of from one to four syllables, regularly, and for particular effects any number of weak or slack syllables may be used. It has one stress, which falls on the only syllable, if there is only one, or, if there are more, then scanning . . . on the first, and so gives rise to four sorts of feet. . . .

The value of the monosyllabic foot and the polysyllabic foot in supporting the meaning of a poetic passage is clearly evident in the first three lines of "The Windhover":

> I caught this morning morning's minion, king-
> dom of daylight's dauphin, dapple-dawn-drawn Falcon in
> his riding
> Of the rolling level underneath him steady air . . .

The impressive solemnity and stateliness of "dapple-dawn-drawn Falcon" with its accented [see *Handbook:* accent, beat] monosyllabic feet contrasts sharply with the rushing sweep of the bird's erratic flight as recorded in the breathless, mainly unaccented "level underneath him steady air." This passage also demonstrates another departure from the expected in Hopkins' verse: the unorthodox carrying over from one line to the next of a word group, a thought group, or, as here, of a segment of a word itself—"king-" appearing in line one and "dom" beginning the second line.

Thus, in spite of its Victorian origins, Hopkins' poetry strikes a modern note in style. Robert Bridges, to whom Hopkins' unpublished poems were entrusted after his death, prevented their publication for almost thirty years—until 1918, in fact—on the ground that the public was not prepared for Hopkins' technical fireworks and would reject fine poetry because of its modern harshness and obscurity. By that time poet laureate of England, Bridges finally edited and published Hopkins' poetry; almost immediate recognition of Hopkins as a "modern" by the postwar literary community justified the editor's caution.

BIBLIOGRAPHY

Kenyon Critics. *Gerard Manley Hopkins.* New York: New Directions, 1945.

Lahey, G. F. *Gerard Manley Hopkins: A Life.* Oxford: Oxford University Press, 1930.

Weyand, Norman, ed. *Immortal Diamond: Studies in Gerard Manley Hopkins.* London: Sheed and Ward, 1949.

"I Wake and Feel the Fell of Dark, not Day"

I wake and feel the fell of dark, not day.
What hours, O what black hoürs we have spent
This night! what sights you, heart, saw; ways you went!
And more must, in yet longer light's delay.
With witness I speak this. But where I say
Hours I mean years, mean life. And my lament
Is cries countless, cries like dead letters sent
To dearest him that lives alas! away.

I am gall, I am heartburn. God's most deep decree
Bitter would have me taste: my taste was me; 10
Bones built in me, flesh filled, blood brimmed the curse.
Selfyeast of spirit a dull dough sours. I see
The lost are like this, and their scourge to be
As I am mine, their sweating selves; but worse.

[*1885*]

Commentary

This is one of Hopkins' "terrible" sonnets, describing a period of despair when even his God seemed either absent or antagonistic. It was a time of physical and psychological torment for the poet, whose daily tasks as schoolmaster-priest wore thin his resistance to sickness, ennui, and discouragement. It was a time too when the impulse toward poetic creativity seemed paralyzed. But Hopkins here blames his plight on his own base, human physicality, the realization of which is the torment the Deity has placed upon him.

The poem offers little verbal difficulty. The double alliterations of the first few lines ("feel the fell," "dark, not day") probably reflect Hopkins' interest in Welsh literature and language, originating with his novitiate in Wales. The monosyllabic alliterations [see *Handbook:* alliteration] contribute to the effect of sadness and solemnity. Further, the use of the word "fell" in line 1 suggests nightfall at daybreak and also suggests the Old English meaning of the word, "cruelty." Note the intense concentration of language in "And more must, in yet longer light's delay." To paraphrase in more normal English constructions is to lengthen the line considerably: "And you, heart, must see more and go more ways, in the darkness caused by light's longer delay." In line 8, "alas! away" suggests a mournful dirge. Line 12 illustrates Hopkins' tendency to coin words like "selfyeast" for his own purposes, and his penchant for upsetting the normal order of subject-verb-object so that the reader must reverse the words to make sense: "A dull dough sours selfyeast of spirit."

The poem is a lyric cry addressed (notice!) to the poet's heart in the first quatrain [see *Handbook:* quatrain]. But it is a heart separated from the rest of the body and given an existence of its own: ". . . what sights you, heart, saw; ways you went!" If we consider the heart as the symbolic core of emotional life, we must take as deliberate the poet's intent to divorce this center from the rest of the body. Indeed, in the sestet of the sonnet, Hopkins diagnoses his affliction as "heartburn." Nor does the burning appear to be purifying fire from which Hopkins will arise purged; the end of the poem sees no way out of his private hell.

Hopkins' plight was compounded by his inability to communicate with God. Nor was this a temporary state, for, though the experience he described was narrowed to a specific night and day, he broadened it to "years" and "life." In this instance, the poet resorted to the homely idea of getting into contact with God by sending him "dead letters"—the implication being that, deprived of heart, they find their way to the dead-letter office as undeliverable. This is logical, for Hopkins does not know the address of the Deity (this is, in fact, his trouble), nor is he able to cry directly to God rather than using an intermediary (the mail,) inasmuch as the poet finds himself at a great distance from God.

Take away wholesome emotion and spiritual communion from a man and he is left only with his material self—his body. Hopkins' disgust with this merely physical husk is couched in unpleasant terms. The appeal is to the sense of taste as possibly the best means of reinforcing the sense of the materially ugly. He is gall, a bitter taste. His body becomes a "dull dough" which has kept the spirit from rising. Hopkins agrees with Coleridge's Ancient Mariner that the most dreadful curse is to be aware of the wretchedness of one's bodily self and yet to be unable to escape from that self. He allies himself, in the last line, with souls in hell whose punishment, like his, is the recognition of their physicality.

The structure of this sonnet shows Hopkins' restiveness under restraint, even though that restraint was self-imposed. First, the poem *is* a sonnet—one of the most conventional and controlled means of poetic utterance. Second, Hopkins does very little in this sonnet to make it modern, "queer," or unconventional in terms of the application of Sprung Rhythm. The lines are all of the traditional iambic variety. All these qualifications should emphasize restraint, resignation, ritual, and regularity. But obviously, though the poet's life may be governed by such patterns externally, his inner life is turbulent. The first line of the sonnet prepares the reader for the turmoil, with its ten spare monosyllabic words, five of them heavy and sharp. Similarly, the fragmented second and third lines, full of pauses, exclamations, repetitions, display the internal emotional struggle. The poet uses sibilants and explosive consonants also to objectify in sound the battle within: "Bones built in me, flesh filled, blood brimmed the curse." And yet he ends the poem with his characteristic two heavy final syllables [see *Handbook:* spondee] ("but worse.") which carry the auditory suggestion of "Amen." It is significant that though Hopkins sees no way out of his predicament in the poem, the last foot is suggestive of the ending of a prayer.

God's Grandeur

The world is charged with the grandeur of God.
  It will flame out, like shining from shook foil;
  It gathers to a greatness, like the ooze of oil
Crushed. Why do men then now not reck his rod?
Generations have trod, have trod, have trod;
  And all is seared with trade; bleared, smeared with toil;
  And wears man's smudge and shares man's smell: the soil
Is bare now, nor can foot feel, being shod.

And for all this, nature is never spent;
  There lives the dearest freshness deep down things; 10
And though the last lights off the black West went
  Oh, morning, at the brown brink eastward, springs—
Because the Holy Ghost over the bent
  World broods with warm breast and with ah! bright wings.

[*1877*]

The Starlight Night

Look at the stars! look, look up at the skies!
  O look at all the fire-folk sitting in the air!
  The bright boroughs, the circle-citadels there!
Down in dim woods the diamond delves! the elves'-eyes!
The grey lawns cold where gold, where quickgold lies!
  Wind-beat whitebeam! airy abeles set on a flare!
  Flake-doves sent floating forth at a farmyard scare!—
Ah well! it is all a purchase, all is a prize.

Buy then! bid then!—What?—Prayer, patience, alms, vows.
Look, look: a May-mess, like on orchard boughs! 10
  Look! March-bloom, like on mealed-with-yellow sallows!
These are indeed the barn; withindoors house

l. 6. *whitebeam . . . abeles:* W. H. Gardner explains that the poet means trees which turn up silvery undersided leaves in the wind.
l. 11. *sallows:* willows.

The shocks. This piece-bright paling shuts the spouse
Christ home, Christ and his mother and all his hallows.
[1877]

Spring

Nothing is so beautiful as spring—
When weeds, in wheels, shoot long and lovely and lush;
Thrush's eggs look little low heavens, and thrush
Through the echoing timber does so rinse and wring
The ear, it strikes like lightnings to hear him sing;
The glassy peartree leaves and blooms, they brush
The descending blue; that blue is all in a rush
With richness; the racing lambs too have fair their fling.

What is all this juice and all this joy?
A strain of the earth's sweet being in the beginning 10
In Eden garden.—Have, get, before it cloy,
Before it cloud, Christ, lord, and sour with sinning,
Innocent mind and Mayday in girl and boy,
Most, O maid's child, thy choice and worthy the winning.
[1877]

The Sea and the Skylark

On ear and ear two noises too old to end
Trench—right, the tide that ramps against the shore;
With a flood or a fall, low lull-off or all roar,
Frequenting there while moon shall wear and wend.

Left hand, off land, I hear the lark ascend,
His rash-fresh re-winded new-skeinèd score
In crisps of curl off wild winch whirl, and pour
And pelt music, till none's to spill nor spend.

How these two shame this shallow and frail town!
How ring right out our sordid turbid time, 10
Being pure! We, life's pride and cared-for crown,

l. 6. *new-skeinèd score:* the lark is pictured as flying in an unwinding movement like yarn unwinding from a spool.

Have lost that cheer and charm of earth's past prime:
Our make and making break, are breaking, down
To man's last dust, drain fast towards man's first slime.
[*1877*]

The Windhover:

TO CHRIST OUR LORD

I caught this morning morning's minion, kingdom of daylight's dauphin, dapple-dawn-drawn Falcon, in his riding
Of the rolling level underneath him steady air, and striding
High there, how he rung upon the rein of a wimpling wing
In his ecstasy! then off, off forth on swing,
As a skate's heel sweeps smooth on a bow-bend: the hurl and gliding
Rebuffed the big wind. My heart in hiding
Stirred for a bird,—the achieve of, the mastery of the thing!

Brute beauty and valour and act, oh, air, pride, plume here
Buckle! *and* the fire that breaks from thee then, a billion
Times told lovelier, more dangerous, O my chevalier! 10

No wonder of it: shéer plód makes plough down sillion
Shine, and blue-bleak embers, ah my dear,
Fall, gall themselves, and gash gold-vermilion.
[*1877*]

l. 3. *rung:* flew in spiralling movements.
l. 9. *Buckle:* probably imperative here.
l. 11. *sillion:* furrow of land for tilling.

Pied Beauty

Glory be to God for dappled things—
For skies of couple-colour as a brinded cow;
For rose-moles all in stipple upon trout that swim;
Fresh-firecoal chestnut-falls; finches' wings;

l. 2. *brinded:* brindled or spotted.
l. 3. *stipple:* pattern of dots.

Landscape plotted and pieced—fold, fallow, and plough;
And áll trádes, their gear and tackle and trim.

All things counter, original, spare, strange;
Whatever is fickle, freckled (who knows how?)
With swift, slow; sweet, sour; adazzle, dim;
He fathers-forth whose beauty is past change: 10
Praise him.

[*1877*]

Hurrahing in Harvest

Summer ends now; now, barbarous in beauty, the stooks arise
Around; up above, what wind-walks! what lovely behaviour
Of silk-sack clouds! has wilder, wilful-wavier
Meal-drift moulded ever and melted across skies?

I walk, I lift up, I lift up heart, eyes,
Down all that glory in the heavens to glean our Saviour;
And, éyes, heárt, what looks, what lips yet gave you a
Rapturous love's greeting of realer, of rounder replies?

And the azurous hung hills are his world-wielding shoulder
Majestic—as a stallion stalwart, very-violet-sweet!— 10
These things, these things were here and but the beholder
Wanting; which two when they once meet,
The heart rears wings bold and bolder
And hurls for him, O half hurls earth for him off under his feet.

[*1877*]

l. 1. *stooks:* sheaves of harvested crops.
l. 14. *hurls earth . . . feet:* probable meaning is that the beholder jumps for joy.

Henry Purcell

The poet wishes well to the divine genius of Purcell
and praises him that, whereas other musicians have given utterance
to the moods of man's mind, he has, beyond that,
uttered in notes the very make and species of man as created
both in him and in all men generally.

Have fair fallen, O fair, fair have fallen, so dear
To me, so arch-especial a spirit as heaves in Henry Purcell,
An age is now since passed, since parted; with the reversal
Of the outward sentence low lays him, listed to a heresy, here.

Not mood in him nor meaning, proud fire or sacred fear,
Or love or pity or all that sweet notes not his might nursle:
It is the forgèd feature finds me; it is the rehearsal
Of own, of abrúpt sélf there so thrusts on, so throngs the ear.

Let him oh! with his air of angels then lift me, lay me! only I'll
Have an eye to the sakes of him, quaint moonmarks, to his pelted
plumage under 10
Wings: so some great stormfowl, whenever he has walked his while

The thunder-purple seabeach plumèd purple-of-thunder,
If a wuthering of his palmy snow-pinions scatter a colossal smile
Off him, but meaning motion fans fresh our wits with wonder.
[*1879*]

Felix Randal

Felix Randal the farrier, O he is dead then? my duty all ended,
Who have watched his mould of man, big-boned and hardy-handsome
Pining, pining, till time when reason rambled in it and some
Fatal four disorders, fleshed there, all contended?

Sickness broke him. Impatient he cursed at first, but mended
Being anointed and all; though a heavenlier heart began some
Months earlier, since I had our sweet reprieve and ransom
Tendered to him. Ah well, God rest him all road ever he offended!

This seeing the sick endears them to us, us too it endears.
My tongue had taught thee comfort, touch had quenched thy tears, 10
Thy tears that touched my heart, child, Felix, poor Felix Randal;

How far from then forethought of, all thy more boisterous years,
When thou at the random grim forge, powerful amidst peers,

l. 1. *farrier:* blacksmith.
l. 13. *random:* rough-hewn of odd-shaped stones.

Didst fettle for the great grey drayhorse his bright and battering
sandal!

[*1880*]

Spring and Fall:

TO A YOUNG CHILD

Márgarét, are you gríeving
Over Goldengrove unleaving?
Leáves, líke the things of man, you
With your fresh thoughts care for, can you?
Áh! ás the heart grows older
It will come to such sights colder
By and by, nor spare a sigh
Though worlds of wanwood leafmeal lie;
And yet you wíll weep and know why.
Now no matter, child, the name: 10
Sórrow's spríngs áre the same.
Nor mouth had, no nor mind, expressed
What heart heard of, ghost guessed:
It ís the blight man was born for,
It is Margaret you mourn for.

[*1880*]

l. 8. *leafmeal:* the meal of dry and crumbled leaves.
l. 13. *ghost:* spirit.

(*Carrion Comfort*)

Not, I'll not, carrion comfort, Despair, not feast on thee;
Not untwist—slack they may be—these last strands of man
In me ór, most weary, cry *I can no more*. I can;
Can something, hope, wish day come, not choose not to be.
But ah, but O thou terrible, why wouldst thou rude on me
Thy wring-world right foot rock? lay a lionlimb against me? scan
With darksome devouring eyes my bruisèd bones? and fan,
O in turns of tempest, me heaped there; me frantic to avoid thee and
flee?

l. 6. *rock:* used here as a verb.

Why? That my chaff might fly; my grain lie, sheer and clear.
Nay in all that toil, that coil, since (seems) I kissed the rod, 10
Hand rather, my heart lo! lapped strength, stole joy, would laugh, chéer.
Cheer whom though? the hero whose heaven-handling flung me, fóot tród
Me? or me that fought him? O which one? is it each one? That night, that year
Of now done darkness I wretch lay wrestling with (my God!) my God.

[*1885*]

"No worst, there is none"

No worst, there is none. Pitched past pitch of grief,
More pangs will, schooled at forepangs, wilder wring.
Comforter, where, where is your comforting?
Mary, mother of us, where is your relief?
My cries heave, herds-long; huddle in a main, a chief
Woe, world-sorrow; on an age-old anvil wince and sing—
Then lull, then leave off. Fury had shrieked 'No lingering! Let me be fell: force I must be brief.'

O the mind, mind has mountains; cliffs of fall
Frightful, sheer, no-man-fathomed. Hold them cheap 10
May who ne'er hung there. Nor does long our small
Durance deal with that steep or deep. Here! creep,
Wretch, under a comfort serves in a whirlwind: all
Life death does end and each day dies with sleep.

[*1885?*]

l. 5. *main:* crowd.
l. 8. *force:* of necessity.

The Habit of Perfection

Elected Silence, sing to me
And beat upon my whorlèd ear,
Pipe me to pastures still and be
The music that I care to hear.

Shape nothing, lips; be lovely-dumb:
It is the shut, the curfew sent
From there where all surrenders come
Which only makes you eloquent.

Be shellèd eyes, with double dark
And find the uncreated light: 10
This ruck and reel which you remark
Coils, keeps, and teases simple sight.

Palate, the hutch of tasty lust,
Desire not to be rinsed with wine:
The can must be so sweet, the crust
So fresh that come in fasts divine!

Nostrils, your careless breath that spend
Upon the stir and keep of pride,
What relish shall the censers send
Along the sanctuary side! 20

O feel-of-primrose hands, O feet
That want the yield of plushy sward,
But you shall walk the golden street
And you unhouse and house the Lord.

And, Poverty, be thou the bride
And now the marriage feast begun,
And lily-coloured clothes provide
Your spouse not laboured-at nor spun.
[*1866*]

l. 24. ***unhouse and house the Lord:*** as priest, he will remove with his hands the consecrated Host from its enclosure on the altar.

The Wreck of the Deutschland

To the
happy memory of five Franciscan Nuns
exiles by the Falk Laws

drowned between midnight and morning of
Dec. 7th, 1875

Part the First

1

Thou mastering me
God! giver of breath and bread;
World's strand, sway of the sea;
Lord of living and dead;
Thou hast bound bones and veins in me, fastened me flesh,
And after it almost unmade, what with dread,
Thy doing: and dost thou touch me afresh?
Over again I feel thy finger and find thee.

2

I did say yes
O at lightning and lashed rod; 10
Thou heardst me truer than tongue confess
Thy terror, O Christ, O God;
Thou knowest the walls, altar and hour and night:
The swoon of a heart that the sweep and the hurl of thee trod
Hard down with a horror of height:
And the midriff astrain with leaning of, laced with fire of stress.

3

The frown of his face
Before me, the hurtle of hell
Behind, where, where was a, where was a place?
I whirled out wings that spell 20

Falk Laws: Falk, as Bismarck's minister of public worship, had instigated the stringent so-called "May Laws" of 1873 against Catholics who resisted in the church-state struggle of the time.
l. 20. *spell:* time of crisis.

And fled with a fling of the heart to the heart of the Host.
My heart, but you were dovewinged, I can tell,
Carrier-witted, I am bold to boast,
To flash from the flame to the flame then, tower from the grace to the grace.

4

I am soft sift
In an hourglass—at the wall
Fast, but mined with a motion, a drift,
And it crowds and it combs to the fall;
I steady as a water in a well, to a poise, to a pane,
But roped with, always, all the way down from the tall 30
Fells or flanks of the voel, a vein
Of the gospel proffer, a pressure, a principle, Christ's gift.

5

I kiss my hand
To the stars, lovely-asunder
Starlight, wafting him out of it; and
Glow, glory in thunder;
Kiss my hand to the dappled-with-damson west:
Since, tho' he is under the world's splendour and wonder,
His mystery must be instressed, stressed;
For I greet him the days I meet him, and bless when I understand. 40

6

Not out of his bliss
Springs the stress felt
Nor first from heaven (and few know this)
Swings the stroke dealt—
Stroke and a stress that stars and storms deliver,
That guilt is hushed by, hearts are flushed by and melt—
But it rides time like riding a river
(And here the faithful waver, the faithless fable and miss).

l. 24. *grace:* "elevating" grace, according to Hopkins, which brings the receiver to a "vital act in Christ."
l. 31. *voel:* a bare hill (Welsh).
l. 39. *instressed:* impressed upon one's being through spiritual intuition or epiphany.

7

It dates from day
Of his going in Galilee; 50
Warm-laid grave of a womb-life grey;
Manger, maiden's knee;
The dense and the driven Passion, and frightful sweat;
Thence the discharge of it, there its swelling to be,
Though felt before, though in high flood yet—
What none would have known of it, only the heart, being hard at bay,

8

Is out with it! Oh,
We lash with the best or worst
Word last! How a lush-kept plush-capped sloe
Will, mouthed to flesh-burst, 60
Gush!—flush the man, the being with it, sour or sweet,
Brim, in a flash, full!—Hither then, last or first,
To hero of Calvary, Christ,'s feet—
Never ask if meaning it, wanting it, warned of it—men go.

9

Be adored among men,
God, three-numberèd form;
Wring thy rebel, dogged in den,
Man's malice, with wrecking and storm.
Beyond saying sweet, past telling of tongue,
Thou art lightning and love, I found it, a winter and warm; 70
Father and fondler of heart thou hast wrung:
Hast thy dark descending and most art merciful then.

10

With an anvil-ding
And with fire in him forge thy will
Or rather, rather then, stealing as Spring
Through him, melt him but master him still:
Whether at once, as once at a crash Paul,
Or as Austin, a lingering-out swéet skíll,
Make mercy in all of us, out of us all
Mastery, but be adored, but be adored King. 80

l. 59. *sloe:* plum-like fruit.
l. 78. *Austin:* Saint Augustine.

Part the Second

11

'Some find me a sword; some
The flange and the rail; flame,
Fang, or flood' goes Death on drum,
And storms bugle his fame.
But wé dream we are rooted in earth—Dust!
Flesh falls within sight of us, we, though our flower the same,
Wave with the meadow, forget that there must
The sour scythe cringe, and the blear share come.

12

On Saturday sailed from Bremen,
American-outward-bound, 90
Take settler and seamen, tell men with women,
Two hundred souls in the round—
O Father, not under thy feathers nor ever as guessing
The goal was a shoal, of a fourth the doom to be drowned;
Yet did the dark side of the bay of thy blessing
Not vault them, the millions of rounds of thy mercy not reeve even
them in?

13

Into the snows she sweeps,
Hurling the haven behind,
The Deutschland, on Sunday and so the sky keeps,
For the infinite air is unkind, 100
And the sea flint-flake, black-backed in the regular blow,
Sitting Eastnortheast, in cursed quarter, the wind;
Wiry and white-fiery and whirlwind-swivellèd snow
Spins to the widow-making unchilding unfathering deeps.

14

She drove in the dark to leeward,
She struck—not a reef or a rock
But the combs of a smother of sand: night drew her
Dead to the Kentish Knock;

l. 88. *cringe:* fall (?).
l. 96. *reeve:* enclose.
l. 107. *combs:* ridges.
l. 108. *Kentish Knock:* a sandbar in the Thames.

And she beat the bank down with her bows and the ride of her keel:
The breakers rolled on her beam with ruinous shock; 110
And canvas and compass, the whorl and the wheel
Idle for ever to waft her or wind her with, these she endured.

15

Hope had grown grey hairs,
Hope had mourning on,
Trenched with tears, carved with cares,
Hope was twelve hours gone;
And frightful a nightfall folded rueful a day
Nor rescue, only rocket and lightship, shone,
And lives at last were washing away:
To the shrouds they took,—they shook in the hurling and horrible airs. 120

16

One stirred from the rigging to save
The wild woman-kind below,
With a rope's end round the man, handy and brave—
He was pitched to his death at a blow,
For all his dreadnough breast and braids of thew:
They could tell him for hours, dandled the to and fro
Through the cobbled foam-fleece, what could he do
With the burl of the fountains of air, buck and the flood of the wave?

17

They fought with God's cold—
And they could not and fell to the deck 130
(Crushed them) or water (and drowned them) or rolled
With the sea-romp over the wreck.
Night roared, with the heart-break hearing a heart-broke rabble,
The woman's wailing, the crying of child without check—
Till a lioness arose breasting the babble,
A prophetess towered in the tumult, a virginal tongue told.

18

Ah, touched in your bower of bone
Are you! turned for an exquisite smart,

l. 111. *whorl:* propeller.
l. 126. *the:* perhaps should read "there."

Have you! make words break from me here all alone,
Do you!—mother of being in me, heart. 140
O unteachably after evil, but uttering truth,
Why, tears! is it? tears; such a melting, a madrigal start!
Never-eldering revel and river of youth,
What can it be, this glee? the good you have there of your own?

19

Sister, a sister calling
A master, her master and mine!—
And the inboard seas run swirling and hawling;
The rash smart sloggering brine
Blinds her; but she that weather sees one thing, one;
Has one fetch in her: she rears herself to divine 150
Ears, and the call of the tall nun
To the men in the tops and the tackle rode over the storm's brawling.

20

She was first of a five and came
Of a coifèd sisterhood.
(O Deutschland, double a desperate name!
O world wide of its good!
But Gertrude, lily, and Luther, are two of a town,
Christ's lily and beast of the waste wood:
From life's dawn it is drawn down,
Abel is Cain's brother and breasts they have sucked the same.) 160

21

Loathed for a love men knew in them,
Banned by the land of their birth,
Rhine refused them. Thames would ruin them;
Surf, snow, river and earth
Gnashed: but thou art above, thou Orion of light;
Thy unchancelling poising palms were weighing the worth,
Thou martyr-master: in thy sight
Storm flakes were scroll-leaved flowers, lily showers—sweet heaven was astrew in them.

22

Five! the finding and sake
And cipher of suffering Christ. 170

l. 150. *fetch:* trick or device.
l. 157. *Gertrude:* a German saint.

Mark, the mark is of man's make
And the word of it Sacrificed.
But he scores it in scarlet himself on his own bespoken,
Before-time-taken, dearest prizèd and priced—
Stigma, signal, cinquefoil token
For lettering of the lamb's fleece, ruddying of the rose-flake.

23

Joy fall to thee, father Francis,
Drawn to the Life that died;
With the gnarls of the nails in thee, niche of the lance, his
Lovescape crucified 180
And seal of his seraph-arrival! and these thy daughters
And five-livèd and leavèd favour and pride,
Are sisterly sealed in wild waters,
To bathe in his fall-gold mercies, to breathe in his all-fire glances.

24

Away in the loveable west,
On a pastoral forehead of Wales,
I was under a roof here, I was at rest,
And they the prey of the gales;
She to the black-about air, to the breaker, the thickly
Falling flakes, to the throng that catches and quails 190
Was calling 'O Christ, Christ, come quickly':
The cross to her she calls Christ to her, christens her wild-worst Best.

25

The majesty! what did she mean?
Breathe, arch and original Breath.
Is it love in her of the being as her lover had been?
Breathe, body of lovely death.
They were else-minded then, altogether, the men
Woke thee with a *we are perishing* in the weather of Gennesareth.
Or is it that she cried for the crown then, 199
The keener to come at the comfort for feeling the combating keen?

l. 176. *rose-flake:* a red rose is the symbol of the martyr.
l. 180. *Lovescape*: Hopkins' editor suggests "the very essence or the *inscape* of Love."

26

For how to the heart's cheering
The down-dugged ground-hugged grey
Hovers off, the jay-blue heavens appearing
Of pied and peeled May!
Blue-beating and hoary-glow height; or night, still higher,
With belled fire and the moth-soft Milky Way,
What by your measure is the heaven of desire,
The treasure never eyesight got, nor was ever guessed what for the hearing?

27

No, but it was not these.
The jading and jar of the cart, 210
Time's tasking, it is fathers that asking for ease
Of the sodden-with-its-sorrowing heart,
Not danger, electrical horror; then further it finds
The appealing of the Passion is tenderer in prayer apart:
Other, I gather, in measure her mind's
Burden, in wind's burly and beat of endragonèd seas.

28

But how shall I . . . make me room there:
Reach me a . . . Fancy, come faster—
Strike you the sight of it? look at it loom there,
Thing that she . . . there then! the Master, 220
Ipse, the only one, Christ, King, Head:
He was to cure the extremity where he had cast her;
Do, deal, lord it with living and dead;
Let him ride, her pride, in his triumph, despatch and have done with his doom there.

29

Ah! there was a heart right
There was single eye!
Read the unshapeable shock night
And knew the who and the why;
Wording it how but by him that present and past,
Heaven and earth are word of, worded by?— 230
The Simon Peter of a soul! to the blast
Tarpeian-fast, but a blown beacon of light.

30

Jesu, heart's light,
Jesu, maid's son,
What was the feast followed the night
Thou hadst glory of this nun?—
Feast of the one woman without stain.
For so conceivèd, so to conceive thee is done;
But here was heart-throe, birth of a brain,
Word, that heard and kept thee and uttered thee outright. 240

31

Well, she has thee for the pain, for the
Patience; but pity of the rest of them!
Heart, go and bleed at a bitterer vein for the
Comfortless unconfessed of them—
No not uncomforted: lovely-felicitous Providence
Finger of a tender of, O of a feathery delicacy, the breast of the
Maiden could obey so, be a bell to, ring of it, and
Startle the poor sheep back! is the shipwrack then a harvest,
does tempest carry the grain for thee?

32

I admire thee, master of the tides,
Of the Yore-flood, of the year's fall; 250
The recurb and the recovery of the gulf's sides,
The girth of it and the wharf of it and the wall;
Stanching, quenching ocean of a motionable mind;
Ground of being, and granite of it: past all
Grasp God, throned behind
Death with a sovereignty that heeds but hides, bodes but abides;

33

With a mercy that outrides
The all of water, an ark
For the listener; for the lingerer with a love glides
Lower than death and the dark; 260

l. 235. *feast followed the night:* Immaculate Conception of the Blessed Virgin, December 8.

l. 250. *Yore-flood:* the Deluge (?).

l. 259. *lingerer:* in Purgatory.

A vein for the visiting of the past-prayer, pent in prison,
The-last-breath penitent spirits—the uttermost mark
Our passion-plungèd giant risen,
The Christ of the Father compassionate, fetched in the storm of his strides.

34

Now burn, new born to the world,
Doubled-naturèd name,
The heaven-flung, heart-fleshed, maiden-furled
Miracle-in-Mary-of-flame,
Mid-numbered He in three of the thunder-throne!
Not a dooms-day dazzle in his coming nor dark as he came; 270
Kind, but royally reclaiming his own;
A released shower, let flash to the shire, not a lightning of fire hard-hurled.

35

Dame, at our door
Drowned, and among our shoals,
Remember us in the roads, the heaven-haven of the Reward:
Our King back, oh, upon English souls!
Let him easter in us, be a dayspring to the dimness of us, be a crimson-cresseted east,
More brightening her, rare-dear Britain, as his reign rolls,
Pride, rose, prince, hero of us, high-priest,
Our hearts' charity's hearth's fire, our thoughts' chivalry's throng's Lord. 280

[*1875*]

The Loss of the Eurydice

FOUNDERED MARCH 24, 1878

The Eurydice—it concerned thee, O Lord:
Three hundred souls, O alas! on board,
Some asleep unawakened, all un-
warned, eleven fathoms fallen

Where she foundered! One stroke
Felled and furled them, the hearts of oak!

l. 6. *furled:* buried.

And flockbells off the aerial
Downs' forefalls beat to the burial.

For did she pride her, freighted fully, on
Bounden bales or a hoard of bullion?— 10
Precious passing measure,
Lads and men her lade and treasure.

She had come from a cruise, training seamen—
Men, boldboys soon to be men:
Must it, worst weather,
Blast bole and bloom together?

No Atlantic squall overwrought her
Or rearing billow of the Biscay water:
Home was hard at hand
And the blow bore from land. 20

And you were a liar, O blue March day.
Bright sun lanced fire in the heavenly bay;
But what black Boreas wrecked her? he
Came equipped, deadly-electric,

A beetling baldbright cloud thorough England
Riding: there did storms not mingle? and
Hailropes hustle and grind their
Heavengravel? wolfsnow, worlds of it, wind there?

Now Carisbrook keep goes under in gloom;
Now it overvaults Appledurcombe; 30
Now near by Ventnor town
It hurls, hurls off Boniface Down.

Too proud, too proud, what a press she bore!
Royal, and all her royals wore.
Sharp with her, shorten sail!
Too late; lost; gone with the gale.

This was that fell capsize,
As half she had righted and hoped to rise
Death teeming in by her portholes
Raced down decks, round messes of mortals. 40

Then a lurch forward, frigate and men;
'All hands for themselves' the cry ran then;
        But she who had housed them thither
Was around them, bound them or wound them with her.

Marcus Hare, high her captain,
Kept to her—care-drowned and wrapped in
        Cheer's death, would follow
His charge through the champ-white water-in-a-wallow,

All under Channel to bury in a beach her
Cheeks: Right, rude of feature, 50
        He thought he heard say
'Her commander! and thou too, and thou this way.'

It is even seen, time's something server,
In mankind's medley a duty-swerver,
        At downright 'No or yes?'
Doffs all, drives full for righteousness.

Sydney Fletcher, Bristol-bred,
(Low lie his mates now on watery bed)
        Takes to the seas and snows
As sheer down the ship goes. 60

Now her afterdraught gullies him too down;
Now he wrings for breath with the deathgush brown;
        Till a lifebelt and God's will
Lend him a lift from the sea-swill.

Now he shoots short up to the round air;
Now he gasps, now he gazes everywhere;
        But his eye no cliff, no coast or
Mark makes in the rivelling snowstorm.

Him, after an hour of wintry waves,
A schooner sights, with another, and saves, 70
        And he boards her in Oh! such joy
He has lost count what came next, poor boy.—

l. 47. *Cheer's death*: despair.

They say who saw one sea-corpse cold
He was all of lovely manly mould,
    Every inch a tar,
Of the best we boast our sailors are.

Look, foot to forelock, how all things suit! he
Is strung by duty, is strained to beauty,
    And brown-as-dawning-skinned
With brine and shine and whirling wind. 80

O his nimble finger, his gnarled grip!
Leagues, leagues of seamanship
    Slumber in these forsaken
Bones, this sinew, and will not waken.

He was but one like thousands more,
Day and night I deplore
    My people and born own nation,
Fast foundering own generation.

I might let bygones be—our curse
Of ruinous shrine no hand or, worse, 90
    Robbery's hand is busy to
Dress, hoar-hallowed shrines unvisited;

Only the breathing temple and fleet
Life, this wildworth blown so sweet,
    These daredeaths, ay this crew, in
Unchrist, all rolled in ruin—

Deeply surely I need to deplore it,
Wondering why my master bore it,
    The riving off that race
So at home, time was, to his truth and grace 100

That a starlight-wender of ours would say
The marvellous Milk was Walsingham Way
    And one—but let be, let be:
More, more than was will yet be.—

l.99. *riving off:* falling off.

O well wept, mother have lost son;
Wept, wife; wept, sweetheart would be one:
        Though grief yield them no good
Yet shed what tears sad truelove should.

But to Christ lord of thunder
Crouch; lay knee by earth low under: 110
        'Holiest, loveliest, bravest,
Save my hero, O Hero savest.

And the prayer thou hearst me making
Have, at the awful overtaking,
        Heard; have heard and granted
Grace that day grace was wanted.'

Not that hell knows redeeming,
But for souls sunk in seeming
        Fresh, till doomfire burn all,
Prayer shall fetch pity eternal. 120

"Patience, hard thing! the hard thing but to pray"

Patience, hard thing! the hard thing but to pray,
But bid for, Patience is! Patience who asks
Wants war, wants wounds; weary his times, his tasks;
To do without, take tosses, and obey.
   Rare patience roots in these, and, these away,
Nowhere. Natural heart's ivy, Patience masks
Our ruins of wrecked past purpose. There she basks
Purple eyes and seas of liquid leaves all day.

   We hear our hearts grate on themselves: it kills
To bruise them dearer. Yet the rebellious wills 10
Of us we do bid God bend to him even so.
   And where is he who more and more distils
Delicious kindness?—He is patient. Patience fills
His crisp combs, and that comes those ways we know.

[*1885*]

Walt Whitman

In the nineteenth century, the American nation was still in what might be called its adolescence. Like most young things that are developing rapidly, the country was frequently awkward, raucous, and self-conscious. Its peculiar and unique characteristics as a nation born of a vision of human equality were beginning to emerge; and it had the vitality, dynamic power, and ebullient hopes of a youth who begins to sense his individuality and potential.

About forty years after the colonies declared their independence, the poet who was to articulate the pride and the aspirations of the growing nation was born to a Huntington, Long Island, couple on May 31, 1819. Walter Whitman, after whom the child was named, was a carpenter. Louisa, the mother, was an uneducated but imaginative woman of Quaker descent whose warm and loving personality exerted a powerful influence on the life and character of her second son. In 1823, the Whitman family moved to Brooklyn, a small town that was to grow into a metropolis within a few decades. Its rapid expansion was comparable to the development of the whole nation. This dynamic quality of the society in which he grew up had a profound influence on the themes and even the techniques of Whitman's poetry.

Whitman left school when he was about twelve and became a printer's apprentice in a newspaper office. For the next twenty years, he was associated with various New York newspapers as reporter and as editor, becoming a very competent journalist though not a particularly outstanding one. Most of Whitman's journalistic writing has been preserved, and it is remarkable in only one way: it reveals no literary talent. In fact, not until Whitman announced in a poem, "I, now thirty-seven years old in perfect health begin, / Hoping to cease not till death," was there any public indication of his poetic talent or of his blossoming genius. About 1851, Whitman left journalism and took up carpentry in Brooklyn.

He made his appearance as a poet in 1855 with a small, privately printed collection of poems bearing the title *Leaves of Grass*. The volume created no great stir in the literary world, but it did bring to the hopeful poet a letter of high praise from Ralph Waldo Emerson who had been sent a complimentary copy. Encouraged, Whitman then began that process of rewriting, editing, and expanding *Leaves of Grass* that was to occupy him for the rest of his career. Like a living organism, Whitman's single book grew through nine separate editions from the embryonic 1855 volume to the large and complete 1892 edition.

A fervent believer in the union of the states, Whitman was profoundly affected by the Civil War. He was in his forties at the beginning of the war, and for two years he devoted his energies as an unofficial nurse to the sick and the wounded in field and army hospitals. In 1864, his health broke down and he returned to his mother's home in Brooklyn to recuperate. He went to Washington in January, 1865, to take a job as clerk in the Indian Bureau of the Department of the Interior. Six months later, the Secretary of the Interior, James Harlan, dismissed him. The Secretary had seen a copy of *Leaves of Grass* and been scandalized by the poet's frank and sensual handling of sex. Fortunately, J. Hubley Ashton, the Assistant Attorney General, was an admirer of Whitman's poetry and the following day appointed him to a position in the Attorney General's office.

Whitman's duties made no excessive demand upon his time and energy, and he retained the position until 1873 when he suffered a stroke. By this time Whitman was an internationally recognized poet, and three books about him as poet and man had already been published. He recovered from the stroke and eventually bought a house in Camden, New Jersey, where he lived until his death in 1892.

Whitman viewed himself as the poet of democracy, an inspired seer who spoke for the common man. In his daily life he attempted to live this role. He wore workman's clothes, a broad-brimmed hat, and a flowing beard that gave him the look of a biblical prophet. He took great pride in his large, healthy physique, and though he never married, he fabricated stories about his masculinity and about fathering children. During the final decades of his life, Whitman was a living legend, vigorously attacked by his critics and as vigorously defended by a growing group of fervid admirers.

Though the biographical details of Whitman's first thirty-six years provide no indications that his genius would suddenly flower, we can, from a study of his poetry, look back and recognize those experiences and those historical and philosophical forces which influenced his thinking and his poetry. As a reporter in a rapidly expanding metropolis, for example, Whitman was keenly aware of the forces that were molding the United States. Today, Americans take for granted the strength, size, and world influence of their country, but 150 or so years ago—a very short time in the span of world history—Americans were deeply involved in the process of establishing a national identity. They took great pride in the growth of their nation as they moved across the massive continent, conquered the wilderness, cultivated the soil, and established communities that grew rapidly into towns and cities. They were very sensitive to criticism, and many, like Whitman, took great pride in the democratic ideal and the American dream of fulfilling the promise of history's long struggle for equality among men. In Whitman, the forces that were welding a nation found a voice and a philosophical justification.

> I chant the chant of dilation or pride,
> We have had ducking and deprecating about enough.
>
> . . .
>
> I speak the pass-word primeval, I give the sign of democracy.
> By God! I will accept nothing which all cannot have their
> counterpart of on the same terms.

Whitman's themes reveal also that he was responsive to the philosophers he read or heard during his formative years. Emerson's concept of the over-soul, for instance, is apparent in Whitman's World Soul. According to this concept, everything in nature contains a droplet of the immortal and indivisible World Soul. Hence all things—a leaf of grass and a human being—are united by the essence they share. This idea is fundamental to Whitman's thought, and most of his other concepts derive from it. His inspiration as poet, he tells us in "Out of the Cradle Endlessly Rocking" derived from a mystical experience in which he recognized that his soul was part of the World Soul, and that he was therefore united to all things, living and dead. It is this message of human and cosmic unity that Whitman chants. Because all men and things in nature are, in essence, one, when Walt Whitman speaks of himself he speaks for all men: the laborer and the intellectual, the failure and the success, the wife and the prostitute. He can also project himself into the cow and the horse; he incorporates within himself "gneiss, coal . . . esculent roots." He knows that "the leaf of grass is no less than the journey-work of the stars." He can transcend time and space because his soul is immortal and is shared by everything everywhere. He can chant without restriction of everything because sensuality and sex, the foul and the clean, the holy and the unholy are all aspects of existence. "I am the poet of the Body and I am the poet of the Soul," he declares.

Whitman's thinking incorporates mysticism, with its belief in intuitive wisdom and inspiration, in the essential brotherhood of all men which can be made manifest through love. It also incorporates aspects of pantheism and of cosmic evolution. Whitman viewed democratic ideals and the union of the individual states into a united nation as the highest stage so far reached in man's progression, but only a stage in a continual development. He was no systematic thinker, and he did not claim to be a philosopher:

> Do I contradict myself?
> Very well then I contradict myself
> I am large, I contain multitudes.

Whitman therefore could be a mystic who celebrated the cosmic unity of all men and all things and, at the same time, a realist and sensualist who celebrated the joys and the pains of physical existence.

In his prefaces to the various editions of *Leaves of Grass,* Whitman had much to say about the role of the poet. In the first edition, he declared that the "United States themselves are essentially the greatest poem," and the American bard must be the incarnation of his country. The duty of the poet, he also said, is to show his fellow men the "path between reality and their souls." In these prefaces, however, Whitman says little about the technique of the poet. His unwillingness to talk about form and technique was, according to Gay Wilson Allen, "imbedded in his fundamental assumptions about his literary intentions. Not only must his form be capable of expressing his mystical ideas, but to admit conscious planning and moulding of the expression would have meant casting doubt on its authenticity and his own sincerity."

Whitman did declare that the three greatest influences upon his style were Italian opera, oratory, and the sea. The declamatory quality of oratory is obvious in all of his work; and in many of his poems such as "Out of the Cradle Endlessly Rocking" the influences of the opera and the sea are readily apparent. Despite his insistence upon the inspired character of his verse, Whitman was a careful revisor, and his work reveals that he utilized throughout his career certain basic techniques. The poetic unit in his verse is the line [see *Handbook:* free verse]. Each line is a complete thought, even if it is not a grammatical unit, a sentence. These line units are frequently developed as parallel units, which, Gay Allen has shown, Whitman probably derived from the Biblical Psalms. In this type of poetic structure, lines are balanced one against another, sometimes synonymously (a second line repeating the idea of the first); sometimes synthetically (the second line responding to the idea of the first); sometimes antithetically (the second line presenting an opposed idea); and sometimes climatically (a series of lines moving to an emotional or logical climax). Whitman's poetry also achieves something approximating the unity of conventional stanzas by connecting a series of lines with repetition of words, phrases, or grammatical forms. Even a casual study of Whitman's style reveals that though the verse may be unconventional, it is by no means artless. He may have been initially inspired, but he developed a distinct and unique technique for expressing his vision.

There have been two major streams of poetry in the United States, the first a traditionally-oriented verse, and the second, fathered by Whitman, an unconventional, free-flowing chant, frequently mystic as in the works of Vachel Lindsay and the more recent "beat" poets. The American nation has reached its maturity since Whitman sang its praises. Many of his dreams and hopes for it remain unfulfilled, but the dream of brotherhood and democratic equality still exerts a powerful influence upon the American character and upon American society. For both Americans and foreigners, Walt Whitman will probably remain the preeminent poet of the American dream.

BIBLIOGRAPHY

Allen, Gay Wilson. *The Solitary Singer.* New York: Macmillan, 1955. (Paper edition, Grove Press, Evergreen Books.)

Allen, Gay Wilson. *Walt Whitman Handbook.* Chicago: Packard, 1946.

Schyberg, Frederik. *Walt Whitman.* New York: Columbia University Press, 1951.

Out of the Cradle Endlessly Rocking

Out of the cradle endlessly rocking,
Out of the mocking-bird's throat, the musical shuttle,
Out of the Ninth-month midnight,
Over the sterile sands and the fields beyond, where the child leaving
his bed wander'd alone, bareheaded, barefoot,
Down from the shower'd halo,
Up from the mystic play of shadows twining and twisting as if they
were alive,
Out from the patches of briers and blackberries,
From the memories of the bird that chanted to me,
From your memories sad brother, from the fitful risings and fallings I
heard,
From under that yellow half-moon late-risen and swollen as if with
tears, 10
From those beginning notes of yearning and love there in the mist,
From the thousand responses of my heart never to cease,
From the myriad thence-arous'd words,
From the word stronger and more delicious than any,
From such as now they start the scene revisiting,
As a flock, twittering, rising, or overhead passing,
Borne hither, ere all eludes me, hurriedly,
A man, yet by these tears a little boy again,
Throwing myself on the sand, confronting the waves,
I, chanter of pains and joys, uniter of here and hereafter 20
Taking all hints to use them, but swiftly leaping beyond them,
A reminiscence sing.

Once Paumanok,
When the lilac-scent was in the air and Fifth-month grass was grow-
ing,
Up this seashore in some briers,
Two feather'd guests from Alabama, two together,
And their nest, and four light-green eggs spotted with brown,

l. 22. *Paumanok:* the Indian name for Long Island.

And every day the he-bird to and fro near at hand,
And every day the she-bird crouch'd on her nest, silent, with bright eyes,
And every day I, a curious boy, never too close, never disturbing them, 30
Cautiously peering, absorbing, translating.

Shine! shine! shine!
Pour down your warmth, great sun!
While we bask, we two together.

Two together!
Winds blow south, or winds blow north,
Day come white, or night come black,
Home, or rivers and mountains from home,
Singing all time, minding no time,
While we two keep together. 40

Till of a sudden,
May-be kill'd, unknown to her mate,
One forenoon the she-bird crouch'd not on the nest,
Nor return'd that afternoon, nor the next,
Nor ever appear'd again.

And thenceforward all summer in the sound of the sea,
And at night under the full of the moon in calmer weather,
Over the hoarse surging of the sea,
Or flitting from brier to brier by day,
I saw, I heard at intervals the remaining one, the he-bird, 50
The solitary guest from Alabama.

Blow! blow! blow!
Blow up sea-winds along Paumanok's shore;
I wait and I wait till you blow my mate to me.

Yes, when the stars glisten'd,
All night long on the prong of a moss-scallop'd stake,
Down almost amid the slapping waves,
Sat the lone singer wonderful causing tears.

He call'd on his mate,
He pour'd forth the meanings which I of all men know. 60

Yes my brother I know,
The rest might not, but I have treasur'd every note,
For more than once dimly down to the beach gliding,
Silent, avoiding the moonbeams, blending myself with the shadows,
Recalling now the obscure shapes, the echoes, the sounds and sights
after their sorts,
The white arms out in the breakers tirelessly tossing,
I, with bare feet, a child, the wind wafting my hair,
Listen'd long and long.

Listen'd to keep, to sing, now translating the notes,
Following you my brother. 70

Soothe! soothe! soothe!
Close on its wave soothes the wave behind,
And again another behind embracing and lapping, every one close,
But my love soothes not me, not me.

Low hangs the moon, it rose late,
It is lagging—O I think it is heavy with love, with love.

O madly the sea pushes upon the land,
With love, with love.

O night! do I not see my love fluttering out among the breakers?
What is that little black thing I see there in the white? 80

Loud! loud! loud!
Loud I call to you, my love!
High and clear I shoot my voice over the waves,
Surely you must know who is here, is here,
You must know who I am, my love.

Low-hanging moon!
What is that dusky spot in your brown yellow?
O it is the shape, the shape of my mate!
O moon do not keep her from me any longer.

Land! land! O land! 90
Whichever way I turn, O I think you could give me my mate back again if you only would,
For I am almost sure I see her dimly whichever way I look.

O rising stars!
Perhaps the one I want so much will rise, will rise with some of you.

O throat! O trembling throat!
Sound clearer through the atmosphere!
Pierce the woods, the earth,
Somewhere listening to catch you must be the one I want.

Shake out carols!
Solitary here, the night's carols! 100
Carols of lonesome love! death's carols!
Carols under that lagging, yellow, waning moon!
O under the moon where she droops almost down into the sea!
O reckless despairing carols.

But soft! sink low!
Soft! let me just murmur,
And do you wait a moment you husky-nois'd sea,
For somewhere I believe I heard my mate responding to me,
So faint, I must be still, be still to listen,
But not altogether still, for then she might not come immediately to me. 110

Hither my love!
Here I am! here!
With this just-sustain'd note I announce myself to you,
This gentle call is for you my love, for you.

Do not be decoy'd elsewhere,
That is the whistle of the wind, it is not my voice,
That is the fluttering, the fluttering of the spray,
Those are the shadows of leaves.

O darkness! O in vain!
O I am very sick and sorrowful. 120

O brown halo in the sky near the moon, drooping upon the sea!
O troubled reflection in the sea!

O throat! O throbbing heart!
And I singing uselessly, uselessly all the night.

O past! O happy life! O songs of joy!
In the air, in the woods, over fields,
Loved! loved! loved! loved! loved!
But my mate no more, no more with me!
We two together no more.

The aria sinking, 130
All else continuing, the stars shining,
The winds blowing, the notes of the bird continuous echoing,
With angry moans the fierce old mother incessantly moaning,
On the sands of Paumanok's shore gray and rustling,
The yellow half-moon enlarged, sagging down, drooping, the face of the sea almost touching,
The boy ecstatic, with his bare feet the waves, with his hair the atmosphere dallying,
The love in the heart long pent, now loose, now at last tumultuously bursting,
The aria's meanings, the ears, the soul, swiftly depositing,
The strange tears down the cheeks coursing,
The colloquy there, the trio, each uttering, 140
The undertone, the savage old mother incessantly crying,
To the boy's soul's questions sullenly timing, some drown'd secret hissing,
To the outsetting bard.

Demon or bird! (said the boy's soul,)
It is indeed toward your mate you sing? or is it really to me?
For I, that was a child, my tongue's use sleeping, now I have heard you,
Now in a moment I know what I am for, I awake,
And already a thousand singers, a thousand songs, clearer, louder and more sorrowful than yours,
A thousand warbling echoes have started to life within me, never to die.

O you singer solitary, singing by yourself, projecting me, 150
O solitary me listening, never more shall I cease perpetuating you,
Never more shall I escape, never more the reverberations,
Never more the cries of unsatisfied love be absent from me,
Never again leave me to be the peaceful child I was before what there
in the night,
By the sea under the yellow and sagging moon,
The messenger there arous'd, the fire, the sweet hell within,
The unknown want, the destiny of me.

O give me the clew! (it lurks in the night here somewhere,)
O if I am to have so much, let me have more!

A word then, (for I will conquer it,) 160
The word final, superior to all,
Subtle, sent up—what is it?—I listen;
Are you whispering it, and have been all the time, you sea waves?
Is that it from your liquid rims and wet sands?

Whereto answering, the sea,
Delaying not, hurrying not,
Whisper'd me through the night, and very plainly before daybreak,
Lisp'd to me the low and delicious word death,
And again death, death, death, death,
Hissing melodious, neither like the bird nor like my arous'd child's
heart, 170
But edging near as privately for me rustling at my feet,
Creeping thence steadily up to my ears and laving me softly all over,
Death, death, death, death, death.

Which I do not forget,
But fuse the song of my dusky demon and brother,
That he sang to me in the moonlight on Paumanok's gray beach,
With the thousand responsive songs at random,
My own songs awaked from that hour,
And with them the key, the word up from the waves,
The word of the sweetest song and all songs, 180
That strong and delicious word which, creeping to my feet,
(Or like some old crone rocking the cradle, swathed in sweet garments,
bending aside,)
The sea whisper'd me.

[*1859, 1881–82*]

Commentary

This poem recreates the mystical experience that made Whitman a poet, the singer of the "here and hereafter." It is an excellent introduction to Whitman not only because it reveals many of his basic ideas, but because it provides insight into the careful structuring of his poetry. The close relationship between form and idea is immediately apparent in the opening line: "Out of the cradle endlessly rocking." The rhythm of the line actually suggests the idea expressed. The careful interweaving of symbols, theme, and form throughout the poem is also apparent in this first line. The poem describes the mystical experience of a young boy. He undergoes a spiritual birth that takes place on the shore of the rolling sea and that is brought about by his spiritual response to the sea. The sea, a symbol of nature, with its endless motion reveals to the boy the ultimate secret of the cosmos—the World Soul, the unity of everything in the universe.

Before the young boy can open his soul to this secret, he must know the meaning of love and of loss. The setting, in nature, is important. By becoming a part of nature, the boy is prepared for the experience. The dominant units of the natural world—land, sea, and sky—are presented and emphasized through various symbols. In the opening lines all the aspects of nature contribute to the boy's intuitive understanding of the universe: "Over the sterile sands and the fields beyond . . . . Down from the shower'd halo, / Up from the mystic play of shadows . . . . Out from the patches of briers and blackberries." The boy's union with nature is effected by his rapport with the mocking-birds, which serve as intermediaries between the inarticulate natural world and the human being. By experiencing the joy of love expressed in their songs and then the pains of loss in the male bird's plaintive call to its mate, the boy becomes a poet, but he still lacks complete understanding. Finally the sound of the sea upon the shore gives him the clue: "Death, death, death, death, death." The poet understands the meaning of death: the absorption of the individual soul into the World Soul. This intuitive recognition of cosmic unity is the secret the sea whispers and it becomes the theme of all the poet's songs.

Structurally, the poem is divided into three parts, which approximate the overture, the drama, and the finale of an opera. In the first twenty-two lines, Whitman sets the tone and suggests the themes and motifs of the musical drama to follow. The introductory character of these opening lines is emphasized by the climactic parallelism of the unit. The series of lines, most of which begin with prepositional phrases, constitute one sentence, the subject and verb of which are delayed until the "I . . . A reminiscence sing" is reached in the final three lines.

In the second section, extending from line 23 to line 129, Whitman uses the recitative and aria of opera. The arias are italicized and their musical quality is emphasized by regularity of meter and traditional sound and rhyme patterns. The passages of recitative revert to the line unit characteristic of Whitman's verse. In the arias, the nature symbols which dominate in the rest of the poem remain prominent. Also Whitman's imagery in these songs conveys and dramatically intensifies the major themes of the entire poem. The close structural relationship between the songs and the rest of the poem is particularly apparent in the repetition of words in the initial line of a number of arias: "Shine! shine! shine!" "Blow! blow! blow!" [see *Handbook:* rest]. The final clue to the mystery of the universe is whispered by the sea with an identical repetition: "Death, death, death, death, death." Through such techniques Whitman unifies his motifs and provides opportunity for the reader to share in the mystical experience.

In the concluding section, all the motifs are united: under the sagging moon, the boy stands on the beach listening to the sea. At the culmination of this spiritual rebirth, Whitman returns to the initial birth image:

> That strong and delicious word which, creeping to my feet,
> (Or like some old crone rocking the cradle, swathed in sweet
> garments, bending aside,)
> The sea whisper'd me.

"Out of the Cradle Endlessly Rocking" makes clear why Whitman could describe himself as the "uniter of here and hereafter," and would declare his purpose to indicate the path between reality and the soul.

FROM *Song of Myself*

I

I celebrate myself, and sing myself,
And what I assume you shall assume,
For every atom belonging to me as good belongs to you.

I loafe and invite my soul,
I lean and loafe at my ease observing a spear of summer grass.

My tongue, every atom of my blood, form'd from this soil, this air,
Born here of parents born here from parents the same, and their
    parents the same,
I, now thirty-seven years old in perfect health begin,
Hoping to cease not till death.

Creeds and schools in abeyance, 10
Retiring back a while sufficed at what they are, but never forgotten,

I harbor for good or bad, I permit to speak at every hazard,
Nature without check with original energy.

3

I have heard what the talkers were talking, the talk of the beginning
    and the end,
But I do not talk of the beginning or the end.

There was never any more inception than there is now,
Nor any more youth or age than there is now,
And will never be any more perfection than there is now,
Nor any more heaven or hell than there is now.

Urge and urge and urge,
Always the procreant urge of the world.
Out of the dimness opposite equals advance, always substance and
    increase, always sex,
Always a knit of identity, always distinction, always a breed of
    life. 10

To elaborate is no avail, learn'd and unlearn'd feel that it is so.

Sure as the most certain sure, plumb in the uprights, well entretied, braced in the beams,
Stout as a horse, affectionate, haughty, electrical,
I and this mystery here we stand.

Clear and sweet is my soul, and clear and sweet is all that is not my soul.

Lack one lacks both, and the unseen is proved by the seen,
Till that becomes unseen and receives proof in its turn.

Showing the best and dividing it from the worst age vexes age,
Knowing the perfect fitness and equanimity of things, while they discuss and I am silent, and go bathe and admire myself.

Welcome is every organ and attribute of me, and of any man hearty and clean, 20
Not an inch nor a particle of an inch is vile, and none shall be less familiar than the rest.

I am satisfied—I see, dance, laugh, sing;
As the hugging and loving bed-fellow sleeps at my side through the night, and withdraws at the peep of the day with stealthy tread,
Leaving me baskets cover'd with white towels swelling the house with their plenty,
Shall I postpone my acceptation and realization and scream at my eyes,
That they turn from gazing after and down the road,
And forthwith cipher and show me to a cent,
Exactly the value of one and exactly the value of two, and which is ahead?

5

I believe in you my soul, the other I am must not abase itself to you,
And you must not be abased to the other.

Loafe with me on the grass, loose the stop from your throat,
Not words, not music or rhyme I want, not custom or lecture, not even the best,
Only the lull I like, the hum of your valvèd voice.

I mind how once we lay such a transparent summer morning,
How you settled your head athwart my hips and gently turn'd over
upon me,
And parted the shirt from my bosom-bone, and plunged your tongue
to my bare-stript heart,
And reach'd till you felt my beard, and reach'd till you held my feet.

Swiftly arose and spread around me the peace and knowledge that pass
all the argument of the earth, 10
And I know that the hand of God is the promise of my own,
And I know that the spirit of God is the brother of my own,
And that all the men ever born are also my brothers, and the women
my sisters and lovers,
And that a kelson of the creation is love,
And limitless are leaves stiff or drooping in the fields,
And brown ants in the little wells beneath them,
And mossy scabs of the worm fence, heap'd stones, elder, mullein and
poke-weed.

6

A child said *What is the grass?* fetching it to me with full hands,
How could I answer the child? I do not know what it is any more
than he.

I guess it must be the flag of my disposition, out of hopeful green
stuff woven.

Or I guess it is the handkerchief of the Lord,
A scented gift and remembrancer designedly dropt,
Bearing the owner's name someway in the corners, that we may see
and remark, and say *Whose?*

Or I guess the grass is itself a child, the produced babe of the vegetation.

Or I guess it is a uniform hieroglyphic,
And it means, Sprouting alike in broad zones and narrow zones,

l. 14. *kelson:* or keelson, a longitudinal beam of timber or metal fastened over a ship's keel to provide structural strength.

Growing among black folks as among white, 10
Kanuck, Tuckahoe, Congressman, Cuff, I give them the same, I receive them the same.

And now it seems to me the beautiful uncut hair of graves.

Tenderly will I use you curling grass,
It may be you transpire from the breasts of young men,
It may be if I had known them I would have loved them,
It may be you are from old people, or from offspring taken soon out of their mothers' laps,
And here you are the mothers' laps.

This grass is very dark to be from the white heads of old mothers,
Darker than the colorless beards of old men,
Dark to come from under the faint red roofs of mouths. 20
O I perceive after all so many uttering tongues,
And I perceive they do not come from the roofs of mouths for nothing.
I wish I could translate the hints about the dead young men and women,
And the hints about old men and mothers, and the offspring taken soon out of their laps.

What do you think has become of the young and old men?
And what do you think has become of the women and children?

They are alive and well somewhere,
The smallest sprout shows there is really no death,
And if ever there was it led forward life, and does not wait at the end to arrest it,
And ceas'd the moment life appear'd. 30

All goes onward and outward, nothing collapses,
And to die is different from what any one supposed, and luckier.

7

Has any one supposed it lucky to be born?
I hasten to inform him or her it is just as lucky to die, and I know it.

l. 11. *Kanuck:* a French Canadian.
Tuckahoe: a poor Virginian who ate a fungus called tuckahoe.
Cuff: a Negro.

I pass death with the dying and birth with the new-wash'd babe,
and am not contain'd between my hat and boots,
And peruse manifold objects, no two alike and everyone good,
The earth good and the stars good, and their adjuncts all good.

I am not an earth nor an adjunct of an earth,
I am the mate and companion of people, all just as immortal and
fathomless as myself,
(They do not know how immortal, but I know.)

Every kind for itself and its own, for me mine male and female,
For me those that have been boys and that love women, 10
For me the man that is proud and feels how it stings to be
slighted,
For me the sweet-heart and the old maid, for me mothers and the
mothers of mothers,
For me lips that have smiled, eyes that have shed tears,
For me children and the begetters of children.

Undrape! you are not guilty to me, nor stale nor discarded,
I see through the broadcloth and gingham whether or no,
And am around, tenacious, acquisitive, tireless, and cannot be
shaken away.

17

These are really the thoughts of all men in all ages and lands,
they are not original with me,
If they are not yours as much as mine they are nothing, or next
to nothing,
If they are not the riddle and the untying of the riddle they are
nothing,
If they are not just as close as they are distant they are nothing.

This is the grass that grows wherever the land is and the water is,
This is the common air that bathes the globe.

20

Who goes there? hankering, gross, mystical, nude;
How is it I extract strength from the beef I eat?

What is a man anyhow? what am I? what are you?
All I mark as my own you shall offset it with your own,
Else it were time lost listening to me.

I do not snivel that snivel the world over,
That months are vacuums and the ground but wallow and filth.

Whimpering and truckling fold with powders for invalids, con-
    formity goes to the fourth-remov'd,
I wear my hat as I please indoors or out.

Why should I pray? why should I venerate and be ceremonious? 10

Having pried through the strata, analyzed to a hair, counsel'd with
    doctors and calculated close,
I find no sweeter fat than sticks to my own bones.

In all people I see myself, none more and not one a barleycorn
    less,
And the good or bad I say of myself I say of them.

I know I am solid and sound,
To me the converging objects of the universe perpetually flow,
All are written to me, and I must get what the writing means.

I know I am deathless,
I know this orbit of mine cannot be swept by a carpenter's
    compass,
I know I shall not pass like a child's carlacue cut with a burnt
    stick at night. 20

I know I am august,
I do not trouble my spirit to vindicate itself or be understood,
I see that the elementary laws never apologize,
(I reckon I behave no prouder than the level I plant my house
    by, after all.)

I exist as I am, that is enough,
If no other in the world be aware I sit content,
And if each and all be aware I sit content.

l. 20. *carlacue:* slang for curlicue.

One world is aware and by far the largest to me, and that is myself,
And whether I come to my own to-day or in ten thousand or ten million years,
I can cheerfully take it now, or with equal cheerfulness I can wait. 30
My foothold is tenon'd and mortis'd in granite,
I laugh at what you call dissolution,
And I know the amplitude of time.

21

I am the poet of the Body and I am the poet of the Soul,
The pleasures of heaven are with me and the pains of hell are with me,
The first I graft and increase upon myself, the latter I translate into a new tongue.

I am the poet of the woman the same as the man,
And I say it is as great to be a woman as to be a man,
And I say there is nothing greater than the mother of men.

I chant the chant of dilation or pride,
We have had ducking and deprecating about enough,
I show that size is only development.

Have you outstript the rest? are you the President? 10
It is a trifle, they will more than arrive there every one, and still pass on.

I am he that walks with the tender and growing night,
I call to the earth and sea half-held by the night.

Press close bare-bosom'd night—press close magnetic nourishing night!
Night of south winds—night of the large few stars!
Still nodding night—mad naked summer night.

Smile O voluptuous cool-breath'd earth!
Earth of the slumbering and liquid trees!
Earth of departed sunset—earth of the mountains misty-topt!

Earth of the vitreous pour of the full moon just tinged with blue! 20
Earth of shine and dark mottling the tide of the river!
Earth of the limpid gray of clouds brighter and clearer for my
sake!
Far-swooping elbow'd earth—rich apple-blossom'd earth!
Smile, for your lover comes.

Prodigal, you have given me love—therefore I to you give love!
O unspeakable passionate love.

24

Walt Whitman, a kosmos, of Manhattan the son,
Turbulent, fleshy, sensual, eating, drinking and breeding,
No sentimentalist, no stander above men and women or apart
from them,
No more modest than immodest.

Unscrew the locks from the doors!
Unscrew the doors themselves from their jambs!

Whoever degrades another degrades me,
And whatever is done or said returns at last to me.

Through me the afflatus surging and surging, through me the
current and index.

I speak the pass-word primeval, I give the sign of democracy, 10
By God! I will accept nothing which all cannot have their
counterpart of on the same terms.

Through me many long dumb voices,
Voices of the interminable generations of prisoners and slaves,
Voices of the diseas'd and despairing and of thieves and dwarfs,
Voices of cycles of preparation and accretion,
And of the threads that connect the stars, and of wombs and of
the father-stuff,
And of the rights of them the others are down upon,
Of the deform'd, trivial, flat, foolish, despised,
Fog in the air, beetles rolling balls of dung.

Through me forbidden voices, 20
Voices of sexes and lusts, voices veil'd and I remove the veil,
Voices indecent by me clarified and transfigur'd.

I do not press my fingers across my mouth,
I keep as delicate around the bowels as around the head and heart,
Copulation is no more rank to me than death is.

I believe in the flesh and the appetites,
Seeing, hearing, feeling, are miracles, and each part and tag of me
is a miracle.

Divine am I inside and out, and I make holy whatever I touch or
am touch'd from,
The scent of these arm-pits aroma finer than prayer,
This head more than churches, bibles, and all the creeds. 30

If I worship one thing more than another it shall be the spread
of my own body, or any part of it,
Translucent mould of me it shall be you!
Shaded ledges and rests it shall be you!
Firm masculine colter it shall be you!
Whatever goes to the tilth of me it shall be you!
You my rich blood! your milky stream pale strippings of my life!
Breast that presses against other breasts it shall be you!
My brain it shall be your occult convolutions!
Root of wash'd sweet-flag! timorous pond-snipe! nest of guarded
duplicate eggs! it shall be you!
Mix'd tussled hay of head, beard, brawn, it shall be you! 40
Trickling sap of maple, fibre of manly wheat, it shall be you!
Sun so generous it shall be you!
Vapors lighting and shading my face it shall be you!
You sweaty brooks and dews it shall be you!
Winds whose soft-tickling genitals rub against me it shall be you!
Broad muscular fields, branches of live oak, loving lounger in my
winding paths, it shall be you!
Hands I have taken, face I have kiss'd, mortal I have ever touch'd,
it shall be you.

l. 34. *colter:* a blade on a plow that makes vertical cuts in the soil.
l. 35. *tilth:* soil prepared for planting.

I dote on myself, there is that lot of me and all so luscious,
Each moment and whatever happens thrills me with joy,
I cannot tell how my ankles bend, nor whence the cause of my faintest wish, 50
Nor the cause of the friendship I emit, nor the cause of the friendship I take again.

That I walk up my stoop, I pause to consider if it really be,
A morning-glory at my window satisfies me more than the metaphysics of books.

To behold the day-break!
The little light fades the immense and diaphanous shadows,
The air tastes good to my palate.

Hefts of the moving world at innocent gambols silently rising, freshly exuding,
Scooting obliquely high and low.

Something I cannot see puts upward libidinous prongs,
Seas of bright juice suffuse heaven. 60

The earth by the sky staid with, the daily close of their junction,
The heav'd challenge from the east that moment over my head,
The mocking taunt, See then whether you shall be master!

31

I believe a leaf of grass is no less than the journey-work of the stars,
And the pismire is equally perfect, and a grain of sand, and the egg of the wren,
And the tree-toad is a chef-d'œuvre for the highest,
And the running blackberry would adorn the parlors of heaven,
And the narrowest hinge in my hand puts to scorn all machinery,
And the cow crunching with depress'd head surpasses any statue,
And a mouse is miracle enough to stagger sextillions of infidels.

I find I incorporate gneiss, coal, long-threaded moss, fruits, grains, esculent roots,
And am stucco'd with quadrupeds and birds all over,

l. 2. *pismire:* an ant.

And have distanced what is behind me for good reasons, 10
But call any thing back again when I desire it.

In vain the speeding or shyness,
In vain the plutonic rocks send their old heat against my approach,
In vain the mastodon retreats beneath its own powder'd bones,
In vain objects stand leagues off and assume manifold shapes,
In vain the ocean settling in hollows and the great monsters lying
low,
In vain the buzzard houses herself with the sky,
In vain the snake slides through the creepers and logs,
In vain the elk takes to the inner passes of the woods,
In vain the razor-bill'd auk sails far north to Labrador, 20
I follow quickly, I ascend to the nest in the fissure of the cliff.

48

I have said that the soul is not more than the body,
And I have said that the body is not more than the soul,
And nothing, not God, is greater to one than one's self is,
And whoever walks a furlong without sympathy walks to his own
funeral drest in his shroud,
And I or you pocketless of a dime may purchase the pick of the
earth,
And to glance with an eye or show a bean in its pod confounds
the learning of all times,
And there is no trade or employment but the young man following
it may become a hero,
And there is no object so soft but it makes a hub for the wheel'd
universe,
And I say to any man or woman, Let your soul stand cool and
composed before a million universes.

And I say to mankind, Be not curious about God, 10
For I who am curious about each am not curious about God.
(No array of terms can say how much I am at peace about God
and about death.)

I hear and behold God in every object, yet understand God not in
the least,
Nor do I understand who there can be more wonderful than myself.

Why should I wish to see God better than this day?
I see something of God each hour of the twenty-four, and each
    moment then,
In the faces of men and women I see God, and in my own face in
    the glass,
I find letters from God dropt in the street, and every one is sign'd
    by God's name,
And I leave them where they are, for I know that wheresoe'er I
    go
Others will punctually come for ever and ever. 20

[*1855, 1881–82*]

When Lilacs Last in the Dooryard Bloom'd

1

When lilacs last in the dooryard bloom'd,
And the great star early droop'd in the western sky in the night,
I mourn'd, and yet shall mourn with ever-returning spring.

Ever-returning spring, trinity sure to me you bring,
Lilac blooming perennial and drooping star in the west,
And thought of him I love.

2

O powerful western fallen star!
O shades of night—O moody, tearful night!
O great star disappear'd—O the black murk that hides the star!
O cruel hands that hold me powerless—O helpless soul of me! 10
O harsh surrounding cloud that will not free my soul.

3

In the dooryard fronting an old farm-house near the white-
    wash'd palings,
Stands the lilac-bush tall-growing with heart-shaped leaves of
    rich green,

When Lilacs . . . Bloom'd: one of four elegies which Whitman wrote for Abraham Lincoln.

With many a pointed blossom rising delicate, with the perfume strong I love,
With every leaf a miracle—and from this bush in the dooryard,
With delicate-color'd blossoms and heart-shaped leaves of rich green,
A sprig with its flower I break.

4

In the swamp in secluded recesses,
A shy and hidden bird is warbling a song.

Solitary the thrush, 20
The hermit withdrawn to himself, avoiding the settlements,
Sings by himself a song.

Song of the bleeding throat,
Death's outlet song of life, (for well dear brother I know,
If thou wast not granted to sing thou would'st surely die.)

5

Over the breast of the spring, the land, amid cities,
Amid lanes and through old woods, where lately the violets peep'd from the ground, spotting the gray debris,
Amid the grass in the fields each side of the lanes, passing the endless grass,
Passing the yellow-spear'd wheat, every grain from its shroud in the dark-brown fields uprisen,
Passing the apple-tree blows of white and pink in the orchards, 30
Carrying a corpse to where it shall rest in the grave,
Night and day journeys a coffin.

6

Coffin that passes through lanes and streets,
Through day and night with the great cloud darkening the land,
With the pomp of the inloop'd flags with the cities draped in black,
With the show of the States themselves as of crape-veil'd women standing,

l. 33. *Coffin . . . streets:* Lincoln's body was taken by special train to Springfield, Illinois. Mourners lined the route which passed through seven states.

With processions long and winding and the flambeaus of the
night,
With the countless torches lit, with the silent sea of faces and the
unbared heads,
With the waiting depot, the arriving coffin, and the sombre faces,
With dirges through the night, with the thousand voices rising
strong and solemn, 40
With all the mournful voices of the dirges pour'd around the
coffin,
The dim-lit churches and the shuddering organs—where amid
these you journey,
With the tolling tolling bells' perpetual clang,
Here, coffin that slowly passes,
I give you my sprig of lilac.

7

(Nor for you, for one alone,
Blossoms and branches green to coffins all I bring,
For fresh as the morning, thus would I chant a song for you
O sane and sacred death.

All over bouquets of roses,
O death, I cover you over with roses and early lilies, 50
But mostly and now the lilac that blooms the first,
Copious I break, I break the sprigs from the bushes,
With loaded arms I come, pouring for you,
For you and the coffins all of you O death.)

8

O western orb sailing the heaven,
Now I know what you must have meant as a month since I
walk'd,
As I walk'd in silence the transparent shadowy night,
As I saw you had something to tell as you bent to me night after
night,
As you droop'd from the sky low down as if to my side, (while
the other stars all look'd on,)
As we wander'd together the solemn night, (for something I
know not what kept me from sleep,) 60
As the night advanced, and I saw on the rim of the west how
full you were of woe,

As I stood on the rising ground in the breeze in the cool transparent night,
As I watch'd where you pass'd and was lost in the netherward black of the night,
As my soul in its trouble dissatisfied sank, as where you sad orb,
Concluded, dropt in the night, and was gone.

9

Sing on there in the swamp,
O singer bashful and tender, I hear your notes, I hear your call,
I hear, I come presently, I understand you,
But a moment I linger, for the lustrous star has detain'd me,
The star my departing comrade holds and detains me. 70

10

O how shall I warble myself for the dead one there I loved?
And how shall I deck my song for the large sweet soul that has gone?
And what shall my perfume be for the grave of him I love?

Sea-winds blown from east and west,
Blown from the Eastern sea and blown from the Western sea, till there on the prairies meeting,
These and with these and the breath of my chant,
I'll perfume the grave of him I love.

11

O what shall I hang on the chamber walls?
And what shall the pictures be that I hang on the walls,
To adorn the burial-house of him I love? 80

Pictures of growing spring and farms and homes,
With the Fourth-month eve at sundown, and the gray smoke lucid and bright,
With floods of the yellow gold of the gorgeous, indolent, sinking sun, burning, expanding the air,
With the fresh sweet herbage under foot, and the pale green leaves of the trees prolific,
In the distance the flowing glaze, the breast of the river, with a wind-dapple here and there,

With ranging hills on the banks, with many a line against the
sky, and shadows,
And the city at hand with dwellings so dense, and stacks of
chimneys,
And all the scenes of life and the workshops, and the workmen
homeward returning.

12

Lo, body and soul—this land,
My own Manhattan with spires, and the sparkling and hurrying
tides, and the ships, 90
The varied and ample land, the South and the North in the
light, Ohio's shores and flashing Missouri,
And ever the far-spreading prairies cover'd with grass and corn.

Lo, the most excellent sun so calm and haughty,
The violet and purple morn with just-felt breezes,
The gentle soft-born measureless light,
The miracle spreading bathing all, the fulfill'd noon,
The coming eve delicious, the welcome night and the stars,
Over my cities shining all, enveloping man and land.

13

Sing on, sing on you gray-brown bird,
Sing from the swamps, the recesses, pour your chant from the
bushes, 100
Limitless out of the dusk, out of the cedars and pines.

Sing on dearest brother, warble your reedy song,
Loud human song, with voice of uttermost woe.

O liquid and free and tender!
O wild and loose to my soul—O wondrous singer!
You only I hear—yet the star holds me, (but will soon depart,)
Yet the lilac with mastering odor holds me.

14

Now while I sat in the day and look'd forth,
In the close of the day with its light and the fields of spring,
and the farmers preparing their crops,

In the large unconscious scenery of my land with its lakes and
forests, 110
In the heavenly aerial beauty, (after the perturb'd winds and the
storms,)
Under the arching heavens of the afternoon swift passing, and
the voices of children and women,
The many-moving sea-tides, and I saw the ships how they sail'd,
And the summer approaching with richness, and the fields all
busy with labor,
And the infinite separate houses, how they all went on, each
with its meals and minutia of daily usages,
And the streets how their throbbings throbb'd, and the cities
pent—lo, then and there,
Falling upon them all and among them all, enveloping me with
the rest,
Appear'd the cloud, appear'd the long black trail,
And I knew death, its thought, and the sacred knowledge of
death.

Then with the knowledge of death as walking one side of me, 120
And the thought of death close-walking the other side of me,
And I in the middle as with companions, and as holding the
hands of companions,
I fled forth to the hiding receiving night that talks not,
Down to the shores of the water, the path by the swamp in the
dimness,
To the solemn shadowy cedars and ghostly pines so still.

And the singer so shy to the rest receiv'd me,
The gray-brown bird I know receiv'd us comrades three,
And he sang the carol of death, and a verse for him I love.

From deep secluded recesses,
From the fragrant cedars and the ghostly pines so still, 130
Came the carol of the bird.

And the charm of the carol rapt me,
As I held as if by their hands my comrades in the night,
And the voice of my spirit tallied the song of the bird.

Come lovely and soothing death,
Undulate round the world, serenely arriving, arriving,
In the day, in the night, to all, to each,
Sooner or later delicate death.

Prais'd be the fathomless universe,
For life and joy, and for objects and knowledge curious, 140
And for love, sweet love—but praise! praise! praise!
For the sure-enwinding arms of cool-enfolding death.

Dark mother always gliding near with soft feet,
Have none chanted for thee a chant of fullest welcome?
Then I chant it for thee, I glorify thee above all,
I bring thee a song that when thou must indeed come, come unfalteringly.

Approach strong deliveress,
When it is so, when thou hast taken them I joyously sing the dead,
Lost in the loving floating ocean of thee,
Laved in the flood of thy bliss O death. 150

From me to thee glad serenades,
Dances for thee I propose saluting thee, adornments and feastings for thee,
And the sights of the open landscape and the high-spread sky are fitting,
And life and the fields, and the huge and thoughtful night.

The night in silence under many a star,
The ocean shore and the husky whispering wave whose voice I know,
And the soul turning to thee O vast and well-veil'd death,
And the body gratefully nestling close to thee.

Over the tree-tops I float thee a song,
Over the rising and sinking waves, over the myriad fields and the prairies wide, 160
Over the dense-pack'd cities all and the teeming wharves and ways,
I float this carol with joy, with joy to thee O death.

15

To the tally of my soul,
Loud and strong kept up the gray-brown bird,
With pure deliberate notes spreading filling the night.

Loud in the pines and cedars dim,
Clear in the freshness moist and the swamp-perfume,
And I with my comrades there in the night.

While my sight that was bound in my eyes unclosed,
As to long panoramas of visions. 170

And I saw askant the armies,
I saw as in noiseless dreams hundreds of battle-flags,
Borne through the smoke of the battles and pierc'd with missiles
I saw them,
And carried hither and yon through the smoke, and torn and
bloody,
And at last but a few shreds left on the staffs, (and all in
silence,)
And the staffs all splinter'd and broken.

I saw battle-corpses, myriads of them,
And the white skeletons of young men, I saw them,
I saw the debris and debris of all the slain soldiers of the war,
But I saw they were not as was thought, 180
They themselves were fully at rest, they suffer'd not,
The living remain'd and suffer'd, the mother suffer'd,
And the wife and the child and the musing comrade suffer'd,
And the armies that remain'd suffer'd.

16

Passing the visions, passing the night,
Passing, unloosing the hold of my comrades' hands,
Passing the song of the hermit bird and the tallying song of my
soul,
Victorious song, death's outlet song, yet varying ever-altering
song,
As low and wailing, yet clear the notes, rising and falling, flood-
ing the night,

Sadly sinking and fainting, as warning and warning, and yet
again bursting with joy, 190
Covering the earth and filling the spread of the heaven,
As that powerful psalm in the night I heard from recesses,
Passing, I leave thee lilac with heart-shaped leaves,
I leave thee there in the dooryard, blooming, returning with
spring.

I cease from my song for thee,
From my gaze on thee in the west, fronting the west, commun-
ing with thee,
O comrade lustrous with silver face in the night.

Yet each to keep and all, retrievements out of the night,
The song, the wondrous chant of the gray-brown bird,
And the tallying chant, the echo arous'd in my soul, 200
With the lustrous and drooping star with the countenance full of
woe,
With the holders holding my hand nearing the call of the bird,
Comrades mine and I in the midst, and their memory ever to
keep, for the dead I loved so well,
For the sweetest, wisest soul of all my days and lands—and this
for his dear sake,
Lilac and star and bird twined with the chant of my soul,
There in the fragrant pines and the cedars dusk and dim.

[*1865, 1881–82*]

Crossing Brooklyn Ferry

I

Flood-tide below me! I see you face to face!
Clouds of the west—sun there half an hour high—I see you also
face to face.

Crowds of men and women attired in the usual costumes, how
curious you are to me!
On the ferry-boats the hundreds and hundreds that cross, returning home, are more curious to me than you suppose,
And you that shall cross from shore to shore years hence are
more to me, and more in my meditations, than you might
suppose.

2

The impalpable sustenance of me from all things at all hours of the day,
The simple, compact, well-join'd scheme, myself disintegrated, every one disintegrated yet part of the scheme,
The similitudes of the past and those of the future,
The glories strung like beads on my smallest sights and hearings, on the walk in the street and the passage over the river,
The current rushing so swiftly and swimming with me far away, 10
The others that are to follow me, the ties between me and them,
The certainty of others, the life, love, sight, hearing of others.

Others will enter the gates of the ferry and cross from shore to shore,
Others will watch the run of the flood-tide,
Others will see the shipping of Manhattan north and west, and the heights of Brooklyn to the south and east,
Others will see the islands large and small;
Fifty years hence, others will see them as they cross, the sun half an hour high,
A hundred years hence, or ever so many hundred years hence, others will see them,
Will enjoy the sunset, the pouring-in of the flood-tide, the falling-back to the sea of the ebb-tide.

3

It avails not, time nor place—distance avails not, 20
I am with you, you men and women of a generation, or ever so many generations hence,
Just as you feel when you look on the river and sky, so I felt,
Just as any of you is one of a living crowd, I was one of a crowd,
Just as you are refresh'd by the gladness of the river and the bright flow, I was refresh'd,
Just as you stand and lean on the rail, yet hurry with the swift current, I stood yet was hurried,
Just as you look on the numberless masts of ships and the thick-stemm'd pipes of steamboats, I look'd.

I too many and many a time cross'd the river of old,
Watched the Twelfth-month sea-gulls, saw them high in the air floating with motionless wings, oscillating their bodies,

Saw how the glistening yellow lit up parts of their bodies and
left the rest in strong shadow,
Saw the slow-wheeling circles and the gradual edging toward the
south, 30
Saw the reflection of the summer sky in the water,
Had my eyes dazzled by the shimmering track of beams,
Look'd at the fine centrifugal spokes of light round the shape of
my head in the sunlit water,
Look'd on the haze on the hills southward and south-westward,
Look'd on the vapor as it flew in fleeces tinged with violet,
Look'd toward the lower bay to notice the vessels arriving,
Saw their approach, saw aboard those that were near me,
Saw the white sails of schooners and sloops, saw the ships at
anchor,
The sailors at work in the rigging or out astride the spars,
The round masts, the swinging motion of the hulls, the slender
serpentine pennants, 40
The large and small steamers in motion, the pilots in their pilot-
houses,
The white wake left by the passage, the quick tremulous whirl
of the wheels,
The flags of all nations, the falling of them at sunset,
The scallop-edged waves in the twilight, the ladled cups, the
frolicsome crests and glistening,
The stretch afar growing dimmer and dimmer, the gray walls of
the granite storehouses by the docks,
On the river the shadowy group, the big steam-tug closely flank'd
on each side by the barges, the hay-boat, the belated
lighter,
On the neighboring shore the fires from the foundry chimneys
burning high and glaringly into the night,
Casting their flicker of black contrasted with wild red and yellow light over the tops of houses, and down into the clefts
of streets.

4

These and all else were to me the same as they are to you,
I loved well those cities, loved well the stately and rapid river, 50
The men and women I saw were all near to me,

Others the same—others who look back on me because I look'd forward to them,
(The time will come, though I stop here to-day and to-night.)

5

What is it then between us?
What is the count of the scores or hundreds of years between us?

Whatever it is, it avails not—distance avails not, and place avails not,
I too lived, Brooklyn of ample hills was mine,
I too walk'd the streets of Manhattan island, and bathed in the waters around it,
I too felt the curious abrupt questionings stir within me.
In the day among crowds of people sometimes they came upon me, 60
In my walks home late at night or as I lay in my bed they came upon me,
I too had been struck from the float forever held in solution,
I too had receiv'd identity by my body,
That I was I knew was of my body, and what I should be I knew I should be of my body.

6

It is not upon you alone the dark patches fall,
The dark threw its patches down upon me also,
The best I had done seem'd to me blank and suspicious,
My great thoughts as I supposed them, were they not in reality meagre?
Nor is it you alone who know what it is to be evil,
I am he who knew what it was to be evil, 70
I too knitted the old knot of contrariety,
Blabb'd, blush'd, resented, lied, stole, grudg'd,
Had guile, anger, lust, hot wishes I dared not speak,
Was wayward, vain, greedy, shallow, sly, cowardly, malignant,
The wolf, the snake, the hog, not wanting in me,
The cheating look, the frivolous word, the adulterous wish, not wanting,
Refusals, hates, postponements, meanness, laziness, none of these wanting,

Was one with the rest, the days and haps of the rest,
Was call'd by my nighest name by clear loud voices of young men as
they saw me approaching or passing,
Felt their arms on my neck as I stood, or the negligent leaning of their
flesh against me as I sat, 80
Saw many I loved in the street or ferry-boat or public assembly, yet
never told them a word,
Lived the same life with the rest, the same old laughing, gnawing,
sleeping,
Play'd the part that still looks back on the actor or actress,
The same old role, the role that is what we make it, as great as we
like,
Or as small as we like, or both great and small.

7

Closer yet I approach you,
What thought you have of me now, I had as much of you—I laid in
my stores in advance,
I consider'd long and seriously of you before you were born.

Who was to know what should come home to me?
Who knows but I am enjoying this? 90
Who knows, for all the distance, but I am as good as looking at you
now, for all you cannot see me?

8

Ah, what can ever be more stately and admirable to me than mast-
hemm'd Manhattan?
River and sunset and scallop-edg'd waves of flood-tide?
The sea-gulls oscillating their bodies, the hay-boat in the twilight, and
the belated lighter?
What gods can exceed these that clasp me by the hand, and with
voices I love call me promptly and loudly by my nighest name
as I approach?

What is more subtle than this which ties me to the woman or man
that looks in my face?
Which fuses me into you now, and pours my meaning into you?

We understand then do we not?
What I promis'd without mentioning it, have you not accepted?

What the study could not teach—what the preaching could not accomplish is accomplish'd, is it not? 100

9

Flow on, river! flow with the flood-tide, and ebb with the ebb-tide!
Frolic on, crested and scallop-edg'd waves!
Gorgeous clouds of the sunset! drench with your splendor me, or the men and women generations after me!
Cross from shore to shore, countless crowds of passengers!
Stand up, tall masts of Mannahatta! Stand up, beautiful hills of Brooklyn!
Throb, baffled and curious brain! throw out questions and answers!
Suspend here and everywhere, eternal float of solution!
Gaze, loving and thirsting eyes, in the house or street or public assembly!
Sound out, voices of young men; loudly and musically call me by my nighest name!
Live, old life! play the part that looks back on the actor or actress! 110
Play the old role, the role that is great or small according as one makes it!
Consider, you who peruse me, whether I may not in unknown ways be looking upon you;
Be firm, rail over the river, to support those who lean idly, yet haste with the hasting current;
Fly on, sea-birds! fly sideways, or wheel in large circles high in the air;
Receive the summer sky, you water, and faithfully hold it till all downcast eyes have time to take it from you!
Diverge, fine spokes of light, from the shape of my head, or any one's head, in the sunlit water!
Come on, ships from the lower bay! pass up or down, white-sail'd schooners, sloops, lighters!
Flaunt away, flags of all nations! be duly lower'd at sunset!
Burn high you fires, foundry chimneys! cast black shadows at nightfall! cast red and yellow light over the tops of the houses!
Appearances, now or henceforth, indicate what you are, 120
You necessary film, continue to envelop the soul,
About my body for me, and your body for you, be hung our divinest aromas,

l. 105. *Mannahatta:* the Indian name for Manhattan meant the dwelling place of Manito-Sod.

Thrive, cities—bring your freight, bring your shows, ample and sufficient rivers,
Expand, being than which none else is perhaps more spiritual,
Keep your places, objects than which none else is more lasting.

You have waited, you always wait, you dumb, beautiful ministers,
We receive you with free sense at last, and are insatiate henceforward,
Not you any more shall be able to foil us, or withhold yourselves from us,
We use you, and do not cast you aside—we plant you permanently within us,
We fathom you not—we love you—there is perfection in you also, 130
You furnish your parts toward eternity,
Great or small, you furnish your parts toward the soul.

[*1856, 1860*]

Passage to India

I

Singing my days,
Singing the great achievements of the present,
Singing the strong light works of engineers,
Our modern wonders, (the antique ponderous Seven outvied,)
In the Old World the east the Suez canal,
The New by its mighty railroad spann'd,
The seas inlaid with eloquent gentle wires;
Yet first to sound, and ever sound, the cry with thee O soul,
The Past! the Past! the Past!

The Past—the dark unfathom'd retrospect! 10
The teeming gulf—the sleepers and the shadows!
The past—the infinite greatness of the past!
For what is the present after all but a growth out of the past?
(As as projectile form'd, impell'd, passing a certain line, still keeps on,
So the present, utterly form'd, impell'd by the past.)

Passage to India: Whitman was inspired by three engineering feats: the laying of the Atlantic cable in 1866, the union of the West and East coasts of the United States by railroads, and the opening of the Suez Canal in 1869. He envisioned these accomplishments as evidence of greater unity among mankind and, therefore, of man's continuing spiritual development.

2

Passage O soul to India!
Eclaircise the myths Asiatic, the primitive fables.

Not you alone proud truths of the world,
Nor you alone ye facts of modern science,
But myths and fables of eld, Asia's, Africa's fables, 20
The far-darting beams of the spirit, the unloos'd dreams,
The deep diving bibles and legends,
The daring plots of the poets, the elder religions;
O you temples fairer than lilies pour'd over by the rising sun!
O you fables spurning the known, eluding the hold of the known,
    mounting to heaven!
You lofty and dazzling towers, pinnacled, red as roses, burnish'd with
    gold!
Towers of fables immortal fashion'd from mortal dreams!
You too I welcome and fully the same as the rest!
You too with joy I sing.

Passage to India! 30
Lo, soul, seest thou not God's purpose from the first?
The earth to be spann'd, connected by network,
The races, neighbors, to marry and be given in marriage,
The oceans to be cross'd, the distant brought near,
The lands to be welded together.

A worship new I sing,
You captains, voyagers, explorers, yours,
You engineers, you architects, machinists, yours,
You, not for trade or transportation only,
But in God's name, and for thy sake O soul. 40

3

Passage to India!
Lo soul for thee of tableaus twain.
I see in one the Suez canal initiated, open'd,
I see the procession of steamships, the Empress Eugenie's leading the
    van,

l. 17. *Eclaircise:* derived from the French *éclaircir,* "to clarify."

I mark from on deck the strange landscape, the pure sky, the level
sand in the distance,
I pass swiftly the picturesque groups, the workmen gather'd,
The gigantic dredging machines.

In one again, different, (yet thine, all thine, O soul, the same,)
I see over my own continent the Pacific railroad surmounting every
barrier,
I see continual trains of cars winding along the Platte carrying freight
and passengers, 50
I hear the locomotives rushing and roaring, and the shrill steam-
whistle,
I hear the echoes reverberate through the grandest scenery in the
world,
I cross the Laramie plains, I note the rocks in grotesque shapes, the
buttes,
I see the plentiful larkspur and wild onions, the barren, colorless,
sage-deserts,
I see in glimpses afar or towering immediately above me the great
mountains, I see the Wind river and the Wahsatch mountains,
I see the Monument mountain and the Eagle's Nest, I pass the Prom-
ontory, I ascend the Nevadas,
I scan the Noble Elk mountain and wind around its base,
I see the Humboldt range, I thread the valley and cross the river,
I see the clear waters of lake Tahoe, I see forests of majestic pines,
Or crossing the great desert, the alkaline plains, I behold enchanting
mirages of waters and meadows, 60
Marking through these and after all, in duplicate slender lines,
Bridging the three or four thousand miles of land travel,
Tying the Eastern to the Western sea,
The road between Europe and Asia.

(Ah Genoese thy dream! thy dream!
Centuries after thou art laid in thy grave,
The shore thou foundest verifies thy dream.)

4

Passage to India!
Struggles of many a captain, tales of many a sailor dead,
Over my mood stealing and spreading they come, 70
Like clouds and cloudlets in the unreach'd sky.

l. 65. *Genoese:* Columbus.

Along all history, down the slopes,
As a rivulet running, sinking now, and now again to the surface rising,
A ceaseless thought, a varied train—lo, soul, to thee, thy sight, they rise,
The plans, the voyages again, the expeditions;
Again Vasco de Gama sails forth,
Again the knowledge gain'd, the mariner's compass,
Lands found and nations born, thou born America,
For purpose vast, man's long probation fill'd,
Thou rondure of the world at last accomplish'd. 80

5

O vast Rondure, swimming in space,
Cover'd all over with visible power and beauty,
Alternate light and day and the teeming spiritual darkness,
Unspeakable high processions of sun and moon and countless stars above,
Below, the manifold grass and waters, animals, mountains, trees,
With inscrutable purpose, some hidden prophetic intention,
Now first it seems my thought begins to span thee.

Down from the gardens of Asia descending radiating,
Adam and Eve appear, then their myriad progeny after them,
Wandering, yearning, curious, with restless explorations, 90
With questionings, baffled, formless, feverish, with never-happy hearts,
With that sad incessant refrain, *Wherefore unsatisfied soul?* and *Whither O mocking life?*

Ah who shall soothe these feverish children?
Who justify these restless explorations?
Who speak the secret of impassive earth?
Who bind it to us? What is this separate Nature so unnatural?
What is this earth to our affections? (unloving earth, without a throb to answer ours,
Cold earth, the place of graves.)

Yet soul be sure the first intent remains, and shall be carried out,
Perhaps even now the time has arrived. 100

l. 76. *Vasco de Gama:* explorer who sailed to India in 1498; the correct spelling is da Gama.

After the seas are all cross'd, (as they seem already cross'd,)
After the great captains and engineers have accomplish'd their work,
After the noble inventors, after the scientists, the chemist, the geologist, ethnologist,
Finally shall come the poet worthy of that name,
The true son of God shall come singing his songs.

Then not your deeds, only O voyagers, O scientists and inventors, shall be justified,
All these hearts as of fretted children shall be sooth'd,
All affection shall be fully responded to, the secret shall be told,
All these separations and gaps shall be taken up and hook'd and link'd together,
The whole earth, this cold, impassive, voiceless earth, shall be completely justified, 110
Trinitas divine shall be gloriously accomplish'd and compacted by the true son of God, the poet,
(He shall indeed pass the straits and conquer the mountains,
He shall double the cape of Good Hope to some purpose,)
Nature and Man shall be disjoin'd and diffused no more,
The true son of God shall absolutely free them.

6

Year at whose wide-flung door I sing!
Year of the purpose accomplish'd!
Year of the marriage of continents, climates and oceans!
(No mere doge of Venice now wedding the Adriatic,)
I see O year in you the vast terraqueous globe given and giving all, 120
Europe to Asia, Africa join'd, and they to the New World,
The lands, geographies, dancing before you, holding a festival garland,
As brides and bridegrooms hand in hand.

Passage to India!
Cooling airs from Caucasus, far, soothing cradle of man,
The river Euphrates flowing, the past lit up again.

Lo soul, the retrospect brought forward,
The old, most populous, wealthiest of earth's lands,

l. 119. *No mere doge:* in Venice each year, the doge officiated at a ceremonial wedding of the sea and the city. A ring was thrown into the Adriatic Sea.
l. 127. *Euphrates:* the cradle of mankind was said to be the Tigris-Euphrates Valley.

The streams of the Indus and the Ganges and their many affluents,
(I my shores of America walking to-day behold, resuming all,) 131
The tale of Alexander on his warlike marches suddenly dying,
On one side China and on the other Persia and Arabia,
To the south the great seas and the bay of Bengal,
The flowing literatures, tremendous epics, religions, castes,
Old occult Brahma interminably far back, the tender and junior Buddha,
Central and southern empires and all their belongings, possessors,
The wars of Tamerlane, the reign of Aurungzebe,
The traders, rulers, explorers, Moslems, Venetians, Byzantium, the Arabs, Portuguese,
The first traveler famous yet, Marco Polo, Patouta, the Moor, 140
Doubts to be solv'd, the map incognita, blanks to be fill'd,
The foot of man unstay'd, the hands never at rest,
Thyself O soul that will not brook a challenge.

The medieval navigators rise before me,
The world of 1492, with its awaken'd enterprise,
Something swelling in humanity now like the sap of the earth in spring,
The sunset splendor of chivalry declining.

And who art thou sad shade?
Gigantic, visionary, thyself a visionary,
With majestic limbs and pious beaming eyes, 150
Spreading around with every look of thine a golden world,
Enhuing it with gorgeous hues.

As the chief histrion,
Down to the footlights walks in some great scena,
Dominating the rest I see the Admiral himself,
(History's type of courage, action, faith,)
Behold him sail from Palos leading his little fleet,
His voyage behold, his return, his great fame,
His misfortunes, calumniators, behold him a prisoner, chain'd,
Behold his dejection, poverty, death. 160

l. 138. *Tamerlane:* a fourteenth-century conqueror of territory from the Persian Gulf to the Ganges.
Aurungzebe: a seventeenth-century Mogul emperor.

l. 140. *Patouta, the Moor:* a fourteenth-century traveler over Africa and Asia.

ll. 155–157. *Admiral . . . Palos:* Columbus, who sailed from the Spanish port of Palos in 1492.

(Curious in time I stand, noting the efforts of heroes,
Is the deferment long? bitter the slander, poverty, death?
Lies the seed unreck'd for centuries in the ground? lo, to God's due occasion,
Uprising in the night, it sprouts, blooms,
And fills the earth with use and beauty.)

7

Passage indeed O soul to primal thought,
Not lands and seas alone, thy own clear freshness,
The young maturity of brood and bloom,
To realms of budding bibles.

O soul, repressless, I with thee and thou with me, 170
The circumnavigation of the world begin,
Of man, the voyage of his mind's return.
To reason's early paradise,
Back, back to wisdom's birth, to innocent intuitions,
Again with fair creation.

8

O we can wait no longer,
We too take ship O soul,
Joyous we too launch out on trackless seas,
Fearless for unknown shores on waves of ecstasy to sail,
Amid the wafting winds, (thou pressing me to thee, I thee to me, O soul,) 180
Caroling free, singing our song of God,
Chanting our chant of pleasant exploration.

With laugh and many a kiss,
(Let others deprecate, let others weep for sin, remorse, humiliation,)
O soul thou pleasest me, I thee.

Ah more than any priest O soul we too believe in God,
But with the mystery of God we dare not dally.

O soul thou pleasest me, I thee,
Sailing these seas or on the hills, or waking in the night,
Thoughts, silent thoughts, of Time and Space and Death, like waters flowing, 190

Bear me indeed as through the regions infinite,
Whose air I breathe, whose ripples hear, lave me all over,
Bathe me O God in thee, mounting to thee,
I and my soul to range in range of thee.

O Thou transcendent,
Nameless, the fibre and the breath,
Light of the light, shedding forth universes, thou centre of them,
Thou mightier centre of the true, the good, the loving,
Thou moral, spiritual fountain—affection's source—thou resevoir,
(O pensive soul of me—O thirst unsatisfied—waitest not there? 200
Waitest not haply for us somewhere there the Comrade perfect?)
Thou pulse—thou motive of the stars, sun, systems,
That, circling, move in order, safe, harmonious,
Athwart the shapeless vastness of space,
How should I think, how breathe a single breath, how speak, if out
of myself,
I could not launch, to those, superior universes?

Swiftly I shrivel at the thought of God,
At Nature and its wonders, Time and Space and Death,
But that I, turning, call to thee O soul, thou actual Me,
And lo, thou gently masterest the orbs, 210
Thou matest Time, smilest content at Death,
And fillest, swellest full the vastnesses of Space.

Greater than stars or suns,
Bounding O soul thou journeyest forth;
What love than thine and ours could wider amplify?
What aspirations, wishes, outvie thine and ours O soul?
What dreams of the ideal? what plans of purity, perfection, strength,
What cheerful willingness for others' sake to give up all?
For others' sake to suffer all?

Reckoning ahead O soul, when thou, the time achiev'd, 220
The seas all cross'd, weather'd the capes, the voyage done,
Surrounded, copest, frontest God, yieldest, the aim attain'd,
As fill'd with friendship, love complete, the Elder Brother found,
The Younger melts in fondness in his arms.

9

Passage to more than India!
Are thy wings plumed indeed for such far flights?

O soul, voyagest thou indeed on voyages like those?
Disportest thou on waters such as those?
Soundest below the Sanscrit and the Vedas?
Then have thy bent unleash'd. 230

Passage to you, your shores, ye aged fierce enigmas!
Passage to you, to mastership of you, ye strangling problems!
You, strew'd with the wrecks of skeletons, that, living, never reach'd
you.

Passage to more than India!
O secret of the earth and sky!
Of you O waters of the sea! O winding creeks and rivers!
Of you O woods and fields! of you strong mountains of my land!
Of you O prairies! of you gray rocks!

O morning red! O clouds! O rain and snows!
O day and night, passage to you! 240

O sun and moon and all you stars! Sirius and Jupiter!
Passage to you!
Passage, immediate passage! the blood burns in my veins!
Away O soul! hoist instantly the anchor!
Cut the hawsers—haul out—shake out every sail!
Have we not stood here like trees in the ground long enough?
Have we not grovel'd here long enough, eating and drinking like mere
brutes?
Have we not darken'd and dazed ourselves with books long enough?

Sail forth—steer for the deep waters only,
Reckless O soul, exploring, I with thee, and thou with me, 250
For we are bound where mariner has not yet dared to go,
And we will risk the ship, ourselves and all.

O brave soul!
O farther farther sail!
O daring joy, but safe! are they not all the seas of God?
O farther, farther, farther sail!

[*1870, 1871*]

l. 229. *Vedas:* the Hindu holy books.

William Butler Yeats

William Butler Yeats was born in Dublin on June 13, 1865. His father, John Yeats, came from a long line of religious Irish Protestants; his mother, Susan Pollexfen, was a County Sligo woman whose family and native rural environment Yeats came to know intimately. In his formative years Yeats much preferred Sligo to cosmopolitan Dublin, and much of his interest in fairy and folk lore was nurtured in the superstitious atmosphere of the place. Though his mother's background and family played a significant role in his development, it was his father's personality that dominated his early years. John Yeats, intellectually uncompromising, had rejected Protestantism when he could not any longer accept its teachings. Moreover, this clergyman's son had become an artist and freethinker. William Butler Yeats was brought up without a faith (though he was allowed to choose for himself a life with or without religion). Instead of religious training, he was subjected to training in classical and modern language and literature, and to the company of artists, writers, and other intellectuals who visited his father.

Living alternately in Dublin and London, Yeats early showed a talent for poetry, though he was academically a very ordinary student. At seventeen, he was writing verses. While in high school, he alienated his fellow students by adopting the pose of the artist—flowing garments, loose red bow tie, and the aloof manner which was later to irritate Irish theater audiences when Yeats lectured them. Barred from Trinity College by lack of tuition funds, Yeats attended an art school where he met the Irish poet George Russell (AE), but by 1885 it had become apparent that Yeats would be a poet.

Yeats rose quickly to prominence in his art. From his first publication in a college periodical in 1885, he went on to publish "The Wanderings of Oisin" in 1889 and "The Countess Kathleen" three years later. He had by this time formed a friendship with William Ernest Henley. Shortly after, he joined the Rhymers Club in London and came under the influence of John Davidson and Walter Pater. Through Arthur Symons he became acquainted with the French Symbolist movement in poetry. During the 1890s Yeats was wholeheartedly a Pre-Raphaelite and very sympathetic to the aesthetic movement in literature.

Simultaneously, Yeats' interests extended in two opposite directions: the movement for Irish independence and serious fascination for magic, theosophy, and spiritualism. He was particularly drawn to involvement in Irish political and military life by his love for the beautiful Irish patriot Maud Gonne, who gave him a first-hand view of the struggle and of her considerable part in it. For a time, indeed, Yeats was a member of the violent Irish Republican Brotherhood. He was also active in the agitation to make contemporary Irishmen aware of their heritage of history and language by reviving the study of Gaelic and publishing long-forgotten heroic tales.

At the same time, Yeats was turning toward private study of theosophy and magic under the aegis of the leader of the Theosophical Movement, Madame Blavatsky, and the founder of the magical Order of the Golden Dawn, MacGregor Mathers. The poet continued to be interested in these matters throughout his life, in later years as an adjunct to the writing of verse, for he insisted that the spirit world gave him metaphors for poetry.

By 1896, Yeats had formed an alliance with Lady Augusta Gregory, a literate philanthropist and patroness of the arts, which was to lead to the formation of the Irish National Theatre. At her estate in Coole, Yeats worked with George Moore and Edward Martyn on plays intended for production at the Dublin theater which was later to become the famous Abbey Players. For about a decade Yeats devoted himself to writing for this institution, producing plays, lecturing the audiences on standards and tastes, and corresponding untiringly concerning the financial end of the operation. This left him little time to devote to the lyric poetry with which he had begun his career.

Recognition came rapidly to Yeats after World War I. He became a senator of the Irish Free State in 1922. In the following year, he was awarded the Nobel Prize for literature. During this period of public acclaim, he lived quietly with the wife he had married in 1917, both devoting their time to deeper study of religion, spiritualism, and the occult. The result was *A Vision,* published in 1925, a strange book of revelation which establishes a semihistorical, semimystical, semimagical system according to which Yeats might govern his life and organize his poetry.

Shortly after the publication of Yeats' "bible," he became ill and selected the climate of the Riviera as best suited to his needs. From 1927 until his death in 1939 he lived quietly but actively in various places in Italy and France, writing poetry devoted to a philosophy of life for old age.

Probably the most significant circumstance of Yeats' life was his lack of a traditional religious framework. He came to an awareness of the material and spiritual world just at the time when the scientific discoveries of the Victorian era were making themselves felt among intellectuals; his father had already fallen away from the faith of his clergyman father. Yeats felt himself deprived of the belief that by tradition would have been his. Thus rudderless in a chaotic world, he had to construct for himself a plausible system by which to live. Hence his intense concern for what folklore might provide, his interest in magic as a way of keeping in touch with unnatural forces, his study of theosophy as a means of reconciling the material world with a higher realm. No system satisfied him entirely. Not until his sixtieth year, with the publication of *A Vision,* was he able to integrate his disparate studies into a fusion that, though it failed to satisfy others, worked for him as a guide to life and the writing of poetry.

Yeats' poetry may meaningfully be divided into "periods." His early work is mistily lyrical, in the Pre-Raphaelite tradition. Action takes place in a half-real, half-unreal world of fairies and mysterious voices. The style is artificial, ornate, heavy with symbolism. The subject matter is slight—the conventional expression of the singer's isolation and melancholy in a world he never made.

From the beginning of the twentieth century to the end of World War I, Yeats was principally concerned with writing verse plays for his theater. Though many of these are esoteric, it is in the nature of the stage that some communication between characters and between actors and audience is necessary. Therefore, the lone, lyric cry had to give way to a more normal interchange of words. In his nondramatic poetry of this time, too, the language and rhythms of ordinary speech begin to impinge on the earlier rarefied utterances. It was during this period that Yeats met Ezra Pound and came under the influence of the modern poetic idiom. His new spare, conversational tone reflects this new influence.

During the years of his life that followed World War I, Yeats wrote his most mature, reflective, and balanced poetry. In poems like "Sailing to Byzantium," he was able at last to fuse the inner vision and the outer life of art and society and history into a meaningful poetic statement. The symbolism is not obscure and private, but evocatively illuminates the relationship of the poet-narrator to his world. The ostensible casualness of the language deepens the sincerity of the tone in the manner of most great poetry. Yeats had not resolved all his personal difficulties, as he was solving his poetic problems. Indeed, as Richard Ellmann points out, he was able to use his uncertainties to produce many of his best poems.

Though extremely vigorous and inventive, the poems of Yeats' last decade reflect a falling off from the earlier work. The poet's principal subject is his age. How to face the decay of the body and the advent of death is treated as both a philosophical and a personal problem. In his poetry as in his life, Yeats refused to bow to inevitable decline. Virility in age, rage for the life of the senses become pervasive themes of a poet who, unlike Wordsworth, was unwilling to settle for the compensations of the spiritual, contemplative life of the philosopher.

When Yeats died in 1939, he ranked with T. S. Eliot as the most widely respected poet of his age. Though there were still pockets of resistance to his aristocratic stance and his habit of lecturing intellectual inferiors on matters of taste, especially in his native Ireland, praise for him as a poet was universal. No such unanimity of opinion greeted his philosophical treatise, *A Vision*. The "system" it describes is a bizarre conglomeration of historical, religious, mythical, and philosophical ideas. Indeed, were it not for the fact that Yeats uses the terminology of *A Vision,* and its accompanying images and symbols, in his later poetry, the work would probably have been forgotten long ago. Its existence is, however, a measure of the complexity of the mature artist and of the distance he had traveled from his earlier days of bardic simplicity.

BIBLIOGRAPHY

Ellmann, Richard. *Yeats: The Man and the Masks.* New York: Macmillan, 1948.

Hone, Joseph. *W. B. Yeats, 1865–1939.* New York: Macmillan, 1943.

Wade, Allan, ed. *The Letters of W. B. Yeats.* New York: Macmillan, 1955.

Sailing to Byzantium

I

That is no country for old men. The young
In one another's arms, birds in the trees,
—Those dying generations—at their song,
The salmon-falls, the mackerel-crowded seas,
Fish, flesh, or fowl, commend all summer long
Whatever is begotten, born, and dies.
Caught in that sensual music all neglect
Monuments of unageing intellect.

II

An aged man is but a paltry thing,
A tattered coat upon a stick, unless 10
Soul clap its hands and sing, and louder sing
For every tatter in its mortal dress,
Nor is there singing school but studying
Monuments of its own magnificence;
And therefore I have sailed the seas and come
To the holy city of Byzantium.

III

O sages standing in God's holy fire
As in the gold mosaic of a wall,
Come from the holy fire, perne in a gyre,
And be the singing-masters of my soul. 20
Consume my heart away; sick with desire
And fastened to a dying animal
It knows not what it is; and gather me
Into the artifice of eternity.

IV

Once out of nature I shall never take
My bodily form from any natural thing
But such a form as Grecian goldsmiths make
Of hammered gold and gold enamelling
To keep a drowsy Emperor awake;

Or set upon a golden bough to sing 30
To lords and ladies of Byzantium
Of what is past, or passing, or to come.

[1927]

Commentary

This poem concentrates several of Yeats' primary concerns into just thirty-two lines of immensely significant poetry. It expresses his belief that the contemporary world is old and sick and ripe for change; it deals with the problem of youth versus age; it weighs the role of body and mind-spirit in human life; and, perhaps most meaningfully, it defines the proper role of the artist as a being out of time, artificial, dealing in artifice and contrivance to create timeless artistic monuments.

None of these themes is struck here for the first or the last time, nor are they literary posturings divorced from the actual life of the poet. Yeats had earlier expressed his belief that in his own time

> Things fall apart; the centre cannot hold;
> Mere anarchy is loosed upon the world. . . .

Believing that his own civilization was doomed, he turns to an earlier and more congenial time and place which nurtured a highly aristocratic and elaborate kind of art, to Yeats an eminently healthy and desirable one. Later, in *A Vision,* Yeats was to imply that through cyclical alternation it would be possible one day to attain a new Byzantium. A desire for such a haven is common only to the old, Yeats says, for youth is too much involved in the natural processes of living, the animal pleasures of the senses. As he grew older, the poet was to extol fiercely the joys of sex, but here he strikes the more natural chord of intellectual compensation for declining physical powers.

What matters most to Yeats is Byzantium as a symbol of the realm of art. For Yeats, art had never been a matter of reproducing nature. On the stage, he insisted that the actors in his plays declaim their speeches artificially. Often the stage directions called for the characters to wear masks or in some other way to render themselves less human to the audience. Yeats pictured the true artist as a man apart from other men, speaking a separate language, dressing in a distinctively different way. He wished to use the raw material of language to create a personal document that should have the impersonality of true art, to create in time a thing of timeless beauty, to create from Irish backgrounds an artistic product that would be universal. Byzantium seemed to him the epitome of eternal, timeless artifice, so strikingly unified in conception and execution as to sum up the impersonal greatness of a civilization whose separate members had long since gone the way of all fish, flesh, or fowl.

The title of the poem is significant in that "Byzantium" has not yet been attained by the narrator. He is in the process of "sailing" toward it merely, with the hope of eventually arriving. The "that" in the first line refers specifically to Ireland and, perhaps, more generally to Yeats' twentieth-century world. In line 5, "commend" may have the meaning of "look with favor upon." In other words, the young—the average man caught up in mere physical processes—approve the very cycle that hastens their decay. In line 7, "sensual music" sums up the rhythmical patterns of the life cycle.

Stanza III introduces several of Yeats' favorite images. In one form or another, he often alludes to "sages," to those who have broken out of the wheel of reincarnation as he would like to do with his poetry and as the great artists of the past were able to do. In line 3, "perne in a gyre" is Yeats' way of describing the imagined spiral descent of the sages, as though unwinding (gyre) from a spool (pern), from their position as mosaic figures on a church wall. By gathering him into the "artifice of eternity," they will be rescuing him from mortality and rebirth as they have previously been rescued.

The poem is a masterpiece of consistent imagery. Most pervasive is the reference to music (the poetic equivalent, for Keats and Yeats, of literature or art). The young making love and the birds in the trees are both "at their song," but, in the undesirable country from which the poet would escape, this "music" is "sensual," merely the inartistic pattern of conception, physical life, and death. Those who make this music have no ear for the music of mind and spirit: the timeless, nonhuman monuments of the artist. The next stanza reinforces the motif of singing. The old man is pictured as a scarecrow, a device to frighten birds (singers) away. But he becomes quite another and more impressive figure if he uses mind-spirit to create art ("sing, and louder sing"). Moreover, he is obligated to study great art of the past in order to create his own (i.e., to attend "singing school"). Such study requires the trip to Byzantium, the supreme monument to the artist's mind and spirit.

The final two stanzas continue to play with the "song" image. The poet invokes as "singing-masters" the "sages," which are both mosaic works of art themselves ("monuments of unageing intellect") and, by extension, spiritual forebears of the artist, and the creators of the mosaics themselves. He will surrender what is yet mortal in him to them and thus place himself out of time. In his new nonhuman state, he might conceivably wish to take any one of a number of forms, but significantly he chooses the form of artificial nightingale who creates beautiful song to delight aristocratic ears. Once again, the bird as singer and creator of song (poet and artist) is introduced, but this time freed from mortality. "Thou wast not born for death, Immortal Bird," Keats said of his symbolic nightingale—and Yeats echoes his predecessor's thought.

The Lake Isle of Innisfree

I will arise and go now, and go to Innisfree,
And a small cabin build there, of clay and wattles made:
Nine bean-rows will I have there, a hive for the honeybee,
And live alone in the bee-loud glade.

And I shall have some peace there, for peace comes dropping slow,
Dropping from the veils of the morning to where the cricket sings;
There midnight's all a glimmer, and noon a purple glow,
And evening full of the linnet's wings.

I will arise and go now, for always night and day
I hear lake water lapping with low sounds by the shore; 10
While I stand on the roadway, or on the pavements grey,
I hear it in the deep heart's core.

[*1890?*]

Innisfree: in boyhood, Yeats was taken by the name and decided to live one day in a place so named.

Never Give All the Heart

Never give all the heart, for love
Will hardly seem worth thinking of
To passionate women if it seem
Certain, and they never dream
That it fades out from kiss to kiss;
For everything that's lovely is
But a brief, dreamy, kind delight.
O never give the heart outright,
For they, for all smooth lips can say,
Have given their hearts up to the play. 10
And who could play it well enough
If deaf and dumb and blind with love?

ll. 9–12. *they . . . love:* Yeats uses an example from the theater; the accomplished actress eschews emotion in order better to act a part requiring display of love.

He that made this knows all the cost,
For he gave all his heart and lost.

[*1904*]

No Second Troy

Why should I blame her that she filled my days
With misery, or that she would of late
Have taught to ignorant men most violent ways,
Or hurled the little streets upon the great,
Had they but courage equal to desire?
What could have made her peaceful with a mind
That nobleness made simple as a fire,
With beauty like a tightened bow, a kind
That is not natural in an age like this,
Being high and solitary and most stern? 10
Why, what could she have done, being what she is?
Was there another Troy for her to burn?

[*1908*]

l. 1. *her:* Yeats' friend Maud Gonne, a beautiful and stately revolutionary in the struggle for Irish freedom; Yeats' love for her was not reciprocated.

l. 12. *Troy:* Yeats here compares Maud Gonne to Helen of Troy.

The Second Coming

Turning and turning in the widening gyre
The falcon cannot hear the falconer;
Things fall apart; the centre cannot hold;
Mere anarchy is loosed upon the world,
The blood-dimmed tide is loosed, and everywhere
The ceremony of innocence is drowned;
The best lack all conviction, while the worst
Are full of passionate intensity.

The Second Coming: though Christian in significance, it is also privately meaningful to Yeats (see *A Vision*) as the harbinger of a new era in civilization—one which comes every 2,000 years.

l. 1. *gyre:* the cycle of civilization in which Yeats lives.

Surely some revelation is at hand;
Surely the Second Coming is at hand. 10
The Second Coming! Hardly are those words out
When a vast image out of *Spiritus Mundi*
Troubles my sight: somewhere in sands of the desert
A shape with lion body and the head of a man
A gaze blank and pitiless as the sun,
Is moving its slow thighs, while all about it
Reel shadows of the indignant desert birds
The darkness drops again; but now I know
That twenty centuries of stony sleep
Were vexed to nightmare by a rocking cradle, 20
And what rough beast, its hour come round at last,
Slouches towards Bethlehem to be born?

[*1919*]

l. 12. *Spiritus Mundi:* Spirit of the World.

Two Songs from a Play

I

I saw a staring virgin stand
Where holy Dionysus died;
And tear the heart out of his side,
And lay the heart upon her hand
And bear that beating heart away;
And then did all the Muses sing
Of Magnus Annus at the spring,
As though God's death were but a play.

Another Troy must rise and set,
Another lineage feed the crow, 10

Play: from *The Resurrection,* written in 1927.
l. 2. *Dionysus*: classical god associated with passion, wine, and the theater.
l. 7. *Magnus Annus:* the so-called "Great Year," which lasts roughly two thousand years by man's reckoning and cyclically brings the celestial heavens to the same point at which they were, astronomically, at the start of the cycle.
l. 9. *Another Troy*: Yeats refers cryptically to the cycle in which the Greeks flourished and declined.

Another Argo's painted prow
Drive to a flashier bauble yet.
The Roman Empire stood appalled:
It dropped the reigns of peace and war
When that fierce virgin and her Star
Out of the fabulous darkness called.

II

In pity for man's darkening thought
He walked that room and issued thence
In Galilean turbulence;
The Babylonian starlight brought 20
A fabulous, formless darkness in;
Odour of blood when Christ was slain
Made all Platonic tolerance vain
And vain all Doric discipline.

Everything that man esteems
Endures a moment or a day.
Love's pleasure drives his love away,
The painter's brush consumes his dreams;
The herald's cry, the soldier's tread
Exhaust his glory and his might: 30
Whatever flames upon the night
Man's own resinous heart has fed.

[1927]

l. 19. *Galilean turbulence:* the newest cycle of the Great Year is Christian, but in its formlessness and violence it has obscured the disciplined classical era which preceded it.

Leda and the Swan

A sudden blow: the great wings beating still
Above the staggering girl, her thighs caressed
By the dark webs, her nape caught in his bill,
He holds her helpless breast upon his breast.

Leda . . . Swan: Zeus, in the form of a swan, courted Leda, and made love to her; and the union produced Helen and Clytemnestra.

How can those terrified vague fingers push
The feathered glory from her loosening thighs?
And how can body, laid in that white rush,
But feel the strange heart beating where it lies?

A shudder in the loins engenders there
The broken wall, the burning roof and tower 10
And Agamemnon dead.
Being so caught up,
So mastered by the brute blood of the air,
Did she put on his knowledge with his power
Before the indifferent beak could let her drop?
[1923]

Byzantium

The unpurged images of day recede;
The Emperor's drunken soldiery are abed;
Night resonance recedes, night-walkers' song
After great cathedral gong;
A starlit or a moonlit dome disdains
All that man is,
All mere complexities,
The fury and the mire of human veins.

Before me floats an image, man or shade,
Shade more than man, more image than a shade; 10
For Hades' bobbin bound in mummy-cloth
May unwind the winding path;
A mouth that has no moisture and no breath
Breathless mouths may summon;
I hail the superhuman;
I call it death-in-life and life-in-death.

Miracle, bird or golden handiwork,
More miracle than bird or handiwork,
Planted on the star-lit golden bough,
Can like the cocks of Hades crow, 20

l. 17. *bird:* the golden nightingale of "Sailing to Byzantium."

Or, by the moon embittered, scorn aloud
In glory of changeless metal
Common bird or petal
And all complexities of mire or blood.

At midnight on the Emperor's pavement flit
Flames that no faggot feeds, nor steel has lit,
Nor storm disturbs, flames begotten of flame,
Where blood-begotten spirits come
And all complexities of fury leave,
Dying into a dance, 30
An agony of trance,
An agony of flame that cannot singe a sleeve.

Astraddle on the dolphin's mire and blood,
Spirit after spirit! The smithies break the flood,
The golden smithies of the Emperor!
Marbles of the dancing floor
Break bitter furies of complexity,
Those images that yet
Fresh images beget,
That dolphin-torn, that gong-tormented sea, 40

[*1930*]

l. 26. *Flames:* purgatorial fires in which the human souls, who come to Byzantium to be released from the round of incarnation, are purged.

He Remembers Forgotten Beauty

When my arms wrap you round I press
My heart upon the loveliness
That has long faded from the world;
The jewelled crowns that kings have hurled
In shadowy pools, when armies fled;
The love-tales wrought with silken thread
By dreaming ladies upon cloth
That has made fat the murderous moth;
The roses that of old time were
Woven by ladies in their hair, 10

The dew-cold lilies ladies bore
Through many a sacred corridor
Where such grey clouds of incense rose
That only God's eyes did not close:
For that pale breast and lingering hand
Come from a more dream-heavy land,
A more dream-heavy hour than this;
And when you sigh from kiss to kiss
I hear white Beauty sighing, too,
For hours when all must fade like dew, 20
But flame on flame, and deep on deep,
Throne over throne where in half sleep,
Their swords upon their iron knees,
Brood her high lonely mysteries.

[*1899*]

September 1913

What need you, being come to sense,
But fumble in a greasy till
And add the halfpence to the pence
And prayer to shivering prayer, until
You have dried the marrow from the bone?
For men were born to pray and save:
Romantic Ireland's dead and gone,
It's with O'Leary in the grave.

Yet they were of a different kind,
The names that stilled your childish play, 10
They have gone about the world like wind,
But little time had they to pray
For whom the hangman's rope was spun,
And what, God help us, could they save?
Romantic Ireland's dead and gone,
It's with O'Leary in the grave.

September 1913: the occasion of labor agitation in Ireland culminating in a strike and a lockout.

l. 8. *O'Leary:* John O'Leary, a nineteenth-century Fenian and patriot.

Was it for this the wild geese spread
The grey wing upon every tide;
For this that all that blood was shed,
For this Edward Fitzgerald died, 20
And Robert Emmet and Wolfe Tone,
All that delirium of the brave?
Romantic Ireland's dead and gone,
It's with O'Leary in the grave.

Yet could we turn the years again,
And call those exiles as they were
In all their loneliness and pain,
You'd cry, 'Some woman's yellow hair
Has maddened every mother's son':
They weighed so lightly what they gave. 30
But let them be, they're dead and gone,
They're with O'Leary in the grave.

[1914]

ll. 20–21. *Fitzgerald . . . Emmet . . . Tone:* patriots in the Irish cause.

Easter 1916

I have met them at close of day
Coming with vivid faces
From counter or desk among grey
Eighteenth-century houses.
I have passed with a nod of the head
Or polite meaningless words,
Or have lingered awhile and said
Polite meaningless words,
And thought before I had done
Of a mocking tale or a gibe 10
To please a companion
Around the fire at the club,
Being certain that they and I
But lived where motley is worn:

Easter 1916: a band of Irish patriots led an abortive revolution on Easter Monday. Fifteen, among them the men named in the poem, were put to death.

All changed, changed utterly:
A terrible beauty is born.

That woman's days were spent
In ignorant good-will,
Her nights in argument
Until her voice grew shrill. 20
What voice more sweet than hers
When, young and beautiful,
She rode to harriers?
This man had kept a school
And rode our wingèd horse;
This other his helper and friend
Was coming into his force;
He might have won fame in the end,
So sensitive his nature seemed,
So daring and sweet his thought. 30
This other man I had dreamed
A drunken, vainglorious lout.
He had done most bitter wrong
To some who are near my heart,
Yet I number him in the song;
He, too, has resigned his part
In the casual comedy;
He, too, has been changed in his turn,
Transformed utterly:
A terrible beauty is born. 40

Hearts with one purpose alone
Through summer and winter seem
Enchanted to a stone
To trouble the living stream.
The horse that comes from the road,
The rider, the birds that range
From cloud to tumbling cloud,

l. 17. *That woman:* Countess Markiewicz, who drew a life term in prison.
l. 24. *This man:* Padraic Pearse, a poet and teacher.
l. 26. *This other:* a writer, Thomas MacDonagh.
l. 31. *This other man:* Maud Gonne's husband, John MacBride.

Minute by minute they change;
A shadow of cloud on the stream
Changes minute by minute; 50
A horse-hoof slides on the brim,
And a horse plashes within it;
The long-legged moor-hens dive,
And hens to moor-cocks call;
Minute by minute they live:
The stone's in the midst of all.

Too long a sacrifice
Can make a stone of the heart.
O when may it suffice?
That is Heaven's part, our part 60
To murmur name upon name,
As a mother names her child
When sleep at last has come
On limbs that had run wild.
What is it but nightfall?
No, no, not night but death;
Was it needless death after all?
For England may keep faith
For all that is done and said.
We know their dream; enough 70
To know they dreamed and are dead;
And what if excess of love
Bewildered them till they died?
I write it out in a verse—
MacDonagh and MacBride
And Connolly and Pearse
Now and in time to be,
Wherever green is worn,
Are changed, changed utterly:
A terrible beauty is born. 80

[*September 25, 1916*]

Death

Nor dread nor hope attend
A dying animal;
A man awaits his end

Dreading and hoping all;
Many times he died,
Many times rose again.
A great man in his pride
Confronting murderous men
Casts derision upon
Supersession of breath; 10
He knows death to the bone—
Man has created death.

[1933]

Among School Children

I

I walk through the long schoolroom questioning;
A kind old nun in a white hood replies;
The children learn to cipher and to sing,
To study reading-books and history,
To cut and sew, be neat in everything
In the best modern way—the children's eyes
In momentary wonder stare upon
A sixty-year-old smiling public man.

II

I dream of a Ledaean body, bent
Above a sinking fire, a tale that she 10
Told of a harsh reproof, or trivial event
That changed some childish day to tragedy—
Told, and it seemed that our two natures blent
Into a sphere from youthful sympathy,
Or else, to alter Plato's parable,
Into the yolk and white of the one shell.

III

And thinking of that fit of grief or rage
I look upon one child or t'other there

l. 9. *Ledaean:* like Leda (or of the line of Leda, i.e., Helen).

l. 15. *Plato's parable:* notion that male and female are halves of one spherical unit.

And wonder if she stood so at that age—
For even daughters of the swan can share 20
Something of every paddler's heritage—
And had that colour upon cheek or hair,
And thereupon my heart is driven wild:
She stands before me as a living child.

IV

Her present image floats into the mind—
Did Quattrocento finger fashion it
Hollow of cheek as though it drank the wind
And took a mess of shadows for its meat?
And I though never of Ledaean kind
Had pretty plumage once—enough of that, 30
Better to smile on all that smile, and show
There is a comfortable kind of old scarecrow.

V

What youthful mother, a shape upon her lap
Honey of generation had betrayed,
And that must sleep, shriek, struggle to escape
As recollection or the drug decide,
Would think her son, did she but see that shape
With sixty or more winters on its head,
A compensation for the pang of his birth,
Or the uncertainty of his setting forth? 40

VI

Plato thought nature but a spume that plays
Upon a ghostly paradigm of things;
Solider Aristotle played the taws
Upon the bottom of a king of kings;
World-famous golden-thighed Pythagoras
Fingered upon a fiddle-stick or strings

l. 26. *Quattrocento:* Italian artists of the fifteenth century.

ll. 43–44. *played the taws . . . king:* Aristotle spanked Alexander, whose teacher he was.

l. 45. *Pythagoras:* classical philosopher who postulated the music of the spheres.

What a star sang and careless Muses heard:
Old clothes upon old sticks to scare a bird.

VII

Both nuns and mothers worship images,
But those the candles light are not as those 50
That animate a mother's reveries,
But keep a marble or a bronze repose.
And yet they too break hearts—O Presences
That passion, piety or affection knows,
And that all heavenly glory symbolise—
O self-born mockers of man's enterprise;

VIII

Labour is blossoming or dancing where
The body is not bruised to pleasure soul,
Nor beauty born out of its own despair,
Nor blear-eyed wisdom out of midnight oil. 60
O chestnut-tree, great-rooted blossomer,
Are you the leaf, the blossom or the bole?
O body swayed to music, O brightening glance,
How can we know the dancer from the dance?

[*1926*]

Robert Frost

Robert Lee Frost, named after the Southern general, was born in San Francisco, California, on March 26, 1875. His father, a rebellious youth, had sympathized with the Southern cause during the Civil War and left his native New England to work as an editor in that West Coast frontier town. When he died in his early thirties of tuberculosis, his widow took their ten-year-old son back to New England where her family had lived for generations. From the age of twelve, Frost spent his summer vacations working on farms or in local factories. He attended high school in Lawrence, Massachusetts, and on graduation was co-valedictorian of his class. The girl with whom he shared the honor, Elinor White, became his wife three years later.

Frost first published a poem in the Lawrence High School magazine, and by the time he completed his secondary studies he had decided to be a poet. His paternal grandfather, who had been unable to make his son a lawyer, now urged his grandson to attend college. Frost reluctantly enrolled at Dartmouth. After two months he returned to Lawrence and spent the next five years teaching school and working as a reporter for the local paper. The families of his parents continued to urge him to return to college, and finally when he was twenty-two and already two years married, he entered Harvard. The poet, who was to spend most of his adult life as a member of college faculties, remained at Harvard for less than two years. He enjoyed the philosophy courses and spent much of his time reading the Greek and Roman classics, but he was dissatisfied and restless. His disappointed grandfather, probably hoping to get the young man to settle down, gave him a farm in New Hampshire with the proviso that he work it for ten years. Frost kept the bargain, supplementing his meager farming income by teaching school. These were important years in the development of the poet. Only a few magazine editors accepted his poems for publication, but Frost was an independent, determined, confident, young man, and doggedly and unassisted he developed his craft.

In 1912, he decided it was time to devote himself exclusively to poetry. With the money he had managed to save, he left the United States and settled with his family in a small rural town in England. The following year, he submitted some of his poems to a London publisher. Within a few months, *A Boy's Will* was in the hands of English reviewers who proclaimed the debut of a new and exceptional poet. Frost came to know several English poets quite well, but they had no influence on his work. He had already explored the vein of his talent and was, as he was to remain throughout his career, aloof from contemporary poetic currents. A second volume, *North of Boston,* was published in 1914, and again the English critics lavished praise on the American poet for his ability to present in simple but unforgettable phrases his trenchant observations, his thoughts and feelings. These two volumes were published by an American firm, and by the time Frost returned to his native country in 1915 he was being hailed throughout the nation as a major poet. For a time Frost retired to a newly-purchased New Hampshire farm, publishing *Mountain Interval* in 1916 and then *New Hampshire* in 1923. Throughout his life, the poet was to own a number of farms somewhere in New England, but he spent most of his time as writer-in-residence at various colleges.

Frost had had to leave the United States to gain recognition, but his countrymen made up for their initial indifference by paying him greater tributes than most American poets have enjoyed. Four volumes of his verse, *New Hampshire* (1923), *Collected Poems* (1930), *A Further Range* (1936), and *A Witness Tree* (1942) were awarded Pulitzer Prizes. These and his many other volumes won him a wide popular audience, and he was honored by many colleges with honorary degrees. Before his death in 1963, Frost reached more people at one time than any poet in American history when he read an inaugural poem at the presidential inauguration of his fellow New Englander, John F. Kennedy.

Even a casual reader of Frost will recognize immediately the significance of the poet's New England background. Frost was exceptionally responsive to his environment, to the minute details of landscape and farm routine, to the character of people molded by the rigors of life on a New England farm. He was a remarkably keen observer, and he reflected upon whatever his senses registered. His poems record the realistic details of his observation and then expand these details into metaphors that convey feeling and idea. "A poem begins," Frost wrote, "with a lump in the throat; a home-sickness or a love-sickness. It is a reaching out toward expression; an effort to find fulfillment. A complete poem is one where an emotion has found its thought and the thought has found the words." Like the earlier New England poet, Emily Dickinson, Frost's keen sensibility responded to the minutiae of a limited environment, but discovered in the familiar a whole spectrum of human emotions and responses.

Sensitive as he was to the world about him, Frost inevitably reflected in his own personality—and hence in his poetry—the practicality, Yankee shrewdness, laconic manner and expression, and the philosophic acceptance of harsh reality that characterized the New Englanders he lived among. Unlike many poets who rage against the conditions of human existence, Frost accepted and recorded the pains and the joys, the beauty and the ugliness that are the constants of life. In nature, he observed the fusion of opposites: the beauty of a fresh flower will deteriorate to withered ugliness; day must go down to darkness. And in the human being are fused the opposing forces of mind and heart: if the heart longs for faith, the mind questions and finds no answers. Neither the beauty nor the ugliness, the light nor the dark, the heart nor the mind can be denied. Frost's acceptance of this dualism made him skeptical of ideals and absolutes and allied him philosophically to the Greek concept of the Golden Mean. The poet himself described his position with the wry humor characteristic of much of his poetry:

> I am not the Platonist Robinson was.* By Platonist I mean one who believes what we have here is an imperfect copy of what is in heaven. The woman you have is an imperfect copy of some woman in heaven or in some one else's bed. Many of the world's greatest—maybe all of them—have been ranged on that romantic side. I am philosophically opposed to having one Iseult for my vocation and another for my avocation. . . . Let me not sound the least bit smug. I define a difference with proper humility. A

* Edward Arlington Robinson, another New England poet.

> truly gallant Platonist will remain a bachelor as Robinson did from unwillingness to reduce any woman to the condition of being used without being idealized.

The effectiveness of Frost's poetry is due, to a great extent, to his ability to enclose and contain opposing extremes within the metaphors he skillfully develops.

Frost's New England heritage is reflected too in his poetic technique. His subjects and his images are derived from the ordinary routine life of the farmer. Perhaps because he had listened so carefully to the laconic, simple speech of the New Englander, Frost rebelled against the over-poetic diction of the late Victorians and responded to Wordsworth's dictum that poets must use the language of the common man. The great English romantic poet was never quite able to achieve his goal, but the American poet did. "All poetry," he wrote, "is the reproduction of actual speech." In discussing his aim to make his poems sound like speech, Frost said, "What I am most interested in emphasizing . . . is the sentence of sound, because to me a sentence is not interesting merely in conveying a meaning of words; it must do something more; it must convey a meaning by sound." What Frost sought to capture was the emotion—anger, tenderness, sorrow—that tone of voice conveys in conversation. And he was successful. In his tightly structured poems, with their conversational rhythms, their restrained epigrammatic phrases, he captures the tones of speech and conveys feeling and meaning through tone.

Frost's interest in the conversational quality of poetry plus his interest in people led him inevitably to the dramatic monologue and the dramatic poem. Many of his poems, such as "The Death of the Hired Man," are dramas presented as dialogues. In that poem the feelings of the husband and wife toward the old man who comes to the only home he knows to die are conveyed as much by the tone of their words as by the meaning of the words. The poet was a careful craftsman, making each of his words bear a heavy responsibility in evoking reader feeling.

> Sometimes [he wrote] I have my doubts of words altogether and I ask myself what is the place of them. They are worse than nothing unless they can do something, unless they amount to deeds as in ultimatums or battle-cries. They must be flat and final like the showdown in poker, from which there is no appeal. My definition

of poetry would be this (if I were forced to give one) words that have become deeds.

In his "talk" poems Frost fused subject matter and form. The simple rural subjects presented in the voice of a bucolic philosopher make his a distinct poetic voice despite his dependence upon traditional forms. During a rich period of poetic experimentation, in which Ezra Pound, T. S. Eliot, and Hart Crane wrote and theorized, the independent New Englander continued along his homely poetic path. He belonged to no poetic school, and his reputation will, for some generations, probably move up and down as poetic fashions change; but that contemplative, wry New England voice has an excellent chance of being heard centuries from now.

BIBLIOGRAPHY

Brower, Reuben A. *The Poetry of Robert Frost.* New York: Oxford University Press, 1963.

Doyle, John Robert, Jr. *The Poetry of Robert Frost.* New York: Hafner, 1962.

Thompson, Lawrance. *Fire and Ice.* New York: Henry Holt, 1942.

Fire and Ice

Some say the world will end in fire,
Some say in ice.
From what I've tasted of desire
I hold with those who favor fire.
But if it had to perish twice,
I think I know enough of hate
To say that for destruction ice
Is also great
And would suffice.

[*1923*]

Commentary

This epigrammatic, reflective lyric with its quiet irony [see *Handbook:* irony], its conversational tone, its traditional verse form, and its metaphorical fusion of opposing extremes exemplifies many of the typical qualities of Frost's poetry.

The conversational tone is established with the initial phrase, "Some say." By using this colloquial expression that so often serves as a prelude to general observations about life, Frost conveys a philosophic attitude and a relaxed, reflective tone. The actual phrase that most people would use would probably be, "Some people say," or "Some people believe." But Frost is economical; he pares his phrases and sentences to their core so that they suggest the *quality* of speech. The repetition of the phrase in the second line is a technique Frost frequently uses to set into dramatic juxtaposition opposing extremes.

The commonplace statement, "Some say the world will end in fire," itself a metaphor, Frost expands to establish an analogy between the physical world and man: fire is equated with human love; ice, with hate. Because ardor is generally described with images of fire, the reader unhesitatingly accepts the equation as a traditional expression of love's intensity. Frost obviously expects such a response and he makes clever use of it. He confesses that he, too, has experienced the fires of passion. The couplet, "From what I've tasted of desire / I hold with those who favor fire," emphasizes the intensity of love and therefore sustains the reader's expectation.

But Frost's aim, as we discover in the second quatrain, is to reveal that love, which is generally associated with creativity and tenderness, is also a destructive emotion. Hate we accept as destructive and by declaring it less destructive than love Frost forces us to view love's intensity from a new perspective. This illumination comes suddenly and dramatically when we reach the final line, "And would suffice." The unexpected concision and restraint and the philosophical tone of the phrase reveal the irony: both love and hate can be cataclysmically destructive, but love is more destructive than hate.

With his analogy, Frost moves from the obvious to the unrealized. The existence in nature of the opposites, fire and ice, and in the human being of the opposed emotions, love and hate, are obvious. What the analogy reveals is that love itself shares the dualism of nature and man and contains both creativity and destructiveness. And love becomes a metaphor to reveal the fusion of opposites in everything. Because the elements that Frost focuses upon are extremes, he also forces his reader to acknowledge the destructiveness of extremes and to accept, at least momentarily, the wisdom of the poet's philosophical middle ground.

The fusion in "Fire and Ice" of opposites in a metaphor that reveals the dualism of existence is typical of Frost's poetry. Also typical is the skill with which he uses his form to intensify his effects and convey meaning. The two quatrains of the poem are composed of iambic tetrameter lines with a rhyme scheme of *abaa, bcbb*. There are two important variations in this traditional form. In the second line, Frost shifts from tetrameter to trimeter. The shortened line places accents on three of the four words and effectively emphasizes the opposition of fire and ice. The final phrase, "And would suffice" carries much of the significance of the poem, and to make that phrase dramatic and forceful, Frost breaks his final line into two dimeters. To make the break emphatic and yet natural, he isolates the final phrase by relating the first dimeter with a rhyme ("great" and "hate") to a preceding line of the quatrain.

Though his verse is traditional, Frost, by means of such variations as these, fused his form and subject-matter. "In making a poem," he once wrote, "you have no right to think of anything but the subject matter. After making it, no right to boast of anything but the form. . . ."

After Apple-picking

My long two-pointed ladder's sticking through a tree
Toward heaven still,
And there's a barrel that I didn't fill
Beside it, and there may be two or three
Apples I didn't pick upon some bough.
But I am done with apple-picking now.
Essence of winter sleep is on the night,
The scent of apples: I am drowsing off.
I cannot rub the strangeness from my sight
I got from looking through a pane of glass 10
I skimmed this morning from the drinking trough
And held against the world of hoary grass.
It melted, and I let it fall and break.
But I was well
Upon my way to sleep before it fell,
And I could tell
What form my dreaming was about to take.
Magnified apples appear and disappear,
Stem end and blossom end,
And every fleck of russet showing clear. 20
My instep arch not only keeps the ache,
It keeps the pressure of a ladder-round.
I feel the ladder sway as the boughs bend.
And I keep hearing from the cellar bin
The rumbling sound
Of load on load of apples coming in.
For I have had too much
Of apple-picking: I am overtired
Of the great harvest I myself desired.
There were ten thousand thousand fruit to touch, 30
Cherish in hand, lift down, and not let fall.
For all
That struck the earth,
No matter if not bruised or spiked with stubble,
Went surely to the cider-apple heap
As of no worth.

One can see what will trouble
This sleep of mine, whatever sleep it is.
Were he not gone,
The woodchuck could say whether it's like his 40
Long sleep, as I describe its coming on,
Or just some human sleep.

[*1914*]

The Death of the Hired Man

Mary sat musing on the lamp-flame at the table
Waiting for Warren. When she heard his step,
She ran on tip-toe down the darkened passage
To meet him in the doorway with the news
And put him on his guard. 'Silas is back.'
She pushed him outward with her through the door
And shut it after her. 'Be kind,' she said.
She took the market things from Warren's arms
And set them on the porch, then drew him down
To sit beside her on the wooden steps. 10

'When was I ever anything but kind to him?
But I'll not have the fellow back,' he said.
'I told him so last haying, didn't I?
If he left then, I said, that ended it.
What good is he? Who else will harbor him
At his age for the little he can do?
What help he is there's no depending on.
Off he goes always when I need him most.
He thinks he ought to earn a little pay,
Enough at least to buy tobacco with, 20
So he won't have to beg and be beholden.
"All right," I say, "I can't afford to pay
Any fixed wages, though I wish I could."
"Someone else can." "Then someone else will have to."
I shouldn't mind his bettering himself
If that was what it was. You can be certain,
When he begins like that, there's someone at him
Trying to coax him off with pocket-money,—
In haying time, when any help is scarce.
In winter he comes back to us. I'm done.' 30

'Sh! not so loud: he'll hear you,' Mary said.

'I want him to: he'll have to soon or late.'

'He's worn out. He's asleep beside the stove.
When I came up from Rowe's I found him here,
Huddled against the barn-door fast asleep,
A miserable sight, and frightening, too—
You needn't smile—I didn't recognize him—
I wasn't looking for him—and he's changed.
Wait till you see.'

'Where did you say he'd been?'

'He didn't say. I dragged him to the house, 40
And gave him tea and tried to make him smoke.
I tried to make him talk about his travels.
Nothing would do: he just kept nodding off.'

'What did he say? Did he say anything?'

'But little.'

'Anything? Mary, confess
He said he'd come to ditch the meadow for me.'

'Warren!'

'But did he? I just want to know.'

'Of course he did. What would you have him say?
Surely you wouldn't grudge the poor old man
Some humble way to save his self-respect. 50
He added, if you really care to know,
He meant to clear the upper pasture, too.
That sounds like something you have heard before?
Warren, I wish you could have heard the way
He jumbled everything. I stopped to look
Two or three times—he made me feel so queer—
To see if he was talking in his sleep.
He ran on Harold Wilson—you remember—

The boy you had in haying four years since.
He's finished school, and teaching in his college. 60
Silas declares you'll have to get him back.
He says they two will make a team for work:
Between them they will lay this farm as smooth!
The way he mixed that in with other things.
He thinks young Wilson a likely lad, though daft
On education—you know how they fought
All through July under the blazing sun,
Silas up on the cart to build the load,
Harold along beside to pitch it on.'

'Yes, I took care to keep well out of earshot.' 70

'Well, those days trouble Silas like a dream.
You wouldn't think they would. How some things linger!
Harold's young college boy's assurance piqued him.
After so many years he still keeps finding
Good arguments he sees he might have used.
I sympathize. I know just how it feels
To think of the right thing to say too late.
Harold's associated in his mind with Latin.
He asked me what I thought of Harold's saying
He studied Latin like the violin 80
Because he liked it—that an argument!
He said he couldn't make the boy believe
He could find water with a hazel prong—
Which showed how much good school had ever done him.
He wanted to go over that. But most of all
He thinks if he could have another chance
To teach him how to build a load of hay—'

'I know, that's Silas' one accomplishment.
He bundles every forkful in its place,
And tags and numbers it for future reference, 90
So he can find and easily dislodge it
In the unloading. Silas does that well.
He takes it out in bunches like big birds' nests.
You never see him standing on the hay
He's trying to lift, straining to lift himself.'

'He thinks if he could teach him that, he'd be
Some good perhaps to someone in the world.
He hates to see a boy the fool of books.
Poor Silas, so concerned for other folk,
And nothing to look backward to with pride, 100
And nothing to look forward to with hope,
So now and never any different.'

Part of a moon was falling down the west,
Dragging the whole sky with it to the hills.
Its light poured softly in her lap. She saw it
And spread her apron to it. She put out her hand
Among the harp-like morning-glory strings,
Taut with the dew from garden bed to eaves,
As if she played unheard some tenderness
That wrought on him beside her in the night. 110
'Warren,' she said, 'he has come home to die:
You needn't be afraid he'll leave you this time.'

'Home,' he mocked gently.

'Yes, what else but home?
It all depends on what you mean by home.
Of course he's nothing to us, any more
Than was the hound that came a stranger to us
Out of the woods, worn out upon the trail.'

'Home is the place where, when you have to go there,
They have to take you in.'

'I should have called it
Something you somehow haven't to deserve.' 120

Warren leaned out and took a step or two,
Picked up a little stick, and brought it back
And broke it in his hand and tossed it by.
'Silas has better claim on us you think
Than on his brother? Thirteen little miles
As the road winds would bring him to his door.
Silas has walked that far no doubt today.

Why doesn't he go there? His brother's rich,
A somebody—director in the bank.'

'He never told us that.'
'We know it though.' 130

'I think his brother ought to help, of course.
I'll see to that if there is need. He ought of right
To take him in, and might be willing to—
He may be better than appearances.
But have some pity on Silas. Do you think
If he had any pride in claiming kin
Or anything he looked for from his brother,
He'd keep so still about him all this time?'

'I wonder what's between them.'

'I can tell you.
Silas is what he is—we wouldn't mind him— 140
But just the kind that kinsfolk can't abide.
He never did a thing so very bad.
He don't know why he isn't quite as good
As anybody. Worthless though he is,
He won't be made ashamed to please his brother.'

'*I* can't think Si ever hurt anyone.'

'No, but he hurt my heart the way he lay
And rolled his old head on that sharp-edged chair-back.
He wouldn't let me put him on the lounge.
You must go in and see what you can do. 150
I made the bed up for him there tonight.
You'll be surprised at him—how much he's broken.
His working days are done; I'm sure of it.'

'I'd not be in a hurry to say that.'

'I haven't been. Go, look, see for yourself.
But, Warren, please remember how it is:
He's come to help you ditch the meadow.

He has a plan. You mustn't laugh at him.
He may not speak of it, and then he may.
I'll sit and see if that small sailing cloud 160
Will hit or miss the moon.'

It hit the moon.
Then there were three there, making a dim row,
The moon, the little silver cloud, and she.

Warren returned—too soon, it seemed to her,
Slipped to her side, caught up her hand and waited.

'Warren?' she questioned. 'Dead,' was all he answered.
[*1914*]

Stopping by Woods on a Snowy Evening

Whose woods these are I think I know.
His house is in the village though;
He will not see me stopping here
To watch his woods fill up with snow.

My little horse must think it queer
To stop without a farmhouse near
Between the woods and frozen lake
The darkest evening of the year.

He gives his harness bells a shake
To ask if there is some mistake. 10
The only other sound's the sweep
Of easy wind and downy flake.

The woods are lovely, dark and deep,
But I have promises to keep,
And miles to go before I sleep,
And miles to go before I sleep.
[*1923*]

West-running Brook

'Fred, where is north?'

'North? North is there, my love.
The brook runs west.'

'West-running Brook then call it.'
(West-running Brook men call it to this day.)
'What does it think it's doing running west
When all the other country brooks flow east
To reach the ocean? It must be the brook
Can trust itself to go by contraries
The way I can with you—and you with me—
Because we're—we're—I don't know what we are.
What are we?'

'Young or new?'

'We must be something. 10
We've said we two. Let's change that to we three.
As you and I are married to each other,
We'll both be married to the brook. We'll build
Our bridge across it, and the bridge shall be
Our arm thrown over it asleep beside it.
Look, look, it's waving to us with a wave
To let us know it hears me.'

'Why, my dear,
That wave's been standing off this jut of shore—'
(The black stream, catching on a sunken rock,
Flung backward on itself in one white wave, 20
And the white water rode the black forever,
Not gaining but not losing, like a bird
White feathers from the struggle of whose breast
Flecked the dark stream and flecked the darker pool
Below the point, and were at last driven wrinkled
In a white scarf against the far shore alders.)
'That wave's been standing off this jut of shore

Ever since rivers, I was going to say,
Were made in heaven. It wasn't waved to us.'

'It wasn't, yet it was. If not to you   30
It was to me—in an annunciation.'

'Oh, if you take it off to lady-land,
As't were the country of the Amazons
We men must see you to the confines of
And leave you there, ourselves forbid to enter,—
It is your brook! I have no more to say.'

'Yes, you have, too. Go on. You thought of something.'

'Speaking of contraries, see how the brook
In that white wave runs counter to itself.
It is from that in water we were from   40
Long, long before we were from any creature.
Here we, in our impatience of the steps,
Get back to the beginning of beginnings,
The stream of everything that runs away.
Some say existence like a Pirouot
And Pirouette, forever in one place,
Stands still and dances, but it runs away,
It seriously, sadly, runs away
To fill the abyss' void with emptiness.
It flows beside us in this water brook.   50
But it flows over us. It flows between us
To separate us for a panic moment.
It flows between us, over us, and *with* us.
And it is time, strength, tone, light, life, and love—
And even substance lapsing unsubstantial;
The universal cataract of death
That spends to nothingness—and unresisted,
Save by some strange resistance in itself,
Not just a swerving, but a throwing back,
As if regret were in it and were sacred.   60
It has this throwing backward on itself
So that the fall of most of it is always
Raising a little, sending up a little.

Our life runs down in sending up the clock.
The brook runs down in sending up our life.
The sun runs down in sending up the brook.
And there is something sending up the sun.
It is this backward motion toward the source,
Against the stream, that most we see ourselves in,
The tribute of the current to the source. 70
It is from this in nature we are from.
It is most us.'

'Today will be the day
You said so.'

'No, today will be the day
You said the brook was called West-running Brook.'

'Today will be the day of what we both said.'

[1929]

T. S. Eliot

Thomas Stearns Eliot was born in St. Louis, Missouri, in 1888. He was a descendant of an old New England family whose first member in America, Andrew Eliot (1627–1704), emigrated from East Coker, England. Future members of the family either entered the ministry or business. The poet's grandfather, the Reverend William Greenleaf Eliot, received a divinity degree from Harvard and went to St. Louis to establish the first Unitarian church there. He climaxed a distinguished career by accepting the chancellorship of Washington University. His second son, Henry Ware Eliot, married Charlotte Stearns, also the descendant of colonial New Englanders. The couple had seven children, of whom the poet was the youngest child and the second son.

Eliot entered Harvard in 1906, took his A.B. degree in three years and an A.M. degree the following year. During his college career he served on the Harvard literary magazine, but his major interest was philosophy. After a year in Paris he returned to Cambridge to complete a Ph.D. dissertation in philosophy. He left Harvard before receiving the degree to study at Oxford in England. Eliot decided to make England his home and, after teaching school for a year, became a banking clerk with Lloyds of London. A man of dignified mein, Eliot eschewed the Bohemian life of poets, dressing conservatively, even to adopting the English clerk's bowler and tightly furled umbrella.

In 1917 his first volume of verse, *Prufrock and Other Observations,* was published. It immediately established him as a major poet, and he became, with his fellow American Ezra Pound, a leader of the revolt against the Georgian school of poetry. He contributed a number of important critical essays to leading literary journals and even established his own publication, *The Criterion*. Despite his involvement in literature, as critic and writer, Eliot retained an attachment to the world of business. When he gave up banking, he joined the publishing firm of Faber & Faber as an editor, a position he retained throughout his life.

"The Waste Land" in 1922 brought Eliot acclaim from readers and critics on both sides of the Atlantic. He was hailed as the voice of his generation and one of the greatest poets of the century. In 1927, the poet became a British citizen and about the same time converted to the Anglican Catholic faith. He declared himself an Anglican in religion, a royalist in politics, and a classicist in literature. An artist who combined great sensibility with penetrating intellect and a passion for artistic perfection, Eliot wrote comparatively few poems, but each was a significant expression of his own spiritual and artistic development. In the latter half of his career, he devoted much of his creative energy to drama, with the aim of infusing new life into poetic drama. His *Murder in the Cathedral* (1935) was successful and has enjoyed numerous revivals. *The Cocktail Party* (1950) had a fair run on Broadway, and *The Confidential Clerk* (1954) also had a Broadway production. It is not, however, as dramatist that Eliot will probably be remembered, but as poet and critic. His poetry and his criticism have had a profound influence upon literary thought and development in England and the United States. Few modern poets and critics have escaped the impress of Eliot's thought and sensibility. A Nobel Prize winner in 1948, he won many other honors from England and America, and he was universally mourned when he died at the age of seventy-six in 1965.

There is, in Eliot's work, a remarkable unity. Each volume of poetry that he published marked a distinct stage in his spiritual development. Until about 1930 and the publication of "Ash Wednesday," it was not clear to Eliot's admirers that he was a religious poet. His early poems, with their tone of world-weary urbanity, sophistication and ironic wit, brilliant and devastating portraits of a hollow society, seemed to be social poems that exposed the sterile soul of modern man. "The Love Song of J. Alfred Prufrock," the major work of this early period, contains few religious allusions and gives little indication that it marked a stage in the poet's religious development. "The Waste Land," too, when it appeared was not recognized as an evocation of the need for religion. Contemporary readers read the poem as an expression of the upheaval in values and the black despair that have characterized the twentieth century. From the perspective of Eliot's later work, we can recognize that the despair the poet expresses has its roots in the absence of religious faith. Eliot provided an important clue to his work, in an essay on Matthew Arnold, when he declared that the poet must penetrate beneath the surface ugliness and beauty of life "to see the boredom, and the horror, and the glory." As a number of critics have since pointed out, Eliot describes in that phrase the three stages in his own spiritual development and the dominant moods of the three stages of his poetic development. The early poems in *Prufrock and Other Observations* convey a sense of futility: modern man is ineffectual and bored because he leads a meaningless life. J. Alfred Prufrock measures out his life with coffee spoons. "The Waste Land" is a profoundly moving evocation of the horror of meaningless existence. "The Hollow Men" (1925) echoes this despair, but the anguish conveyed is the anguish of indecision, the inability to escape the stupor of spiritual aridity and make the final commitment to faith. "Ash Wednesday" (1930) depicts the moment of commitment, and the *Four Quartets,* "East Coker" (1940), "Burnt Norton" (1941), "The Dry Salvages" (1941), and "Little Gidding" (1943), are religious poems, expressing the glory of faith.

Though Eliot's poetry was clearly rooted in his own spiritual experiences, it cannot be considered personal poetry. The response of Eliot's contemporaries to his poetry indicates how forcefully he had voiced his generation's feeling of malaise. Many of his ardent admirers felt keen disappointment when the poet joined the Anglican Church. They could not follow Eliot in his religious commitment and somehow felt betrayed that the man who had expressed so perfectly their own feelings had moved into areas of experience alien to them. But even Eliot's religious poetry transcends personal experience. One of his fundamental concepts is that poetry must not be a Wordsworthian "spontaneous overflow of feeling." Eliot broke from this tradition because he considered it too effusively personal; he believed that the poet's task was to objectify personal feeling and experience so that they could express universal rather than individual experience. To communicate effectively, the poet had to view his own feelings from a broad perspective and discover in them the constants of human experience. Eliot's own state of mind, for instance, during the period in which he wrote "The Waste Land" is made to reflect the spiritual crisis of his generation and also to see that crisis as a common experience throughout human history during periods in which religious faith is flickering.

Out of this aim Eliot's theory of the "objective correlative" developed. The poet sought an image, an allusion, a dramatic situation, a myth that would evoke a particular response in the reader. By means of his structure and techniques, the poet orchestrates these responses to evoke a unified and total experience, mood, feeling. In an Eliot poem, meaning derives from feeling. Frequently, two images which seem to have no logical connection are juxtaposed, but the feelings evoked by the images are related. Because we are accustomed to an intellectually obvious logic in more traditional poetry, an Eliot poem is at first confusing. But once we understand that Eliot's work requires full participation from his reader and that there is an emotional rather than an intellectual logic in the structuring of his poetry, we are ready to appreciate the experience it affords.

Because he believed that poetic communication must take place on the level of feeling, Eliot sought the image that would fuse idea and feeling. As a result, it is possible to feel the emotional impact of an Eliot poem before we fully comprehend its meaning. During the forty-odd years since the publication of "The Waste Land," critics and scholars have explicated the many erudite and esoteric allusions and myths that Eliot crammed into that poem, but perceptive readers of the poem during the 1920s were deeply moved by it even if they did not recognize all the allusions and quotations.

Eliot's use of literary allusions and quotations and ancient myths adds to the complexity of his poetry but also adds much to its profundity. He believed that a sense of history, a recognition of the continuity in human experience was an essential attribute for a poet. Great poets, such as Dante, not only express their own feelings but those of their age and those of men in any age. The myths of the ancient and medieval worlds, the poetry of the greatest poets in all periods of history are the common heritage of modern man, and Eliot believed that by incorporating allusions from these older works into his poetry he could expand the significance of his own poetry and provide an intense experience for his readers. When, for instance, he has Prufrock say, "I am not Prince Hamlet nor was meant to be," he forces his reader to recall Shakespeare's play and to view Prufrock from the perspective of Hamlet's character and career. Such allusions serve to involve the reader in the creation of poetry by drawing upon his memory of past experiences and responses to strengthen his response. Such allusions are generally incorporated into Eliot's poetic structure sufficiently to be effective even if we do not recognize them, but when we do, maximum response is achieved. Eliot worked for compression in the poetic line. He sought to pack into each phrase as many nuances as possible [see *Handbook:* ambiguity] and at the same time to startle the reader into fresh perceptions. With a brilliant image, for instance, he captures the whole character of Prufrock's society: "the women come and go / Talking of Michelangelo."

Eliot's characteristic device of juxtaposing startling images is derived from the French symbolists, particularly Laforgue. From this poet also, Eliot probably derived his technique of mixing colloquial with esoteric words. And from the metaphysical writers of the seventeenth century, Eliot adapted the technique of uniting disparate ideas and images to convey idea and feeling in one explosive metaphor.

Another technique that Eliot adopted to objectify experience was to create characters and scenes. "The Love Song of J. Alfred Prufrock" is a dramatic monologue. The opening lines establish a dramatic situation: "Let us go then, you and I . . . Let us go and make our visit." We attend Prufrock as he goes to make his visit, following the circuitous paths of his thoughts and feelings as he moves toward and then away from his moment of decision. By the end of the poem, we know Prufrock thoroughly and we know his world. Chaotic though this or any Eliot poem may at first seem, it is in reality tightly structured and tightly controlled. Everything in the poem, from the epigraph to the spacing of the lines on the page contributes to the totality of effect. Eliot rejected the Georgian poets' emphasis upon meter and rhyme because he believed that verse technique had to develop from the feeling and thought of the poem rather than being superimposed upon them.

Eliot's influence upon the twentieth century has been incalculable, not only because of the effectiveness of his poetry but also because he was a poetic theorist. At the beginning of his career, he saw a need for a revitalization of poetry, and by means of his critical essays and his own poetic practices he made poetry a vital literary vehicle in an age dominated by prose. Eliot's contemporaries have accorded him a pedestal among the greatest of poets in the English language, and it is very possible that future literary historians will refer to the first half of the twentieth century as the Age of Eliot.

BIBLIOGRAPHY

Eliot, T. S. *Selected Essays, 1917–1932.* New York: Harcourt, Brace, 1932.
Gardner, Helen. *The Art of T. S. Eliot.* New York: E. P. Dutton, 1959.
Matthiessen, F. O. *The Achievement of T. S. Eliot.* New York: Oxford University Press, 1947.
Williamson, George. *A Reader's Guide to T. S. Eliot.* New York: Noonday Press, 1957.

The Hollow Men

Mistah Kurtz—he dead.

A penny for the Old Guy

I

We are the hollow men
We are the stuffed men
Leaning together
Headpiece filled with straw. Alas!
Our dried voices, when
We whisper together
Are quiet and meaningless
As wind in dry grass
Or rats' feet over broken glass
In our dry cellar 10

Shape without form, shade without colour,
Paralysed force, gesture without motion;

Those who have crossed
With direct eyes, to death's other Kingdom
Remember us—if at all—not as lost
Violent souls, but only
As the hollow men
The stuffed men.

II

Eyes I dare not meet in dreams
In death's dream kingdom 20
These do not appear:
There, the eyes are
Sunlight on a broken column
There, is a tree swinging
And voices are
In the wind's singing
More distant and more solemn
Than a fading star.

Let me be no nearer
In death's dream kingdom 30
Let me also wear
Such deliberate disguises
Rat's coat, crowskin, crossed staves
In a field
Behaving as the wind behaves
No nearer—

Not that final meeting
In the twilight kingdom.

III

This is the dead land
This is cactus land 40
Here the stone images
Are raised, here they receive
The supplication of a dead man's hand
Under the twinkle of a fading star.

Is it like this
In death's other kingdom
Waking alone
At the hour when we are
Trembling with tenderness
Lips that would kiss 50
Form prayers to broken stone.

IV

The eyes are not here
There are no eyes here
In this valley of dying stars
In this hollow valley
This broken jaw of our lost kingdoms

In this last of meeting places
We grope together
And avoid speech
Gathered on this beach of the tumid river 60

Sightless, unless
The eyes reappear
As the perpetual star
Multifoliate rose
Of death's twilight kingdom
The hope only
Of empty men.

V

Here we go round the prickly pear
Prickly pear prickly pear
Here we go round the prickly pear 70
At five o'clock in the morning.

Between the idea
And the reality
Between the motion
And the act
Falls the Shadow

For Thine is the Kingdom

Between the conception
And the creation
Between the emotion 80
And the response
Falls the Shadow

Life is very long

Between the desire
And the spasm
Between the potency
And the existence
Between the essence
And the descent
Falls the Shadow 90

For Thine is the Kingdom

For Thine is
Life is
For Thine is the

This is the way the world ends
This is the way the world ends
This is the way the world ends
Not with a bang but a whimper.

[1925]

Commentary

"The Hollow Men" (1925), published three years after "The Waste Land," dramatizes the despair of one who knows life is meaningless without God and yet is not able to make the final commitment to faith. Many critics have described the poem as the nadir of Eliot's spiritual despair, but others have recognized that the means of salvation are clearly indicated in the poem. Helen Gardner in *The Art of T. S. Eliot* notes that two types of images predominate. The images of sterility, boredom, and despair are similar to those in "Prufrock" and "The Waste Land." But other images point forward to the images of "Ash Wednesday," in which salvation through faith is achieved.

The hollow men described in the poem are like the flowing crowds in the "Unreal City" passage of "The Waste Land." These lost souls, who walk with downcast eyes, are the souls in Dante's Inferno who dwell on the dark plain in front of the gates of hell. Eliot's incorporation of Dante's words in this passage, "I had not thought death had undone so many," provides the clue to the character of his "Unreal City" people. In Dante's Canto III from which the quotation is taken, Dante reaches the Acheron, the river that borders hell. He hears the sighs and deep wailings of those souls who "lived without blame, and without praise." They had never been really alive, had never committed themselves to either good or evil, had cared for nothing but themselves. Among these lost souls were the angels who did not rebel with Satan nor remain loyal to God. Such souls cannot enter hell because the wicked "would have some glory over them." The death-in-life represented by Dante's souls is the spiritual state of modern man. In section IV of "The Hollow Men," Eliot refers again to Dante's third canto in his image, "this last of meeting places" where the hollow men are "Gathered on this beach of the tumid river."

Other clues to the character of the hollow men are provided by the two epigraphs. "Mistah Kurtz—he dead" is a quotation from Joseph Conrad's "Heart of Darkness." Kurtz is a European whose mission is to bring the light of European civilization into the heart of the

African darkness. The cultural values Kurtz embodies and which he is to teach the natives are eroded during his sojourn in the primitive world of the savage. The thin veneer of civilization wears away, and Kurtz becomes one of the savages he had come to enlighten. The allusion to Kurtz suggests that the values of the hollow men are cultural rather than religious and, therefore, are superficial and intrinsically meaningless. The other epigraph alludes to the custom among English children of begging pennies for fireworks to celebrate Guy Fawkes Day. On November 5 each year, an effigy of the seventeenth-century man who conspired to blow up King James and the members of Parliament is burned. These effigies, made of straw, are grotesque caricatures, and the epigraph suggests that the hollow men with "headpiece filled with straw" are likewise grotesques.

Aside from the various images of aridity and sterility which are used to describe the hollow men and their world, there are three major images that reveal the speaker's inability to make the final abnegation of self necessary for faith and salvation: the four kingdoms of death, the eyes, and the star.

The inevitability of death generates much human thought about the meaning of life, and because each of us must live in the presence of his own death, we live, in a sense, in death's kingdom. Death's other Kingdom (capitalized) is the afterlife. Death's dream kingdom appears to be the world of imagination, and the twilight kingdom is occupied by one who vacillates, unable to commit himself to God.

Two sets of eyes appear in the poem. One is an objectification of the idea that man lives in the sight of God. The other set, which appears only in the dream kingdom, probably symbolizes worldly values. The third symbol, the star, is invested with its traditional religious significance: the star that guided the wise men to the birthplace of Jesus.

Having established the general character of the hollow men and the significance of these major symbols, we can now consider each of the five sections of the poem. In section I, by his characteristic fusion of images, Eliot conveys the spiritual sterility of the hollow men and their world. The emphasis, as it is in "The Waste Land," is on dryness. Life-giving water is absent, and voices, grass, cellar are dry. In the existence of the hollow men there is a furtive quality, the manifestation of their fear, their refusal or inability to face the essential questions of life. They huddle together speaking in whispers. The image of "rat's feet over broken glass" evokes the sound of rattling bones, and the phrase "in our dry cellar" may suggest the terror of death that is deep within their empty souls. They exist in a state of paralysis between life and death. In the final stanza of section I are introduced the symbols of the eyes and death's other Kingdom. Allusion to those who faced the eyes of God and entered the other Kingdom emphasizes the inaction of the hollow men.

The shift in section II from the first person plural to the first person singular separates the protagonist of the poem from the rest of his society. He too suffers from the malaise of his fellow men, but he has moved into another state. He seems to have recognized the necessity of responding to the eyes, but he is still unable to do so. He records the attempt to make life meaningful without faith by seeking the natural or artistic beauty available in life. But the sunlight falls on a broken column, attesting the impermanence of art, and the voices cannot provide the guidance of the perpetual star: they are "more distant . . . than a fading star." The desire to escape from the overwhelming question is expressed in "Let me be no nearer" that opens and "No nearer—" that closes this stanza. The desire to escape the "eyes I dare not meet" is also expressed in the need for disguises. The character of the disguises reveals a sense of shame. The stanza concludes with an expression of fear—fear of meeting the eyes, through death, in a state of indecision. The protagonist cannot escape from the twilight kingdom.

Section III pictures the reality of the dead land. The false gods of cultural values are insignificant and provide no relief. The second stanza conveys the sense of uncertainty that prevents commitment. Is death's other Kingdom simply a mirror of this life? At the same time the image also conveys the intense need for belief and the frustration of not being able to believe.

Section IV expresses the despair and disgust that accompanies the failure to achieve faith. The eyes that represent the possibility of faith are gone and we are on the banks of Dante's river among the lost souls who neither lived nor died. Out of this moment of despair comes the full and complete recognition that only through faith is salvation possible. The symbol of the eyes merges into the perpetual star, and the star merges into the rose, the symbol in Dante's Paradise of the Virgin Mary. The rose of many leaves probably symbolizes the church by imaging the rose windows of cathedrals. In short, only total commitment through the church can bring salvation. Faith alone can make life meaningful for the inhabitant of the twilight kingdom. But for the empty men it is only a hope because they cannot achieve that abnegation of self that faith demands.

The inability to make the final and necessary surrender of self is symbolized in section V by the falling Shadow. Between the series of pairs, all of which express potential and fulfillment, the "Shadow" falls. Prayers, expressing the need and desire for faith, are cut short. The child's nursery rhyme with which the section opens conveys the meaninglessness of life in a spiritually sterile world and this rhyme is matched by the final lines of the poem.

Eliot skillfully utilizes his form to convey feeling. The verse is stripped to essentials. The monotonous two-beat line which dominates has the character of a chant, and in the pattern of the verse is expressed the sense of frustration and despair of the hollow men.

The Love Song of J. Alfred Prufrock

S'io credesse che mia risposta fosse
A persona che mai tornasse al mondo,
Questa fiamma staria senza piu scosse.
Ma perciocche giammai di questo fondo
Non torno vivo alcun, s'i'odo il vero,
Senza tema d'infamia ti rispondo.

Let us go then, you and I,
When the evening is spread out against the sky
Like a patient etherised upon a table;
Let us go, through certain half-deserted streets,
The muttering retreats
Of restless nights in one-night cheap hotels
And sawdust restaurants with oyster-shells:
Streets that follow like a tedious argument
Of insidious intent
To lead you to an overwhelming question . . . 10
Oh, do not ask, "What is it?"
Let us go and make our visit.

In the room the women come and go
Talking of Michelangelo.

The yellow fog that rubs its back upon the window-panes,
The yellow smoke that rubs its muzzle on the window-panes
Licked its tongue into the corners of the evening,
Lingered upon the pools that stand in drains,
Let fall upon its back the soot that falls from chimneys,
Slipped by the terrace, made a sudden leap, 20
And seeing that it was a soft October night,
Curled once about the house, and fell asleep.

S'io credesse . . . rispondo: Dante's Inferno, xxvii, 61–66. The speaker is Guido da Montefeltro, who has been asked to identify himself. "If I believed my answers were being made to one who could ever return to this world, this flame would gleam no more; but since, if what I hear is true, never from this abyss did living man return, I answer thee without fear of infamy."

And indeed there will be time
For the yellow smoke that slides along the street,
Rubbing its back upon the window-panes;
There will be time, there will be time
To prepare a face to meet the faces that you meet;
There will be time to murder and create,
And time for all the works and days of hands
That lift and drop a question on your plate; 30
Time for you and time for me,
And time yet for a hundred indecisions,
And for a hundred visions and revisions,
Before the taking of a toast and tea.

In the room the women come and go
Talking of Michelangelo.

And indeed there will be time
To wonder, "Do I dare?" and, "Do I dare?"
Time to turn back and descend the stair,
With a bald spot in the middle of my hair— 40
[They will say: "How his hair is growing thin!"]
My morning coat, my collar mounting firmly to the chin,
My necktie rich and modest, but asserted by a simple pin—
[They will say: "But how his arms and legs are thin!"]
Do I dare
Disturb the universe?
In a minute there is time
For decisions and revisions which a minute will reverse.

For I have known them all already, known them all:—
Have known the evenings, mornings, afternoons, 50
I have measured out my life with coffee spoons;
I know the voices dying with a dying fall
Beneath the music from a farther room.
So how should I presume?

l. 29. *works and days:* Hesiod's eighth-century B.C. account of daily life, *Works and Days,* is interspersed with moral precepts.

l. 52. *dying fall:* in Shakespeare's *Twelfth Night,* I. i. 1–4, occur the following lines:
If music be the food of love, play on;
Give me excess of it, that, surfeiting
The appetite may sicken, and so die.
That strain again! It had a dying fall.

And I have known the eyes already, known them all—
The eyes that fix you in a formulated phrase,
And when I am formulated, sprawling on a pin,
When I am pinned and wriggling on the wall,
Then how should I begin
To spit out all the butt-ends of my days and ways? 60
  And how should I presume?

And I have known the arms already, known them all—
Arms that are braceleted and white and bare
[But in the lamplight, downed with light brown hair!]
Is it perfume from a dress
That makes me so digress?
Arms that lie along a table, or wrap about a shawl.
  And should I then presume?
  And how should I begin?

. . .

Shall I say, I have gone at dusk through narrow streets 70
And watched the smoke that rises from the pipes
Of lonely men in shirt-sleeves, leaning out of windows? . . .

I should have been a pair of ragged claws
Scuttling across the floors of silent seas.

. . .

And the afternoon, the evening, sleeps so peacefully!
Smoothed by long fingers,
Asleep . . . tired . . . or it malingers,
Stretched on the floor, here beside you and me.
Should I, after tea and cakes and ices,
Have the strength to force the moment to its crisis? 80
But though I have wept and fasted, wept and prayed,
Though I have seen my head [grown slightly bald] brought in
    upon a platter,
I am no prophet—and here's no great matter;
I have seen the moment of my greatness flicker,
And I have seen the eternal Footman hold my coat, and snicker,
And in short, I was afraid.

l. 83. *prophet:* Saint John the Baptist.

And would it have been worth it, after all,
After the cups, the marmalade, the tea,
Among the porcelain, among some talk of you and me,
Would it have been worth while, 90
To have bitten off the matter with a smile,
To have squeezed the universe into a ball
To roll it toward some overwhelming question,
To say: "I am Lazarus, come from the dead,
Come back to tell you all, I shall tell you all"—
If one, settling a pillow by her head,
  Should say: "That is not what I meant at all.
  That is not it, at all."

And would it have been worth it, after all,
Would it have been worth while, 100
After the sunsets and the dooryards and the sprinkled streets,
After the novels, after the teacups, after the skirts that trail
    along the floor—
And this, and so much more?—
It is impossible to say just what I mean!
But as if a magic lantern threw the nerves in patterns on a
    screen:
Would it have been worth while
If one, settling a pillow or throwing off a shawl,
And turning toward the window, should say:
  "That is not it at all,
  That is not what I meant, at all." 110

. . .

No! I am not Prince Hamlet, nor was meant to be;
Am an attendant lord, one that will do
To swell a progress, start a scene or two,
Advise the prince; no doubt, an easy tool,
Deferential, glad to be of use,
Politic, cautious, and meticulous;
Full of high sentence, but a bit obtuse;
At times, indeed, almost ridiculous—
Almost, at times, the Fool.

I grow old . . . I grow old . . . 120
I shall wear the bottoms of my trousers rolled.

l. 94. *Lazarus:* see *John* XI: 11–44.

Shall I part my hair behind? Do I dare to eat a peach?
I shall wear white flannel trousers, and walk upon the beach.
I have heard the mermaids singing, each to each.

I do not think that they will sing to me.

I have seen them riding seaward on the waves
Combing the white hair of the waves blown back
When the wind blows the water white and black.

We have lingered in the chambers of the sea
By sea-girls wreathed with seaweed red and brown 130
Till human voices wake us, and we drown.

[1917]

Journey of the Magi

'A cold coming we had of it,
Just the worst time of the year
For a journey, and such a long journey:
The ways deep and the weather sharp,
The very dead of winter.'
And the camels galled, sore-footed, refractory,
Lying down in the melting snow.
There were times we regretted
The summer palaces on slopes, the terraces,
And the silken girls bringing sherbet. 10
Then the camel men cursing and grumbling
And running away, and wanting their liquor and women,
And the night-fires going out, and the lack of shelters,
And the cities hostile and the towns unfriendly
And the villages dirty and charging high prices:
A hard time we had of it.
At the end we preferred to travel all night,
Sleeping in snatches,
With the voices singing in our ears, saying
That this was all folly. 20

l. 1. *'A cold coming . . .'*: the speaker is one of the Magi, recalling the journey.

ll. 1–5. are actually from a sermon by Bishop Lancelot Andrewes (1555–1626) in which the Bishop expands upon the text "Behold there came wise men from the East."

Then at dawn we came down to a temperate valley,
Wet, below the snow line, smelling of vegetation;
With a running stream and a water-mill beating the dark-
        ness,
And three trees on the low sky,
And an old white horse galloped away in the meadow.
Then we came to a tavern with vine-leaves over the lintel,
Six hands at an open door dicing for pieces of silver,
And feet kicking the empty wine-skins.
But there was no information, and so we continued
And arrived at evening, not a moment too soon   30
Finding the place; it was (you may say) satisfactory.

All this was a long time ago, I remember,
And I would do it again, but set down
This set down
This: were we led all that way for
Birth or Death? There was a Birth, certainly,
We had evidence and no doubt. I had seen birth and death,
But had thought they were different; this Birth was
Hard and bitter agony for us, like Death, our death.
We returned to our places, these Kingdoms,   40
But no longer at ease here, in the old dispensation,
With an alien people clutching their gods.
I should be glad of another death.

[*1927*]

l. 24. *three trees:* the three crosses on Calvary.
l. 27. *Six hands:* the poet is recalling the betrayal of Jesus and the soldiers playing dice at the foot of the cross.

A Song for Simeon

Lord, the Roman hyacinths are blooming in bowls and
The winter sun creeps by the snow hills;
The stubborn season has made stand.
My life is light, waiting for the death wind,

A Song for Simeon: the passage in *Luke* (II: 25–35) begins: "And, behold, there was a man in Jerusalem, whose name was Simeon; and the same man was just and devout, waiting for the consolation of Israel: and the Holy Ghost was upon him." Simeon is the speaker in the poem.

Like a feather on the back of my hand.
Dust in sunlight and memory in corners
Wait for the wind that chills towards the dead land.

Grant us thy peace.
I have walked many years in this city,
Kept faith and fast, provided for the poor, 10
Have given and taken honour and ease.
There went never any rejected from my door.
Who shall remember my house, where shall live my children's children
When the time of sorrow is come?
They will take to the goat's path, and the fox's home,
Fleeing from the foreign faces and the foreign swords.

Before the time of cords and scourges and lamentation
Grant us thy peace.
Before the stations of the mountain of desolation,
Before the certain hour of maternal sorrow, 20
Now at this birth season of decease,
Let the Infant, the still unspeaking and unspoken Word,
Grant Israel's consolation
To one who has eighty years and no to-morrow.

According to thy word.
They shall praise Thee and suffer in every generation
With glory and derision,
Light upon light, mounting the saints' stair.
Not for me the martyrdom, the ecstasy of thought and prayer,
Not for me the ultimate vision. 30
Grant me thy peace.
(And a sword shall pierce thy heart,
Thine also.)
I am tired with my own life and the lives of those after me,
I am dying in my own death and the deaths of those after me.
Let thy servant depart,
Having seen thy salvation.

[*1928*]

Marina

Quis hic locus, quae regio, quae mundi plaga?

What seas what shores what grey rocks and what islands
What water lapping the bow
And scent of pine and the woodthrush singing through the fog
What images return
O my daughter.

Those who sharpen the tooth of the dog, meaning
Death
Those who glitter with the glory of the hummingbird, meaning
Death
Those who sit in the stye of contentment, meaning 10
Death
Those who suffer the ecstasy of the animals, meaning
Death

Are become unsubstantial, reduced by a wind,
A breath of pine, and the woodsong fog
By this grace dissolved in place

What is this face, less clear and clearer
The pulse in the arm, less strong and stronger—
Given or lent? more distant than stars and nearer than the eye

Whispers and small laughter between leaves and hurrying feet 20
Under sleep, where all the waters meet.

Marina: in *Pericles, Prince of Tyre,* to which Shakespeare contributed the last two acts, Pericles miraculously finds his daughter Marina who had been born in a storm at sea and then lost during her childhood in another storm. Pericles presumes her dead but continues to search for her. Now an old man, he recalls his pilgrimage.

Quis . . . plaga?: in Seneca, *Hercules Furens,* the words: "What place is this; what region; what quarter of the universe?" are uttered by Hercules when he comes to his senses after a spell of madness during which he killed his wife and children. The awakening of Hercules contrasts with that of Pericles when he finds his daughter, a symbol of idealized beauty and of discovered faith.

Bowsprit cracked with ice and paint cracked with heat.
I made this, I have forgotten
And remember.
The rigging weak and the canvas rotten
Between one June and another September.
Made this unknowing, half conscious, unknown, my own.
The garboard strake leaks, the seams need caulking.
This form, this face, this life
Living to live in a world of time beyond me; let me 30
Resign my life for this life, my speech for that unspoken,
The awakened, lips parted, the hope, the new ships.

What seas what shores what granite islands towards my timbers
And woodthrush calling through the fog
My daughter.

[1930]

Dylan Thomas

Dylan Thomas was born in Swansea, Wales, on October 22, 1914. The child of understanding middle-class parents, the poet seems to have had a routinely pleasant childhood in the bustling city that fronts the sea. His father has been remembered by his students and by his son as a dedicated and popular English master at the Swansea Grammar School who inspired in his pupils a liking for the learning he provided. As a student in the school at which his father taught, young Dylan did not distinguish himself academically, for he much preferred life to the acquisition of scholastic skills. The poet participated in extracurricular activities such as editing the school periodical and appearing in the school dramatic productions with more genuine interest than he gave to studies.

Thomas knew early in his school career that he wanted to be a poet, and he therefore arranged his life accordingly. Refusing to apply for a scholarship which would ensure him a higher academic education, he left school at seventeen to take the only kind of position in Wales that would give him a salary and allow him to write. He became a reporter on the *Herald of Wales*, a job in which he was often assigned to report news of local poetic activity. In his spare time, he wrote poems.

Two years later, Thomas left Swansea for London as the first step in his plan to become a professional poet. Speaking to a group of writers in later years, the poet explained his going to London in this way:

> I am a Welshman who does not live in his own country, mainly because he still wants to eat and drink, be rigged and roofed, and no Welsh writer can hunt his bread and butter in Wales unless he pulls his forelock to the *Western Mail*, Bethesdas on Sunday, and enters public-houses by the back door. . . .

That Thomas had made the right move, so far as his career was concerned, is clear from the almost immediate recognition which sophisticated literary magazines afforded his work. He immediately found a publisher for his first book, *Eighteen Poems* (1934) and another collection appeared two years later. During this period he also wrote poetry for such periodicals as the *Criterion* and *The Adelphi*. By the end of the 1930s his improving fortunes allowed him to marry Caitlin Macnamara, an Irish girl to whom he was introduced by the painter, Augustus John, and to settle briefly in Laugharne, Wales. In 1939, his first son was born.

World War II found Thomas, judged physically unfit for military service, employed in various quasi-literary cultural activities. He worked for the B.B.C., he supplied scripts for documentaries sponsored by the Ministry of Information, and he participated in broadcasts on artistic subjects. In addition, Thomas continued to write poetry and he published short fiction. By 1946, he had settled, with his wife and their three children, in a village near Oxford, where he could enjoy the nonacademic activities of the university: good conversation, the conviviality of pub life, and intellectual companions. William Jay Smith recalls the Thomases at Oxford:

> . . . A. L. Rowse had invited us to lunch, and I shall never forget the first sight of Dylan and Caitlin in those august surroundings, Dylan in a bright checked suit and rakish pancake cap, Caitlin all gold and red, completely the dancer. . . . They were "country". . . and they didn't mind letting the world know that there was something more important than literature, and that was life.

From 1946 until his death in 1953, the poet was actually in a period of decline, though ostensibly his fortunes rose steadily. As a script writer for films, he earned a substantial sum of money, but he detested the work. Convivial drinking turned into alcoholism by imperceptible degrees. His marriage was not working out successfully. Above all, his creative inspiration was drying up. One critic points out that Thomas wrote only seven poems in the last six years of his life. Nor did Thomas' frenzied pace of living help to right the balance. He traveled to Iran on business, he visited Italy for his son's health, he traveled in middle Europe. Most deceptive of all events in his gradual deterioration were his three triumphal tours of the United States to read his poetry, speak on literature, and be lionized by the intellectually aware and the morbidly curious. His fourth visit in 1953 was his last. He died wretchedly in New York in the autumn of that year, worn out physically and emotionally at the age of thirty-nine.

The influence of Wales upon Thomas cannot be overestimated. Though he left it for England, as Joyce fled from Ireland, he found, as Joyce did, that his thought, his vision of life, his literary nature owed more to the country of his childhood than to his adult environment. Suzanne Roussillat, who interviewed Thomas on the facts of his life, reports the strong effect on his personality of his Nonconformist religious training and his Welsh training in the Bible. Another writer points out that Thomas' grandfather was a Welsh preacher who enthralled his congregation by his incantatory sermons as Thomas was later to weave a spell by the musical rendition of his poetry. Like Gerard Manley Hopkins, who was not perhaps a direct influence, Thomas had a reservoir of things Welsh.

Suzanne Roussillat feels that the natural scenery of Wales, and particularly the vistas of Swansea, exerted the strongest influence on Thomas. The mistiness of the sky, the expanse of Swansea Bay meeting the sky in the distance, the sea and the hills, are responsible, she believes, for the basic imagery of Thomas' poetry. On the other hand, what man has done to nature in Swansea becomes central to much of Thomas' prose:

> I was born in a large Welsh industrial town at the beginning of the Great War: an ugly, lovely town (or so it was, and is, to me), crawling, sprawling, slummed, unplanned, jerry-villa'd, and smug-suburbed by the side of a long and splendid-curving shore where truant boys and sandfield boys and old anonymous men . . . idled, and paddled, watched the dock-bound boats. . . .

A reading of Thomas' poems turns up more fundamental interests than landscape. Stated broadly, the poet's theme is man in nature. Unlike Wordsworth, however, Thomas is relatively indifferent to the form which natural surroundings take. His preoccupation, as many critics have pointed out, is with the *process* by which man becomes part of his natural world (conception and birth), and the inevitable journey toward death which being born entails (childhood, maturity, old age). Understandably, therefore, Thomas is concerned with religion and with Freud.

The poet speaks of his poems as "written for the love of Man and in praise of God." Elsewhere, in reply to a question concerning the use of his poetry, he speaks of it almost in apocalyptic terms as movement "from an overclothed blindness to a naked vision." "My poetry," he says, "is the record of my individual struggle from darkness towards some measure of light, and what of the individual struggle is still to come benefits by the sight and knowledge of the faults and fewer merits in that concrete record." But Thomas is not unique in striving for revelation, or at least for awareness of the truth. If his poetry is useful to others, he declares, its usefulness lies in its "individual recording of that same struggle with which they are necessarily acquainted."

Thus, Thomas' attempt to plumb the meaning of his own existence, the process which advances the organism from the womb to the tomb, is also an attempt to define the role of mankind caught up in the flux of natural mutability. In microcosm, man reenacts in his life process the natural movements of the macrocosm. By celebrating these processes in man and nature, the poet, if successful, celebrates the divine scheme which generates them and harmoniously vindicates the ways of God to man. In their celebration, Thomas uses a language rich in Hebrew and Christian references so that the religious contents of a poem are immediately apparent even when precise "meaning" eludes the reader. His imagery is sacramental, as Hopkins' often is. The reader perceives that he is present at a religious rite as he reads the poem—though often the doctrine being preached is unclear.

Like religion, the doctrines of Freud are naturally associated with Thomas' purpose in writing poetry. The initiation of the process of life lies in the act of copulation, which implies love—or sex, at least. Yet this act of love is the first step in the drama of degeneration and death. Love, sex, birth, childhood, death—these are the province of Freud, by whom Thomas freely admitted being influenced:

> Whatever is hidden should be made naked. To be stripped of darkness is to be clean, to strip of darkness is to make clean. Poetry, recording the stripping of the individual darkness, must,

> inevitably, cast light upon what has been hidden for too long, and by so doing, make clean the naked exposure. Freud cast light on a little of the darkness he had exposed. Benefiting by the sight of the light and the knowledge of the hidden nakedness, poetry must drag further into the clean nakedness of light more even of the hidden causes than Freud could realize.

Thomas preferred to use the imagery and symbols of Freud's "Interpretation of Dreams" rather than to versify Freudian doctrine. Worms, apples, fingers, hair, fluids, stairs, and entrances testify to the influence of psychoanalysis and its literature, but Thomas' intention is artistic and religious, not scientific.

It is interesting, too, that as Thomas advanced as a poet, in confidence and virtuosity, he relied less and less on even the Freudian vocabulary. *Eighteen Poems* in 1934 and *Twenty-Five Poems* in 1936 are drenched in the idiom, but when the shock of recognition wears off, the reader is left with the weary task of "translating" scientific language into meaningful poetic idiom. By the time of *Deaths and Entrances* (1946), the language is subdued. Freudian imagery is sometimes present, but it is subordinated to poetic balance. The poetry expresess Thomas' point of view more simply, and there are even long "narrative" poems to spell the lyrics.

Thomas' career is a study in contradictions. Because he had undoubted poetic talents, he attained almost immediate success with London critics. But his removal to London and the life which being a successful poet entails proved the first step in his physical deterioration. Had his American tours not been so triumphal, his last years would certainly have been less frenzied and his death, perhaps, long postponed. The acclaim of such recognized authorities on poetry as Edith Sitwell may not have turned the head of the poet barely out of his teens, yet his apprenticeship to poetry might have been more selective and eclectic had not his youthful voice been acclaimed as mature and "authentic." Thomas is known most widely as a "difficult" poet; yet an enormous audience (for poetry) bought his books and listened to his voice on recordings as he recited his "impossibly obscure" verses. Most serious of all, the intensity of the adulation resulted in a diminishing of his poetic gifts, or, at the very least, led to a situation in which his undiminished talents could not be utilized. Dylan Thomas died in 1953 as a fully developed myth. It is only now that a very human being is emerging from the legend.

BIBLIOGRAPHY

Brinnin, John Malcolm. *Dylan Thomas in America*. Boston: Little, Brown, 1955.

Maud, Ralph. *Entrances to Dylan Thomas' Poetry*. Pittsburgh: University of Pittsburgh Press, 1963.

Tindall, W. Y. *A Reader's Guide to Dylan Thomas*. New York: Noonday Press, 1964.

"The force that through the green fuse drives the flower"

The force that through the green fuse drives the flower
Drives my green age; that blasts the roots of trees
Is my destroyer.
And I am dumb to tell the crooked rose
My youth is bent by the same wintry fever.

The force that drives the water through the rocks
Drives my red blood; that dries the mouthing streams
Turns mine to wax.
And I am dumb to mouth unto my veins
How at the mountain spring the same mouth sucks. 10

The hand that whirls the water in the pool
Stirs the quicksand; that ropes the blowing wind
Hauls my shroud sail.
And I am dumb to tell the hanging man
How of my clay is made the hangman's lime.

The lips of time leech to the fountain head;
Love drips and gathers, but the fallen blood
Shall calm her sores.
And I am dumb to tell a weather's wind
How time has ticked a heaven round the stars. 20

And I am dumb to tell the lover's tomb
How at my sheet goes the same crooked worm.

[1933]

Commentary

This poem is a typical statement of Thomas' concern with process—in this instance, the process of existence, the drama played out in the life of every man, and, on a larger scale, in the evolutionary movement of nature. Ironically, in an eloquent exposition of the process, the poet repeatedly declares in his refrain that he is powerless to verbalize to man and nature the significance of this immutable mutability.

We have already said enough about the importance to Thomas of this theme. Perhaps it is necessary merely to restate the obsessive quality of his concern with it and the infinitely varied treatments of it as the major motif of poetry composed over a period of many years.

As compared with much of Thomas' work, the poem is short and deceptively simple. However, the poet's inclination to assign to words as many associative meanings as the lines will bear adds considerable complexity to ostensibly straightforward sentences. Thus, in the first stanza, "green" age refers to the time of the narrator's youth but also allies him with the natural environment by association with "green fuse." "Blasts" has the primary meaning of "destroys," but it will later be associated with "the blowing wind" of the third stanza, which "Hauls my shroud sail." In stanza three, "quicksand" is used with its denotative meaning, as a deathtrap and grave for man; but it may also refer to the quick sand (two words) of the hourglass that appears to fall in "ropes" and is a traditional symbol for the passing of time, an essential element in the process the poet is describing. The "hanging man" is Everyman caught up in process, hanging between birth and death, eventually to rest in the "lime" (quicklime of the grave) to which the "hangman" (Time) consigns him. That grave in earth is nurtured by the organic remains of those, like Thomas, who have earlier suffered death and burial at the same remorseless and methodical hands.

The rest of the poem makes the role of time in the process explicit. It is the lips of Time that have sucked dry the veins of the poet and the mountain springs as a "leech" sucks blood. But even though "Love" be the victim of this bloodletting, in a sense the process is benevolent, for age and approaching death ease love's fevers. The masterful use of associative meanings in the last stanza emphasizes the paradox of man's fate. To have been a "lover" is to have experienced the ultimate in living; but the "lover" is in the "tomb" reserved for all men. The narrator, using on one level, the images of sex ("sheet" and "crooked worm") to suggest his own part in sexual experience and his own contribution to the evolutionary process of life, is, at the same time, suggesting that the sexual act prefaces the onset of death. The same sheet that warms the lovers is their winding sheet, and the "crooked worm" of the phallus is the maggot that devours corpses.

The reader will notice that, in dealing with Thomas' poem, it has not been possible, as it was in introductions to the poems of the other poets in this volume, merely to define difficult words in the text before proceeding to a systematic analysis of the meaning of the poem. Like Joyce's in *Finnegans Wake,* Thomas' use of words is multidimensional, and meaning can be arrived at only by examining the word in a very special and particular context. Thus, by "defining" some of the more troublesome words, we have partially explicated the poem as a whole.

Thomas' poem is a pessimistic reflection on the transiency of man's earthly condition and, on a larger scale, on the impermanence of all natural things at the hands of Time, the destroyer. It is at the same time a statement of the bard's impotence to convey the meaning of this universal movement toward dissolution and change. Nor would man stop the process if he could, since such a termination would mean refusal to create new life, a withdrawal from sex, the end of love. Thus, the implication is, man is caught in a cyclical trap of his own choice.

The poem sets up two forces, in equilibrium, regulating the universal process: the force of creation (for man and nature) and the complementary force of time, which begins to operate at the moment of creation (it "blasts the *roots* of trees"—that is, attacks them at their very source). Significantly, the narrator cannot tell the "crooked rose," rather than another developing thing, of the force which bends both him and it because, in traditional English poems, the rose has been a symbol of sexual love or of the destroying power of time (the "Gather ye rosebuds" theme). Time is seen as a leech, drying up the waters (symbols of life) and sucking the blood from man's veins. The creative hand which sets life into motion ("whirls the water in the pool") through the instrument of time prepares the grave for living things: the quicksand or the rope of sand in an hourglass which represents the running out of time for mortal creatures. At this point, the poem reeks with images of death: shroud, hanging man, clay, hangman's lime, tomb, sheet, and worm.

But apparently, each sensible thing in nature must discover for itself the meaning of the two-headed force in its own cycle of existence. The "hanging man," the individual still caught at some point of process, cannot be informed meaningfully of the fate of earlier individuals whose journey from birth to death has assured the present sufferer of a similar grave. And by a macabre twist, this grave will be filled with earth enriched by the physical elements of his predecessors. The poem ends with the lover in the tomb and with the narrator in the process of loving again and, consequently, in the process of creating life again which will be subject to the ravages of time and the respite that death brings.

Though Thomas has often been accused of verbal excesses, close examination shows that often his word associations, bizarre as they may be, are just. In fact, much of the power of his poetry resides in the controlled imaginativeness of his verbal displays. Moreover, Thomas is careful to carry on his verbal experiments in a verse form sometimes traditional and fixed and always obviously organized, symmetrical, balanced, and logical. In this poem, the first four stanzas follow such a predictable pattern in terms of sentence structure, line length, tone—in everything but rhyme scheme. And the final two lines—almost, but not quite, a couplet ("tomb", "worm")—deliberately miss the finality of a Shakespearean sonnet ending. The very regularity of the verses adds to the incantatory effect of Thomas' reading and gives added sharpness to the verbal gymnastics within the lines.

"Especially when the October wind"

Especially when the October wind
With frosty fingers punishes my hair,
Caught by the crabbing sun I walk on fire
And cast a shadow crab upon the land,
By the sea's side, hearing the noise of birds,
Hearing the raven cough in winter sticks,
My busy heart who shudders as she talks
Sheds the syllabic blood and drains her words.

Shut, too, in a tower of words, I mark
On the horizon walking like the trees 10
The wordy shapes of women, and the rows
Of the star-gestured children in the park.
Some let me make you of the vowelled beeches,
Some of the oaken voices, from the roots
Of many a thorny shire tell you notes,
Some let me make you of the water's speeches.

Behind a pot of ferns the wagging clock
Tells me the hour's word, the neural meaning
Flies on the shafted disk, declaims the morning
And tells the windy weather in the cock. 20
Some let me make you of the meadow's signs;
The signal grass that tells me all I know
Breaks with the wormy winter through the eye.
Some let me tell you of the raven's sins.

Especially when the October wind
(Some let me make you of autumnal spells,
The spider-tongued, and the loud hill of Wales)
With fists of turnips punishes the land,
Some let me make you of the heartless words.
The heart is drained that, spelling in the scurry 30
Of chemic blood, warned of the coming fury.
By the sea's side hear the dark-vowelled birds.

[1932, 1934]

"After the funeral"

(IN MEMORY OF ANN JONES)

After the funeral, mule praises, brays,
Windshake of sailshaped ears, muffle-toed tap
Tap happily of one peg in the thick
Grave's foot, blinds down the lids, the teeth in black,
The spittled eyes, the salt ponds in the sleeves,
Morning smack of the spade that wakes up sleep,
Shakes a desolate boy who slits his throat
In the dark of the coffin and sheds dry leaves,
That breaks one bone to light with a judgment clout,
After the feast of tear-stuffed time and thistles 10
In a room with a stuffed fox and a stale fern,
I stand, for this memorial's sake, alone
In the snivelling hours with dead, humped Ann
Whose hooded, fountain heart once fell in puddles
Round the parched worlds of Wales and drowned each sun
(Though this for her is a monstrous image blindly
Magnified out of praise; her death was a still drop;
She would not have me sinking in the holy
Flood of her heart's fame; she would lie dumb and deep
And need no druid of her broken body). 20
But I, Ann's bard on a raised hearth, call all
The seas to service that her wood-tongued virtue
Babble like a bellbuoy over the hymning heads,
Bow down the walls of the ferned and foxy woods
That her love sing and swing through a brown chapel,
Bless her bent spirit with four, crossing birds.
Her flesh was meek as milk, but this skyward statue
With the wild breast and blessed and giant skull
Is carved from her in a room with a wet window
In a fiercely mourning house in a crooked year. 30
I know her scrubbed and sour humble hands
Lie with religion in their cramp, her threadbare
Whisper in a damp word, her wits drilled hollow,
Her fist of a face died clenched on a round pain;
And sculptured Ann is seventy years of stone.
These cloud-sopped, marble hands, this monumental

Argument of the hewn voice, gesture and psalm,
Storm me forever over her grave until
The stuffed lung of the fox twitch and cry Love
And the strutting fern lay seeds on the black sill. 40

[1933, 1938]

"And death shall have no dominion"

And death shall have no dominion.
Dead men naked they shall be one
With the man in the wind and the west moon;
When their bones are picked clean and the clean bones gone,
They shall have stars at elbow and foot;
Though they go mad they shall be sane,
Though they sink through the sea they shall rise again;
Though lovers be lost love shall not;
And death shall have no dominion.

And death shall have no dominion. 10
Under the windings of the sea
They lying long shall not die windily;
Twisting on racks when sinews give way,
Strapped to a wheel, yet they shall not break;
Faith in their hands shall snap in two,
And the unicorn evils run them through;
Split all ends up they shan't crack;
And death shall have no dominion.

And death shall have no dominion.
No more may gulls cry at their ears 20
Or waves break loud on the seashores;
Where blew a flower may a flower no more
Lift its head to the blows of the rain;
Though they be mad and dead as nails,
Heads of the characters hammer through daisies;
Break in the sun till the sun breaks down,
And death shall have no dominion.

[1933, 1936]

Ceremony after a fire raid

I

Myselves
The grievers
Grieve
Among the street burned to tireless death
A child of a few hours
With its kneading mouth
Charred on the black breast of the grave
The mother dug, and its arms full of fires.

Begin
With singing 10
Sing
Darkness kindled back into beginning
When the caught tongue nodded blind,
A star was broken
Into the centuries of the child
Myselves grieve now, and miracles cannot atone.

Forgive
Us forgive
Us your death that myselves the believers
May hold it in a great flood 20
Till the blood shall spurt,
And the dust shall sing like a bird
As the grains blow, as your death grows, through our heart.

Crying
Your dying
Cry,
Child beyond cockcrow, by the fire-dwarfed
Street we chant the flying sea
In the body bereft.
Love is the last light spoken. Oh 30
Seed of sons in the loin of the black husk left.

II

I know not whether
Adam or Eve, the adorned holy bullock
Or the white ewe lamb
Or the chosen virgin
Laid in her snow
On the altar of London,
Was the first to die
In the cinder of the little skull,
O bride and bride groom 40
O Adam and Eve together
Lying in the lull
Under the sad breast of the head stone
White as the skeleton
Of the garden of Eden.
I know the legend
Of Adam and Eve is never for a second
Silent in my service
Over the dead infants
Over the one 50
Child who was priest and servants,
Word, singers, and tongue
In the cinder of the little skull,
Who was the serpent's
Night fall and the fruit like a sun,
Man and woman undone,
Beginning crumbled back to darkness
Bare as the nurseries
Of the garden of wilderness.

III

Into the organpipes and steeples 60
Of the luminous cathedrals,
Into the weathercocks' molten mouths
Rippling in twelve-winded circles,
Into the dead clock burning the hour
Over the urn of sabbaths
Over the whirling ditch of daybreak
Over the sun's hovel and the slum of fire
And the golden pavements laid in requiems,

Into the bread in a wheatfield of flames,
Into the wine burning like brandy, 70
The masses of the sea
The masses of the sea under
The masses of the infant-bearing sea
Erupt, fountain, and enter to utter for ever
Glory glory glory
The sundering ultimate kingdom of genesis' thunder.

[*1944*]

Fern Hill

Now as I was young and easy under the apple boughs
About the lilting house and happy as the grass was green,
The night above the dingle starry,
Time let me hail and climb
Golden in the heydays of his eyes,
And honoured among wagons I was prince of the apple towns
And once below a time I lordly had the trees and leaves
Trail with daisies and barley
Down the rivers of the windfall light.

And as I was green and carefree, famous among the barns 10
About the happy yard and singing as the farm was home,
In the sun that is young once only,
Time let me play and be
Golden in the mercy of his means,
And green and golden I was huntsman and herdsman, the calves
Sang to my horn, the foxes on the hills barked clear and cold,
And the sabbath rang slowly
In the pebbles of the holy streams.

All the sun long it was running, it was lovely, the hay
Fields high as the house, the tunes from the chimneys, it was air 20
And playing, lovely and watery
And fire green as grass.
And nightly under the simple stars
As I rode to sleep the owls were bearing the farm away
All the moon long I heard, blessed among stables, the night jars
Flying with the ricks, and the horses
Flashing into the dark.

And then to awake, and the farm, like a wanderer white
With the dew, come back, the cock on his shoulder: it was all
Shining, it was Adam and maiden, 30
The sky gathered again
And the sun grew round that very day.
So it must have been after the birth of the simple light
In the first, spinning place, the spellbound horses walking warm
Out of the whinnying green stable
On to the fields of praise.

And honoured among foxes and pheasants by the gay house
Under the new made clouds and happy as the heart was long,
In the sun born over and over,
I ran my heedless ways, 40
My wishes raced through the house high hay
And nothing I cared, at my sky blue trades, that time allows
In all his tuneful turning so few and such morning songs
Before the children green and golden
Follow him out of grace,

Nothing I cared, in the lamb white days, that time would take me
Up to the swallow thronged loft by the shadow of my hand,
In the moon that is always rising,
Nor that riding to sleep
I should hear him fly with the high fields 50
And wake to the farm forever fled from the childless land.
Oh as I was young and easy in the mercy of his means,
Time held me green and dying
Though I sang in my chains like the sea.

[*1945*]

"When, like a running grave"

When, like a running grave, time tracks you down,
Your calm and cuddled is a scythe of hairs,
Love in her gear is slowly through the house,
Up naked stairs, a turtle in a hearse,
Hauled to the dome,

Comes, like a scissors stalking, tailor age,
Deliver me who, timid in my tribe,
Of love am barer than Cadaver's trap
Robbed of the foxy tongue, his footed tape
Of the bone inch, 10

Deliver me, my masters, head and heart,
Heart of Cadaver's candle waxes thin,
When blood, spade-handed, and the logic time
Drive children up like bruises to the thumb,
From maid and head,

For, sunday faced, with dusters in my glove,
Chaste and the chaser, man with the cockshut eye,
I, that time's jacket or the coat of ice
May fail to fasten with a virgin o
In the straight grave, 20

Stride through Cadaver's country in my force,
My pickbrain masters morsing on the stone
Despair of blood, faith in the maiden's slime,
Halt among eunuchs, and the nitric stain
On fork and face.

Time is a foolish fancy, time and fool.
No, no, you lover skull, descending hammer
Descends, my masters, on the entered honour.
You hero skull, Cadaver in the hangar
Tells the stick, 'fail.' 30

Joy is no knocking nation, sir and madam,
The cancer's fusion, or the summer feather
Lit on the cuddled tree, the cross of fever,
Nor city tar and subway bored to foster
Man through macadam.

I damp the waxlights in your tower dome.
Joy is the knock of dust, Cadaver's shoot
Of bud of Adam through his boxy shift,
Love's twilit nation and the skull of state,
Sir, is your doom. 40

Everything ends, the tower ending and,
(Have with the house of wind), the leaning scene,
Ball of the foot depending from the sun,
(Give, summer, over), the cemented skin,
The actions' end.

All, men my madmen, the unwholesome wind
With whistler's cough contages, time on track
Shapes in a cinder death; love for his trick,
Happy Cadaver's hunger as you take
The kissproof world. 50

[1934]

"I dreamed my genesis"

I dreamed my genesis in sweat of sleep, breaking
Through the rotating shell, strong
As motor muscle on the drill, driving
Through vision and the girdered nerve.

From limbs that had the measure of the worm, shuffled
Off from the creasing flesh, filed
Through all the irons in the grass, metal
Of suns in the man-melting night.

Heir to the scalding veins that hold love's drop, costly
A creature in my bones I 10
Rounded my globe of heritage, journey
In bottom gear through night-geared man.

I dreamed my genesis and died again, shrapnel
Rammed in the marching heart, hole
In the stitched wound and clotted wind, muzzled
Death on the mouth that ate the gas.

Sharp in my second death I marked the hills, harvest
Of hemlock and the blades, rust
My blood upon the tempered dead, forcing
My second struggling from the grass. 20

And power was contagious in my birth, second
Rise of the skeleton and
Rerobing of the naked ghost. Manhood
Spat up from the resuffered pain.

I dreamed my genesis in sweat of death, fallen
Twice in the feeding sea, grown
Stale of Adam's brine until, vision
Of new man strength, I seek the sun.

[*1934*]

"I make this in a warring absence"

I make this in a warring absence when
Each ancient, stone-necked minute of love's season
Harbours my anchored tongue, slips the quaystone,
When, praise is blessed, her pride in mast and fountain
Sailed and set dazzling by the handshaped ocean,
In that proud sailing tree with branches driven
Through the last vault and vegetable groyne,
And this weak house to marrow-columned heaven,

Is corner-cast, breath's rag, scrawled weed, a vain
And opium head, crow stalk, puffed, cut, and blown, 10
Or like the tide-looped breastknot reefed again
Or rent ancestrally the roped sea-hymen,
And, pride is last, is like a child alone
By magnet winds to her blind mother drawn,
Bread and milk mansion in a toothless town.

She makes for me a nettle's innocence
And a silk pigeon's guilt in her proud absence,
In the molested rocks the shell of virgins,
The frank, closed pearl, the sea-girls' lineaments
Glint in the staved and siren-printed caverns, 20
Is maiden in the shameful oak, omens
Whalebed and bulldance, the gold bush of lions,
Proud as a sucked stone and huge as sandgrains.

These are her contraries: the beast who follows
With priest's grave foot and hand of five assassins
Her molten flight up cinder-nesting columns,
Calls the starved fire herd, is cast in ice,
Lost in a limp-treed and uneating silence,
Who scales a hailing hill in her cold flintsteps
Falls on a ring of summers and locked noons. 30

I make a weapon of an ass's skeleton
And walk the warring sands by the dead town,
Cudgel great air, wreck east, and topple sundown,
Storm her sped heart, hang with beheaded veins
Its wringing shell, and let her eyelids fasten.
Destruction, picked by birds, brays through the jaw-bone,
And, for that murder's sake, dark with contagion
Like an approaching wave I sprawl to ruin.

Ruin, the room of errors, one rood dropped
Down the stacked sea and water-pillared shade, 40
Weighed in rock shroud, is my proud pyramid;
Where, wound in emerald linen and sharp wind,
The hero's head lies scraped of every legend,
Comes love's anatomist with sun-gloved hand
Who picks the live heart on a diamond.

'His mother's womb had a tongue that lapped up mud,'
Cried the topless, inchtaped lips from hank and hood
In that bright anchorground where I lay linened,
'A lizard darting with black venom's thread
Doubled, to fork him back, through the lockjaw bed 50
And the breath-white, curtained mouth of seed.'
'See,' drummed the taut masks, 'how the dead ascend:
In the groin's endless coil a man is tangled.'

These once-blind eyes have breathed a wind of visions,
The cauldron's root through this once-rindless hand
Fumed like a tree, and tossed a burning bird;
With loud, torn tooth and tail and cobweb drum
The crumpled packs fled past this ghost in bloom,
And, mild as pardon from a cloud of pride,
The terrible world my brother bares his skin. 60

l. 39. *rood:* cross.

Now in the cloud's big breast lie quiet countries,
Delivered seas my love from her proud place
Walks with no wound, nor lightning in her face,
A calm wind blows that raised the trees like hair
Once where the soft snow's blood was turned to ice.
And though my love pulls the pale, nippled air,
Prides of to-morrow suckling in her eyes,
Yet this I make in a forgiving presence.

[*1937*]

"There was a saviour"

There was a saviour
Rarer than radium,
Commoner than water, crueller than truth;
Children kept from the sun
Assembled at his tongue
To hear the golden note turn in a groove,
Prisoners of wishes locked their eyes
In the jails and studies of his keyless smiles.

The voice of children says
From a lost wilderness 10
There was calm to be done in his safe unrest,
When hindering man hurt
Man, animal, or bird
We hid our fears in that murdering breath,
Silence, silence to do, when earth grew loud,
In lairs and asylums of the tremendous shout.

There was glory to hear
In the churches of his tears,
Under his downy arm you sighed as he struck,
O you who could not cry 20
On to the ground when a man died
Put a tear for joy in the unearthly flood
And laid your cheek against a cloud-formed shell:
Now in the dark there is only yourself and myself.

Two proud, blacked brothers cry,
Winter-locked side by side,
To this inhospitable hollow year,
O we who could not stir
One lean sigh when we heard
Greed on man beating near and fire neighbour 30
But wailed and nested in the sky-blue wall
Now break a giant tear for the little known fall,

For the drooping of homes
That did not nurse our bones,
Brave deaths of only ones but never found,
Now see, alone in us,
Our own true strangers' dust
Ride through the doors of our unentered house.
Exiled in us we arouse the soft,
Unclenched, armless, silk and rough love that breaks all rocks. 40

[*1940*]

Robert Lowell

Robert Trail Spence Lowell, Jr., born in Boston on March 1, 1917, is the descendant of two distinguished New England families. His grandfather, a well-known Episcopal minister and the headmaster of St. Mark's School, was a younger brother of the poet James Russell Lowell. His mother's family was descended from Edward Winslow, one of the Pilgrim fathers. Robert Lowell, Sr. was a graduate of the U. S. Naval Academy, but at the insistence of his wife he resigned his commission to enter the business world. In a poem entitled "Commander Lowell," the poet portrays his father as never having adjusted to civilian life. A prose autobiographical sketch, "91 Revere Street," published in the 1959 volume *Life Studies,* describes the poet's childhood in a house at the foot of Beacon Street. On that street the descendants of the Boston Brahmins lived next door to the ascendant Irish and Italian families. "We are barely perched," Mrs. Lowell is quoted as saying, "on the outer rim of the hub of decency." In this delightful, amusing sketch, Lowell focuses attention upon his parents and their friends, but he does provide some glimpses of himself as an observant child, sometimes recalcitrant and rebellious, living among the heirlooms of his ancestry.

He attended St. Mark's and then, following the family tradition, entered Harvard. After one year, he left Cambridge to complete his studies at Kenyon College. This display of independence preceded a more violent break with family tradition when, in 1940, Lowell converted to Roman Catholicism. Sometime after the Japanese bombing of Pearl Harbor, the poet attempted to enlist in the Navy but was rejected. When he was drafted into service in 1943, he declared himself a conscientious objector. At his trial, he stated that he considered the bombing of civilians in European cities by the Allies morally indefensible. Lowell was sentenced to Federal prison for a year and a day. After five months he was released, and a short time later, in 1944, his first volume of poems, *Land of Unlikeness,* was published. It was well received by the critics, and in 1946 a second collection, *Lord Weary's Castle,* established him as the leading poet of his generation. He received the 1947 Pulitzer Prize for that volume, was awarded a Guggenheim grant, and was appointed a consultant in poetry at the Library of Congress. A British edition of his poems in 1950 was enthusiastically reviewed by the English critics. After the publication of *The Mills of the Kavanaughs* in 1951, Lowell produced no new volume for eight years. His 1959 *Life Studies,* which received the National Book Award in 1960, contained several poems recording a nervous breakdown and a stay in a mental hospital.

For a number of years Lowell served as an associate professor at Boston University. More recently, he has made his home in New York City, where he lives with his second wife, Elizabeth Hardwicke, the critic and novelist, and their daughter. In the spring of 1965, national attention became focused upon the poet when he displayed once again the moral independence that characterized his career. He refused an invitation from President Johnson to attend a Festival of the Arts at the White House, explaining in an eloquent letter that attendance would imply support of the administration's war policies in Vietnam.

Robert Lowell is still in mid-career, and though he is now a mature and skilled poet, his technique and style may undergo further development and his attitudes and beliefs may alter. In 1960, he reportedly told his audience at the National Book Award ceremony, "When I finished *Life Studies,* I was left hanging on a question mark. I am still hanging there. I don't know whether it is a death-rope or a lifeline." His 1965 volume *For the Union Dead* clearly indicates that it was a lifeline. But these two later collections mark a change from the poetry of *Lord Weary's Castle*. The tone is much quieter, more objective, more intimate. The violent social denunciations of the earlier poems have been muted by a new attitude of acceptance. The religious imagery which dominates the early poetry is missing. Several poems in the 1965 collection even reveal a shift in religious attitude. And the verse forms and metrical patterns tend to be less traditional. Because these two volumes probably indicate a transitional period in the poet's development, we have concentrated our attention upon the work of the earlier period.

The poet of *Lord Weary's Castle* is a tortured, angry, young man, his sensibilities rubbed raw by the horrors of life, by the failure of the past to provide meaningful spiritual values, by the brutality and the pain men inflict upon one another. Death hovers as a palpitant horrifying force. Many of the poems are set in graveyards or are elegies. Images of erosion and decay, of impermanence, abound. A heritage of blood guilt blackens the present. It is almost as if Lowell had concluded early in life that he was not among the elect, chosen according to Calvin's doctrine, for salvation. Tortured by the knowledge, he set out to defy this authoritative exclusion. Such a supposition serves to focus upon the ambivalent attitudes that produce much of the vital tension in the poetry. Lowell is fascinated enough by his Puritan heritage to dwell upon it constantly, and at the same time he denounces it for its hypocrisy and its failure to transmit to the present more than a passion for material splendor. His satiric thrusts at Jonathan Edwards' fire and brimstone preaching, for example, are offset by his own jeremiads, in which he sees the modern world consumed by the fire of its sins. His religious break with the Protestantism of his ancestors, too, is not complete and final; it does not provide him sufficient spiritual security to make him indifferent to the wrongs of his ancestors; he must proclaim his own salvation and reveal the blindness of those who have not found Jesus.

These ambivalences and tensions are captured in vivid, powerful images: "Children, the raging memory drools / Over the glory of past pools." This image in "The Drunken Fisherman" denounces the New England Quaker fishermen who slaughtered whales for gold. Lowell's vision in these poems is cosmic. Each poem is usually anchored in a specified place: Black Rock, Connecticut, where the poet lived for a time after his release from prison; Dunbarton cemetery, where his maternal ancestors are buried; the Public Gardens in Boston Commons. But with Biblical allusions and images, Lowell transforms the Charles River into the Acheron; Boston becomes Babylon doomed to destruction; World War II is made to reflect the eternal war between Cain and Abel, as well as the barbarousness of modern man and the chaos of his world. This poetry of protest, of intense dissatisfaction with the spiritual aridity of modern life is, at the same time, intensely religious poetry that takes the form of jeremiads, revelations, fantasies, and passionate outbursts against materialism, tyranny, injustice, and cruelty. Faith seems to provide a desperate refuge rather than a consistent spiritual peace; it does not evoke expressions of brotherly love nor does it provide insight into the beauties of life.

The excellence of Lowell's poetic expression is due, to a great extent, to the vigor of his imagination, but he also has a penetrating intellect that is capable of fusing disparate images and of sustaining a series of interlocked ironies and interlocked images throughout a poem until they resonate with a multiplicity of feelings and meanings. His poetry, with its allusions (mainly Biblical but in the later poetry increasingly mythical), with its mixture of esoteric and colloquial diction, its metaphysical wit, requires careful, sensitive reading. Lowell was, unquestionably, in his earlier period at least, an admirer of T. S. Eliot, and his picture of the modern world is not unlike Eliot's "Waste Land." The older poet's influence is also apparent in many of Lowell's poetic techniques: the use of epigraphs, the incorporation of references and quotations from other writers into his verse. Lowell, too, finds dramatic poetry congenial, and in *The Mills of the Kavanaughs,* a long dramatic monologue depicting the demise of an old New England family, he introduces an ancient myth to parallel the present. He has also, interestingly enough, followed Eliot into the poetic drama. His verse play *The Old Glory* was given an off-Broadway production in 1964, and part of it was later redone for television. In his verse technique, however, Lowell remained traditional, using regular metrical patterns and established rhyme schemes, almost as if he required such restraint. Surprisingly, the formal patterns restrain without diminishing the intensity of the imagery and they contribute to the dynamic quality of the poetry. It is difficult to predict the direction of Lowell's future work, but he has already demonstrated his poetic talent by adding a number of great poems to our English and American poetic heritage.

BIBLIOGRAPHY

Staples, Hugh B. *Robert Lowell: The First Twenty Years.* New York: Farrar, Straus, 1962.

Children of Light

Our Fathers wrung their bread from stocks and stones
And fenced their gardens with the Redman's bones;
Embarking from the Nether Land of Holland,
Pilgrims unhouseled by Geneva's night,
They planted here the Serpent's seeds of light;
And here the pivoting searchlights probe to shock
The riotous glass houses built on rock,
And candles gutter by an empty altar,
And light is where the landless blood of Cain
Is burning, burning the unburied grain. 10

[*1944–46*]

Commentary

"Children of Light" is an expression of disillusionment with the present, which is the creation of the past. Like the transmitted stain of man's original sin, the sins of the parents are visited upon the children. The poem is developed on a series of interlocked images that focus upon the central image of light. In the manner of the seventeenth-century metaphysical poets, Lowell ironically inverts the connotations of his image to fuse idea and feeling. Typically, too, his words develop multiple resonances within the structure of his sentences.

The title has religious connotations: light is associated with God and Jesus and salvation of the soul. But the children of light are not God's children; they are modern Americans, heirs of their Puritan forebears. And the light in the modern world is not that of spiritual illumination but the product of the "Serpent's seeds of light": the pivoting searchlights searching the dark skies for enemy bombers, and the destructive flames of war.

How is World War II related to the Pilgrim heritage? Lowell establishes the relationship in the first half of his ten line poem. The opening line emphasizes the Pilgrim's struggle to provide for his material needs. This struggle developed into the pursuit of material comfort and wealth in the modern world. The modern American inherits the blood guilt of the Puritans whose original sin was their slaughter of the Indians. The cruelty of the Pilgrims and their distortion of spiritual values to provide for material comforts were made possible because the Pilgrim fathers were disciples of the Genevan, Calvin, who forsook the true religion.

Lowell, in a pun, views the Pilgrims as emigrants from the dark underworld, the "Nether Land." They are the devil's servants: "Pilgrims unhouseled by Geneva's night." This line contains the central clue to Lowell's light image. "Housel" refers to the Eucharist, the miraculous conversion of the body and blood of Christ into the bread and wine which the Roman Catholic receives at the sacrament of Communion. Calvin's doctrines do not accept this sacrament which permits man to share the light of God through Christ. The deluded Pilgrims who saw themselves as servants of the Lord were actually servants of the devil and planted in the New World, which they viewed as a latter day Garden of Eden, the devil's seeds that have bloomed into the destructive chaos of the modern world.

In the second half of the poem, Lowell presents the modern world—at war, godless, and bloated with material wealth. As the poem progresses, the initial images begin to resonate as they are inverted. The light of the Eucharist, as we have noted, becomes the light of the devil, which is the beam of the searchlights and the fire of war. Each line is now rich with multiple meanings. In the sixth line, the probing searchlights merge into the bombings with the phrase "to shock." The following line "The riotous glass houses built on rock" evokes multiple associations. The glass houses could be the cathedrals built according to the instructions of Jesus upon "this rock." The adjective "riotous" suggests the presence of the moneychangers in the temple of the Lord. The glass houses also evoke the modern skyscrapers on the rock of Manhattan, and they suggest the modern houses, impermanent and vulnerable, built upon the Pilgrims' Plymouth Rock. The image of the candles flickering out in empty churches emphasizes the absence of the true Eucharistic light. The devil's seeds of light become the fire burning the rich produce of the seeds that the Pilgrims planted—"excess" grain in a world of want.

Though this summary presents the general meaning of the poem, it has not yet plumbed the rich texture of Lowell's poem. Besides the interlocked images of light, there are a number of others. The bread, for instance, wrung out of the chopped logs and stones by the colonists, develops into the seeds planted in the gardens and then reaches its climax with the image of the unburied grain in the final line. But that grain planted in the original gardens fenced with the bones of murdered Indians is also, Lowell's reference to Cain indicates, the unburied bodies of the war dead. The Pilgrims had committed the sin of Cain in the New World, and the blood guilt is transmitted and the crime repeated. Cain, exiled from the sight of the Lord, is landless. That crucial adjective Lowell has prepared for by emphasizing land in the third line of the poem: "Embarking from the Nether Land of Holland."

The repetition of "burning" in the final line suggests, of course, the eternal fires of hell, but it also echoes the passage in "The Fire Sermon" of T. S. Eliot's "The Waste Land." Eliot's note to the line in which he repeats "burning" four times refers his reader to the Buddha's Fire Sermon, which Eliot says "corresponds in importance to the Sermon on the Mount." In that sermon the Buddha tells the priests that all things are on fire, and when the priests ask with what are they on fire, Buddha answers: "With the fire of passion, with the fire of hatred, with the fire of infatuation, with birth, old age, death, sorrow, lamentation, misery, grief, despair, are they on fire." All these things attach man to the physical world and cause him to ignore the spiritual.

In this short poem with its iambic tetrameter meter and its halves, each containing a pair of couplets separated by a line, Lowell's ability to make his words, images, and lines resonant with meaning and feeling is readily apparent. One of the less complex of Lowell's poems, its richness indicates the profound poetic experience his more complex poems afford.

In the Cage

The lifers file into the hall,
According to their houses—twos
Of laundered denim. On the wall
A colored fairy tinkles blues
And titters by the balustrade;
Canaries beat their bars and scream.
We come from tunnels where the spade
Pick-axe and hod for plaster steam
In mud and insulation. Here
The Bible-twisting Israelite 10
Fasts for his Harlem. It is night,
And it is vanity, and age
Blackens the heart of Adam. Fear,
The yellow chirper, beaks its cage.

[*1946*]

l. 10. *Israelite:* member of a Negro religious cult.

The Blind Leading the Blind

Nothing will hustle: at his own sweet time
My father and his before him humanized
The seedy fields and heaped them on my house
Of straw; no flaring, hurtling thing surprised
Us out of season, and the corn-fed mouse
Reined in his bestial passions. Hildesheim
Survived the passing angel; who'd require
Our passion for the Easter? Satan snored
By the brass railing, while his back-log roared
And coiled its vapors on St. Gertrude's blue stone spire: 10

A land of mattocks; here the brothers strode,
Hulking as horses in their worsted hose

The Blind Leading the Blind: after the famous painting of the same title by Breughel.

l. 6. *Hildesheim:* a city in Germany.

And cloaks and shin-guards—each had hooked his hoe
Upon his fellow's shoulder; by each nose
The aimless waterlines of eyeballs show
Their greenness. They are blind—blind to the road
And to its Maker. Here my father saw
The leadman trip against a pigpen, crash,
Legs spread, his codpiece split, his fiddle smash . . .
These mammoth vintners danced their blood out in the straw. 20

[*1946*]

Where the Rainbow Ends

I saw the sky descending, black and white,
Not blue, on Boston where the winters wore
The skulls to jack-o'-lanterns on the slates,
And Hunger's skin-and-bone retrievers tore
The chickadee and shrike. The thorn tree waits
Its victim and tonight
The worms will eat the deadwood to the foot
Of Ararat: the scythers, Time and Death,
Helmed locusts, move upon the tree of breath;
The wild ingrafted olive and the root 10

Are withered, and a winter drifts to where
The Pepperpot, ironic rainbow, spans
Charles River and its scales of scorched-earth miles
I saw my city in the Scales, the pans
Of judgment rising and descending. Piles
Of dead leaves char the air—
And I am a red arrow on this graph
Of Revelations. Every dove is sold
The Chapel's sharp-shinned eagle shifts its hold
On serpent-Time, the rainbow's epitaph. 20

In Boston serpents whistle at the cold.
The victim climbs the altar steps and sings:

l. 8. *Ararat:* the landing place of Noah's ark.
l. 12. *Pepperpot:* the towers on the Charles Street Bridge look like pepperpots.
l. 18. *Revelations:* a clue to the source of much of the poem's imagery, the book of *Revelations*.

"Hosannah to the lion, lamb, and beast
Who fans the furnace-face of IS with wings:
I breathe the ether of my marriage feast."
At the high altar, gold
And a fair cloth. I kneel and the wings beat
My cheek. What can the dove of Jesus give
You now but wisdom, exile? Stand and live,
The dove has brought an olive branch to eat. 30

[*1946*]

In Memory of Arthur Winslow

I

Death from Cancer

This Easter, Arthur Winslow, less than dead,
Your people set you up in Phillips' House
To settle off your wrestling with the crab—
The claws drop flesh upon your yachting blouse
Until longshoreman Charon come and stab
Through your adjusted bed
And crush the crab. On Boston Basin, shells
Hit water by the Union Boat Club wharf:
You ponder why the coxes' squeaking dwarf
The *resurrexit dominus* of all the bells. 10

Grandfather Winslow, look, the swanboats coast
That island in the Public Gardens, where
The bread-stuffed ducks are brooding, where with tub
And strainer the mid-Sunday Irish scare
The sun-struck shallows for the dusky chub
This Easter, and the ghost
Of risen Jesus walks the waves to run
Arthur upon a trumpeting black swan
Beyond Charles River to the Acheron
Where the wide waters and their voyager are one. 20

Arthur Winslow: the poet's maternal grandfather.
l. 2. *Phillips' House:* a private pavillion in a Boston hospital.
l. 10. *resurrexit dominus:* God is risen.

II

Dunbarton

The stones are yellow and the grass is gray
Past Concord by the rotten lake and hill
Where crutch and trumpet meet the limousine
And half-forgotten Starks and Winslows fill
The granite plot and the dwarf pines are green
From watching for the day
When the great year of the little yeomen come
Bringing its landed Promise and the faith
That made the Pilgrim Makers take a lathe
And point their wooden steeples lest the Word be dumb. 10

O fearful witnesses, your day is done:
The minister from Boston waves your shades,
Like children, out of sight and out of mind.
The first selectman of Dunbarton spreads
Wreaths of New Hampshire pine cones on the lined
Casket where the cold sun
Is melting. But, at last, the end is reached;
We start our cars. The preacher's mouthings still
Deafen my poor relations on the hill:
Their sunken landmarks echo what our fathers preached. 20

III

Five Years Later

This Easter, Arthur Winslow, five years gone
I came to mourn you, not to praise the craft
That netted you a million dollars, late
Hosing out gold in Colorado's waste,
Then lost it all in Boston real estate.
Now from the train, at dawn
Leaving Columbus in Ohio, shell
On shell of our stark culture strikes the sun
To fill my head with all our fathers won
When Cotton Mather wrestled with the fiends from hell. 10

l. 4. *Hosing out gold:* Arthur Winslow was a mining engineer.
l. 10. *Cotton Mather:* a Puritan minister and writer.

You must have hankered for our family's craft:
The block-house Edward made, the Governor,
At Marshfield, and the slight coin-silver spoons
The sheriff beat to shame the gaunt Revere,
And General Stark's coarse bas-relief in bronze
Set on your granite shaft
In rough Dunbarton; for what else could bring
You, Arthur, to the veined and alien West
But devil's notions that your gold at least
Could give back life to men who whipped or backed the King? 20

IV

A Prayer for My Grandfather to Our Lady

Mother, for these three hundred years or more
Neither our clippers nor our slavers reached
The haven of your peace in this Bay State:
Neither my father nor his father. Beached
On these dry flats of fishy real estate
O Mother, I implore
Your scorched, blue thunderbreasts of love to pour
Buckets of blessings on my burning head
Until I rise like Lazarus from the dead:
Lavabis nos et super nivem dealbabor. 10

"On Copley Square, I saw you hold the door
To Trinity, the costly Church, and saw
The painted Paradise of harps and lutes
Sink like Atlantis in the Devil's jaw
And knock the Devil's teeth out by the roots;
But when I strike for shore
I find no painted idols to adore:
Hell is burned out, heaven's harp-strings are slack.
Mother, run to the chalice, and bring back
Blood on your finger-tips for Lazarus who was poor." 20

[*1944–46*]

l. 12. *Governor:* Edward Winslow (1595–1655).
l. 15. *General Stark:* another Lowell ancestor.
l. 10. *Lavabis . . . dealbabor:* the original in the psalm "Wash me, and I shall be whiter than the snow;" Lowell alters to the plural "us."
l. 11. *Copley Square:* Boston Square.

Mr. Edwards and the Spider

I saw the spiders marching through the air,
Swimming from tree to tree that mildewed day
In latter August when the hay
Came creaking to the barn. But where
The wind is westerly,
Where gnarled November makes the spiders fly
Into the apparitions of the sky,
They purpose nothing but their ease and die
Urgently beating east to sunrise and the sea;

What are we in the hands of the great God? 10
It was in vain you set up thorn and briar
In battle array against the fire
And treason crackling in your blood;
For the wild thorns grow tame
And will do nothing to oppose the flame;
Your lacerations tell the losing game
You play against a sickness past your cure.
How will the hands be strong? How will the heart endure?

A very little thing, a little worm,
Or hourglass-blazoned spider, it is said, 20
Can kill a tiger. Will the dead
Hold up his mirror and affirm
To the four winds the smell
And flash of his authority? It's well
If God who holds you to the pit of hell,
Much as one holds a spider, will destroy,
Baffle and dissipate your soul. As a small boy

On Windsor Marsh, I saw the spider die
When thrown into the bowels of fierce fire:
There's no long struggle, no desire 30
To get up on its feet and fly—
It stretches out its feet
And dies. This is the sinner's last retreat;
Yes, and no strength exerted on the heat
Then sinews the abolished will, when sick
And full of burning, it will whistle on a brick.

But who can plumb the sinking of that soul?
Josiah Hawley, picture yourself cast
Into a brick-kiln where the blast
Fans your quick vitals to a coal— 40
If measured by a glass,
How long would it seem burning! Let there pass
A minute, ten, ten trillion; but the blaze
Is infinite, eternal: this is death,
To die and know it. This is the Black Widow, death.

[*1946*]

The Drunken Fisherman

Wallowing in this bloody sty,
I cast for fish that pleased my eye
(Truly Jehovah's bow suspends
No pots of gold to weight its ends);
Only the blood-mouthed rainbow trout
Rose to my bait. They flopped about
My canvas creel until the moth
Corrupted its unstable cloth.

A calendar to tell the day;
A handkerchief to wave away 10
The gnats; a couch unstuffed with storm
Pouching a bottle in one arm;
A whiskey bottle full of worms;
And bedroom slacks: are these fit terms
To mete the worm whose molten rage
Boils in the belly of old age?

Once fishing was a rabbit's foot—
O wind blow cold, O wind blow hot,
Let suns stay in or suns step out:
Life danced a jig on the sperm-whale's spout— 20
The fisher's fluent and obscene
Catches kept his conscience clean.
Children, the raging memory drools
Over the glory of past pools.

Now the hot river, ebbing, hauls
Its bloody waters into holes;

A grain of sand inside my shoe
Mimics the moon that might undo
Man and Creation too; remorse,
Stinking, has puddled up its source; 30
Here tantrums thrash to a whale's rage.
This is the pot-hole of old age.

Is there no way to cast my hook
Out of this dynamited brook?
The Fisher's sons must cast about
When shallow waters peter out.
I will catch Christ with a greased worm,
And when the Prince of Darkness stalks
My bloodstream to its Stygian term . . .
On water the Man-Fisher walks. 40

[*1944–46*]

Colloquy in Black Rock

Here the jack-hammer jabs into the ocean;
My heart, you race and stagger and demand
More blood-gangs for your nigger-brass percussions,
Till I, the stunned machine of your devotion,
Clanging upon this cymbal of a hand,
Am rattled screw and footloose. All discussions

End in the mud-flat detritus of death.
My heart, beat faster, faster. In Black Mud
Hungarian workmen give their blood
For the martyre Stephen, who was stoned to death. 10

Black Mud, a name to conjure with: O mud
For watermelons gutted to the crust,
Mud for the mole-tide harbor, mud for mouse,
Mud for the armored Diesel fishing tubs that thud
A year and a day to wind and tide; the dust
Is on this skipping heart that shakes my house,

House of our Savior who was hanged till death.
My heart, beat faster, faster. In Black Mud

Colloquy in Black Rock: the colloquy appears to be between the poet and his heart.

Stephen the martyre was broken down to blood:
Our ransom is the rubble of his death. 20

Christ walks on the black water. In Black Mud
Darts the kingfisher. On Corpus Christi, heart,
Over the drum-beat of St. Stephen's choir
I hear him, *Stupor Mundi*, and the mud
Flies from his hunching wings and beak—my heart,
The blue kingfisher dives on you in fire.

[*1944–46*]

l. 22. *Corpus Christi:* the feast celebrating the Holy Eucharist.
l. 23. *St. Stephen:* the first Christian martyr.
l. 24. *Stupor Mundi:* the astonishment of the world.

The Quaker Graveyard in Nantucket

(FOR WARREN WINSLOW, DEAD AT SEA)

Let man have dominion over the fishes of the sea and the fowls of the air and the beasts and the whole earth, and every creeping creature that moveth upon the earth.

[*Genesis*]

I

A brackish reach of shoal off Madaket,—
The sea was still breaking violently and night
Had steamed into our North Atlantic Fleet,
When the drowned sailor clutched the drag-net. Light
Flashed from his matted head and marble feet,
He grappled at the net
With the coiled, hurdling muscles of his thighs:
The corpse was bloodless, a botch of reds and whites,
Its open, staring eyes
Were lustreless dead-lights 10
Or cabin-windows on a stranded hulk
Heavy with sand. We weight the body, close
Its eyes and heave it seaward whence it came,
Where the heel-headed dogfish barks its nose
On Ahab's void and forehead; and the name

Is blocked in yellow chalk.
Sailors, who pitch this portent at the sea
Where dreadnaughts shall confess
Its hell-bent deity,
When you are powerless 20
To sand-bag this Atlantic bulwark, faced
By the earth-shaker, green, unwearied, chaste
In his steel scales: ask for no Orphean lute
To pluck life back. The guns of the steeled fleet
Recoil and then repeat
The hoarse salute.

II

Whenever winds are moving and their breath
Heaves at the roped-in bulwarks of this pier,
The terns and sea-gulls tremble at your death
In these home waters. Sailor, can you hear
The Pequod's sea wings, beating landward, fall
Headlong and break on our Atlantic wall
Off 'Sconset, where the yawing S-boats splash
The bellbuoy, with ballooning spinnakers,
As the entangled, screeching mainsheet clears
The blocks: off Madaket, where lubbers lash 10
The heavy surf and throw their long lead squids
For blue fish? Sea-gulls blink their heavy lids
Seaward. The winds' wings beat upon the stones,
Cousin, and scream for you and the claws rush
At the sea's throat and wring it in the slush
Of this old Quaker graveyard where the bones
Cry out in the long night for the hurt beast
Bobbing by Ahab's whaleboats in the East.

III

All you recovered from Poseidon died
With you, my cousin, and the harrowed brine
Is fruitless on the blue beard of the god,

ll. 23–24. *Orphean lute to pluck life back:* Orpheus brought his wife back from the Underworld, but at the final moment violated the condition upon which he could bring her back to life; he looked around at her and lost her.

l. 5. *Pequod:* Captain Ahab's boat in Melville's *Moby Dick.*

l. 1. *Poseidon:* god of the sea.

Stretching beyond us to the castles in Spain,
Nantucket's westward haven. To Cape Cod
Guns, cradled on the tide,
Blast the eelgrass about a waterclock
Of bilge and backwash, roil the salt and sand
Lashing earth's scaffold, rock
Our warships in the hand 10
Of the great God, where time's contrition blues
Whatever it was these Quaker sailors lost
In the mad scramble of their lives. They died
When time was open-eyed,
Wooden and childish; only bones abide
There, in the nowhere, where their boats were tossed
Sky-high, where mariners had fabled news
Of IS, the whited monster. What it cost
Them is their secret. In the sperm-whale's slick
I see the Quakers drown and hear their cry: 20
"If God himself had not been on our side,
If God himself had not been on our side,
When the Atlantic rose against us, why,
Then it had swallowed us up quick."

IV

This is the end of the whaleroad and the whale
Who spewed Nantucket bones on the thrashed swell
And stirred the troubled waters to whirlpools
To send the Pequod packing off to hell:
This is the end of them, three-quarters fools,
Snatching at straws to sail
Seaward and seaward on the turntail whale,
Spouting out blood and water as it rolls,
Sick as a dog to these Atlantic shoals:
Clamavimus, O depths. Let the sea-gulls wail 10

For water, for the deep where the high tide
Mutters to its hurt self, mutters and ebbs.
Waves wallow in their wash, go out and out,
Leave only the death-rattle of the crabs,
The beach increasing, its enormous snout

l. 10. *Clamavimus*: from Psalm 130, "Out of the depths have I cried unto thee, O Lord."

Sucking the ocean's side.
This is the end of running on the waves;
We are poured out like water. Who will dance
The mast-lashed master of Leviathans
Up from this field of Quakers in their unstoned graves? 20

V

When the whale's viscera go and the roll
Of its corruption overruns this world
Beyond tree-swept Nantucket and Wood's Hole
And Martha's Vineyard, Sailor, will you sword
Whistle and fall and sink into the fat?
In the great ash-pit of Jehoshaphat
The bones cry for the blood of the white whale,
The fat flukes arch and whack about its ears,
The death-lance churns into the sanctuary, tears
The gun-blue swingle, heaving like a flail, 10
And hacks the coiling life out: it works and drags
And rips the sperm-whale's midriff into rags,
Gobbets of blubber spill to wind and weather,
Sailor, and gulls go round the stoven timbers
Where the morning stars sing out together
And thunder shakes the white surf and dismembers
The red flag hammered in the mast-head. Hide,
Our steel, Jonas Messias, in Thy side.

VI

Our Lady of Walsingham

There once the penitents took off their shoes
And then walked barefoot the remaining mile;
And the small trees, a stream and hedgerows file
Slowly along the munching English lane,
Like cows to the old shrine, until you lose
Track of your dragging pain.
The stream flows down under the druid tree,
Shiloah's whirlpools gurgle and make glad

Our Lady of Walsingham: based upon a description of the shrine by E. L. Watkin in *Catholic Art and Culture.*

The castle of God. Sailor, you were glad
And whistled Sion by that stream. But see: 10

Our Lady, too small for her canopy,
Sits near the altar. There's no comeliness
At all or charm in that expressionless
Face with its heavy eyelids. As before,
This face, for centuries a memory,
Non est species, neque decor,
Expressionless, expresses God: it goes
Past castled Sion. She knows what God knows,
Not Calvary's Cross nor crib at Bethlehem
Now, and the world shall come to Walsingham. 20

VII

The empty winds are creaking and the oak
Splatters and splatters on the cenotaph,
The boughs are trembling and a gaff
Bobs on the untimely stroke
Of the greased wash exploding on a shoal-bell
In the old mouth of the Atlantic. It's well;
Atlantic, you are fouled with the blue sailors,
Sea-monsters, upward angel, downward fish:
Unmarried and corroding, spare of flesh
Mart once of supercilious, wing'd clippers, 10
Atlantic, where your bell-trap guts its spoil
You could cut the brackish winds with a knife
Here in Nantucket, and cast up the time
When the Lord God formed man from the sea's slime
And breathed into his face the breath of life,
And blue-lung'd combers lumbered to the kill.
The Lord survives the rainbow of His will.

[*1945–46*]

l. 16. *Non . . . decor:* there is no attractiveness, nor is there loveliness.

A Handbook of Poetry

A Handbook of Poetry

SELECTED FROM

Encyclopedia of Poetry and Poetics

ALEX PREMINGER, *Editor*

The contents of this *Handbook* should prove useful in two ways to students using this anthology. As a glossary, it may be used in dictionary fashion to provide definitions and background material on items suggested by the editors' introductions and by the poetry itself. The editors have therefore selected from the *Encyclopedia* all those articles which, in their opinion, would be helpful to students using this college text, often editing the articles to eliminate subject matter beyond the scope of an undergraduate anthology. Second, as an introduction to the study of poetry in college, the *Handbook* may be used as a primer and read as a textbook.

For students approaching the *Handbook* as a primer, the editors would suggest first familiarity with general terms applicable to all poetry: the articles on form, imagery, symbol, tone color, meter, metrical variation, ambiguity, irony, paradox, and the like. To study the mechanics of prosody, the student should address himself to a second, and more technical category of articles: those on the foot, on scansion, on the types of poetic feet (iamb, trochee, dactyl, anapaest), caesura, defective foot, line, line endings, meter, rhyme, rhyme scheme, and stanza. Those interested in specific verse forms and stanzaic arrangements will find articles on the ballad, blank verse, couplet, free verse, "In Memoriam" stanza, ode, quatrain, sonnet, terza rima, Spenserian stanza, and others. In addition, there are numerous articles on more special technical devices in poetry: assonance, broken rhyme, enjambement, and so forth.

To enable students more easily to relate the *Handbook* to the anthology, the editors have inserted references to appropriate articles in the *Handbook* at relevant places in their introductions. In addition, following many of the entries in the *Handbook* the editors have inserted, in brackets, illustrative examples from the poetry selections in the anthology so that readers may see how the principles enunciated in the *Encyclopedia* are exemplified in specific poems.

ACCENT. The vocal emphasis with which a syllable is spoken relative to the emphasis received by contiguous syllables.

ALEXANDRINE. In French prosody, a line of 12 syllables. The a. has been, since the sixteenth century, the standard meter of French poetry, in which it has had an importance comparable to that of the quantitative hexameter in Latin poetry or blank verse in English poetry; it has been used especially in dramatic and narrative forms.

ALLEGORY (Gr. *allos*, "other," and *agoreuein*, "to speak"). A term denoting a technique of literature which in turn gives rise to a method of criticism. As a technique of literature, a. is a technique of fiction-writing, for there must be some kind of narrative basis for allegory. We have a. when the events of a narrative obviously and continuously refer to another simultaneous structure of events or ideas, whether historical events, moral or philosophical ideas, or natural phenomena. The myth and the fable are forms closely related to, or frequently used for, a., and the works usually called allegories are genres of fiction: epic (Dante's *Divina Commedia*), romance (Spenser's *Faerie Queene*), prose fiction (Bunyan's *Pilgrim's Progress*), or drama (*Everyman*). It is continuity that distinguishes a. from ambiguity or simple allusion. Fiction-writing has two aspects: (1) a progression of incidents which are imitations of actions, and (2) elements of meaning or thought which represent a poetic use of ideas. Hence there are two main types of a.: historical or political a., referring to characters or events beyond those purportedly described in the fiction; and moral, philosophical, religious, or scientific allegories, referring to an additional set of ideas. If the allegorical reference is continuous throughout the narrative, the fiction "is" an a. If it is intermittent, if a. is picked up and dropped again at pleasure, as in many works of Ariosto, Goethe, Ibsen, and Hawthorne, we say only that the fiction shows allegorical tendencies. A. is thus not the name of a form or a genre, but of a structural principle in fiction.

A. may be simple or complex. In simple a. the fiction is wholly subordinate to the abstract "moral," hence it often impresses the literary critic as naive. An example is the fable, which is directed primarily at the set of ideas expressed in its moral. Simple historical allegories (simple at least as regards their literary structure) occur in some of the later prophecies of the Bible, such as the a. of the four kingdoms in Daniel. More complex historical and political allegories tend to develop a strongly ironic tone, resulting from the fact that the allegorist is pretending to talk about one series of incidents when he is actually talking about another.

ALLITERATION. Any repetition of the same sound(s) or syllable in two or more words of a line (or line group), which produces a noticeable artistic effect. . . . A. may occur involuntarily or by choice. It can produce emphasis and euphony (or cacophony!) comparable to the striking effects of end rhyme. The most common type of a. is that of initial sounds (hence the term "initial rhyme" or "head rhyme"), especially of consonants or consonant groups; a. of initial vowels is less frequent since they do not have the same acoustic impact as consonants. [See Shakespeare, Sonnet 73, line 8: "Death's *s*econd *s*elf, that *s*eals up all in rest"; Lowell, "The Drunken Fisherman," line 22: "Catches *k*ept his *c*onscience *c*lean."]

AMBIGUITY. Term introduced by William Empson, who devoted a book, *Seven Types of Ambiguity* (1930), to an examination of its critical applicability and usefulness. . . . Most readers of poetry, Empson felt, reduced the meaning of a given word to a single denotation. For example, he found that Shakespeare editors differed strongly about the meaning of a word like *rooky* (*Macbeth*). Learned reasons were given why a single meaning, and no other meaning, was *the* correct one. Empson inferred that if collectively the editors saw multiple meanings in *rooky,* then Elizabethan audiences must also have seen multiple meanings, and that Shakespeare himself must have seen them "since he was no less sensitive to words than they." In explaining his method, Empson confesses an indebtedness to the analysis of a Shakespeare sonnet by Robert Graves in *A Survey of Modernist Poetry* (1938). (The method was also employed by Graves in *Poetic Unreason* [1925].) And both Graves and Empson had been anticipated by Frederick C. Prescott in *The Poetic Mind* (1922). Prescott used Freudian terminology, "displacement," "condensation," etc., but his analyses bring out the same sort of thing that Empson does. For example, Prescott analyzes two lines from a speech of Hotspur's against Henry IV: "We must have bloody noses and crack'd crowns/ And pass them current too. God's me, my horse."— "Here the 'crack'd crowns' are first cracked coins, secondly broken heads, and thirdly royal crowns upset. Note too that the third meaning is at once farthest from the literal, the most latent, perhaps the most unconscious (in Hotspur's mind), and the most far-reaching (involving the whole dramatic action)."

Many readers have felt that Empson's insistence on *seven* types of a. is unnecessary and mistaken. William York Tindall, who finds Empson's readings "exemplary," finds the division into seven types "pretentious." There seems little doubt, however, that Empson has helped to teach at least one generation of poetry readers to find more complicated meanings in poetry than they had hitherto been prepared to find. Again, in Mr. Ransom's words, "The ordinary critic cannot read them (Empson's analyses) and be the same critic again. . . ." Mr. Empson summarizes this method in these words: "We call it ambiguous . . . when we recognize that there could be a puzzle as to what the author meant, in that alternate views might be taken without sheer misreading. . . . An ambiguity, in ordinary speech, means something very pronounced, and as a rule witty or deceitful. I propose to use the word in an extended sense, and shall think relevant to my subject any verbal nuance, however slight, which gives room for alternative reactions to the same piece of language."

ANAPAEST, anapest (Gr. "beaten back," i.e., either a "reversed" dactyl or a verse begun with a "beat" of the foot). A metrical unit, in quantitative verse, of 2 short syllables followed by 1 long one:

x x ′
[to dispute]

[See Browning, "Prospice," lines 27–28: "O thou soul of my soul! I shall clasp thee again,/ And with God be the rest!"]

ASSONANCE. Sometimes called "vocalic rhyme," denotes vowel identity in the tonic syllables, sometimes supported by the same device in the succeeding unstressed syllables, of words whose consonants differ or, if partly the same, avoid creating rhyme (grave / fate; votive / notice; glory / holy) and which (1) echo each other in the same line or in different portions of a poem, or which (2) appear at the end of successive or alternating lines. [See Frost, "Stopping by Woods," line 3: "He will not see me stopping here"; Eliot, "The Love Song of J. Alfred Prufrock," line 10: "To lead you to an overwhelming question."]

BALLAD. The "folk," "popular," or "traditional" b. is a short narrative song preserved and transmitted orally among illiterate or semiliterate people. Story-songs of this kind have been collected in all European countries, and though each national balladry has its distinctive characteristics, certain constants hold for all bona fide specimens: (1) Ballads focus on a single crucial episode or situation. The ballad begins usually at a point where the action is decisively directed toward its catastrophe. Events leading up to this crucial and conclusive episode are told in a hurried, summary fashion. Little attention is given to describing settings; indeed, circumstantial detail of every sort is conspicuously absent. (2) Ballads are dramatic. We are not told about things happening: we are shown them happening. Every artistic resource of the genre is pointed toward giving an intensity and immediacy to the action and toward heightening the emotional impact of the climax. Protagonists are allowed to speak for themselves, which means, of course, that dialogue bulks large in ballads. At strategic moments, dialogue erupts into the narrative. Such speeches are sparingly tagged; we must frequently deduce the speaker from what is being said. (3) Ballads are impersonal. The narrator seldom allows his own subjective attitude toward the events to intrude. Comments on motives are broad, general, detached. There may be an "I" in a ballad, but the singer does not forget that he is the deputy of the public voice and is not speaking from private judgment. Bias there is in ballads, of course, but it is the bias of a party, community, or nation, not an individual's particularistic point of view.

Stylistically the ballad is a species apart. This is because the b., like folk song in general but unlike all the literary genres, is an oral phenomenon, and, as a consequence, preserves traces of the archaic modes of preliterature. The story is the key thing in a b., all other artistic possibilities are subordinated to it. The language is plain and formulaic. A small stock of epithets and adjectives serves for all the ballads in a given language. There are few arresting figures of speech and no self-conscious straining after novel turns of phrase. And because the emphasis is on a single line of action precipitously developed, there is not time in a b. for careful delineation of character or for extensive research into psychological motivation. The heavy amount of repetition and parallelism one finds in the ballads may appear to be merely decorative rhetoric, but it is not so. Repetition in heightened passages was brilliantly explained by Coleridge as the singers' effort to discharge emotion that could not be exhausted in one saying. Much repetition is mnemonic: in a story being recited or sung, crucial facts must be firmly planted in the memory since the hearer cannot turn back a page to refresh himself about a fact that slipped by in a moment of inattention.

BALLAD METER, or common meter. . . . In the characteristic ballad stanza the first and third lines are iambic tetrameter, the second and fourth lines iambic trimeter. Only the second and fourth lines rhyme. A typical quatrain:

The ladies cracked their fingers white,
The maidens tore their hair,
All for the sake of their true loves,
For them they ne'er saw mair.

[Note variations in ballad construction in Keats: "La Belle Dame sans Merci"; Wordsworth, "Strange Fits of Passion Have I Known."]

BEAT. Regularly recurring metrical emphasis in accentual poetic lines. The term is often used instead of "stress" by prosodists who are pressing the analogies between verse and music and who are thinking of the metrical foot as an almost exact parallel with the musical bar. The expression "a 5-beat line" emphasizes the "ideal" or "normal" accentual pattern and suggests that the number of syllables may vary as long as the five structural beats are present. See METER [See Hopkins, "The Habit of Perfection," line 1: "Elécted Sílence, síng to mé" and note regularity of this 4-beat line.]

BLANK VERSE. Unrhymed iambic pentameter lines. Neither originally nor exclusively English, b.v. is nevertheless the distinctive poetic form of our language; it is the medium of nearly all verse drama and of much narrative and reflective verse. B.v. was introduced with the first substantial body of poetry written in Standard Modern English: Surrey's b.v. translations from the *Aeneid,* written ca. 1540, were printed by Tottel in 1557. In Tottel's *Miscellany,* also 1557, the work of Wyatt, Surrey, and others (including two short b.v. poems by Grimald) introduced the iambic line and decisively marked the course that poetry in the modern English tongue would take.

Some verse forms, like the triolet, the ballad measure, the limerick, seem to carry in themselves a suggestion of meaning or tone regardless of the language set to them; others, like the sonnet or the heroic couplet, have acquired a strong traditional manner from their exemplary employment during one literary period or by one great master. B.v. has no inherent tone. Except for free verse, it is the form closest to the form of our speech. Its stresses alternate as our English speech stresses tend to do, and its measure of 5 strong stresses marked by the juncture of the line end, a measure readily apprehended without counting, both simulates and accommodates the way we make phrases and clauses as we speak. This is perhaps the reason no one poet, not even Shakespeare or Milton, has stamped b.v. forever with the mark of his own style as Pope did the heroic couplet. The freedom of the form is also a challenge; lacking the extrinsic mark of rhyme, poets must prove themselves in b.v. by their powers of conception and by their deployment of the sound-patterns of the language in interaction with the ideal pattern of the metrical form. The shifts of dominance in this interaction constitute the metrical history of b.v. [See Wordsworth, "The Old Cumberland Beggar"; Milton, "Paradise Lost"; Browning, "How It Strikes a Contemporary," and note the distinctive tone which each poet imparts to the verse form.]

BROKEN RHYME. Refers to the division of a word (not the rhyme) at the end of a line in order to produce a rhyme: for*get*ful/*debt* (Pope); *tu*-tor/*U*-niversity (George Canning). Poets from Shakespeare to Ogden Nash have used b.r. for comic or satiric effects; yet Hopkins has taken it as a resource for serious poetry, e.g., in *The Windhover* and *To what serves Mortal Beauty?* [See Hopkins, "The Windhover," first quatrain, for rhyming of "king- / dom" with "wimpling wing."]

CAESURA, cesura. A rhetorical and extrametrical pause or phrasal break within the poetic line. If the pause occurs near the beginning of the line, it is called initial c.; if near the middle of the line, medial; if near the end, terminal. [See Whitman, "Song of Myself," stanza 5, line 3: "Loafe with me on the grass, loose the stop from your throat"; Tennyson, "The Lotos-Eaters," stanza 2, line 1: "A land of streams! some, like a downward smoke."]

CLICHÉ. A phrase or figure which from overuse, like a dulled knife, has lost its cutting edge; a trite expression. Clichés in verse result when the poet's inspiration arises from other poems rather than from a fresh response to experience. Examples of poetic clichés are: fettered soul, eagle-eyed, break of day, rolling wave, purling brook, whispering breeze, ruby lips, pearly teeth, white as snow. Good poets sometimes use clichés intentionally for ironical purposes.

CONCEIT. An intricate or far-fetched metaphor, which functions through arousing feelings of surprise, shock, or amusement; in earlier usage, the imagination or fancy in general. . . . The poet compares elements which seem to have little or nothing in common, or juxtaposes images which establish a marked discord in mood. . . .

The metaphysical c. is usually intended in critical discussions of the c. Within this type of c. one may perceive two general forms: (1) the extended, in which the initial analogy is subjected to a detailed and ingenious development, as in Donne's famous figure from *A Valediction: Forbidding Mourning:*

If they be two, they are two so
As stiffe twin compasses are two;
Thy soule, the fixt foot, makes no show
To move, but doth, if th' other doe . . .

[p. 42]

(2) the condensed, in which the ingenious analogy or discordant contrast is expressed with a telling brevity, as at the opening of T. S. Eliot's *The Love-Song of J. Alfred Prufrock:*

When the evening is spread out against the sky
Like a patient etherised upon a table

[p. 432]

The lines of Eliot will serve to typify two important aspects of the c.: its subtle use of controlled connotation to enrich the meaning of the poem, with the associated dependence on the imaginative sensitivity of the reader, and its consistent evocation of paradox (q.v.).

The faculty of wit, the capacity for finding likenesses between the apparently unlike, is central to the c., and the presence of this faculty largely determines the success of a given c. For the emotion evoked by a good c. is not simply surprise, or, in Dr. Johnson's terms, wonder at the perversity which created the c., but rather a surprised recognition of the ultimate validity of the relationship presented in the c., which thus serves not as an ornament but as an instrument of vision.

COUPLET. Two lines of verse, usually rhymed. Ever since the advent of rhymed verse, the c. has counted as one of the principal units of versification in the Western literatures, whether as a stanzaic form in extended composition, as a subordinate element in other stanzaic forms, or as an independent poem of an epigrammatic nature. The c. composed of two lines of iambic pentameter—the so-called heroic couplet . . . —is the most important c. form in English poetry. As perfected by Dryden and Pope, the heroic c. is "closed"—syntax and thought are fitted neatly into the envelope of rhyme and meter—and in this form it dominates the poetry of the neoclassical period: "Know then thyself, presume not God to scan; / The proper study of Mankind is Man" (Pope, *Essay on Man*). Although the heroic c. is generally associated with its eighteenth-century masters, one should recognize that it is a form of great antiquity, used by Chaucer in *The Legend of Good Women* and most of *The Canterbury Tales,* by Marlowe, Chapman, and other Elizabethans, and by Donne, whose free use of enjambement [q.v.] achieves effects utterly different from those of Pope and Dryden. [See Pope's poetry in text for supreme examples in English literature.]

DACTYL (Gr. "finger"). . . . In accentual verse, an accented syllable followed by two unaccented ones:

ˊ x x
ˊx x ; tenderly

DEFECTIVE FOOT. In a conventional metrical line, a foot which lacks one or more unstressed syllables. In this example,

This is the forest primeval,

the last foot is defective: the normal pattern calls for a final dactyl, but the clause ends with a trochee instead. The term "defective" is unfortunate, for a foot lacking one or more syllables can be considered "faulty" only by those who are gratified by absolute metrical monotony. [See Wordsworth, "Ode: Intimations of Immortality," stanza 2, lines 10–15: "Waters on a starry night" lacks technically an introductory unstressed syllable to fit the meter of the other lines.]

DIDACTIC POETRY. Poetry which is primarily intended to instruct. Most commonly, the label is used for poetry which teaches a moral. It can also refer to poetry which conveys factual information, like astronomy, mathematics, or rhetoric; or systematic philosophy. Aesthetically it seems to be the first stage in the evolution of literary forms: the earliest literature we possess, Eastern, Hebrew, Greek, is in verse and uses meter as a mnemonic device to make the hearer remember and thereby learn what is being said. The seed of all literature is the proverb, the gnomic line, the memorizable rhyme ("Thirty days hath September"), and from such seeds d. poetry evolved in antiquity as it was to do again in northern Europe in the early centuries of the Christian era. [See Pope's "Essay on Man" for prime example of the type.]

DISSONANCE. The quality of being harsh or inharmonious in rhythm or sound; akin to cacophony. . . . Insofar as the terms may be distinguished, cacophony is what is harsh-sounding in itself, d. is that which is discordant or inharmonious with what surrounds it. By extension the term may refer to poetic elements other than sound that are discordant with their immediate context. Donne and Browning have made notable use of d. [see Wordsworth, "Lines" (Tintern Abbey), lines 90–92:

> *. . . but hearing oftentimes*
> *The still, sad music of humanity,*
> *Nor harsh nor grating, though of ample power*

See also Lowell, "Quaker Graveyard," part II, lines 4–12.]

ELEGY (from Gr. *elegeia,* "lament"). A lyric, usually formal in tone and diction, suggested either by the death of an actual person or by the poet's contemplation of the tragic aspects of life. In either case, the emotion, originally expressed as a lament, finds consolation in the contemplation of some permanent principle. [See Milton's "Lycidas" for example of the form.]

END-STOPPED. A term applied to poetic lines in which both meaning and meter undergo a pause at the end of the line. End-stopped lines, like closed couplets [q.v.], are characteristic of the heroic couplets of English eighteenth-century poetry: "Hope springs eternal in the human breast; / Man never is, but always to be, blest" (Pope) and of the alexandrine verse of the French neoclassicists. The term "end-stopped" is opposed to *run-on,* or *enjambé (see* ENJAMBEMENT), terms which are used to describe the free and uninterrupted carryover of the grammatical structure from one line to the other, as in most English blank verse and most romantic poetry. The relative occurrence of end-stopped lines has been used as a means of determining the chronology of Shakespeare's plays and of other works.

ENJAMBEMENT, or enjambment. The completion, in the following poetic line, of a clause or other grammatical unit begun in the preceding line; the employment of "run-on" lines which carry the sense of a statement from one line to another without rhetorical pause at the end of the line:

> . . . *Yet I know her for*
> *A spleeny Lutheran* . . .
> (Shakespeare. HENRY VIII, 3.2)

The term is also applied to the carrying over of meaning from one couplet or stanza to the next.

E., a device widely used by the Elizabethans and by Milton, fell into disrepute in eighteenth-century poetry but was revived by the romantic poets, who saw in it a symbol of liberation from neoclassical rules. Keats's *Endymion* supplies some extreme examples of e. [See Lowell, "Colloquy in Black Rock," lines 2–3:

> *My heart, you race and stagger and demand*
> *More blood-gangs for your nigger-brass percussions*

See also Tennyson, "Ulysses," lines 6–7:

> *I cannot rest from travel; I will drink*
> *Life to the lees* . . .]

EPISTLE, verse. A poem addressed to a particular patron or friend, written in a familiar style. Two types of verse epistles exist: the one on moral and philosophical subjects which stems from Horace's *Epistles* and the other on romantic and sentimental subjects which stems from Ovid's *Heroides*.

EUPHONY. The quality of having a pleasant and smooth-flowing sound, free from harshness; the opposite of cacophony. E. arises largely from ease of articulation. The vowel sounds, which demand no cessation of breath, are considered more euphonious than the consonants, with the longer vowels being preferred to the shorter. Of the consonant sounds the most euphonious are the liquids and semi-vowels: *l, m, n, r, y, w*. Poe, considering long *o* the most sonorous vowel and *r* the most reproducible consonant, chose "Nevermore" as refrain word for *The Raven,* a word combining three vowels, four liquids, and a soft *v*. Opinions differ as to the order in which the other consonants follow, but in general those most easily produced are felt to be most pleasing. E. results not only from choice of sounds but from their arrangement. Sounds may be arranged so that they flow easily into each other, or may be placed in difficult combinations, demanding more muscular effort. Meter also will play a role, sometimes clogging a line with heavy accents, sometimes spacing them out more agreeably.

FOOT. A measurable, patterned unit of poetic rhythm. The concept of the f. has been imported into modern accentual-syllabic prosody (see

METER) from classical quantitative practice, and disagreement over the nature (and even the "existence") of the f. has been traditional since the late Renaissance. The English f. is customarily defined by the orthodox as a measure of rhythm consisting of 1 accented (stressed, "long") syllable (or 2, as in the spondee) and 1 or more unaccented (unstressed, "short," "slack") syllables. The poetic line in a more or less regular composition, say the traditional prosodists, consists of a number of feet from 1 to 8; conventionally, the feet are to be roughly of the same kind, although metrical variations (q.v.), produced by the occasional "substitution" of different feet, are permissible so long as these substitutions do not efface for long the repeated pattern of the prevailing f.

In traditional English accentual or accentual-syllabic verse . . . , the following feet are the most common:

IAMB (iambus); iambic, x ' as in *destroy* (x ')

ANAPAEST (anapest); anapaestic x x ' *intervene* (x x ')

TROCHEE; trochaic ' x *topsy* (' x)

DACTYL; dactylic ' x x *merrily* (' x x)

SPONDEE; spondaic ' ' *amen* (' ')

PYRRHIC x x *the sea* | *son of* | *mists* (x ' x x)

Iambic and anapaestic feet are called ascending or rising feet; trochaic and dactylic, descending or falling. . . . Some prosodists recognize also a monosyllabic f. consisting of 1 stressed syllable. The exemplification of these feet by single words, above, of course distorts their nature: it is important to remember that f. divisions do not necessarily correspond to word divisions, and that the structure of a f. is determined contextually by the nature of the feet which surround it.

FORM. In poetry, simply defined, is the manner in which a poem is composed as distinct from what the poem is about. The latter may be called the subject or the substance of the poem, its subject matter or content as distinct from its form or manner. "Form" being a term with a variety of denotations, some of them closely connected with particular systems of philosophy, poetic f. also admits of several meanings, some so divergent from each other that they are contradictory.

To take first one of the commonest meanings, the f. of a poem may be its meter, poetry being usually composed in verse. Modern alternatives to regular verse such as free verse and patterned prose would also constitute the formal element of the poem in this meaning of the term. Alternatively, the words used in the poem, its language and diction, may be considered the f., as distinct from the thought or subject matter of the poem. By extension, f. may be the style in which the composition is written. Most of these meanings are implied when one speaks of the "cult of form" or formalism in poetry, which is making art consist essentially in the skillful handling of words and phrases, verse and rhyme, style and diction. Formalists believe that the value of a poem depends exclusively on the quality of its f., in that sense. . . .

The organic concept of f. and content has as its logical corollary that there is no such thing in art as the same f. with different content: alteration in one produces alteration in the other. Hence the rejection of the common concept of genre or kind as an empty form into which a separate matter is poured, as in a mold or vessel (cf. Schlegel). The ultimate consequence of this argument is the rejection, by Croce and others, of genres and kinds from the domain of criticism, f. being conceived as individual and as unique as matter, or as "the efficient equivalent" of a poem's unity.

FREE VERSE. A term popularly, but not accurately, used to describe the poems of Walt Whitman and others whose verse is based not on the recurrence of stress accent in a regular, strictly measurable pattern, but rather on the irregular rhythmic cadence of the recurrence, with variations, of significant phrases, image patterns, and the like. F.v. treats the device of rhyme with a similar freedom and irregularity. The following quotation, from Whitman's *Song of Myself*, is fairly typical:

I celebrate myself, and sing myself
And what I assume you shall assume,
For every atom belonging to me as good be-
longs to you.

I loafe and invite my soul,
I lean and loafe at my ease observing a spear
of summer grass.

[p.344]

There are two opinions about the form and Whitman's use of it. Some say that his practice is no more than rhythmical prose. Others that it has distinctively "poetic" qualities. Both of these opinions are consistent with the following addition to the definition given above in paragraph one: whenever and however, either by the agency of the eye or ear, a persistent irregularity of the metrical pattern is established in a poem, it can justly be called f.v. The irregularity involves both the eye and the ear. Whether the measure be written down with a view to the appearance of the poem on the printed page or to the sound of the words as spoken or sung is of no consequence so long as the established irregularity is maintained. . . .

The crux of the question is measure. In f.v. the measure has been loosened to give more play to vocabulary and syntax—hence, to the mind in its excursions. The bracket of the customary foot has been expanded so that more syllables, words, or phrases can be admitted into its confines. The new unit thus created may be called the "variable foot," a term and a concept already accepted widely as a means of bringing the warring elements of freedom and discipline together. It rejects the standard of the conventionally fixed foot and suggests that measure varies with the idiom by which it is employed and the tonality of the individual poem. Thus, as in speech, the prosodic pattern is evaluated by criteria of effectiveness and expressiveness rather than mechanical syllable counts. The verse of genuine poetry can never be "free," but f.v., interpreted in terms of the variable foot, removes many artificial obstacles between the poet and the fulfillment of the laws of his design.

IAMB (Gr. *iambos,* a word of unknown etymology but certainly very ancient). A metrical unit, in quantitative verse, of a short syllable followed by a long:

⌣ –
⌢ – ; *amans*

x ʹ
[re peat]

[See Shakespeare, all sonnets; Keats, "The Eve of St. Agnes."]

IMAGERY. An image is the reproduction in the mind of a sensation produced by a physical perception. Thus, if a man's eye perceives a certain color, he will register an image of that color in his mind—"image," because the subjective sensation he experiences will be an ostensible copy or replica of the objective color itself. The mind may also produce images when not reflecting direct physical perceptions, as in the attempt to remember something once perceived but no longer present, or in the undirected drifting of the mind over experience, or in the combinations wrought out of perception by the imagination, or in the hallucinations of dreams and fever, and so on.

More specifically in literary usage, *imagery* refers to images produced in the mind by language, whose words and statements may refer either to experiences which could produce physical perceptions were the reader actually to have those experiences, or to the sense-impressions themselves. When Archibald MacLeish says, in *Ars Poetica,* that a poem should be "Dumb / As old medallions to the thumb," he not only *means* that the language of poetry should make important use of i., he also *exemplifies* what he means by expressing it in terms of i.: a poem, he implies, should make its impact upon the imagination rather than upon the intellect, much as a person feels an old coin with his fingers (a physical perception). When, however, he says "A poem should not mean / But be," his meaning is the same but his language is not, for this statement is abstract rather than concrete and imagery-bearing, dealing as it does with an idea or concept rather than a perception or sensation. This combination of meaning and imagery may indicate the confusion which can result when "i." is applied to literary study, for it is used variously to refer to the meaning of a statement involving images, to the images themselves, or to the combination of meaning and images.

IN MEMORIAM STANZA. So called from its use in Tennyson's *In Memoriam*. A stanza of 4 lines of iambic tetrameter, rhyming abba:

I hold it true, whate'er befall;
I feel it when I sorrow most;
'Tis better to have loved and lost
Than never to have loved at all.
(IN MEMORIAM, 27)

INSCAPE AND INSTRESS. Inscape in the aesthetic of Gerard Manley Hopkins, who coined the term, refers to the principle of physical distinctiveness in a natural or artistic object. Rooted in the Scotist concept of *haecceitas* or "thisness," inscape is whatever uniquely differentiates a thing from whatever was, is, or shall be. Hopkins himself somewhat inadequately defined the term in a letter to Robert Bridges as "design" or "pattern." (*The Letters of G. M. H. to Robert Bridges,* ed. C. C. Abbott, 1935, p. 66.) In his critical study of Hopkins, W. A. M. Peters gives a more elaborate definition of inscape as "the outward reflection of the inner nature of a thing, or a sensible copy or representation of its individual essence." (*G. M. H.: A Critical Study Toward the Understanding of His Poetry,* 1948, p. 2.) W. H. Gardner states simply that inscape is "the name for that 'individually-distinctive' form (made up of various sense-data) which constitutes the rich and revealing 'one-ness' of the natural object." (*Poems and Prose of G.M.H.,* 1953, p. xx.)

Inscape and instress are closely related terms—inscape, the principle of individuation, and instress, the force which sustains and emanates from inscape. In the words of Gardner, instress is essentially the "sensation of inscape," the impulse "which acts on the senses and, through them, actualizes the inscape in the mind of the beholder" (*op. cit.,* p. xxi). Peters notes that instress is the force that "holds the inscape together" as well as "the power that ever actualizes the inscape" (pp. 14–15). For Hopkins, instress is the energy by which "all things are upheld."

IRONY. . . . Modern discussions have tended to emphasize two main categories of i.: simulation (verbal i) and dramatic i.

Verbal i. is a form of speech in which one meaning is stated and a different, usually antithetical, meaning is intended. In understatement the expressed meaning is mild, and the intended meaning intense; as, for example, Mercutio's comment on his death-wound, "No, 'tis not so deep as a well, nor so wide as a church door; but 'tis enough, 'twill serve." In overstatement, a device especially common in American folk humor, the reverse is true. Often a statement becomes ironic because of its context. When one looks out of his window at a rain storm and remarks to a friend, "Wonderful day, isn't it?" the statement can only be understood in an ironic sense. When Hamlet rejects the idea of suicide with the remark, "Thus conscience does make cowards of us all," his remark is unconsciously ironic because *conscience* is a sacramental word associated with moral goodness, whereas *coward* has pejorative connotations. The same kind of i. is illustrated in Comus' speech of seduction, where a true principle (natural fertility) is used to prove an untrue doctrine (libertinism). Often, i. can arise from explicit or implicit contradiction, as when Marvell begins his proposition to his coy mistress with the remark that time is short, and ends with the observation that love can make time pass more quickly ("Thus, though we cannot make our sun / Stand still, yet we will make him run.") Finally, foreshadowing is often ironic. Hamlet's speech on the fall of the sparrow has one meaning in its immediate context and a somewhat different one when considered in connection with Hamlet's own "fall" at the end of the scene.

Naïveté is a special form of i. half way between verbal and dramatic i. Basically, it is a pose of innocence or simplicity. Socrates used it; it appears frequently in the literature stemming from St. Paul's remark that the wisdom of God is the folly of this world, and the wisdom of this world is the folly of God. The tradition of ironic naïveté can be traced in *The Praise of Folly,* Shakespeare's fools and clowns, *Gulliver's Travels,* Blake's *Songs of Innocence,* Dickens' *Barnaby Rudge,* Dostoevski's *Idiot,* and Faulkner's *Sound and the Fury.* An extremely rudimentary example of this form of i. is the stanza,

The golf links lie so near the mill
That almost every day
The laboring children can look out
And see the men at play.
(Sarah N. Cleghorn)

Dramatic i. is a plot device according to which (a) the spectators know more than the protagonist; (b) the character reacts in a way contrary to that which is appropriate or wise; (c) characters or situations are compared or contrasted for ironic effects, such as parody; (d) there is a marked contrast between what the character understands about his acts and what the play demonstrates about them.

Tragedy is especially rich in all forms of dramatic i. The necessity for a sudden reversal or catastrophe in the fortunes of the hero (Aristotle's *peripety,* which, he said, is found in all true tragedy) means that the fourth form of i. (form d) is almost inevitable. *Oedipus Rex* piles i. on i. For example, form (a) is present because of the fact that the audience becomes increasingly conscious as the play progresses that Oedipus is rushing blindly to his doom. Form (b) is present because of Oedipus' insistence on pursuing his investigation to its bitter climax (and the fact that his basic motivation is a desire for justice and public welfare is a further i.—his fall is in part caused by his nobility). Form (c) is illustrated in the parallel between blind Tiresias (who can "see" morally) and the figure of Oedipus when he, too, has gained "vision" after blinding himself. Form (d) is, of course, present in the contrast between what Oedipus hopes to accomplish and what he finally does accomplish.

LINE. A formal structural division of a poem, consisting of one or more feet arranged as a separate rhythmical entity. The line . . . is a "unit of attention," but it is not necessarily a unit of sense: in fact, poems are rather rare in which individual lines constitute complete sense units. For this reason, line divisions, unless they happen to coincide with sense pauses (whether indicated by punctuation or not), are often as unrelated to the rhetoric of poetic assertions as foot divisions. Lines are commonly classified according to their length in feet:

monometer	a line of 1 foot
dimeter	2 feet
trimeter	3 feet
tetrameter	4 feet
pentameter	5 feet
hexameter	6 feet (see also ALEXANDRINE)
heptameter	7 feet
octameter	8 feet

Because the memory can retain a rhythmical pattern of only a limited duration, heptameters and longer lines tend to receive from reader or hearer an unconscious restructuring: the heptameter commonly breaks into a tetrameter and a trimeter (as in ballad meter, q.v.), the octameter into two tetrameters, and so on. Line divisions frequently function like foot divisions in providing a form of counterpoint to the rhetorical and syntactical design in a poem. Although generalization on this point is traditionally hazardous, it may be suggested that short lines (trimeter and shorter) tend to imply levity of tone, and that the pentameter line (or a line of similar duration, measured by whatever system of scansion) has proved the most flexible in English.

LINE ENDINGS. Divided prosodically into two general types depending upon the position of the final stress in relation to the other syllables near the end of the iambic or anapaestic line. A *masculine ending* (generally productive of an effect of some force or weight) has the stress on the final syllable of the line:

x
Upon the moon I fixed my eye
(Wordsworth, STRANGE FITS OF PASSION [p. 163])

A *feminine ending* has the last stress on the penultimate (or even the antepenultimate) syllable and most often requires terminal extrametrical syllables:

/ x / x / x x
Whatever ails me, now a-late especially,
/ x x
I can as well be hanged as refrain seeing her
(Middleton, THE CHANGELING 2.1)

Feminine ending is very common in the blank verse of the Elizabethan and Jacobean drama, where it is frequently used to give the verse a suggestion of colloquial informality, lightness, or irregularity. The term *weak ending* is sometimes used to describe masculine ending with a secondary (instead of primary) degree of stress. [For feminine endings, see Keats's "Endymion," lines 1–2:

A thing of beauty is a joy for ever:
Its loveliness increases; it will never
Pass into nothingness . . .]

LOGAOEDIC (Gr. "prose-poetic"). Term invented by metricians of Roman imperial times as a general description of mixed anapaestic and iambic or dactylic and trochaic cola (ascending and descending rhythm respectively) in Greek lyric verse. [See Hopkins' poetry for a revival in modern times of the Logaoedic idea.]

LYRIC. The term used to designate one of the three general categories of poetic literature, the others being narrative and dramatic. Although the differentiating features between these arbitrary classifications are sometimes moot, l. poetry may be said to retain most pronouncedly the elements of poetry which evidence its origins in musical expression—singing, chanting, and recitation to musical accompaniment. Though the drama and epic as well as the l. may have had their genesis in a spontaneously melodic expression which soon adapted itself to a ritualistic need and thus became formalized, music in dramatic and epic poetry was secondary to other elements of the works, being mainly a mimetic or mnemonic device. In the case of l. poetry, however, the musical element is intrinsic to the work intellectually as well as aesthetically: it becomes the focal point for the poet's perceptions as they are given a verbalized form to convey emotional and rational values. . . .

Though the attributes of brevity, metrical coherence, subjectivity, passion, sensuality, and particularity of image are frequently ascribed to the l. genre, there are schools of poetry obviously l. which are not susceptible to such criteria. Milton's mood poems, *L'Allegro* and *Il Penseroso,* as well as the most famous of the English elegies are "brief" in only the most relative sense. Much of the vers libre of the present age contradicts the rule of metrical coherence. Imagist lyrics are hardly "empassioned" in the ordinary sense of the word. The "lucubrations" of the metaphysicals are something less than sensual in the romantic meaning of the term. The problem of subjectivity must always plague the critic of the Elizabethan love l. And, finally, the common artistic admission that the universal can be expressed best, and perhaps solely, through the particular image largely invalidates any distinction between the l. and non-l. on a metaphoric or thematic basis.

METAPHOR. A condensed verbal relation in which an idea, image, or symbol may, by the presence of one or more other ideas, images, or symbols, be enhanced in vividness, complexity, or breadth of implication.

The nature and definition of metaphorical terms and of the relations between them have both been matter for much speculation and disagreement. It is unlikely therefore that a more specific definition will at first be acceptable. The metaphorical relation has been variously described as comparison, contrast, analogy, similarity, juxtaposition, identity, tension, collision, fusion; and different views have been held regarding the nature, operation, and function of metaphor in poetry. In recent years the view has gathered weight that m. is the radical process in which the internal relationships peculiar to poetry are achieved; some critics maintaining that m. marks off the poetic mode of vision and utterance from the logical or discursive mode; others, usually on anthropological evidence, that all language is m. . . . W. B. Stanford's definition [is given here:] "Metaphor is the process and result of using a term (X) normally signifying an object or concept (A) in such a context that it must refer to another object or concept (B) which is distinct enough in characteristics from A to ensure that in the composite idea formed by the synthesis of the concepts A and B and now symbolized in the word X, the factors A and B retain their conceptual independence even while they merge in the unity symbolized by X."

METER. More or less regular poetic rhythm; the measurable rhythmical patterns manifested in verse; or the "ideal" patterns which poetic rhythms approximate. If "m." is regarded as the ideal rhythmical pattern, then "rhythm" becomes "m." the closer it approaches regularity and predictability. The impulse toward metrical organization seems to be a part of the larger human impulses toward order: m. is what results when the rhythmical movements of colloquial speech are heightened, organized, and regulated so that pattern emerges from the relative phonetic haphazard of ordinary utterance. M. is thus one of the fundamental and most subtle techniques of order available to the poet, like rhyme, line division, stanza form, and over-all structure.

Most theorists agree that poetic m., even when most primitive, produces a pleasant effect, but there is widespread disagreement among critics and scholars over the reason for the universal popularity of metered compositions. According to some theorists (mostly rationalists), m. is pleasant because it focuses attention and refines awareness; according to others (mostly romanticists), on the contrary, it is pleasant because it produces a lulling, drugging, or hypnotic effect. One theory holds that, since the beat in most accentual poetries is slightly faster than the normal heart-beat, the apprehension of poetic m. produces a physically exhilarating effect on hearer or reader: his heart-beat, the theory contends, actually speeds up to "match" the slightly faster poetic rhythm. The pleasure universally resulting from foot-tapping and musical time-beating seems to suggest that the pleasures of m. are definitely physical and that they are as intimately connected with the rhythmic quality of man's total experience as are the similar alternating and recurring phenomena of breathing, walking, and love-making. Perhaps one could untangle some of the disagreements about the pleasures of m. by suggesting that the quality of the apprehender will determine the nature of the pleasure in each case: children and the unsophisticated receive from m. primarily physical pleasure which manifests itself in foot- or finger-tapping, head-nodding, and the like; on the other hand, the more experienced and sensitive reader will probably derive most of his metrical pleasure from the higher level of rhetorical attention which m. enforces ("Meter keeps the mind on the stretch," one critic has observed), or from an intellectual delight in witnessing order and containment brought out of chaos and flux. Medieval theories of m., in fact, frequently assume that the pleasure man takes in m. is an image of the pleasure he takes in the observation of the principle of order in a universe which is itself will and order incarnate. . . .

In poetry, which is the most organic and "total" mode of verbal expression, m. (like the other formal elements) serves as one of the primary correlatives of meaning: since m. is an indispensable contributor to meaning, it follows that the m. of a poem, in and by itself, means something, and even that the m. maintains a portion, at least, of its meaning whether symbolic sounds are attached to it or not. A good illustration of this basic alliance of m. with meaning (perhaps through association only) is the function of m. in the limerick, where the short anapaestic lines are themselves expressive of light impudence. The fact that a "translation" of a limerick into another m. (say, iambic tetrameter) seriously impairs the comic tone which is a part of the total expression indicates the large burden of meaning which m. alone carries. In the same way, most sensitive English poets have discovered that triple meters (anapaestic, dactylic) tend to have something vaguely comic, light, or superficial about them (some, like Longfellow in *Evangeline,* apparently have made the discovery too late), and they tend to eschew such meters in favor of duple rhythms for the treatment of more or less serious subjects. Taking a somewhat more complex illustration than a limerick, we can see the relationship of m. to meaning in Shakespeare's 129th sonnet:

> *Th'expense of spirit in a waste of shame*
> *Is lust in action; and till action, lust*
> *Is perjured, murd'rous, bloody, full of blame,*
> *Savage, extreme, rude, cruel, not to trust;*

Here the metrical disorder and violence of the 4th line is intimately allied with the violence and extremity of the statement, and indeed both creates and is created by that violence. One has only to imagine the same statement expressed in a regular anapaestic m. to perceive how m. and meaning are indissolubly married here. In a good poem, thus, limerick or sonnet, rhythmical pattern (together with expressive variations from it) is a constituent and a source of significance; it is never a mere embellishment, appliquéd from the outside onto what would otherwise be "prose" utterance; it issues from the pressure of feeling and reasoning at every point in the poem (see METRICAL VARIATIONS).

In addition to serving as a major technique for the reinforcement of meaning, m. performs more general functions in a poem. It often establishes a sort of "distance" between both poet and subject and reader and subject by interposing a film of unaccustomed rhythmical ritual between observer and experience. It can thus help to control emotion and inhibit cliché responses in both poet and reader. This ritual "frame" in which m. encloses what is often perfectly everyday experience resembles the frame or artificial border of a painting. It reminds the apprehender unremittingly that he is not experiencing the real object of the "imitation" (in the Aristotelian sense) but is experiencing instead that object transmuted into symbolic form. M., as a device of artificiality and unnaturalness, is thus a primary technique of artifice in poetry, just as similar conventions (the palpably artificial stone flesh of statues, for example) are primary techniques of artifice in the other arts. M. also tends to suggest (since ordinary people don't speak in meter) the vatic rôle of the poet, just as it tends to invest with a mysterious air of permanence and authority the words which are cut to its pattern. The strange power of m. to burnish the commonplace has even tempted some thinkers to regard metrical patterns as Platonic forms, themselves inherently and permanently beautiful, which the poet perceives unconsciously and toward which he constantly impels his own utterance.

If one regards absolutely regular m. (as some Platonists do) as the "ideal," then one becomes extraordinarily sensitive to those points in the poem where the "sense" pattern of the language rhythm lies at some distance from the normal or "base" abstract rhythm of the presumed metrical scheme. Prosodists and critics who have studied closely this frequent distance between a poem's "ideal" and "real" m. have developed a theory of prosodic "tension": these theorists maintain that one of the sources of metrical power and pleasure is just this tension between perfect and imperfect metrical patterns. To these theorists, the perpetual tension between "metrical" and real rhythms constitutes the sort of "play" or "suspension" (or even the Coleridgean reconciliation of opposites) which is the secret source of illumination and delight in all art.

METRICAL VARIATIONS. A term covering the techniques of departing from metrical regularity for the purposes of either sheer variety or rhetorical reinforcement. Strictly speaking, m.v. are possible only in verse composed with a more or less regular base rhythm; they do not exist as such in cadenced or free verse.

"Substitution" (according to conventional graphic scansion) is the most frequent technique of metrical variation. Here, once a basic metrical pattern has been established, the rhythm may be varied by the introduction of a "substitute" foot to replace one or more of the normal ones. In the following example,

An aged man is but a paltry thing,
A tattered coat upon a stick, unless
Soul clap its hands and sing, and louder sing
For every tatter in its mortal dress, . . .
(Yeats, SAILING TO BYZANTIUM [p. 383])

each line uses a substitution for one of the "expected" iambic feet. . . . These substitutions serve both to alleviate the metrical monotony of the long-continued iambic pentameter and to allow the metrical structure to "give" and shape itself according to the rhetorical pressures of the statement. In the following lines by Matthew Arnold,

Listen! you hear the grating roar
Of pebbles which the waves draw back, and
fling,
At their return, up the high strand,
Begin, and cease, and then again begin, . . .
(DOVER BEACH)

one can see substitutions used with even stronger intentions of sense reinforcement. Against an iambic background, the initial trochaic substitution in line 1 constitutes an unexpected reversal of the metrical movement which emphasizes a shift in the address; in line 2, the spondaic substitution in the fourth position suggests the slowness of the sea wave as it coils back upon itself, gathering force to shoot itself up the beach; in line 3, the pyrrhic substitution in the 1st position suggests the speed with which the wave "flings" itself up the sand; and in line 4, the return to iambic regularity, after these suggestive variations, transmits a feeling of the infinite, monotonous continuance of the wave's process. In English verse, the most common substitution is the replacement of the initial iamb by a trochee, as in the first line of the Arnold example. . . .

As the examples above help illustrate, the fundamental principles of metrical variation are these: (1) a succession of stressed syllables without the expected intervening unstressed syllables tends to transmit an effect of slowness, weight, or difficulty; (2) a succession of unstressed syllables without the expected intervening stressed syllables tends to suggest an effect of rapidity, lightness, or ease; and (3) an unanticipated reversal in the rhythm (as in the first line of the Arnold passage, above) suggests a new direction of thought, a new tone of voice, or a change in poetic address.

The fact that m.v. such as these can be illustrated by scansion and analyzed dispassionately should not cause the reader to believe that, from the point of view of the poet (as least the good poet), they are anything but instinctual. Many poets whose work can be analyzed metrically according to the foot system would be astonished to be told that they have indulged in "substitution": the genuine poet composes according to the rhythms which his utterance supplies, and, although these rhythms frequently turn out to consist of "normal" and "substitute" feet, they do not necessarily begin that way.

NEAR RHYME. The repetition in accented syllables of the final consonant-sound without correspondence of the preceding vowel- or consonant-sounds, and either with or without "feminine" unaccented syllables following (which should be largely identical). E.g., *grope-cup, maze-coze, drunkard-conquered.* It is a special case of CONSONANCE, and is called by such various names as slant rhyme, half rhyme (also applied to rich consonance), oblique rhyme, para-rhyme. [See Lowell, "A Prayer for My Grandfather," line 11: "On Copley Squ*are,* I saw you hold the d*oor*": Tennyson, "The Lotos-Eaters," Choric song, stanza I, lines 7–8: "blissful . . . / cool."]

OCTAVE, octet. A group of 8 lines, either a stanza or part of a stanza, as the first 8 lines of a sonnet are called the octave, or octet. "I have finished the First Canto, a long one, of about 180 octaves," Byron, *Letter to Murray.*

ODE (Gr. *aeidein* "to sing," "to chant"). In modern usage the name for the most formal, ceremonious, and complexly organized form of lyric poetry, usually of considerable length. It is frequently the vehicle for public utterance on state occasions, as, for example, a ruler's birthday, accession, funeral, the unveiling or dedication of some imposing memorial or public work. The o. as it has evolved in contemporary literatures generally shows a dual inheritance from classic sources, combining the reflective or philosophic character of the Horatian o. with the occasional character of the Pindaric o. [See Wordsworth, "Ode: Intimations of Immortality," and the odes of Keats in this book.]

ONOMATOPOEIA. Strictly, o. refers to the formation or use of words which imitate sounds, such as *hiss, snap, buzz, clash, murmur*. Broadly, the term refers to combinations of words in which any correspondence is felt between sound and sense, whether of sound, of motion, or of mood. In Tennyson's

> *The moan of doves in immemorial elms*
> *And murmuring of innumerable bees,*

only *moan* and *murmuring* are strictly onomatopoetic, but their reinforcement by the repeated *m*'s, *n*'s, and *r*'s *of immemorial, innumerable,* and *elms* makes the whole passage onomatopoetic in the broader sense.

Whether sounds of themselves can suggest meaning has been much disputed. Riding and Graves in *A Survey of Modernist Poetry* (1928) point out that the suggestiveness of Tennyson's lines is lost if their sounds are reproduced in a line of different meaning: "More ordure never will renew our midden's pure manure." Experimental evidence, however, indicates that sounds do have limited capacity for suggesting meaning; e.g. agreement will be almost universal as to which of the nonsense words *taketa* or *naluma* should go with a curved diagram and which with an angular one (W. Kohler, *Gestalt Psychology,* 1947). Undoubtedly this capacity has been often exaggerated and many purely fanciful correspondences discovered. Pope's dictum that "the sound must seem an echo to the sense" seems a reasonable view, since an echo comes after rather than before the event it accompanies. Most readers would agree that Tennyson's lines are more appropriate to their meaning than the following revision:

> *The moan of doves in stately ancient oaks*
> *And quiet murmuring of countless bees.*

The importance of o. to poetry has also been much disputed, some considering it the crowning technical achievement of the poet, others decrying it as a technical bauble quite removed from the essential nature of poetry. The historical record indicates that great poetry has existed without it, but that great poets in all languages have sought it. [See Keats, "Ode to a Nightingale," stanza II: "With beaded bubbles winking at the brim, / And purple-stainéd mouth"; Hopkins, "The Windhover," line 6: "As a skate's heel sweeps smooth on a bow-bend."]

PARADOX. A statement which seems untrue but proves valid upon close inspection. E.g.: "The longest way round is the shortest way home;" or, "When my love swears that she is made of truth / I do believe her, though I know she lies" (Shakespeare, Sonnet 138). . . .

As a widely employed critical term, p. is peculiar to twentieth-century criticism. The rediscovery of Donne and Marvell undoubtedly played a part in its usage, as well as our general awareness of the need for the ironic mind. It is in Cleanth Brooks' *The Well Wrought Urn* that p. is most closely examined. Brooks says, in "The Language of Paradox," that p. is a form of indirection, and indirection is a general characteristic of poetic language and structure. Brooks brings a good deal of evidence to bear in support of his thesis, showing examples of p. in a poet like Wordsworth, whom one might expect to be a poet of simple, direct statement. An issue that he touches on but probably does not develop sufficiently is the difference between *verbal paradoxes* and *paradoxical situations*. Because he does not sufficiently stress this distinction, Brooks is sometimes accused of reducing poetry to "screaming paradoxes." Obviously, as his analysis of Wordsworth's *Composed upon Westminster Bridge* shows, Brooks does not insist merely on witty paradoxes. He is more concerned, and rightly so, to show that many interesting and good poems are written from insights that dramatically enlarge or in some way startlingly modify our commonplace conceptions and understandings, and these we call paradoxical. A good poet might, for example, take Eliot's p., "Liberty is a different sort of pain from prison," and make it into a full poem. Whether he kept Eliot's own verbal p. or chose to render the idea either by a series of examples or of simple direct statements would be of little significance. His poem would remain paradoxical.

PERSONIFICATION. As a manner of speech endowing things or abstractions with life, has been a feature of European poetry since Homer. Psychologically and rhetorically it may be described as "a means of taking hold of things which appear startlingly uncontrollable and independent" (T. B. L. Webster). But the famous personifications of Strength and Force in *Prometheus Bound* parallel and challenge the figures of gods in myths, and according to a theory now current, . . . personifications replace mythical figures when rational attitudes supersede the primitive imagination. [See Eliot, "Prufrock," line 16ff.:

> *The yellow smoke that rubs its muzzle on the*
> *windowpanes*
> *Licked its tongue into the corners of the evening* . . .

See also Milton, "Lycidas," line 103: "Next Camus, reverend Sire, went footing slow . . ."]

PUN. A figure of speech depending upon a similarity of sound and a disparity of meaning. For a successful p., the reader must recognize multiple meanings in a context where all these meanings can be applied. The figure is apparently as old as language, possessing irresistible appeal and appearing in all literatures. . . .

Only in the present day, with a revival of interest in the metaphysical poets and greater scholarly interest in medieval and Renaissance rhetoric, has there been any kind of rehabilitation of the p. as a figure of speech and any serious interest in it found in criticism. The allusiveness of modern verse is related to punning, the original context of the quotation standing for the second sense of the word, and here frequently modern poetry makes an approach to the serious wit of the Renaissance (e.g., Eliot's *The Waste Land,* "When lovely woman stoops to folly and . . ." and "Good night, sweet ladies, good night . . ."). However, another influence, the exuberant word-play in Joyce's *Ulysses* and the mass of interlingual puns in *Finnegans Wake* (balmheartzyheat—*Barmherzigkeit*) is working to keep the comic aspect of the p. dominant. [See Keats, "Ode on a Grecian Urn," Stanza V:

> *O Attic shape! Fair attitude! with* brede
> *Of marble men and maidens* overwrought

See also Donne, "A Hymne to God the Father," pun on done and Donne and, last stanza, play on sun and Son.]

QUATRAIN. A stanza of 4 lines, rhymed or unrhymed. It is, with its many variations, the most common of all stanzaic forms in European poetry. Most rhyming quatrains fall into one of the following categories: abab, or its variant xbyb (in which x and y represent unrhymed lines), a category which includes the familiar ballad meter and the elegiac stanza or heroic quatrain; abba, the so-called envelope stanza, of which Tennyson's *In Memoriam* stanza (q.v.) is a type; aabb, in which an effect of internal balance or antithesis is achieved through the use of opposed couplets, as in Shelley's *The Sensitive Plant.* Less common quatrains are the Omar Khayyám stanza, rhyming aaxa, and the monorhymed quatrain (e.g., Gottfried Keller's *Abendlied*). Quatrains interlinked by rhyme are also to be found, as are those displaying such complications as the alternation of masculine and feminine rhyme and the use of irregular line length. The q. has been used in Western poetry primarily as a unit of composition in longer poems, but the term is also applied to the two component parts of the octave (q.v.) of a sonnet. As a poem complete in itself, the q. lends itself to epigrammatic utterance; Landor and Yeats have shown mastery in the composition of such poems.

REFRAIN. A line, or lines, or part of a line, repeated at intervals throughout a poem, usually at regular intervals, and most often at the end of a stanza; a burden, chorus, or repetend. (*Burden* usually indicates a whole stanza; a *chorus* is a refrain joined in by a group; a *repetend* need not occur *throughout* a poem.) The r. seems a universal feature of primitive poetry and tribal verse, an accompaniment of communal dance and communal labor. Probably the very beginnings of poetry are to be found in iterated words and phrases. Refrains occur in the Egyptian *Book of the*

Dead, in the Hebrew Psalms, in the Greek idyls of Theocritus and Bion, in the Latin epithalamiums of Catullus, in the Anglo-Saxon *Deor's Lament;* they blossom in the medieval ballads, in Provencal fixed forms, in Renaissance lyrics, and in poetry of the romantic period.

A r. may be as short as a single word or as long as a stanza. Though usually recurring as a regular part of a metrical pattern, it may appear irregularly throughout a poem, and it may be used in free verse. In stanzaic verse it usually occurs at the end of a stanza, but may appear at the beginning or in the middle. It may be used in such a way that its meaning varies or develops from one recurrence to the next (Poe discusses this use in "The Philosophy of Composition"), or it may be used each time with a slight variation of wording appropriate to its immediate context (Rossetti's *Sister Helen,* Tennyson's *Lady of Shalott* [p. 249]).

The r. may be a nonsense phrase, apparently irrelevant to the rest of the poem, or relevant only in spirit ("With a hey, and a ho, and a hey nonino"), or it may very meaningfully emphasize some important aspect of the poem—theme, characters, or setting. The r. furnishes pleasure in its repetition of familiar sound; it serves to mark off rhythmical units, and at the same time to unify the poem; and it may be very skillfully used to reinforce emotion and meaning.

REST. A term adapted from music and generally definable as a pause that counts in the metrical scheme. Most writers seem to restrict this definition to situations where a pause seems to compensate . . . for the absence of an unstressed syllable or syllables in a foot. The standard example is Tennyson's

> xx ´ xx ´xx ´
> *Break, break, break,*
> x x ´ x x ´ x ´
> *At the foot of thy crags, O sea!*

However, others have suggested that a rest may take the place of an entire foot.

RHYME. NATURE AND FUNCTION. The spelling "rhyme" became common in the seventeenth century and is now more usual than the older "rime." The main meaning of the word is: a metrical rhetorical device based on the sound-identities of words. The minor meanings can be summarily disposed of before the main one is elaborated: (1) a poem in rhymed verse (cf. Mrs. Browning's *Rhyme of the Duchess May* which has a "Pro-rhyme" before and an "Epi-rhyme" after); (2) rhymed verse in general (e.g., "Pope's Homer is in rhyme"); (3) any kind of echoing between words besides the one specified by the main meaning above (e.g., assonance, consonance, alliteration, etc.); (4) unison or accord (e.g., J. R. Lowell, *Among My Books:* "of which he was as unaware as the blue river is of its rhyme with the blue sky"); (5) a word that echoes another (e.g., " 'Love' is a hackneyed rhyme for 'dove' ") or the sound common to two or more words (e.g., "The meanings of the words are just as important as their rhymes"); (6) a complement to "reason" (in such phrases as: "without rhyme or reason"). . . .

The functions of r. are metrical and rhetorical. From the metrical point of view end- or final r. is a device to mark the ends of lines and link them in couplets, stanzas, or verse paragraphs. It has an organizing effect, therefore, in respect of metrical units longer than the foot. It might be regarded as an ornamental stress falling on and confirming the metrical stresses at the ends of the lines. But middle-and-end r. is sometimes used to mark the ends of the two halves of a line. Such rhyming is sporadic in many ballads, as well as elsewhere. When it is systematic, it simply results from two short lines having been put down as one to save space.

R. in verse is not limited to the ends of lines and half-lines. One word may echo another anywhere in its immediate neighborhood and apart from the metrical scheme. The purpose of such inner, internal, or medial rhymes is then more rhetorical than metrical, as where Browning builds up a seriocomic climax with them in:—

> *How* sad *and* bad *and* mad *it was—*
> *But then, how it was sweet!*

or where Swinburne suggests the darting flight of the bird in:—

> *Sister, my sister,* O fleet sweet *swallow.*

Rhetorical, too, rather than metrical is the practice of Shakespeare and his fellow-dramatists intermingling a good deal of end-r. with their blank verse, generally in couplets, but sometimes in greater complication; they were particularly partial to rhymed couplets for ending a speech or pointing a maxim.

RHYME SCHEME. The arrangement of rhyming words, usually at the ends of lines, though sometimes internally, which gives the poem its characteristic pattern. R. schemes may be fixed or variable, simple or complex. The sonnet and the Spenserian stanza, for example, have fixed patterns, but stanza forms not traditionally fixed may be shaped to the needs of the individual poem. Among the more useful r. schemes in English verse are those of the couplet, which often suggests the epigrammatic package of meaning as in Pope, and the quatrain, which allows for some flexibility of arrangement (for example, alternating, abab, as in Gray's *Elegy Written in a Country Churchyard;* enclosing, abba, as in Tennyson's *In Memoriam;* and intermittent, xbyb, as in Coleridge's *The*

Rime of the Ancient Mariner). Some r. schemes involve the repetition of whole lines . . . and others require the repetition of "rhyming" words . . . . Because rhyming words must carry a semantic as well as a phonetic value, the r. scheme has a great deal to do with the emergence of meaning aesthetically embodied in the stanza or the poem. [Thus, Yeats' "Leda and the Swan" has the following rhyme scheme: abab cdcd efgefg; Lowell's "In the Cage" has the following scheme: ababcdcdeffgeg.]

RUNNING RHYTHM, common rhythm. Term coined by Gerard Manley Hopkins to denote the standard rhythm of English verse measured by feet of 2 or 3 syllables (with only occasional extra unaccented syllables). The rhythm is said to be rising if the stress occurs at the end of the foot, falling if the stress occurs at the beginning of the foot. . . . If the stress occurs between 2 unstressed (or "slack") syllables the rhythm, according to Hopkins, is "rocking." Running rhythm, in Hopkins' conception, is opposed to sprung rhythm (q.v.).

SATIRE. Says Dr. Johnson, is "a poem in which wickedness or folly is censured"; and more elaborate definitions are rarely more satisfactory. No strict definition can encompass the complexity of a word which signifies, on one hand, a kind of literature, and on the other, a spirit or tone which expresses itself in many literary genres. . . .

In addition to attacking vice and folly on nearly all levels, the formal satirist has from the beginning felt impelled to justify his ungrateful art. His *apologiae* (Horace, 1.4; 2.1; Persius, 1; Juvenal, 1; Régnier, 12; Boileau, 9; Pope, *Epistle to Dr. Arbuthnot*) are conventional; they project an image of the satirist as a plain honest man, wishing harm to no upright person, but appalled at the evil he sees about him and forced by his conscience . . . to write s. Readers have not always been convinced. While the influence of Roman practice on later satirists in matters of theme, point of view, tone, literary and rhetorical device, etc., has been enormous, relatively few poets have attempted to adapt precisely the Roman form. Boileau and Pope are great exceptions. . . .

By and large the satiric spirit seems to fuse most readily with the comic genres: when s. was prohibited by law in Elizabethan England, and it was ordered that the verses of Hall and Marston be burned, the satirists turned promptly to the comic drama ("comicall satyre") as the form most appropriate for their purposes. But, as in all generalizations about s., the qualifications are important. Juvenal deliberately sought to rise above the prescriptive bounds of the comic; at the end of the scarifying Sixth S. he enforces a comparison in theme and tone with Sophocles. In the modern Age of S. Alexander Pope catches beautifully, when he likes, the deft Horatian tone; but his wit (like that of Dryden in *Absalom and Achitophel*) is also a serious wit, deeply probing and prophetic. The last lines of the *Dunciad* rise to a terrifying sublimity as they celebrate the restoration of chaos, the obliterating triumph of the anti-Logos. Such passages transcend easy generic distinctions.

The private motivations of the satirist we cannot know. The public function of s.—how it works in its social, psychological, cultural dimensions—we understand only obscurely. (Approaches to these problems by way of psychoanalytic theory, cultural anthropology, etc., are promising; e.g., the work of E. Kris and E. H. Gombrich on caricature in Kris, *Psychoanalytic Explorations in Art* [1952].) But the public motivation of the satirist is explicit and self-justificatory; he writes, so he claims, to reform. His audience may be small (a few "right-thinking men") but it must share with him commitment to certain intellectual and moral beliefs which validate his critique of aberration. Ridicule, which in some cultures may kill and in our own kills symbolically, depends on shared assumptions against which the aberrant stands in naked relief. The greatest s. has been written in periods when ethical and rational norms were sufficiently powerful to attract widespread assent, yet not so powerful as to compel absolute conformity—those periods when the satirist could be of his society and apart from it; could exercise the "double vision." Neoclassic poets had available to them as a kind of implicit metaphor the mighty standard of the classical past; witness the success in the period of the mock-heroic genres. These mock not primarily the ancient forms (although there may be affectionate laughter at some aspects of the epic) but present society, which in the context of past grandeur shows contemptible and mean.

The twentieth century, like the nineteenth, lacks such available norms; but unlike the nineteenth (Byron's *Vision of Judgment* and *Don Juan* and Heine's *Atta Troll* are hardly characteristic of their period) it has a taste for s. Yet though this may be a satirical age, it is hardly an age of great verse s. The alienation of poet from society is notorious; and when the poet has struggled through to the adoption of beliefs and values adequate to his needs, it is a question whether they will serve as metaphors for poetry. Three exceptions (to speak only of poets writing in English) may be noted: Yeats, his vision radically private, and Eliot, his values at the time of *The Waste Land* generally religious, have both written powerful s.; and Auden, his orientation at first social-political, later religious, has demonstrated that a poet writing consciously within the eighteenth-century satiric tradition can speak sharply, eloquently, effectively—can speak *satirically*—even to our fragmented society. [See Pope's "The Rape of the Lock."]

SCANSION. The system of describing more or less conventional poetic rhythms by visual symbols for purposes of metrical analysis and study. . . . In performing s. of a line or group of lines, the reader first marks stressed and unstressed syllables, not according to any preconceived pattern, but according to the degree of sense emphasis transmitted by the syllables. For example:

x ' x ' x ' x ' x '
I sometimes think that never blows so red
x ' x ' ' ' x ' x '
The Rose as where some buried Caesar bled;
x ' x ' x x x ' x '
That every Hyacinth the Garden wears
' x x ' x ' ' x '
Dropt in her lap from some once lovely head.
(*FitzGerald,* The Rubaiyat)

After ascertaining whether the lines are generally in ascending or descending rhythm, the reader next marks the feet, as follows:

x ' x ' x ' x ' x '
I some|times think | that ne|ver blows | so red|
x ' x ' ' ' x ' x '
The Rose | as where|some bur|ied Cae|sar bled;|
x ' x ' x x x ' x '
That ev|ery Hy|acinth | the Gar|den wears|
' x x ' x ' ' ' x
Dropt in | her lap | from some | once love|ly
'
head.|

S. does not make rhythm: it reveals it by transferring it from a temporal into a spatial dimension. By giving the reader a visual representation of the metrical situation underlying the words of the poem, s. helps to make clear the function of metrical variations (q.v.): in the fourth line of FitzGerald's stanza, for example, the s. makes visually apparent the substitution of a trochee for the expected iamb in the first position; this variation reinforces the suddenness and the rapidity of the fall of the drops of blood.

The s. of the following stanza also serves to reveal in visual symbols meaningful variations from the expected metrical pattern:

x ' x ' x ' x '
Her lips| were red, | her looks | were free,|
x ' x ' x x '
Her locks |were yel|low as gold:|
x ' x ' x ' x x
Her skin | was white | as lep|rosy,|
x ' x ' x ' x '
The Night|mare Life|-in-Death | was she,|
x ' ' ' x '
Who thicks | men's blood | with cold.|
(*Coleridge,* RIME OF THE ANCIENT MARINER)

Here the s. of the last line reveals that a spondaic substitution has occurred in the second position, and that the added metrical weight performs the function of reinforcing the sense of the slow, heavy movement of chilled and thickened blood.

SESTET(T), *sestette, sestetto.* (a) The minor division or last 6 lines of an Italian type sonnet, preceded by an octet (see OCTAVE). Sometimes the octet states a proposition or situation and the s. a conclusion, but no fast rules for content can be formulated. The rhyme scheme of the s. varies. (b) Any separable 6-line section of a stanza, but s. is not generally used to describe an entire stanza. [See particularly the sonnets of Milton for the final sestet.]

SIMILE. A comparison of one thing with another, explicitly announced by the word "like" or "as."

Aristotle granted that good similes "give an effect of brilliance," but preferred metaphor to simile because s., being longer, was less attractive, and because the s. "does not say outright that 'this' *is* 'that' . . . the hearer is less interested in the idea." (*Rhetoric* 1410a.) As a figure of speech, s. merges with and to some extent overlaps the "prosaic" metaphor of comparison, substitution, or description, differing from it only by the presence of "like" or "as" (see e.g. *Rhetoric* 1406a, 1410a). Not every s. is a metaphor, though some similes can be compressed or converted into metaphors; and only some metaphors can be expanded into similes. . . .

Whereas metaphor is a mode of condensation and compression, s. through its descriptive function readily leads to diffuseness and extension, even to the digressive development of the figurative scene, action, or object as an object of beauty in itself. Homer's brief similes (e.g. Thetis rises out of the sea like a mist, Apollo descends like the night, "And with them followed a cloud of foot-soldiers") suggest clearly their origin in metaphor; for, although comparison is explicitly indicated by the word "like" or "as," the two things are not primarily compared but identified, yet without any loss of individual character. Such a use of the metaphor in s.-form may be a natural mark of young and vital speech. (See Bowra, *Tradition and Design.*) Indeed Chaucer's characteristic brief similes are of this kind: "hir eyen greye as glas," "His eyen twynkled in his heed aryght, / As doon the sterres in the frosty nyght."

SONNET (fr. It. *sonetto,* a little sound or song). A 14-line poem in iambic pentameter (normally iambic hexameter in France) whose rhyme scheme has, in practice, been widely varied despite the traditional assumption of limited freedom in this respect. The three most widely recognized forms of the s., with their traditional rhyme schemes, are the Italian or Petrarchan (octave: *abbaabba;* sestet: *cdecde* or *cdcdcd* or a similar combination that avoids the closing couplet), the Spenserian (*abab bcbc cdcd ee*), and the English or Shakespearean (*abab cdcd efef* gg). With respect to the Italian pattern (by far the most widely used of the three) it will be observed that a two-part division of thought is invited, and that the octave offers an admirably unified pattern and leads to the *volta* or "turn" of thought in the more varied sestet. The effect of the *abbaabba* octave is truly remarkable. It is actually a blend of 3 brace-rhyme quatrains, since the middle 4 verses, whose sounds overlap the others and echo their pattern, impress the reader with a similar rhyme pattern, thus, ab*baab*ba. Normally, too, a definite pause is made in thought development at the end of the eighth verse, serving to increase the independent unity of an octave that has already progressed with the greatest economy in rhyme sounds. Certainly it would be difficult to conceive a more artistically compact and phonologically effective pattern. The sestet, in turn, leads out of the octave, and, if the closing couplet is avoided, assures a commendable variety within uniformity to the poem as a whole. The Spenserian and Shakespearean patterns, on the other hand, offer some relief to the difficulty of rhyming in English and invite a division of thought into 3 quatrains and a closing or summarizing couplet; and even though such arbitrary divisions are frequently ignored by the poet, the more open rhyme schemes tend to impress the fourfold structure on the reader's ear and to suggest a stepped progression toward the closing couplet. Such matters of relationship between form and content are, however, susceptible of considerable control in the hands of a skilled poet, and the ultimate effect in any given instance may override theoretical considerations in achievement of artistic integrity. . . .

In England the s. has had a fruitful history. Wyatt (1503–1542) brought the form from Italy but showed an immediate preference (possibly influenced by the work of minor writers while he was abroad) for a closing couplet in the sestet. Wyatt did, however, adhere to the Petrarchan octave, and it was Surrey (1517–1547) who established the accepted *abab cdcd efef* gg, a pattern more congenial to the comparatively rhyme-poor English language. This pattern was used extensively in the period, but by no means exclusively for there was wide variety in rhyme schemes and line lengths. It was brought to its finest representation by Shakespeare. . . . The period also saw many s. cycles, beginning with Sidney's *Astrophel and Stella* (1580) and continuing in the sequences of . . . Spenser . . . and Shakespeare; with a shift to religious themes shortly thereafter in John Donne's *Holy Sonnets* [p. 56]. It remained for Milton to introduce the true Italian pattern, to break from sequences to occasional sonnets, to give a greater unity to the form by frequently permitting octave to run into sestet (the "Miltonic" sonnet, but anticipated by the Elizabethans), and a greater richness to the texture by employing his principle of "apt numbers, fit quantity of syllables, and the sense variously drawn out from one verse into another," as in his blank verse. . . . [The sonnet was] reestablished in the early nineteenth [century] by Wordsworth (also under Milton's influence but easing rhyme demands by use of an *abbaacca* octave in nearly half of his more than 500 sonnets); and by Keats, whose frequent use of the Shakespearean pattern did much to reaffirm it as a worthy companion to the generally favored Miltonic-Italian. . . . Few writers in the present century (W. H. Auden and Dylan

Thomas might be named) have matched the consistent level of production found in the earlier work, although an occasional single s., such as Yeats's "Leda and the Swan," has rare beauty. . . .

During the past century s. themes in both Europe and America have broadened to include almost any subject and mood, even though the main line of development has remained remarkably stable. Structurally, even within the traditional patterns, the type has reflected the principal influences evident in modern poetry as a whole: the sprung rhythm of Hopkins and free-verse innovations have frequently led to less metronomic movement within the iambic norm; substitutions for exact rhymes have supplied fresher sound relationships; and a more natural idiom has removed much of the artificiality that had long been a burden. This adaptability within a tradition of eight centuries' standing suggests that there will be no diminution of interest in and use of the form in the foreseeable future, and that the inherent difficulties that have kept the numbers of truly fine sonnets to an extremely small percentage of those that have been written will deter neither versifier nor genius from testing for himself the challenge of what Rossetti called

> . . . *a moment's monument,—*
> *Memorial from the Soul's eternity*
> *To one dead deathless hour.*

SONNET CYCLE or sequence. A series of sonnets on a given theme or to a given individual. The effect is that of stanzas in a longer work, but with the difference that each sonnet retains its integrity as an independent poem. When this is not the case, as in William Ellery Leonard's moving *Two Lives* (1925), the sonnet loses much of its force as a type and becomes in fact "stanzaic." At times the sequence will be given added unity by use of repetition, either of rhymes or of lines, between the different poems, as in the "crown of sonnets." From the earliest times the cycle has been used to amplify the limited scope of the single sonnet and to reflect the many facets of the chosen theme. [This text provides selections from the sonnet cycle of Shakespeare.]

SPENSERIAN STANZA. An important stanza in English poetry, composed of 9 iambic lines, the first 8 being pentameter and the last hexameter (alexandrine), rhyming ababbcbcc. The form was invented by Edmund Spenser for his *The Faerie Queene*. [See Keats, "The Eve of St. Agnes," written in Spenserian stanza form.]

SPONDEE (Gr. "used at a libation" poured to the accompaniment of the 2 long notes). In classical metric, a unit consisting of 2 long syllables:

(– –; *fect*)

Meters entirely composed of spondees are rare, but do occur. . . .

In the common meters, a s. may replace dactyl, iamb, trochee, or anapaest. In English stressed verse, the s. (´´; ámén) is rarer than might be expected, the instance of 2 equally stressed syllables in the same foot being almost wholly confined to compound words or 2 adjacent monosyllables:

x ´ ´ ´ x ´ ´ ´
The long|day wanes;|the slow|moon climbs
(Tennyson, ULYSSES [p. 226])

It is the basis of no English verse, occurring only as a variation. Most English attempts at the foot in classical imitations result in trochees.

SPRUNG RHYTHM. Term coined by Gerard Manley Hopkins to describe what he thought to be his most important metrical rediscovery. As Hopkins describes it, "Sprung rhythm . . . is measured by feet of from one to four syllables, regularly, and for particular effects any number of weak or slack syllables may be used. It has one stress, which falls on the only syllable, if there is only one, or, if there are more, then scanning as above, on the first, and so gives rise to four sorts of feet, a monosyllable and the so-called accentual Trochee, Dactyl, and the First Paeon. . . . Sprung Rhythm cannot be counterpointed. . . ." Sprung (or "abrupt") rhythm differs from running rhythm . . . in that it may use rests, monosyllabic feet. . . .

Hopkins points out that s. rhythm is found in nursery rhymes, and a good illustration of the rhythm is to be found in

One, two,
Buckle my shoe.

Here, line 1 is in s., line 2 in running rhythm. Another example given by Hopkins is

March dust, April showers
Bring forth May flowers

where, if "showers" and "flowers" are considered monosyllables, both lines are in s. rhythm. These examples will make clear that s. rhythm is essentially a system of overstressing; the poet practicing s. rhythm composes almost as if the spondee were a normal English foot. As has been said of s. rhythm, "Its external distinguishing feature is the free occurrence of juxtaposed stresses without intermediate unstressed syllables."

S. rhythm, by approximating the movements of emotion-charged natural speech, suggests a tone of frank sincerity and intimate emotional involvement. Good examples of the tone most natural to s. rhythm are Hopkins' poems *At the Wedding March* and *Spring and Fall: To a Young Child* [p. 314].

STANZA (It. "station, stopping-place"). A basic structural unit in verse composition, a sequence of lines arranged in a definite pattern of meter and rhyme scheme which is repeated throughout the work. Stanzas range from such simple patterns as the couplet or the quatrain (qq.v.) to such complex stanza forms as the Spenserian (q.v.) or those used by Keats in his odes. The term "stanza" is sometimes restricted to verse units of 4 lines or more, "couplet" and "tercet" being the preferred terms for the shorter forms. The term is also sometimes employed to designate irregular formal divisions found in nonstanzaic poetry (e.g., *Paradise Lost*), but the term "verse paragraph" is here more expressive and less confusing.

Some narrative poetry, particularly of the epic type, is nonstanzaic (i.e., stichic) in structure (e.g., the *Iliad,* the *Aeneid, Paradise Lost, The Ring and the Book*) and thus achieves an effect of linear development in which the narrative line in itself provides the essential structure. Such compositions as Pope's *Rape of the Lock* (in couplets) and Dante's *Divina Commedia* (in tercets, or, more properly, in terza rima) achieve a similar effect. True stanzaic composition, as in Spenser's *Faerie Queene* (Spenserian stanza), Ariosto's *Orlando Furioso* (ottava rima), and Chaucer's *Troilus and Criseyde* (rhyme royal), lends itself to a kind of tension between narrative structure and lyric, elegiac, didactic, or satiric digression. Although the essence of stanzaic composition lies in the regular repetition of the pattern, stanzaic verse often employs variation, not only through metrical substitution but also through irregularities in s. form, as in Coleridge's *Ancient Mariner,* with its subtle rhetorical embroideries on the basic ballad measure.

SYMBOL. The word "symbol" derives from the Greek verb, *symballein,* meaning "to put together," and the related noun, *symbolon,* meaning "mark," "token," or "sign," in the sense of the half-coin carried away by each of the two parties of an agreement as a pledge. Hence, it means basically a joining or combination, and, consequently, something once so joined or combined as standing for or representing in itself, when seen alone, the entire complex. This term in literary usage refers most specifically to a manner of representation in which what is shown (normally referring to something material) means, by virtue of association, something *more* or something *else* (normally referring to something immaterial). Thus a literary s. unites an image (the analogy) and an idea or conception (the subject) which that image suggests or evokes—as when, for example, the image of climbing a staircase (the difficulty involved in the effort to raise oneself) is used to suggest the idea of "raising" oneself spiritually or becoming purified (T. S. Eliot's *Ash Wednesday*).

A s. thus resembles what are known traditionally as "figures of speech" (cf. IMAGERY), which themselves comprise "tropes," or departures (turns) from the commonplace modes of signification, and "schemes," or artful elaborations of the forms of words and sentences. A s. is like a trope, in that a simile, metaphor, personification, allegory (qq.v.), and so on, each represent a manner of speaking in which what is said means something more or something else. But a s. is not a trope, and may be distinguished in terms of how it relates subject and analogy in a poem. In the other figures mentioned, what is said (analogy) is distinct from what is meant (subject), and their relationship is based upon a stated or implied resemblance within difference.

A s., on the other hand, puts the analogy in place of the subject (and may thus be thought of as an "expanded" metaphor—and, conversely, recurring metaphors in a given work are often spoken of as symbolic) so that we read what is said (climbing a staircase) as if that were what is meant, but are made to infer, by virtue of the associations provoked by what is said and the manner in which it is expressed, something more or something else as the additional or true meaning, spiritual purification). Thus, an idea which would be difficult, flat, lengthy, or unmoving when expressed prosaically and by itself, may be made intelligible, vivid, economical, and emotionally effective by the use of symbols.

A s., then, may be called, for purely technical purposes, a "pseudo-subject." Nor need the relationship between what is said and what is to be inferred be based, as in metaphor and simile, merely upon resemblance, for many images have become potentially symbolic not through likeness only but also through one sort of association or another—as when the loss of a man's hair symbolizes the loss of strength (Samson) or the rejection of worldly desires (monastic and ascetic practice), not because of any resemblance between them but rather because a primitive and magical connection has been established between secondary sex characteristics, virility, and desire. Of course, an associative relationship may be established having resemblance as its basis when a metaphor or simile is repeated so often, either in the work of a single author or in literary tradition, that the analogue can be used alone to summon up the subject with which it was once connected. Similarly, many interpreters have pointed out that poets tend to use the metaphors and similes of their earlier work as symbols in their later work because of the associative relations thus established. Critics rightly warn, moreover, that symbolic associations of imagery should be made neither too explicit nor too fixed, for implications of this sort are best felt rather than explained, and vary from work to work depending upon the individual context.

The first question, however, which faces the reader of a poem is whether or not a given image is indeed symbolic to begin with. This question may be answered in at least three related ways: (1) the connection between s. and thing symbolized may be made explicit in the work, as with the "Sea of Faith" in Arnold's *Dover Beach;* (2) the image may be presented in such a way as to discourage a merely literal interpretation, as with Byzantium in Yeats's *Sailing to Byzantium,* since no such thing actually exists, or to encourage a more than merely literal interpretation, as with the garden in Marvell's poem of that name, since, although it does actually exist, it is made into something more by virtue of the speaker's reactions to it; or (3) the pressure of implicit association may be so great as to demand a symbolic interpretation, as with Ulysses in Tennyson's poem of that name, since that figure has received such extensive previous treatment in myth, legend, and literature (cf. Homer and Dante). Because there is today a tendency to apply symbolic interpretation rather loosely, it bears emphasizing at this point that an image in a work is not symbolic unless a literal interpretation fails to do it justice; that is to say, a negative test often helps—an image is literal until proved otherwise, and if a literal interpretation can account satisfactorily for its place and function in the work then it is probably not symbolic.

Once the presence of symbols has been established, however, the next question is how to interpret their place and function in the work. This question may be answered in terms of at least three overlapping areas of inquiry: (1) the source of their imagery in experience, whether from the natural world, the human body, man-made artifacts, and so on; (2) the status of their imagery in a given work, whether presented literally as an actual experience (so that it symbolizes something more) or non-literally as a dream or vision (so that it symbolizes something else altogether); and (3) the way in which their imagery has acquired associative power, whether mainly by virtue of universal human experience . . . or particular historical conventions, or the internal relationships which obtain among the elements of a given work (whereby one thing becomes associated with another by virtue of structural emphasis, arrangement, position, or development—this aspect, is, of course, involved to some degree in all works containing symbols), or some private system invented by the poet, or some combination. Regarding the third area of inquiry, examples of universally understood symbols would include climbing a staircase (or mountain) as spiritual purification, crossing a body of water as some sort of spiritual transition, sunset as death and sunrise as rebirth, and so on; examples of conventional symbols would include the transmutation of lead to gold as redemption, the lily as chastity and the rose as passion, the tiger as Christ, and so on; examples of internal-relationship symbols would include the wall as the division between the primitive and the civilized or natural chaos and human order in Robert Frost, the guitar and the color blue as the aesthetic imagination in Wallace Stevens, the island as complacency and the sea as courage in W. H. Auden, and so on; and examples of private symbols would include the phases of the moon as the cycles of history combined with the psychology of individuals in W. B. Yeats, embalmment as an obstacle that cannot be overcome in the attempt to resurrect the spirit in Dylan Thomas. . . .

In Frost's famous poem, *Birches,* for example, the speaker talks of climbing to the top of a birch tree and swinging on it back down to earth again in such a way that the reader is given to understand that this action means something more than just climbing up and swinging down. That is to say, in the context of this poem the action comes to mean for its speaker a temporary release from the difficulties and responsibilities of daily life (climbing up and away from earth toward heaven) and a subsequent return to those mundane limitations once again refreshed (swinging back down to earth). Climbing, then, stands for his desire to get away, while swinging down stands for his recognition that he must, after all, live out his life on earth where the gods have placed him. Thus this action, which at first seemed to be the speaker's subject, turns out ultimately to be an analogue of his subject (which in no way, of course, diminishes the value and interest of the imagery in itself).

According to the three areas of inquiry outlined above, this symbolic imagery may first be analyzed as coming from the natural world in combination with actions of the human body: earth, heaven, tree, climbing up and swinging down. It is presented, secondly, as literal occurrence. And thirdly, its associative power derives from universal experience—earth as limitation and heaven as release—in combination with internal relationships—the act of swinging from a birch as seen in this context.

Yeats's *Sailing to Byzantium* [p. 383], on the other hand, is rather more complicated in its symbolism. Here the speaker talks of sailing the seas and coming to the holy city of Byzantium, but, because this cannot be taken literally, what he actually means (again the warning against being too specific in explaining the meaning of symbols must be recalled) is that he wants to divest himself of mortality and its limitations and dwell —probably through the forms of art—in eternity. Notice, however, in the first place, that Byzantium as a symbolic image is derived from manmade artifact (although sailing as transition is not); secondly, that it is presented as a vision and not as something which has literally happened or could literally happen; and thirdly, that, in addition to internal relationships, the associative power of this image depends for its force upon—or at least is aided greatly by—a knowledge of exactly what it meant to Yeats in his private symbology. Thus the symbolism of different writers may be distinguished, characterized, and interpreted. (Even here, however, such categories must be applied flexibly, for Yeats's Byzantium image, although it does indeed have crucial private associations, is also related to the universal image of the "holy city" [e.g., Jerusalem] as fulfillment or redemption.)

Historically, men once tended to see the physical world in terms of spiritual values, not only by way of generating universal symbols (the world as a body, for example, or man's body as a state, and so on) but also of developing—through myth, lore, legend, craft, and learning—special conventions. And it is one of the doctrines of modern criticism that, partly due to the Protestant Reformation, partly to the changes gradually effected in school curricula, partly to the growth of science, and partly to the mere passing of time, not only have many conventional symbols been rendered meaningless to poets and readers alike but also the very power of seeing the physical world in terms of spiritual values has disappeared. Thus symbolism has been called in the twentieth century the "lost" or the "forgotten" language.

Certain twentieth-century poets, following the lead of the nineteenth-century French "symbolists" (Baudelaire, Verlaine, Rimbaud, and Mallarmé each in his own way explored afresh the possibilities of the private symbolism of vision and dreams), and partly under the influence of a renewal of interest in Donne, Blake, and Hopkins, have attempted not only a revival of conventional religious and legendary symbolism, as has Eliot in *Ash Wednesday*, for example, but also have tried, in what they have felt to be a collapse of spiritual values, to invent their own symbolic conventions (Yeats is only the most obvious, with Ezra Pound, Hart Crane, Wallace Stevens, and Dylan Thomas working along similar if less systematic lines). Other poets, such as Frost, William Carlos Williams, and E. E. Cummings, have by and large been content to use natural, literal, universal, and contextual symbols. . . .

Thus, if symbolism refers generally to the use of one thing to stand for another, then its specific meanings will vary according to the framework in which this relationship is viewed. A s. is a device of the poetic art when it refers to something in the poem as standing for something else in the poem; it is a power of poetic language when it refers to the way words and rhythms can evoke mystery; it is a function of the whole poem when it refers to the kinds of meaning a literary work can stand for; it is a form of therapeutic disguise when it refers to the ways in which a poem stands for the working out of the author's inner disturbances; and it is an index of cultural values when it refers to the ways in which man's products reveal his attitudes. Since the word is thus capable of such protean meanings—some of them overlapping at certain points—it is obviously best, when using the term, to specify the exact sense intended.

TERZA RIMA. A verse form composed of iambic tercets rhyming aba bcb, etc., the second line of the first tercet supplying the rhyme for the second tercet, the second line of the second tercet supplying the rhyme for the third, and so on, thus giving an effect of linkage to the entire composition. In t.r., the conclusion of a formal unit is generally signified by the occurrence of a single line which completes the rhyme structure by rhyming with the middle line of the preceding tercet, thus: xyx y.

T.r. was invented by Dante as an appropriate form for his *Divina Commedia*. . . .

The form makes even greater demands on poets who write in a language less rich in rhymes than Italian. T.r. was introduced into English by Chaucer in his *Complaint to his Lady* and was used by Wyatt and by Daniel. Some of the English romantics experimented with the form, Byron in *The Prophecy of Dante* and Shelly in *Prince Athanase* and *The Triumph of Life*. The latter poet's *Ode to the West Wind* is composed of five sections, each rhyming aba bcb cdc ded ee.

TONE-COLOR. Characteristic auditory quality of a speech-sound or musical instrument (Germ. *Tonfarbe, Klangfarbe;* Fr., Eng. *timbre*). Extended to cover the kinesthetic "feel" of articulation and utterance. The relations of both aspects of tone-color to sound-associations are here examined. . . .

It is clear that every sound (-collocation) has multiple affinities. The whole picture is distorted by lexical associations. Thus one word (or set) may attract others *in the language* (*swing, sway, swirl, swill, swish, swash, swoop, swat, switch*) and/or *in verse*. . . .

Nevertheless, potential associations are activated in certain milieux. In "And the dull wheel hums doleful through the day" (Crabbe) the monotony is conveyed by the doubled *d-l,* lingering *l*'s and *m,* driving *d*'s, flat British *u*'s. In "Liberty . . . o'er Spain, / Scattering contagious fire into the sky, / Gleamed. My soul spurned the chains of its dismay" (Shelley) the release and ardor are expressed by the swishing *s*'s, leaping *sp*'s, flinging *sk*'s, gay *ā/ai*'s. In "The horrid crags, by toppling convent crown'd, / The cork-trees hoar that clothe the shaggy steep, / The mountain-moss by scorching skies imbrown'd" (Byron), the scene is suggested by the gasping *h*'s, dark *or*'s and *ŏ*'s, rugged *kr*'s, hard-edged *k*'s and *ag*'s, sweeping *mount/m-own'd,* abrupt *p*'s, dizzy *sk*'s and spiring *trees/steep.* In Mallarmé's swan-sonnet the *i*'s illuminate white bird, frozen winter, spiritual intensity, sterility. Rilke uses *i*-sounds similarly in the unicorn Sonnet to Orpheus, but almost confined to certain lines, set in contrast with *a*-sounds in the first quatrain and *au* in the second, and in modulation with *ei* in the sestet. (Tone-colors can also be used for themselves alone without "program.")

To systematize is possible. Depending on the language (see below), vowels like [e, i, y] tend to be appropriate to height, intensity, sharpness, thinness, delicacy, minuteness, insignificance, pallidity, purity, rarefaction, mobility; but such as [ɑ, ɒ, ɔ] to the opposite notions; like [u, o] to hollowness, roundness, solemnity, gloom, depth, softness, malleability, liquidity; but such as [a, æ, ɛ] to their opposites; like [y, ø, œ] to preciosity, charm, melancholy; but such as [ʌ, ɑ] to their antitheses; rounded vowels generally to interest, rich hue or form; but others to the reverse; vowels like [u, y, i] to mystery, tenderness, cool tints; but such as [a, ɑ, ɒ] to their contraries; short vowels can be brisk or trite, long vowels operatic (diphthongs plastically expressive). *Consonants—resonants* (nasals, liquids) can suggest harmony, flow, protraction (especially as finals), malleability; *stops:* the opposites; *voiceless:* levity, agitation; *voiced:* the converse; *hissing*: scorn, tenuity; *hushing:* swarm, effusion; *both the last:* speed, harshness; *r*'s: roughness, menace, warmth; *labials:* warm emotions; *velars:* cold emotions; *stops juxtaposed:* obstacle shapes; *fricatives combined with other consonants:* movement shapes.

TROCHEE, *choree* (respectively from Gr. "running" and "belonging to the dance"). A metrical unit, in quantitative verse, of a long syllable followed by a short:

–⏑ ; *ante* (–⏑ marked over *ante*)

The rhythm of the trochaic foot was therefore the reverse of the iambic (q.v.), i.e. "falling" instead of "rising. . . ."

The term has been adopted into English for the accentual foot of a stressed followed by an unstressed syllable:

ˊ x; silver (ˊ x marked over *silver*)

Though common in Middle English verse, the trochaic base was almost wholly absent from English poetry until the end of the sixteenth century when it was employed both in lyric and in dramatic monologues and songs:

ˊ x | ˊ x | ˊ x | ˊ x
Honour, | *riches,* | *marriage*|*-blessing*
(Shakespeare, TEMPEST 4.1.06)

The 4-foot line remained predominant until Blake, whose innovations in length and variation opened up the way for subsequent developments. The nineteenth century saw more frequent and broader use, chiefly, however, as substitution in predominantly iambic lines; but by itself it has never been a favorite in English, owing no doubt to the difficulty of finding words or phrases to begin the line with a stressed syllable (cf. the variations in Milton's *L'Allegro* and *Il Penseroso* [pp. 99–107]). Used mechanically, as in *Hiawatha,* the trochee becomes monotonous; but in short passages it is often handled with success.

TRUNCATION, catalexis. The omission of the last (generally unstressed) syllable or syllables in a line of conventional metrical structure. A line lacking one syllable of the normal number is called catalectic; one lacking two is called brachycataletic. . . . Truncation is frequent in trochaic verse, where the line of complete trochaic feet tends to create an effect of monotony. The following trochaic lines exhibit t.: "Simple maiden, void of art, / Babbling out the very heart" (Ambrose Philips). T. is also frequently employed in dactylic lines to avoid an effect of excessive bounciness; Hood's second line is truncated: "Take her up tenderly, / Lift her with care."